Related Books of Interest

GW00597211

Mastering XPages
A Step-by-Step Guide to XPages Application Development and the XSP Language

By Martin Donnelly, Mark Wallace, and Tony McGuckin

ISBN: 0-13-248631-8

The first complete, practical guide to XPages development—direct from members of the XPages development team at IBM Lotus. Martin Donnelly, Mark Wallace, and Tony McGuckin have written the definitive programmer's guide to utilizing this breakthrough technology. Packed with tips, tricks, and best practices from IBM's own XPages developers, *Mastering XPages* brings together all the information developers need to become experts—whether you're experienced with Notes/Domino development or not. The authors start from the very beginning, helping developers steadily build your expertise through practical code examples and clear, complete explanations. Readers will work through scores of real-world XPages examples, learning cutting-edge XPages and XSP language skills and gaining deep insight into the entire development process. Drawing on their own experience working directly with XPages users and customers, the authors illuminate both the technology and how it can be applied to solving real business problems.

XPages Portable Command Guide
A Compact Resource to XPages Application Development and the XSP Language

By Martin Donnelly, Maire Kehoe, Tony McGuckin, and Dan O'Connor

ISBN: 0-13-294305-0

Now, there's a perfect portable XPages quick reference for every working developer. Straight from the experts at IBM, *XPages Portable Command Guide* offers fast access to working code, tested solutions, expert tips, and example-driven best practices. Drawing on their unsurpassed experience as IBM XPages lead developers and customer consultants, the authors explore many lesser known facets of the XPages runtime, illuminating these capabilities with dozens of examples that solve specific XPages development problems. Using their easy-to-adapt code examples, you can develop XPages solutions with outstanding performance, scalability, flexibility, efficiency, reliability, and value.

Related Books of Interest

IBM Lotus Connections 2.5
Planning and Implementing Social Software for Your Enterprise

By Stephen Hardison, David M. Byrd, Gary Wood,
Tim Speed, Michael Martin, Suzanne Livingston,
Jason Moore, and Morten Kristiansen
ISBN: 0-13-700053-7

In *IBM Lotus Connections 2.5*, a team of IBM
Lotus Connections 2.5 experts thoroughly introduces the newest product and covers every facet
of planning, deploying, and using it successfully. The authors cover business and technical
issues and present IBM's proven, best-practices
methodology for successful implementation. The
authors begin by helping managers and technical
professionals identify opportunities to use social
networking for competitive advantage—and by
explaining how Lotus Connections 2.5 places full-
fledged social networking tools at their fingertips.
IBM Lotus Connections 2.5 carefully describes
each component of the product—including
profiles, activities, blogs, communities, easy social
bookmarking, personal home pages, and more.

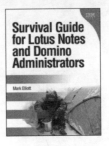

Survival Guide for Lotus Notes and Domino Administrators

By Mark Elliott
ISBN: 0-13-715331-7

Mark Elliott has created a true encyclopedia of
proven resolutions to common problems and has
streamlined processes for infrastructure support.
Elliott systematically addresses support solutions
for all recent Lotus Notes and Domino
environments.

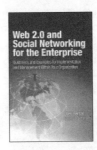

Web 2.0 and Social Networking for the Enterprise
Guidelines and Examples for Implementation and Management Within Your Organization

By Joey Bernal
ISBN: 0-13-700489-3

Related Books of Interest

The Social Factor
Innovate, Ignite, and Win through Mass Collaboration and Social Networking

By Maria Azua
ISBN: 0-13-701890-8

Business leaders and strategists can drive immense value from social networking "inside the firewall." Drawing on her unsurpassed experience deploying innovative social networking systems within IBM and for customers, Maria Azua demonstrates how to establish social networking communities, and then leverage those communities to drive extraordinary levels of innovation. *The Social Factor* offers specific techniques for promoting mass collaboration in the enterprise and strategies to monetize social networking to generate new business opportunities.

Whatever your industry, *The Social Factor* will help you learn how to choose and implement the right social networking solutions for your unique challenges...how to avoid false starts and wasted time...and how to evaluate and make the most of today's most promising social technologies—from wikis and blogs to knowledge clouds.

Listen to the author's podcast at:
ibmpressbooks.com/podcasts

Lotus Notes Developer's Toolbox
Elliott
ISBN: 0-13-221448-2

DB2 9 for Linux, UNIX, and Windows
DBA Guide, Reference, and Exam Prep, 6th Edition
Baklarz, Zikopoulos
ISBN: 0-13-185514-X

The Art of Enterprise Information Architecture
A Systems-Based Approach for Unlocking Business Insight
Godinez, Hechler, Koening, Lockwood, Oberhofer, Schroeck
ISBN: 0-13-703571-3

Enterprise Master Data Management
An SOA Approach to Managing Core Information
Dreibelbis, Hechler, Milman, Oberhofer, van Run, Wolfson
ISBN: 0-13-236625-8

Mainframe Basics for Security Professionals
Getting Started with RACF
Pomerantz, Vander Weele, Nelson, Hahn
ISBN: 0-13-173856-9

XPages Extension Library

June 2012.

Paul cris

Paul Henn.

XPages Extension Library

A Step-by-Step Guide to the Next Generation of XPages Components

Paul Hannan, Declan Sciolla-Lynch, Jeremy Hodge, Paul Withers, and Tim Tripcony

IBM Press
Pearson plc

Upper Saddle River, NJ • Boston • Indianapolis • San Francisco
New York • Toronto • Montreal • London • Munich • Paris • Madrid
Cape Town • Sydney • Tokyo • Singapore • Mexico City

ibmpressbooks.com

IBM Press Program Managers: Steven M. Stansel, Ellice Uffer
Cover design: IBM Corporation

Associate Publisher: Greg Wiegand
Marketing Manager: Stephane Nakib
Acquisitions Editor: Mary Beth Ray
Publicist: Heather Fox
Development Editor: Eleanor Bru
Editorial Assistant: Vanessa Evans
Technical Editors: Brian Benz, Chris Toohey
Managing Editor: Kristy Hart
Cover Designer: Alan Clements
Project Editor: Jovana Shirley
Copy Editor: Gill Editorial Services
Indexer: Lisa Stumpf
Compositor: Gloria Schurick
Proofreader: Mike Henry
Manufacturing Buyer: Dan Uhrig

Published by Pearson plc
Publishing as IBM Press

IBM Press offers excellent discounts on this book when ordered in quantity for bulk purchases or special sales, which may include electronic versions and/or custom covers and content particular to your business, training goals, marketing focus, and branding interests. For more information, please contact:

U.S. Corporate and Government Sales
1-800-382-3419
corpsales@pearsontechgroup.com

For sales outside the U.S., please contact:

International Sales
international@pearsoned.com

The Library of Congress cataloging-in-publication data is on file.

ISBN-13: 978-0-13-290181-9

ISBN-10: 0-13-290181-1

Text printed in the United States on recycled paper at R.R. Donnelley in Crawfordsville, Indiana.
First printing May 2012

To Katie and Alec, my family—Paul H.
To my wonderful wife, Terri, for all her support—Declan
To the IBM Lotus XPages team for giving us all this
Open Source ExtLib goodness—Jeremy
To Mandy, my wife—Paul W.
To Paul Hannan: This book was your vision, and it owes its existence to your
persistence, diligence, and enthusiasm.—Tim

Contents

Foreword

XPages is a truly groundbreaking technology. Its initial release in 2009 revolutionized web application development on Notes®/Domino® and brought new life and vibrancy to the developer community. As a runtime framework built on top of standards-based technologies and open source libraries, it greatly simplified the art of web development for the existing community and removed barriers to entry for non-Domino developers. Suddenly, it was a breeze to create a web page that pulled data from a Domino view or extracted a set of fields from a Notes document. The process of weaving these pages together to form compelling web applications became a no-brainer. In a nutshell, the advent of XPages meant that cranking out a half-decent Domino web application was easy and fast.

The good news is that after the 2009 revolution, XPages evolution continued apace. Within just nine months of XPages' official debut, we shipped a new release in Notes/Domino 8.5.1, which included lots of new features and, most notably, support for the Notes Client. This meant that users could take XPages web applications offline and run them locally in Notes! While we were working hard to push out more XPages technology, its adoption continued to grow. By Lotusphere® 2010, we were getting invaluable customer feedback on real-world XPages application development—the good, the bad, and the ugly. (It was mostly good!) A key theme emerged from the community at this time, one that really resonated with us. The message was simple: Yes, it was indeed easy and fast to write XPages web applications, but developing truly sleek and professional applications remained difficult and required expertise that was often beyond the core skill set of the typical Domino developer. Solving this would be our next big challenge.

One means of enabling the community to write better applications was through technical empowerment. Opening the XPages application programming interfaces (APIs) would allow developers to add their own XPages components to the framework and consume assets from other third parties. Thus, for Notes/Domino 8.5.2, we released the first public XPages APIs and integrated the OSGi framework into the Domino server. As a means of illustrating how to use the APIs, we decided to provide a set of sample artifacts. The thinking was that if customers learned from these samples to build their own controls and shared them with each other across the community, developing top-drawer web applications would be easier to achieve. This led to the creation of a new XPages extension project, initially named Porus.

According to Plato, Porus was the personification of plenty, so this new library was intended to provide an abundance of new capabilities. True to its name, Porus quickly grew and soon boasted a large set of new controls, datasources, and other XPages assets. In fact, it was so effective that we wanted to build our next generation of XPages application templates on top of it, and that's where we ran into a problem: The library was simply too big to fit into the next Notes/Domino maintenance release. Moreover, we didn't want to wait for the next release. We wanted our customers to benefit from all the bountiful goodies of Porus as quickly as possible, and that meant being able to install it on top of the latest Notes/Domino release (8.5.2). What to do?

With the benefit of 20-20 hindsight, perhaps moving our internal Porus library to a public open source model out on OpenNTF.org was the obvious next move, but this was not so clear cut at the time. You must bear in mind that none of the core XPages runtime or Notes/Domino platform code is available as open source, so going down this road would be a new departure for us. The advantages of an open source model, however, were appealing. First, we could share our library with the development community more or less immediately and then update it when needed. This would allow us to deliver before the next Notes/Domino maintenance release and be independent of its constraints. It would also allow us to provide all the benefits of our Extension Library (ExtLib) while they are their most relevant to the community. The IT industry evolves at a rapid pace, so what's new and cool today can be old hat tomorrow; the timeliness of technology delivery can be a crucial factor in its success or failure. Being at the bleeding edge requires an agile delivery model, and we recognized that our traditional model simply could not adapt and respond quickly enough to the rapidly mutating demands of the market.

Of course, we had firsthand experience of the dynamic nature of open source systems by virtue of the fact that XPages depends on such components. The Dojo JavaScript library, which is at the core of XPages, is a perfect example. It typically provides two major releases per year, plus some maintenance updates. Not only do these releases constantly add new features and fixes, they target the latest browsers available in the market. With the most popular browsers piling through major release after major release in quick-fire succession and auto-updating themselves on end-user desktops, the Dojo project is well adapted to what is required to stay relevant in the modern IT world. The Notes/Domino product release cycle, on the other hand, is a heavyweight process. The last months in our release cycles are spent solidifying the products, with no new features being added, to minimize quality risks. On the one hand, this process helps to produce high-quality software, but on the other, it doesn't keep pace with the overall evolution rate of the modern industry.

Quite apart from speed and agility, however, is the critical element of transparency. Twenty-first century developers no longer want black boxes of code that they can use blindly. They expect to go further: They want to understand what the code does and how it works. They want to be able to debug it, to extend it. They want to share with a community. If you don't provide these capabilities, developers will find a way to get access to your code anyway. By nature, script languages are delivered in source form (if sometimes obfuscated), and even compiled languages such as Java™ or C# can be easily introspected.

September 1, 2010 was a landmark date for XPages, because it was when the XPages ExtLib was introduced as an open source project on OpenNTF.org. The response was amazing. The community latched on to this project from the get-go and ran with it. Today it proudly stands well clear of the field as the most active project on OpenNTF, with more than 26,000 downloads.

Despite the XPages ExtLib's runaway adoption success, other issues arose. Soon it became clear that although the open source model gave us many benefits, it was by no means perfect. Open source projects are often started by developers who put a greater emphasis on the code itself, leaving other pieces, such as documentation, test, accessibility, and support, behind. This is generally not acceptable for enterprise software intended for production. In fact, installing open source software in production environments is prevented by policy in many organizations. Perhaps even more significant is the fact that open source projects generally rely heavily on a small set of core developers. Open source repositories, like SourceForge and GitHub, are full of static projects that individuals started in their spare time and then left behind as the founders moved on to new pastures. For these projects to be successful, organizations that are prepared to stand behind the projects must endorse them. Without this endorsement, the use of open source software inevitably carries a certain amount of risk.

At this juncture, it was natural to wonder if we had gone full circle. To give customers the latest and greatest cutting-edge technology, we had to put a greater emphasis on code development. The open source model helped us achieve this. To give customers a system that IBM® fully supports and endorses, we needed to reinvest in all the aforementioned elements that we had sacrificed along the way for speed of innovation. Was it impossible to have both? We thought long and hard on this problem to come up with alternative distribution models that could satisfy the largest spectrum of users, from the early adopters to the more risk-averse conservative consumers. Our strategy can be summarized in three practices:

- We continue to deliver source code as early and frequently as possible to OpenNTF.org. Early adopters can continue to consume these offerings, which are supported not by IBM but by the ExtLib community. Thus, answers to questions and fixes to problems can be delivered promptly.

- Periodically, we package a subset of the ExtLib functionality available on OpenNTF.org and include this in an Upgrade Pack (UP) for Notes/Domino. Such UPs are fully supported by IBM and install on top of the latest shipping version of the Notes/Domino platform.

- The latest UP, plus any important subsequent features or fixes from OpenNTF, is always rolled into the next release of the product. Thus, between Notes/Domino release cycles, there is the potential for multiple UPs.

This three-tiered model has numerous advantages. It allows us to continue to get real feedback from the early adopters—the consumers of the OpenNTF project. By the time the code actually makes the official UP, or later into the core product, it has already been used in many projects, making it robust as we fix and deliver the open source project on a frequent basis. Also, regardless of the distribution mode, the source code is always provided. On December 14, 2011, we delivered on this proposed model by shipping our first UP: Notes/Domino 8.5.3 UP1. There are more to come!

In a long-standing software organization, like Notes/Domino, UP was a real revolution—2009 all over again! It was the first time IBM Collaboration Solutions (aka Lotus®) had delivered significant pieces of software in this way. It was a huge challenge, but we successfully achieved it because of the high level of commitment of the XPages team, the help of the broader Notes/Domino application development teams, and, most importantly, the great support of the community. Thanks to all of you, the Upgrade Pack has been a tremendous success.

Speaking of success, the release of the first XPages book, *Mastering XPages*, at Lotusphere 2011 exceeded our initial expectations. Despite having shipped three times the normal stock levels to the Lotusphere bookstore, because of the high number of online preorders, the book was completely sold out by Tuesday morning. That had never happened before. Coincidentally, this was also the first Lotusphere that discussed the ExtLib. So with the buzz of *Mastering XPages* in full flow, we floated the idea of another book, dedicated to the ExtLib. This proposal was a little different. By this time we were surfing the social wave; given the open source model on which the project rested, we wanted to get the community involved. Later that same Tuesday, the idea of a new ExtLib book was tweeted, proposing that a different author write each chapter. This social technique worked well. We rapidly got a list of volunteers from the community, which demonstrated both the great commitment of our community as well as the power of social media today. As a result, we ended up with a team of great experts, la crème de la crème, contributing to this book.

You'll note as you leaf through the chapters that the XPages ExtLib is moving to Social. We added numerous social-oriented features, which are certainly going to evolve rapidly over time. Take advantage of them, add social capabilities to your applications, and connect them to the world. There are fantastic opportunities opening up in this space. At the time *Mastering XPages* was published in 2011, we claimed we were at the beginning of a great XPages odyssey. Without a doubt, the success of the ExtLib has proven this. But we're not done; the story relentlessly continues. Further adventures in Social and Mobile will be our major themes going forward, and the XPages ExtLib will continue to be at the core of our innovation.

Enjoy the ExtLib as much as we do!

—Philippe Riand and Martin Donnelly, XPages Architects

Preface

Lotusphere 2011 was memorable in a lot of ways. It was another rip-roaring success for XPages as it continues to gain traction, make converts out of once-skeptics, and project a vision of what application development is going to look like in the years to come. The same event was also notable for the publication of the first real technical book on this technology, *Mastering XPages* by Martin Donnelly, Mark Wallace, and Tony McGuckin. Its approach was to document XPages in a way that hadn't been done before. It created a fantastic stir at Lotusphere 2011 that has reverberated throughout the coming year. Lotusphere, similar to other events, brings like-minded people together to meet face to face and talk. It was at Lotusphere 2011 that a group of XPagers (anyone who develops XPages applications) was talking about how wonderful the *Mastering XPages* book was and expressing how they couldn't wait until the next XPages book was written. This started the ball rolling.

We all have ideas. Some of these ideas never see the light of day, which is not necessarily a bad thing. Other ideas don't go away. The idea for another XPages book began to snowball. By the end of Lotusphere week, more than a few of us nearly swore in blood that we would write this book. And so we did.

The initial target for publication of this book was Lotusphere 2012. When we started to write this book in June 2011, that target was realistic. But as the long summer progressed, those busy bees in the XPages development team were deep into a process of reshaping the XPages ExtLib so IBM would fully support it. Add on the new support for relational databases and the new features to support social application development released to OpenNTF in the latter half of the year; the authors were effectively writing about a moving target. Each moving target stops occasionally to catch its breath.

A milestone was developing with the release of the Lotus Notes Domino 8.5.3 Upgrade Pack (UP) in December 2011. It was a significant release, because it was the first of its type in the

20-year history of Lotus Notes Domino. New features were being released to the market between major releases of the core project, which brought forth the fully IBM-supported version of the XPages Extension Library (ExtLib). What better event to base a book around?

This Book's Approach

The main desire for this book is to collate the knowledge of the XPages ExtLib and to communicate that knowledge to you, the reader. We seek to do this in a progressive way, starting with the basics and finishing with the more technical areas. And it's these advanced areas that we believe will take XPages application development to new heights.

Most chapters, apart from Chapter 13, "Get Social," use one or two applications for reference: the XPages ExtLib Demo application (**XPagesExt.nsf**) and the TeamRoom XL template (**teamrm8xl.ntf**). At the time of writing, both of these applications contain examples for 100% of the controls and components available from the XPages ExtLib. In these examples, we will take you through how to use these controls, describe what the various properties are for, and in some cases recommend how you can take advantage of such controls.

This book targets the December 2011 releases of the XPages ExtLib, be it in the form of the Lotus Notes Domino 8.5.3 UP 1 release or the release to the OpenNTF project. The feature set encapsulated in these releases represents a high point in the story of the technology. But this is not to say that this story is complete—far from it. There may be another book in the offing that will tell the story of how this technology will reach its next high point. Only time will tell.

We recommend that before picking up this book, you become familiar with XPages. One excellent shortcut for this is reading the *Mastering XPages* book, which will give you a firm grounding before you step into the XPages ExtLib. However, you don't have to be an expert in XPages. A basic knowledge of XPages is all you need to take advantage of the ExtLib and build better, more efficient applications more quickly.

Some Conventions

This book employs a few conventions of note that will make reading smooth.

User-interface elements, such as menus, buttons, links, file paths, folders, sample XPages, and Custom Control and so on in Domino Designer or in applications, are styled in the text as bold, for example, "Go to the **Download/Releases** section." Attributes and their options that are selectable from the All Properties view in Designer are also in bold.

Code, be it programming script, markup, or XSP keywords in the text, is typically styled in mono font size. For example, "Developers who have used the Dojo dialog in the past will know that it is opened via Client-Side JavaScript using the `show()` function and closed using the `hide()` function."

Also, in code, the XPages XML markup examples that typically form the listings throughout the book have split multiple attributes to a new line. This makes it easier to read the markup.

Those experienced with reading XPages markup will recognize the default prefix used for the core controls namespace: `xp`, as in `xp:viewPanel` or `xp:button`. They will also recognize that Custom Controls have their own prefix: xc as in xc:layout from the Discussion XL template. The XPages ExtLib namespace has its own prefix, xe, which is used for the more than 150 ExtLib controls; for example, xe:dataView.

How This Book Is Organized

This book is divided into four parts, each a progression for you to navigate through various levels of XPages ExtLib knowledge.

Part I, "The Extension Library, Installation, Deployment, and an Application Tour": This part is aimed at getting you started with the XPages ExtLib. It explains what it is and how you install and deploy it, and it demonstrates in a production-ready application how and why it is used.

- **Chapter 1, "The Next Generation of XPages Controls":** This chapter introduces you to the XPages ExtLib, explains why the controls and components contained within will take XPages application development to the next level, and describes some of the areas that are likely to help grow the XPages technology even further.

- **Chapter 2, "Installation and Deployment of the XPages Extension Library":** This chapter describes the various ways to install and deploy versions of the ExtLib, be it IBM Lotus Notes Domino R8.5.2 or R8.5.3, or server, Domino Designer, or Notes Client.

- **Chapter 3, "TeamRoom Template Tour":** The purpose of this chapter is twofold. First, it is to gently introduce you to the XPages ExtLib. Second, it is to demonstrate how an existing template was modernized with this exciting new technology with features that are built entirely using the ExtLib in a production-ready application.

Part II, "The Basics: The Applications Infrastructure": This is the part of the book where each of more than 150 controls in the XPages ExtLib is described. These six chapters are laid out in a way that a typical Domino application developer might expect; start with a form, and then move on to views and to the overall navigation and layout. That is not to say that you have to read these chapters in that sequence to get a full understanding of the controls. An XPages app developer typically starts with the application layout and navigation before moving on to view and form controls. The sequence in how you read them is up to you. Each chapter can be taken in a standalone fashion.

- **Chapter 4, "Forms, Dynamic Content, and More!":** This chapter, along with Chapters 5 and 6, describes those controls that are typically used in the form of an XPage. With the use of Form Layout, Post, and Dynamic Content and Switch controls, you can quickly take advantage of these prebuilt and preformatted components to deploy complex layouts and design patterns.

- **Chapter 5, "Dojo Made Easy":** Whether you are familiar with Dojo or not, this chapter is aimed at how you can take advantage of this toolkit, which has been encapsulated into the Dojo controls for the XPages ExtLib. Without the ExtLib, configuring Dojo components can be tricky. The controls in the ExtLib make it easier.

- **Chapter 6, "Pop-Ups: Tooltips, Dialogs, and Pickers":** The ExtLib contributes tooltips for displaying additional content, dialogs for displaying or managing content, and pickers for facilitating selection of values. The XPages ExtLib makes this easier for developers, overcoming some of the challenges of integrating Dojo and XPages. This chapter describes all this.

- **Chapter 7, "Views":** Before the ExtLib, there were three available core container controls for displaying a collection of documents: the View Panel, the Data Table, and the Repeat Control. The ExtLib provides some new controls to help you take the display of a data collection to new levels. This chapter describes each one of these new view controls.

- **Chapter 8, "Outlines and Navigation":** For the end user to be able to switch between the different views in the application, you need to create an application layout and navigation. This chapter covers both the Dojo layout controls and navigation controls that have been added to the XPages ExtLib.

- **Chapter 9, "The Application's Layout":** In this chapter, you learn use of the Application Layout control, which helps you meet the challenge of creating an effective application interface that is not only pleasing, but intuitive and consistent, allowing users to predict what behaviors will produce the desired effect. All this is despite the difficulties presented when developing applications with the browser as your target platform.

Part III, "Bell and Whistles: Mobile, REST, RDBMS, and Social": In this part of the book, the big four deliverables to the XPages ExtLib in 2011 are described. If Part II of this book marks a step up in developing XPages applications, this part marks another. The next four chapters effectively describe the direction application development will progress in the coming years. Each of these chapters stands alone.

- **Chapter 10, "XPages Goes Mobile":** Mobile is the technology of the age. Owning a mobile device is no longer a luxury but a necessity. This fact is becoming increasingly important in business, as desktops and laptops are being superseded by tablets and smartphones. This transition has many challenges, ranging from the user interface (UI) design to security. XPages and the ExtLib are in place to meet these mobile challenges. This chapter shows how to meet and overcome these obstacles.

- **Chapter 11, "REST Services":** REpresentational State Transfer (REST) is important to the new Web 2.0 programming model. New technologies like OpenSocial and Android are embracing REST services to allow remote clients access to Server-Side data. The XPages ExtLib has RESTful services in place, so a whole range of exciting data-handling options open for the XPages developer.

- **Chapter 12, "XPages Gets Relational":** This chapter reviews concepts behind integrating relational data and the new relational database components that the ExtLib provides, including JDBC, the Connection Pool and Connection Manager, the datasources, and the Java and Server-Side JavaScript (SSJS) APIs included to integrate relational data into an XPages application.

- **Chapter 13, "Get Social":** Social and social business are the buzzwords of the age. This chapter uses a definition of social applications in the context of XPages, custom application development, and IBM Lotus Domino/IBM XWork Server. It describes the new requirements, maps them to technologies, and shows how the ExtLib helps implement these new requirements.

NOTE: At the time we were writing this manuscript, we were using the product called LotusLive™. This product has since been renamed IBM SmartCloud™ for Social Business.

Part IV, "Getting Under the Covers with Java": Gaining a fuller understanding of XPages Extensibility can be achieved with a little knowledge of Java. In this part of the book, the aim is to help you round out this knowledge and enable you to get the most out of the ExtLib.

- **Chapter 14, "Java Development in XPages":** With the addition of XPages to IBM Lotus Notes Domino, the capacity for inclusion of Java in applications has never been easier or more powerful. This chapter provides a glimpse into some of the many ways Java can take your applications to the next level, as well as a few ways that you can get even more use out of some of the XPages ExtLib controls already described in previous chapters.

Acknowledgments

Books aren't produced by one person. If they were, there would be very few of them. It takes a team of people to get a book to its rightful place on the shelf. That's stating the obvious, we know, but it's to make the point that we would like to thank a whole ream of people who have helped us get this book out the door.

First, we would like to thank the contributing authors for helping out on the book. Without Niklas Heidloff, Stephen Auriemma, Lorcan McDonald, and Simon McLoughlin, we wouldn't be where we are.

A sincere expression of gratitude has to go to the technical reviewers, Brian Benz and Chris Toohey. You guys rock! Your patience, insight, and expertise were a great help to us. Thanks for sticking with us through our adventure.

Thanks for all the leadership help of the Notes Domino Application Development team, especially Eamon Muldoon, Martin Donnelly, Philippe Riand, Pete Janzen, and Maureen Leland for supporting this book from the beginning to the end.

Still at IBM, we would like to thank the following people, who helped put the XPages ExtLib on the map: Andrejus Chaliapinas, Brian Gleeson, Darin Egan, Dan O'Connor, Dave Delay, Edel Gleeson, Elizabeth Sawyer, Graham O'Keeffe, Greg Grunwald, Jim Cooper, Jim Quill, Joseph J Veilleux, Kathy Howard, Kevin Smith, Lisa Henry, Maire Kehoe, Mark Vincenzes, Michael Blout, Mike Kerrigan, Padraic Edwards, Peter Rubinstein, Rama Annavajhala, Robert Harwood, Robert Perron, Teresa Monahan, Tony McGuckin, and Vin Manduca.

Going back to the beginning, we would like to thank Philippe Riand (yes, him again) for lighting the fire with that Twitter post (https://twitter.com/#!/philriand/status/32730855042457601) at Lotusphere 2011. This tweet reverberated, and the XPages community and the wider Lotus Community responded. It is safe to say that without this community, the idea for the book would never have gotten off the ground, so a great big thank-you to all. There aren't enough pages available to thank everyone in the community, but we would like to mention Bruce Elgort, Darren Duke, David Leedy, John Foldager, John Roling, Matt White, Michael Bourak, Michael Falstrup, Nathan T. Freeman, Per Henrik Lausten, Phil Randolph, René Winkelmeyer, Tim Clark, Tim Malone, and Ulrich Krause for the help and inspiration in achieving liftoff and flight.

Still in the community, we would like to thank all those who have participated in the ExtLib project through OpenNTF who have been the early adopters of this technology. Without your feedback, this project likely wouldn't have gotten off the runway.

Finally, we would like to thank Mary Beth Ray, Chris Cleveland, Ellie Bru, Vanessa Evans, Jovana Shirley, Lori Lyons, Steven Stansel, Ellice Uffer, and Karen Gill at IBM Press and Pearson Education for being such wonderful partners in this project.

About the Authors

This book has many authors, all from the XPages community.

Paul Hannan is a senior software engineer in the IBM Ireland software lab in Dublin and a member of the XPages runtime team. He has worked on XPages since it was known as XFaces in Lotus Component Designer. Previous to this, he worked on JSF tooling for Rational® Application Developer, and before that on Notes Domino 6 back to Notes 3.3x and Lotus ScreenCam. A native of County Sligo, Paul now lives in Dublin with his wife Katie and son Alec. A recent convert (dragged kicking and screaming) to opera (not the web browser), Paul also enjoys thinking about stuff, taking pictures, commanding the remote control, and playing with his son and his Lego.

Declan Sciolla-Lynch was born in Dublin, Ireland and now lives in Pittsburgh, Pennsylvania. Declan has been working with IBM Lotus Notes/Domino for more than 15 years. He wrote one of the first XPages learning resources on his blog and is widely considered one of the community's XPages gurus. Declan has spoken at Lotusphere on a number of occasions and has contributed popular projects to OpenNTF, the community's open source hub. He is also an IBM Champion. He and his wife have three dogs and three cats and go to Disney theme parks whenever they get a chance.

Jeremy Hodge, from southern Michigan, is a software architect with ZetaOne Solutions Group and has more than 15 years' experience in the software design industry. He has designed and implemented applications in the vertical market application, custom application, Software as a Service (SaaS), and off-the-shelf product spaces in many platforms and languages, including IBM Lotus Notes/Domino, C/C++/Objective-C, Java, Object Pascal, and others. He has served as the subject matter expert for courses with IBM Lotus Education, including those on XPages applications. He blogs on XPages at XPagesBlog.com and his personal blog at hodgebloge.com.

Paul Withers is senior Domino developer and team leader at Intec Systems Ltd, an IBM Premier Business partner in the UK. He is an IBM Champion for collaboration solutions and the cohost of The XCast XPages podcast. Paul has presented at Lotusphere and various Lotus User Groups across Europe. He has written blogs, wiki articles, and a NotesIn9 episode. He has authored reusable XPages controls and an application, XPages Help Application, on OpenNTF. Outside of work, Paul is a Reading FC supporter and netball umpire in the England Netball National Premier League.

Tim Tripcony leads the Transformer ExtLib development team at GBS, creating XPage components and other JSF artifacts that extend the native capabilities of the Domino platform. He maintains a popular technical blog, Tip of the Iceberg (TimTripcony.com), offering tips on cutting-edge Domino development techniques. He frequently speaks at user group meetings and technical conferences, including Lotusphere. Tim is a globally recognized expert on advanced XPage and JSF development and has been designated an IBM Champion.

Contributing Authors

Niklas Heidloff is a software architect working for the software group in IBM. He is focused on invigorating the application development community and promoting XPages as IBM's web and mobile application development platform for collaborative and social applications. In this role, he is the technical committee chair and a director of the Board of Directors of the open source site OpenNTF.org. Previously, Niklas was responsible for other application development areas in the IBM Lotus Domino space, including composite applications. Before this, he worked on IBM Lotus Notes, IBM WebSphere® Process Choreographer, and IBM Workplace Client Technology. In 1999, he joined IBM as part of the Lotus Workflow team. Niklas studied at the university in Paderborn, Germany, and has a degree in Business Computing (Diplom Wirtschaftsinformatiker).

Stephen Auriemma is an advisory software engineer currently working in the IBM Littleton software lab on an XPages and Domino Access (REST). Stephen has a master's degree in computer science from Boston University. In the past, he worked as a developer on various projects, including Composite Applications for Notes 8.0, the open source project on Apache called Xalan for IBM Research, and Domino Offline Services for Lotus. Stephen started his career with IBM in 1996, providing development technical support for Notes programmability. He lives in Chelmsford, Massachusetts, with his wife and two daughters, Jessica and Amanda.

Simon McLoughlin is a graduate software developer in the IBM Ireland software lab in Dublin working for the XPages mobile team. A graduate of the Institute of Technology, Tallaght, he was responsible for reworking and adding the mobile front end to the Discussion and Team-Room templates delivered with the XPages ExtLib. In college, he studied computer science. In his last year there, he joined with IBM on a research project; the result was a smartphone push alert system to alert native iPhone/Android users that a server undergoing a long run test was running low on resources or approaching some critical state. This project finished in the top 3 for the

Irish software awards for the student category of most commercially viable/innovative. Living in Dublin, Simon enjoys experimenting with new mobile technology and suffers greatly from an addiction to computer games.

Lorcan McDonald is a senior software engineer on the XPages team in the Dublin office of the IBM Ireland software lab. He is the tech lead on the XPages Mobile controls project and has worked on the Domino platform for three years, split between the XPages Runtime team and Quickr® Domino. Before coming to IBM, Lorcan worked on financial web applications for the credit card and trading industries. Born and raised in Sligo, he has been living in Dublin for more than a decade. He never stops thinking about computing problems. He has been known to perform and record music as 7800 beats, presumably via some sort of web interface.

PART I

The Extension Library, Installation, Deployment, and an Application Tour

CHAPTER 1

The Next Generation of XPages Controls

With the release of IBM Lotus Notes Domino 8.5.2 came many exciting new features, one of which is the XPages Extensibility application programming interface (API). It is the notion of extending the core XPages controls with customized controls. The XPages Extensibility framework allows developers to expand upon existing XPages capabilities, build their own artifacts, and move beyond the out-of-the-box features that come with XPages. It allows developers to create and provide their own solutions. Theoretically, consumers no longer need IBM to answer their request for new XPages controls; they can build the controls in-house immediately, without waiting years for them to be part of a release. The power to do this comes with XPages Extensibility.

A prime example of this extensibility is the XPages Extension Library. It's a set of controls and artifacts that form one of the biggest releases to open source by IBM. The controls are easily consumable and deployable, enabling efficient, effective, and fast development. They are the next generation of XPages controls designed to elevate application development and become more up-to-date to meet the software challenges of today and maybe even tomorrow. The extensibility infrastructure facilitates this; only the imagination of the application developers and their ability to create hold it back.

The release of IBM Lotus Notes Domino 8.5.3 in October 2011 allowed for even further progression of the XPages Extension Library. Core changes in the code made it possible for many more exciting features: REST services, mobile support, social business application support, and relational data support.

The release of the IBM Lotus Notes Domino 8.5.3 Upgrade Pack 1 demonstrates that IBM is taking the XPages Extension Library seriously. It's no longer a toy. It's IBM supported and ready for production.

So How Did We Get Here?

XPages has come a long way since 2009, when it was released as part of IBM Lotus Notes Domino R8.5.0. It was revolutionary for Domino because it truly facilitated the modernization of Domino web application development. XPages is the web-application framework for Notes Domino and the recommended approach for anyone writing new web applications or extending or upgrading existing applications to modern web standards. It is an important addition to Domino and application development. Form-based editing for web development is still valid, although XPages provides a more user-friendly method that is standardized and familiar to web developers while adhering to the Domino developer philosophy: creating an enterprise-fit application with minimum fuss.

XPages is on its fourth release, as a runtime feature on the Domino server in R8.5, and as a tooling feature on the Domino Designer, which runs on the Eclipse platform. The XPages development experience features what Domino developers have been calling out for years: drag and drop, source editors, property sheets, resource bundling, and so on. An XPage is the main design element, and along with Custom Controls, it appears in the navigator with instances of controls that can be built in an intuitive what-you-see-is-what-you-get (WYSIWYG) way. Developers can then immediately deploy these XPages to a Domino server. Building web applications should be easy; it is with XPages.

In the beginning, XPages provided a set number of controls, which meant having less to learn but dealing with more restrictions. Soon developers found themselves using similar techniques repeatedly. Custom Controls were developed to prevent this duplication throughout the application. A Custom Control is similar to an XPage. The beauty of Custom Controls is that they are reusable in the application. They also appear in their own palette once they are created, waiting to be of service to developers on the application. Custom Controls can easily be selected and dropped to the design pane of the XPage, much like Subforms are to Notes Forms. All this is fine as long as development is taking place within the same application. But using the same Custom Control on another application means copying the instance to the other application for use there. The procedure works but is not always elegant.

Then Came Domino R.8.5.2, and the Extensibility Door Opened

XPages Extensibility offers a way to break free. Rather than being constricted by building controls based on standard XPages components, Extensibility provides a method for developers to extend the XPages runtime framework.

It allows them to build their own XPages artifacts and user interface controls from the ground up, featuring their own behaviors and functionality that they and others can then consume within any XPages applications and potentially on any XPages server. The developers now have the *power* in a sense. They no longer need to ask IBM to enhance their software tools hoping that someday IBM will address it. If developers have the ability and the knowledge, they can enhance the tools themselves now. They can create their own controls to solve their business needs. With XPages Extensibility, what was thought impossible has become probable.

OpenNTF and the Controls Too Good Not to Release

The XPages Extension Library is currently the best example available of the power of XPages Extensibility. It contains more than 150 controls and complex properties built from scratch and covers a wide range of use cases. The list of controls is growing, allowing Domino to break new ground in areas where it traditionally feared to tread: working with relational data, developing mobile applications, provisioning REST services, and making social connections for business, among others. And all this is available free from OpenNTF.org (http://extlib.openntf.org).

OpenNTF is an organization, founded in 2002, that is devoted to enabling groups or individuals all over the world to collaborate on IBM Lotus Notes/Domino applications and release them as open source. The OpenNTF Alliance, formed in 2009, also provides a framework for the community so that open source applications may be freely distributed, using widely accepted licensing terms. The mission of the OpenNTF Alliance is to increase the quality and quantity of templates, applications, and samples that are shared by the community so the community can grow and be successful.

IBM decided to share the XPages Extension Library with this community because it felt that these controls were too good *not* to release; IBM didn't want to wait any longer to get feedback from the community. This feedback is being used for the betterment of the product, which is evident from the number of changes and updates since the XPages Extension Library's release in September 2010. It can only get better.

To Extensibility and Beyond

Extensibility is one of the main tracks for future XPages core development. The next set of enhancements is being built upon it. Depending on the enterprise needs, because of all the advantages extensibility brings, all future developments of XPages will be done through the XPages Extension Library. Does there need to be a way to interface with relational databases? Do you need to handle REST services better? Do you want to build a UI that is smartphone friendly? Do you have a goal of breaking down the barriers to social business? Or do you just want to build XPages applications easier, faster, and better? All this is possible with extensibility and in the next generation of XPages controls that are part of the Extension Library.

What Makes an XPages Control Next Generation?

It's said that every generation throws a hero up the pop charts. This is certainly true with software development continually responding to the world's technology needs. Software is always evolving; sometimes it succeeds, and other times it fails. Technology without evolution becomes tomorrow's trash; technology is constantly looking for the next generation.

Saying that something is the *next generation* doesn't always mean that it is so. In the dotcom bubble burst, many things that were touted as being the *next generation* turned out not to be for reasons like revenue generation. Commentators need to be mindful of this when saying something is *next generation*.

So for XPages, let's start at what might be called the first generation. In the first couple of releases of IBM Lotus Notes Domino 8.5x, the set of controls that came with XPages and what is represented on the Designer palette could have been called *next generation* at the time. XPages certainly revolutionized the way web applications were created in Domino. This was *next generation* stuff. The tag *next generation* has a certain life span, however. With success, the next generation becomes the norm; it becomes everyday stuff that is indispensible.

XPages is now the norm; it's the recommended way to build Domino web applications and web-based solutions. But it isn't standing still, resting on its laurels; it's evolving. And with the Extension Library, a clearer picture is emerging of what the next generation of the XPages controls might look like.

Certain themes are popping up of what the next generation of XPages controls might involve:

- Make application development faster.
- Provide the tools that developers need to take the drudgery out of application development and allow them to put in more creativity.
- Make applications perform better, scale better, and provide best practices out of the box.
- Give developers shortcuts to learning.
- Give developers the tools that will enable them to create applications that will harness the new technologies to respond to the business needs of tomorrow.
- Give developers the power to compete and to succeed.

The next generation of XPages controls may help application developers do these things. They are here in the form of the XPages Extension Library.

What Is the XPages Extension Library?

Let's start with the standard definition of the XPages Extension Library. It's a library that provides a set of new XPages artifacts that are ready to use. It's provided as an open source project (http://extlib.openntf.org) on OpenNTF, which is an organization devoted to getting groups of individuals together to collaborate on Lotus Notes/Domino applications and tools, and release them as open source to the general public to be downloaded from the OpenNTF website.

The entire source code is available from plugins when the Extension Library is installed, either through OpenNTF or the Upgrade Pack, in Designer. IBM contributed it to support the enhancement of Notes/Domino application development. The code contains a set of new XPages controls that supplement the existing ones by providing new capability. It is built atop IBM Lotus Notes Domino R8.5.2, using the XPages Extension API provided with that release, and is carried through to subsequent releases. As such, it is also a nice example of how to use this API. The XPages Extension Library saves application developers from writing their own user interface controls for most use cases. For all other use cases, developers require some Java programming skills to take full advantage of the XPages extensibility.

An alternative or additional definition could be that the XPages Extension Library represents a way in which IBM software is released more frequently. Instead of having to wait years, releases of XPages features and bug fixes can occur monthly. Releasing software in smaller chunks makes it more agile, which benefits IBM, its business partners, and customers who are developing applications. Decreasing development time and time to market makes the release cycle more attractive and more flexible, lowers costs, and increases user satisfaction. Releasing the Extension Library becomes a no-brainer from a software development point of view.

Most of the controls in the XPages Extension Library started life as Custom Controls. Developers can reuse these controls in an elegant and effective way by making them part of the XPages runtime framework. This is done with extensibility. Chapter 12 of the *Mastering XPages* book published by IBM Press takes developers through this process step by step. The XPages Extension Library could be defined as a collection of glorified Custom Controls for everyone to use and share.

Today the XPages Extension Library is the most popular project (more than 1,300 downloads per month) on OpenNTF. Its long-term plan is to incorporate some of these projects into core IBM product, providing a certain criteria is met. The first step along this path is the Upgrade Pack release of the XPages Extension Library into Notes Domino R8.5.3. Because of the easier deployment with the release of Domino 8.5.3, users will be able to build XPages applications with the Extension Library out of the box.

The way the XPages Extension Library has evolved on OpenNTF from a technical point of view projects how the library will develop in the future. The XPages Extension Library started life on OpenNTF as a series of plugins: the com.ibm.xsp.extlib library. In October 2011, a second library of plugins was delivered to OpenNTF: the com.ibm.xsp.extlibx library. Now the XPages Extension Library contains two libraries with distinct sets of plugins. The original library, ExtLib, contains all the controls and features that have been consumed back into the IBM software product range. The first release of this library is in the first Upgrade Pack to IBM Lotus Notes/Domino R8.5.3.

The second and latest plugin to the XPages Extension Library is ExtLibx. It contains all new controls and features and is an incubation phase for the latest library developments. The features from the ExtLibx may at some point become part of the core product like ExtLib. This important incubation phase allows IBM to quickly deliver to its business partners and customers the innovation, ideas, and technology drivers that will keep XPages at the cutting edge. Examples of these would be the relational data management system feature for XPages and the new tools for social business. Hatching from incubation with maturity, stability, and a sound business use case and these features, ExtLibx may become part of the core product, ExtLib.

With IBM now supporting the XPages Extension Library through the Upgrade Packs, we're at a point where full adoption of the XPages Extension Library has been made easy. It is time to come to grips with this *next generation* technology.

Making Domino Application Development Easier, Faster, and Better

One of the main goals of the Extension Library is to make the Domino web application development easier, faster, and better. It's about taking common design patterns, building these into reusable controls, and then incorporating them into libraries for deployment.

This, in the long run, lowers the cost of application development. Take, for example, the Application Layout control from the library. It will enable developers in minutes to create a layout for an application that might have previously taken hours or perhaps days to do with conventional XPages controls. This frees up time, allowing developers to concentrate on the trickier aspects on the development of the application. This in turn saves on cost while making the application better at the same time.

Another goal is to provide developers with some handy controls that can make their applications easier to use. Take the `KeepSessionAlive` control, for example. Simply dropping this to an XPage transforms the way this page behaves on the browser, enabling the user to create and edit documents without necessarily submitting data over a long period. The data that the user has worked upon in that session will still be there until the user is ready to commit the data to storage.

By upgrading to Notes Domino 8.5.2 and 8.5.3, businesses automatically gain performance and scalability enhancements. On performance, developers or administrators only get so much from the server's configuration; the rest has to come from the configuration of the application. Chapter 16 of *Mastering XPages* can help developers bring their application up to scratch, teaching them the techniques they need to know to make the application perform better. One example of this involves changing the way a certain control or action is used or executed. Let's take the Open Page simple action as an example. Using it without a Server-Side JavaScript (SSJS) request effectively wastes server processing in that the POST-based request (a request issued by the browser when the contents of the web page are submitted to the server) is sent to the server, which then returns a Client-Side redirect response to the browser. Then the browser executes the Client-Side redirect to send back to the server a GET-based request (a request sent from a browser when a user enters a new URL address or navigates to another web page typically) for the target of the Open Page simple action. This same action can be accomplished without the server processing expense by using the **parameters complex** property and eliminating four server lifecycle phases, a double request scenario, and a reduction in server CPU usage.

This performance technique is built into some XPages Extension Library controls. The Data View control contains navigation links that use the GET-based request. The Change Dynamic Content action uses this technique, too, where applying the same parameters produces the same result: performing best practices out of the box.

What Are the Most Important Controls and Why?

Learning 150 controls at once can be daunting. It might be more advantageous to learn just a few important controls that will give an application that extra punch without too much effort.

Picking the top five controls is open to opinion, but the following are what we consider the five most important controls:

- Application Layout
- Page Navigator
- Dynamic Content
- Dynamic View
- Data View

These controls will be explained in full later in this book, but it's worth focusing on them a little here.

Two of these controls—the Application Layout and the Dynamic View—can modernize most Domino applications to XPages without too much effort or time. Developers can configure the Application Layout control to present the application's look and feel. Developers can configure the Dynamic View control to display all the Notes views in the database. After that, developers can use a couple of other Extension Library controls, such as Form controls, to read and use document content. Using these controls can take the pain out of XPages development.

Rather than create numerous XPages to perform various functions like creating documents and displaying collections in views, developers can use a Dynamic Content control to display everything on one XPage. A Dynamic Content control is a panel that displays a section or facet of a page or dynamic page part. It creates its children from a facet definition, based on the facet name. It can also save developers needless server transitions by using a Change Dynamic Simple Action or changing the show parameter in an action. A good example of using the Dynamic Content control is in the TeamRoom template that has been extended with the XPages Extension Library. In the allDocuments XPage, a switch control drives the views displayed by the Dynamic Content control. It displays the contents of the All Documents view by default, with options to display All by date, All by author, All by team views, or even filter the selected view. It's flexible, and it's contained in one XPage.

Finally, another useful control to learn is the Data View. A more advanced way to view a data collection, Data View is a control based upon the conventional View Panel control. Data View is flexible, although complex. Once the richness of the Data View is mastered, this control will be a friend to developers. Again, the TeamRoom contains many fine examples, and the Data View is used throughout that template more than any other control to display view collection data from a Notes view.

XPages Learning Shortcuts

Application development should aim to be easy so that almost everyone can do it. It should be like driving a car from point A to point B without needing to know exactly how the internal combustion engine works. It shouldn't be a requirement that the developer knows *everything*, although it does help to know *something*.

By setting a number of options on the Application Layout control, developers can create the backbone of the application with little effort. All they need to know and understand is what these options are, what they do, and what effect they have. Building a layout for an application from scratch, without the shortcuts from the Extension Library, can be challenging, especially if the design specification isn't complicated. Being an expert in the Cascading Style Sheets (CSS) language will certainly help developers here, but creating a custom look and feel for an application is time consuming. Before the Extension Library, certain shortcuts were available in XPages, such as the OneUI theme and the application layout framework projects. (Go to **OpenNTF** and search for the **XPages Framework** project.) These projects, which are Custom Controls that developers add to their application, are reference themes and styling already present on the Notes Domino installation. This, in one step, simplifies what the developer needs to know. The Application Layout control from the Extension Library does this and more.

The Application Layout control is but one example from the Extension Library that helps developers take shortcuts without compromising quality. By the very nature of the Extension Library, just about each control gives developers the shortcuts they need to work on the main features and purpose of a project.

Bells and Whistles: Welcome to the Future

The XPages Extension Library isn't just about the controls; it also has its eye on the challenges facing application development. Technology provides new ways for societies and communities to collaborate. This is a world that is becoming more mobile; people expect wireless and don't want to be tied to a desk. Technology serves up data, regardless of its source, in a consumable and more usable way. Bringing this world into the application gives it a new dimension and enables it to become an application of the future.

Get Social

Social business is the industry buzzword of the year, or at least the most commonly used word to describe enterprise-level collaboration. It's a new way of doing business and the greatest leap forward of our age. Isn't it?

Social business is not new. It's been around for years—since mankind started to trade goods and services, and since neighbors traded surplus goods with each other and got something bartered in return. They found out what they needed and what was needed in exchange by being social, communicating infinite needs and wants to neighbors and friends.

The way we socialize and the way we do business has changed throughout the millennia. Early trading centered on forest clearings, river junctions, and where paths met. When this activity increased, permanent settlements were established, and markets formed. Ideas and innovations were exchanged alongside traded goods at a faster rate. Villages became towns, and towns became cities. All this happened because of social business.

What's new are the tools used for business. Face-to-face conversations have always occurred, whether at crossroads, town hall meetings, public houses, or other meeting places where ideas and knowledge are exchanged. An advancement came when newspapers and printed media made it possible for information to be broadcast over greater distances. Today, though, in the electronic and digital age, business is global. The tools used for social business have made this happen, and they continue to evolve.

Software development is at the forefront of this social business evolution. IBM Software is in this space and has been for years. Lotus Notes and Domino, the collaboration and business platform, has been the leader in this field, and it continues to evolve. XPages Extensibility opens the door for further expansion through social enablers, making it easy for developers to connect to and incorporate aspects from social networking tools into their applications. Whether displaying a user's information or accessing social data from different systems, the addition of the social tools in the Extension Library takes collaboration to a new level.

Upwardly Mobile

Mobile is the technology of the age. Owning a mobile device is no longer a luxury but a necessity. This fact is becoming increasingly important in business as desktops and laptops are being superseded by tablets and smartphones. This transition has many challenges, ranging from the user interface (UI) design to security. XPages and the Extension Library are in place to meet these mobile challenges by taking existing web applications and rendering a native look-and-feel on the device. It's secure; no data is stored on the device. It's a regular Domino application running on a mobile device. The Extension Library provides controls that are easy to use, enabling the developer to build a mobile interface onto existing applications rapidly.

These features have been built into the Discussion and TeamRoom templates that have been released as part of the IBM-supported version of the Extension Library. Applying these templates in the IBM Notes Domino R8.5.3 Upgrade Pack, along with the library, makes for a compelling leap forward. Enterprise applications become usable from mobile devices with more or less a flick of the switch.

Relational Data

If the enhancements for mobile represent future technologies, then the implementation for support to access relational databases represents the technologies now. With the release of IBM Lotus Notes Domino 8.5.3 and the associated XPages Extension Library, the door is open to utilize XPages as the integration point between disparate systems.

With these advancements, relational data can be exercised in the same manner as data from the Domino database forming data collections and editing data. This enables developers to provide wide-ranging solutions without having to configure intermediary systems to handle the exchanges between Domino and other information management systems.

This is an enhancement that was requested for many years. Solutions were tried with varying degrees of success. The solution provided by the XPages Extension Library is more elegant. If the relational database has a JDBC driver, it works.

RESTful Web Services

Further data-handling enhancements are now available in the form of REpresentational State Transfer (REST). REST is a set of principles that define a communication protocol used when constructing a web application. REST is important to the new Web 2.0 programming model. New technologies like IBM Connections, OpenSocial, Google Services, Android, and Microsoft® are embracing REST web services to allow remote clients access to server-side data. REST isn't tied to one operating system, machine, or technology. For the Web, it's design once, run anywhere. The XPages Extension Library has RESTful web services in place, so a range of exciting data-handling options is available for the XPages developer. The options come ready to use out of the box, with extra options in place to allow for more advanced configurations with servlets.

It's staggering what capabilities the XPages Extension Library can deliver. The original list of controls and artifacts provided by the initial release, along with newer mobile, relational, REST, and social capabilities, makes the library the most essential tool for application development. Its empowerment is breathtaking.

Doing It Yourself with Java

A book on the XPages Extension Library would not be complete without mentioning Java. It's the programming language that is becoming more and more prevalent in Notes Domino. With the notion of extensibility in XPages and using it directly in applications, Java has become an element that people can no longer ignore. For developers who want to be able to use a managed bean in an XPages application or build their own controls for an Extension Library, knowledge of Java programming is necessary. It's not essential that they know everything about this programming language but enough to allow them to take their first steps.

For typical Domino developers, using Java in applications involves stepping out of their comfort zone somewhat. Chapter 14, "Java Development in XPages," will get them comfortable again. XPages gives extra capacity for the inclusion of Java into Domino applications and makes these applications even more powerful. Chapter 14 provides a glimpse into some of the many ways Java can take an application to the next level, as well as a few ways developers can get even more use out of some of the Extension Library controls.

Conclusion

This chapter introduced the XPages Extension Library and described its components that make it essential to application development in the future. The next chapters in this Part, "Installation and Deployment of the XPages Extension Library," and "TeamRoom Template Tour," will ease you gently into using the library before getting deeper into the new controls. The next generation of XPages controls is here. All that's needed is to let them out of the box.

CHAPTER 2

Installation and Deployment of the XPages Extension Library

Users wishing to begin utilizing the new controls from the XPages Extension Library (ExtLib) in an application need to install the library to both the Domino Designer and the Domino server, as well as consider various deployment strategies for the Notes Client end users. This chapter is written for the XPages developer and the administrator of the Domino environment. It shows how to deploy the ExtLib for various scenarios.

Until the release of the IBM Lotus Notes Domino 8.5.3 Upgrade Pack 1 in December 2011, a common misconception was that the installation, deployment, and maintenance of the ExtLib was quite an undertaking. However, the ExtLib is constantly evolving to meet the needs of the enterprise while delivering expected feature functionality to users. Thus, it became necessary to maintain the Extension Library post-initial setup. This chapter illustrates how you can easily deploy the Extension Library in your IBM Lotus Notes Domino or IBM XWork environment. It takes you through downloading the latest releases to enabling automated deployment.

The ExtLib from OpenNTF requires IBM Lotus Domino Server version 8.5.2 or higher to work, whereas the IBM supported version of the ExtLib requires IBM Lotus Domino Server version 8.5.3 to work. The ExtLib does not work on Domino 8.5.1 or lower, because the server does not include any of the required extension points that ExtLib hooks into to provide the additional controls and artifacts.

Downloading the ExtLib

You can download the ExtLib from two places: the OpenNTF website (http://extlib.openntf.org) for IBM Lotus Notes Domino 8.5.2 and above or as part of the IBM Lotus Domino 8.5.3 Upgrade Packs available from Passport Advantage® (http://www.ibm.com/software/passportadvantage) for IBM Lotus Notes Domino 8.5.3 or above. There are two available places for download because of license and, more significantly, because the download from Passport Advantage is fully supported by IBM.

Customers and business partners have access to Passport Advantage. Once you're there, it's easy to navigate to the Online section to sign in and download the build. For IBM Lotus Notes Domino 8.5.3 Upgrade Pack 1, the build part number that locates the downloadable file is CI5GIEN. There is only one download for the complete Upgrade Pack; the zip file contains all platform installs for the server, client, and designer client. It isn't possible to take one part of this install; you must download all parts under the same part number.

After you've downloaded the file, extract the contents of the zip file to a temporary folder. The extract zip contains three folders: **client**, **designer**, and **domino**, along with a **readme.txt** file. The readme is small but contains a link to the Lotus Notes and Domino Application Development Wiki (http://www-10.lotus.com/ldd/ddwiki.nsf), which contains the documentation to accompany the Upgrade Pack. The three folders contain the install executables for each platform that Lotus Notes Domino 8.5.3 supports.

You can also download the ExtLib from the OpenNTF project under the same name (http://extlib.openntf.org).

Once you're at the site, go to the **Download/Releases** section, as shown in Figure 2.1, and select the latest release.

TIP

It is best to use the same release of ExtLib on the servers as what the developers and end users are using in the organization.

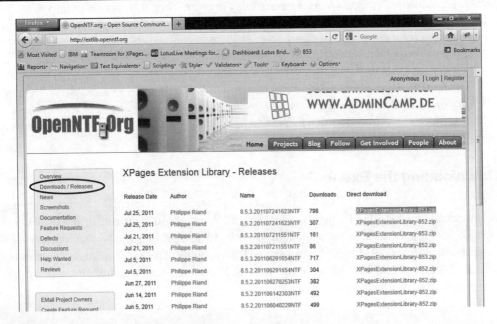

Figure 2.1   ExtLib download and releases.

The downloaded file from the OpenNTF project is in zip format. It contains numerous files; an example of which from the 8.5.3 release in January 2012 is shown in Listing 2.1.

Listing 2.1   Files Extracted from the ExtLib Download

```
discussion8xl.ntf
doclib8xl.ntf
DominoDataServiceDoc.zip
Extension Library REST Services.pdf
ExtLib-Notes85.zip
FirebugLiteLicense
LICENSE
NOTICE
readme.pdf
SLF4JLicense
srcOpenNTF-designer.zip
srcOpenNTF.zip
srcOpenNTFSamples.zip
teamrm8xl.ntf
updateSiteOpenNTF-designer.zip
updateSiteOpenNTF.zip
updateSiteOpenNTFSamples.zip
WebSecurityStore.ntf
XPages Extension Library - Slides.pdf
XPages Goes Relational.odp
XPages-Doc.zip
XPagesExt.nsf
XPagesJDBC.nsf
XPagesSBT.nsf
```

The **src*.zip** files contains the open source files for the ExtLib. Developers proficient in Java can use those files to explore the controls and customize them for their own use.

Developers interested in enhancing and exploring the ExtLib through the modification of the Java source files can reference the Javadoc documentation found in **XPages-Doc.zip**. Extract the files to a local directory. Loading **index.html** in a web browser gives you one-click access to information on the various ExtLib controls, their properties, and more (see Figure 2.2).

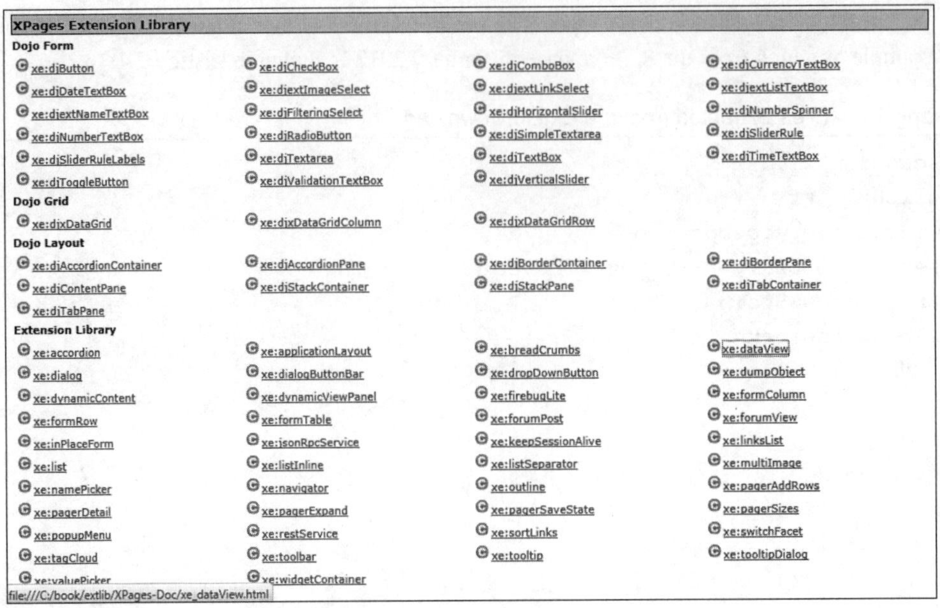

Figure 2.2   ExtLib documentation from the download from the OpenNTF website.

The PDF files, **XPages Extension Library - Slides.pdf**, **Extension Library REST Services.pdf**, and **readme.pdf**, and the **XPages Goes Relational.odp** file, give developers and server administrators an introduction to this OpenNTF project. From the high-level architectural overview to instructions on how to use some controls, developers and administrators have what they need to go beyond the introductory level.

The ExtLib demonstration application, **XPagesExt.nsf**, is a powerful education tool in itself, but it does require a configured instance of the ExtLib to render. (An online demo of this application is available. Go to http://xpages.info/, select the **Demo** tab, and then go to the **Live XPages Development Controls from OpenNTF** section. Note, however, that the version of the application being demonstrated won't likely match the version downloaded.) This application will show the developer live, working examples of most of the ExtLib controls. By exploring this application in Domino Designer, developers are given an application they can reverse-engineer. This allows the discovery of the technological principles behind the XPages contained within the application and shows how certain controls are used in each of the examples.

Along with the **XPagesEXT.nsf**, the download contains a number of other demo apps. The file **XPagesJDBC.nsf** demonstrates the Relational support from the ExtLib, while **XPagesSBT.nsf** is the app that shows off the capabilities of the Social Enabler from the ExtLib. Both of these applications demonstrate the experimental features in the ExtLib.

TIP

It is advised that you put this application on the Domino server so that the user can refer to it when needed. Many of the examples demonstrated in this application are described in later chapters.

The Notes Domino templates, Discussion (**discussion8xl.ntf**) and TeamRoom (**teamrm8xl.ntf**) are also part of the ExtLib download. These are fully functional templates that are ready to use enterprise environments and are also a showcase for the features of the ExtLib.

The most important files in the archive are the **updateSiteOpenNTF*.zips**, which contain the ExtLib Eclipse plugins. These files contain everything that the administrator and developer need to deploy ExtLib on both servers and end users' machines.

Installing the ExtLib via the Upgrade Pack

If you're installing the ExtLib for the first time on a system that has *never* had it deployed, this process is relatively straightforward. You must have a licensed version of the product to install the Upgrade Pack. The install executable locates the installed product on the system and completes the installation of the Upgrade Pack as long as that product isn't running. The Upgrade Pack installer is an addon that installs to an existing install. It doesn't contain a standalone edition of the product.

For more information on installing the Upgrade Pack to Lotus Notes Domino 8.5.3 and beyond, refer to the online documentation available from the Lotus Notes and Domino Application Development wiki (http://www-10.lotus.com/ldd/ddwiki.nsf).

Installing the Upgrade Pack on a system that has the OpenNTF version of the Extension Library installed is likely to cause problems, chief being that the runtime will not function as expected and possibly not at all. The systems do use the same class files, plugin names, and so forth, but that is where the similarities end. Mismatches will occur particularly if the release data stamp of either is out of sequence. Even if they are within sequence, there is no guarantee that they will work together; in addition, IBM doesn't support this configuration. So before installing the Upgrade Pack, manually remove any previous version of the Extension Library from your designated system that originated from an OpenNTF release.

The Upgrade Pack uses an add-on installer. Future Upgrade Packs should be able to install over the previous version without breaking the functionality of the server, so removing the previous version of the Extension Library isn't a requirement.

Deploying ExtLib to Developers in Designer

Developers need to install the Extension Library to Domino Designer before they can begin using the various controls in their applications. The great advantage of installing the ExtLib into the Designer is that developers can begin creating applications with the library and see the result of their endeavors when they run the XPages application in the Notes Client (XPiNC) locally. Developers can also preview the application locally in the web browser, but this requires an additional manual step post-installation of the Extension Library from OpenNTF: copying the runtime ExtLib files to the same location as the existing XPages runtime files, which is usually the **osgi** folder off the Designer root. One of the many advantages of installing the Designer executable (**853UpgradePack1_20111208-0717.exe**) from the Upgrade Pack is that it installs the Extension Library runtime to the local preview HTTP server as well as to XPiNC with the design runtime.

If developers want to use the preview server in Windows® Vista or Windows 7, they need to launch Lotus Notes\Designer via Run as Administrator.

If end users are required to use the ExtLib controls in XPiNC applications, administrators need to deploy the ExtLib to all who use Notes Client. (The various deployment strategies are described in "Deploying the Extension Library to End Users," later in this chapter.) XPages developers can take advantage of this same end user deployment strategy and skip the following ExtLib installation instructions.

If, however, developers are planning to create only server-based web applications, they need to have the ExtLib deployed to their machines, and the administrators need to deploy the ExtLib to the server machines.

Developers can take care of manual deployment using an update site from OpenNTF or using the installer executable from the Upgrade Pack. If administrators are using automatic server deployments, as described later in this chapter under the "Automatic Server Deployment in Domino for 8.5.3" section, it is recommended that developers use the same update site to ensure that the developers are running the same version of ExtLib as the servers.

For OpenNTF release, the first step in a manual deployment is to verify in Domino Designer that the **Preferences** option to **Enable Eclipse Plug-in Install** is selected, as in Figure 2.3. If this menu option is not visible, the Domino administrator may have disabled it via a policy document and need to re-enable it before continuing.

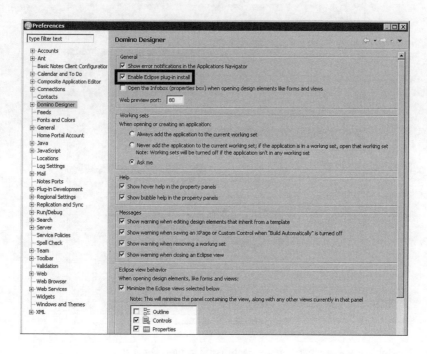

Figure 2.3   Enable Eclipse Plugin Install in Domino Designer.

Start the installation process by selecting the **File** → **Application** → **Install** menu options, as in Figure 2.4.

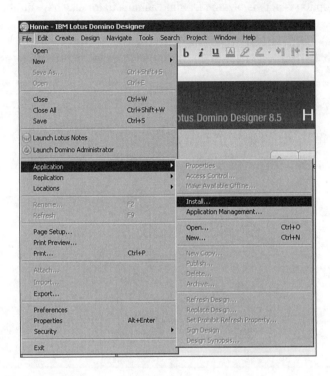

Figure 2.4   Begin the installation of the ExtLib on Domino Designer.

In the next dialog box, select the **Search for New Features to Install** option, as shown in Figure 2.5. Then click **Next** to continue.

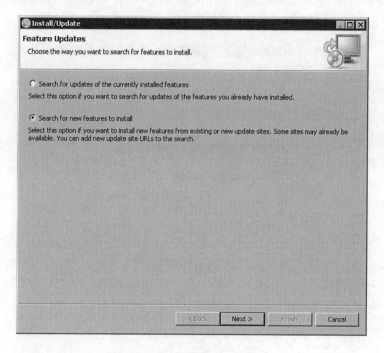

Figure 2.5　　Select the Search for New Features to Install option.

The dialog that follows may appear empty; regardless, you need to add the location of the new update site. If you're using the update site downloaded from OpenNTF, select the **Add Zip/Jar Location** button and then select the **updateSite.zip** file, as shown in Figure 2.6.

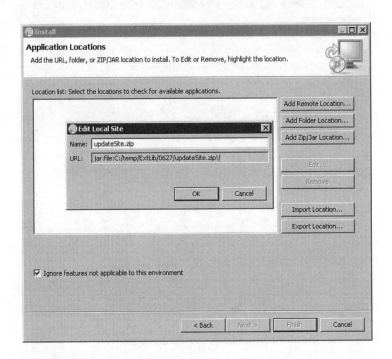

Figure 2.6   Installing from the updateSite.zip file.

If you're using the update site created for your automatic server deployments, select the **Add Remote Location** button and fill in a name and URL for the update site (see Figure 2.7).

Figure 2.7   The server deployment database or update site.

Regardless of which update site you added or which method you used, click the **Finish** button. You're next shown a list of features you can install into the Domino Designer client (see Figure 2.8).

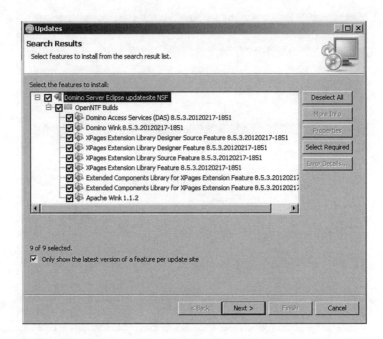

Figure 2.8   ExtLib update site version.

You may select all the available features to install as illustrated, or just select one if desired, and then click **Next** and then **Accept** to accept the Apache license agreement, if you're using the OpenNTF version. Click **Next** and then **Finish**.

Because the plugins don't have a digital signature, depending on the client's security settings, a dialog box may appear asking if the user still wants to perform the install, as in Figure 2.9. Select the option **Install This Plug-in**, and then click **OK**.

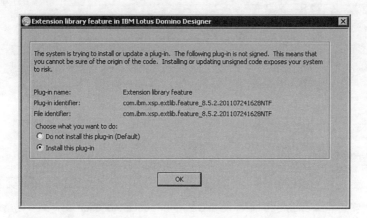

Figure 2.9   Plugin install confirmation.

After the plugin has been installed, the user must restart the Lotus Notes Client to complete the install.

Once Designer has restarted, the developer can quickly verify that the installation of the Extension Library has been successful. Create a new application and then an XPage within this application. When this XPage launches, the palette on the right side becomes populated with the newly installed extended controls, as in Figure 2.10.

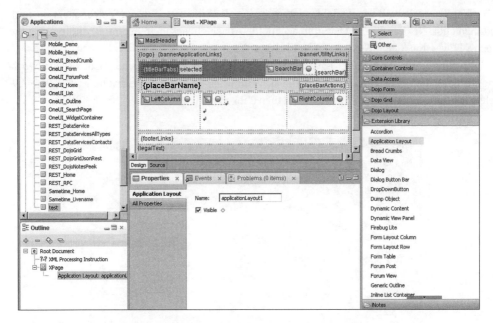

Figure 2.10   The new extended controls in Designer post installation.

The palette may seem cluttered with the extra options available from the Extension Library, but you can remedy this in Designer 8.5.3 by using **Palette Profiles**. Add these by selecting **File → Preferences** from the main menu, and then select **Domino Designer** and then **Palette** from the dialog box. From here, select the **New** button to create a name for the profile. Then select the desired palette drawers to appear in this profile. The user can then switch to this palette profile and tidy up the XPages palette.

Taking this one step further, the XPages developer can run applications that use the extended controls in the Notes Client locally. The ExtLib Demo application comes with the OpenNTF download. This application provides examples of most of the extended controls available on the library. It is a valuable education tool that can help the XPages developer get started on the extended controls.

You can also preview this application in the Notes Client, as shown in Figure 2.11. Do this by selecting **Design → Preview in Notes Client**.

Figure 2.11   Running the ExtLib Demo application in the Notes Client.

Uninstalling the Extension Library from Designer

Uninstalling the Extension Library from Domino Designer is straightforward. The reasons for uninstalling can vary. One reason might be to install a previous version of the Extension Library to what is currently installed. Another could be to keep the development environment tidy and not have multiple versions of the library cluttering the file system.

The way the Extension Library is uninstalled differs depending on the installation type. If installed through the Upgrade Pack, the ExtLib is uninstalled along with the rest of the Upgrade Pack through the **Program and Features** program, as you would do with any other installation in Windows. Uninstalling the Extension Library that originated from OpenNTF is completely different.

In Designer, select **File → Application → Application Management** to launch the **Application Management** dialog. From this dialog, you have several options for the management of the plugin, namely **Disable**, **Uninstall**, and **Show Properties**, as shown in Figure 2.12.

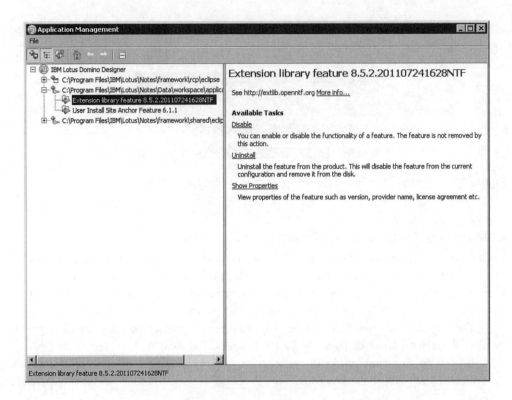

Figure 2.12   The Application Management dialog with the Extension Library highlighted.

Select the **Uninstall** option for the Extension Library feature. A message prompt then appears to confirm the selection of this option. After you've confirmed the option, the user is prompted to restart Designer; this completes the uninstallation of the Extension Library.

Server Deployment

The way the ExtLib is deployed to Domino or XWork servers depends on the source of the download. If you're using the Upgrade Pack, an AddOn installer is provided for server installations. If you're using releases from OpenNTF, which doesn't have an installer executable, other methods are required to deploy the ExtLib.

Automatic Server Deployment in Domino 8.5.3

Domino 8.5.3 (which was released in September 2011) contains a feature that makes it easy for the administrator to deploy and update an Extension Library from OpenNTF without manually copying files to the Domino Server. Using a standard Notes Storage Facility (NSF) based on **updateSite.ntf**, the administrator can dynamically deploy OSGi plugins to the server.

This new feature is optional and simple to use. By default, the dynamic contribution is turned off. To enable it, you must add a variable to the **notes.ini** that contains the database paths allowed to contribute dynamic plugins: **OSGI_HTTP_DYNAMIC_BUNDLES= updateSite1.nsf,updateSite2.nsf**, for example. For each database specified in OSGI_HTTP_ DYNAMIC_BUNDLES, the server administrator needs to create a database based on the **updateSite.ntf** template and then create replicas in all the servers (upon which the above variable must be set) of the cluster or domain. This enables the deployment of Extension Library almost seamlessly.

For the server's administrator, the steps to enable this feature are straightforward, although they're configured in a number of places. The first step is to create a database on the server using the Eclipse update site (**updateSite.ntf**) template. Select **File → Application → New**, which launches the New Application dialog. From here, select a server where the application is to be created. Then on the same dialog select a server upon which the **updateSite.ntf** template resides, as in Figure 2.13.

Figure 2.13 The New Application dialog where the update site application is created.

Selecting the **OK** button on this dialog creates the application. Then it is a matter of modifying the application's Access Control List (ACL) for those who are to be allowed to create documents, and thus deploy plugins to the server. Modify the ACL of the databases to only allow trusted users (**Author Access at a Minimum**). No one else should have access. Also, set the **Do Not Show in Open Application Dialog** flag on the database.

The application is now ready to begin deploying the Extension Library. On the view, **Main Features**, select the **Import Local Update Site** action button. This launches a dialog that allows you to select a **site.xml** file from an Eclipse plugin project, as in Figure 2.14. For the ExtLib, this is located in the **updateSite.zip** file, which when extracted contains the **site.xml** file and two folders: **Features** and **Plugins**. Select **OK** on this dialog to begin the import process.

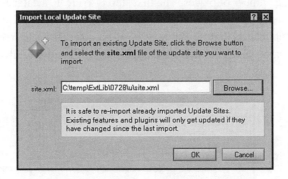

Figure 2.14   The Import Local Update Site dialog with the site.xml file from the ExtLib updateSite zip file.

Once the import is complete, the view of the update site database is updated with a document representing the import of the plugin, as shown in Figure 2.15.

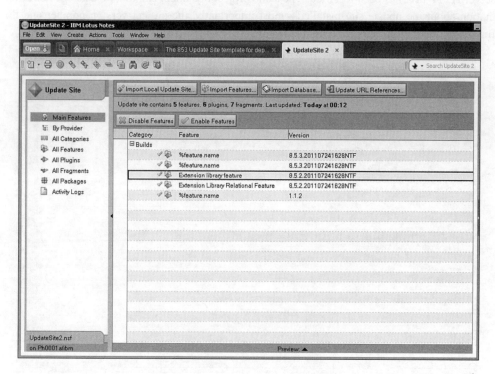

Figure 2.15   The updated site installation has been completed.

After it's installed, the default state of the update site is to be enabled. You can disable this same project document, which means that it will not be picked up by the OSGi runtime when the server HTTP task has been restarted. The same project document can tell the user a lot of information about the update site installed—most importantly, the project version number and the fragments and plugins bundled with this feature (see Figure 2.16).

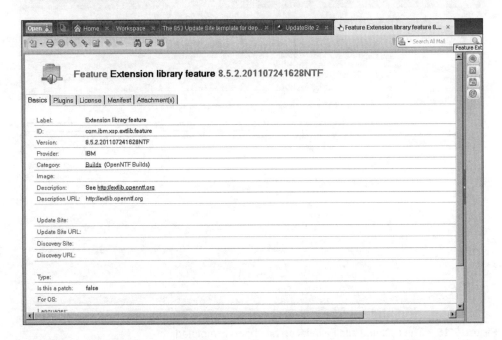

Figure 2.16   The update site document.

All that is left to do here is to put the reference to this update site database in the **notes.ini**, **OSGI_HTTP_DYNAMIC_BUNDLES=updateSite1.nsf**, for example. As long as this same **notes.ini** variable is set on other Domino servers, this application can be replicated to these servers; the Extension Library is deployed here as well.

After you change the **notes.ini** variable, you will need to restart the server's HTTP task. This can be done by either restarting the entire Domino server or by issuing the command Restart Task HTTP on the server console. When the HTTP task starts back up or when the server's HTTP Task has been restarted using the Restart Task HTTP command in the server's console, a highlighted message appears on the server console indicating that the NSF-based plugin is being installed on the server (see Listing 2.2).

Listing 2.2   Server Console Output of the NSF-Based Plugins Deployment

```
restart task http
29.11.2011 10:47:04    HTTP Server: Using Web Configuration View
29.11.2011 10:47:15    JVM: Java Virtual Machine initialized.
29.11.2011 10:47:15    HTTP Server: Java Virtual Machine loaded
29.11.2011 10:47:16    HTTP Server: DSAPI Domino Off-Line Services HTTP
extension Loaded successfully
29.11.2011 10:47:18    HTTP JVM: CLFAD0330I: NSF Based plugins are being
installed in the OSGi runtime. For more information please consult the
log
29.11.2011 10:47:29    XSP Command Manager initialized
29.11.2011 10:47:29    HTTP Server: Started
```

When the server is restarted or the server's Http task has been restarted, the OSGi launcher introspects the update site databases, automatically detects the features, and dynamically loads the associated plugins in the OSGi runtime. Internally, the OSGi launcher references each plugin using a URL with a proprietary protocol that knows how to access the attachment plugin.

The URL format follows:

osginsf:<dbPath>/<documentUNID>/<pluginJarName>

For example:

osginsf:updateSite.nsf/1234…890/com.ibm.extlib.demo_1.0.0_02102011.jar

Deployed in this way, the plugins are not physically installed on the Domino server. Also, after the HTTP task is shut down, the plugins are not persisted anywhere on the server. If there is more than one version of the same feature, the Domino OSGi launcher uses only the latest version; any older versions are ignored. The launcher only compares the major, minor, and service parts of the version. If two features have the same major, minor, and service parts, the Domino OSGi launcher relies on the last modified date of the feature document.

Deploying the OSGi plugins using this method is easy, but not just anyone can be allowed to import plugins to the server. Many security safeguards are built in to this feature. As with any code running from an NSF, be careful about what code you trust and who created it.

The first layer of security is that the server's administrator can enable/disable NSF-based plugin contributions. By default, the feature is disabled; to enable it, the administrator uses the **OSGI_HTTP_DYNAMIC_BUNDLES notes.ini** variable containing the list of comma-separated NSF paths that are authorized to contribute dynamic plugins. This **notes.ini** variable must be either manually entered into the **notes.ini** file or automatically added using a server configuration document. The Domino Administrator cannot use the **set config** method of adding this **notes.ini** variable from the Domino console.

The next layer of security is the ACL of the update site database. The ACL should only allow the Domino Administrator access to create documents in the database. End users should only have reader access to this database.

The OSGi runtime also checks document signatures. Documents storing the plugins and fragments are signed when they're imported into the database. If they are not signed or the signature has been tampered with, the OSGi runtime will not load them, and a warning message will be added to the log.

Additionally, for the plugin/fragment to be loaded, the person who signed the document must be included in the **Sign or Run Unrestricted Methods and Operations** field in the **Security** tab of the server document. If that's not the case, the OSGi runtime adds a warning to the log, and the plugin is not loaded.

Automatic Server Deployment in Domino 8.5.2

Although the dynamic OSGI deployment feature is not available in Domino 8.5.2, the administrator can still automatically deploy the Extension Library plugins to the Domino server using an additional OpenNTF project called **Plugins Deployment for Domino**.

This project is principally a modified Domino **updateSite.ntf** template that contains one additional form, where the administrator can specify the features and plugins to be deployed into the Domino server, along with a LotusScript class (triggered by various agents) that copies the plugins and features into the designated locations on the server and issues (if checked) a restart HTTP command on the console. Because the ability to deploy into the server file system is powerful, the administrator needs to carefully control access to any database created with this template. (Read-only is okay.) The database solves for 8.5.2 the problem of deploying extension libraries. Keeping a replica on each server eases the rollout of updates.

The administrator can download the latest release of the project from OpenNTF by navigating to http://plugindeploy.openntf.org (see Figure 2.17) and going to the **Downloads/Releases** section of the project.

Figure 2.17 The home page of the Plugins Deployment for Domino project for pre-R8.5.3 Domino ExtLib installations.

Once you have downloaded the zip file, unpack it and copy the **newupdatesite.ntf** to the Domino server's Data directory.

You then need to sign the template with an ID that is allowed to run unrestricted agents using the Domino Administrator client.

After you have completed this step, you can create a new database on the server using this template. Once the database has been created, it automatically launches on the Notes Client.

This database is similar to the current update site application that is distributed with Domino 8.5.2 with the exception of a couple of new views and agents that do the server deployment.

The next step is to import the Extension Library update site into this database. Select the **Import Local Update Site** action button. In the dialog that appears, click the **Browse** button and select the **site.xml** file from an unpacked **updateSite.zip**. Then click **OK**. The site then imports into the database; the user should see, depending on the release of ExtLib, a number of **Features**, **Plugins,** and **Fragments** in the update site database, as shown in Figure 2.18.

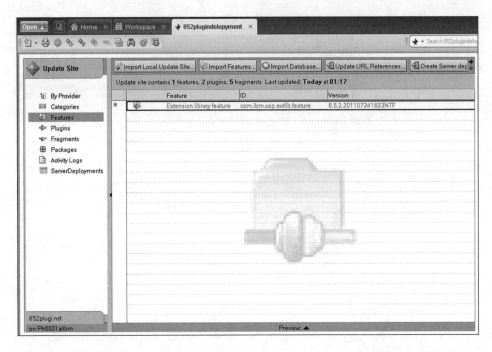

Figure 2.18   Features view of the 8.5.2 updated site application with the Extension Library installed.

Next, click on the **Create Server Deployment** action button to bring the user into a new document in the database. Select to which servers to deploy the ExtLib, and then select the features and all the plugins/fragments to be deployed. It is recommended that you select the **Restart HTTP After Deployment** box so that the Domino server will know to start using ExtLib immediately, as in Figure 2.19.

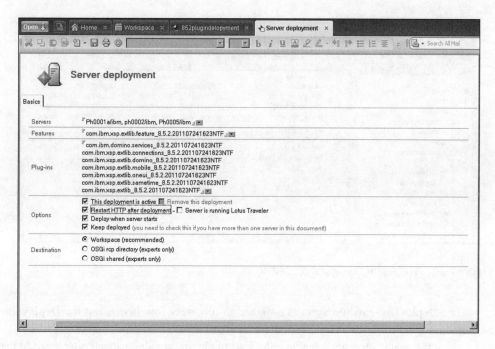

Figure 2.19   New server deployment document.

If the Domino server is also running IBM Lotus Traveler, it is recommended that you select the **Server Is Running Lotus Traveler** box so that the deployment agent will know that it needs to shut down and restart Traveler as part of the process. If you don't do this, the HTTP task can't restart correctly.

Before the new server deployment document can start working, you need to perform one last step: enable the deployment agents. Open the database in the Domino Designer client and select the **Agents** section of the design. Select and enable the two agents, **DeployOnSchedule** and **DeployOnServerStart**, as highlighted in Figure 2.20.

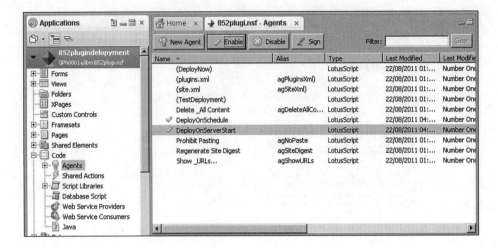

Figure 2.20   The Agent Configuration Setting for pre-8.5.3.

The **DeployOnSchedule** agent is designed to run every four hours, and the **DeployOn-ServerStart** agent runs when your Domino server is restarted.

Once the agents have been enabled, the ExtLib plugins are automatically deployed to the selected Domino servers. The administrator can verify this by looking in the Activity Log contained within the same application.

Manually Deploying Libraries to a Server

Manually deploying libraries to a server requires the administrator to have access to the server's file system so that the required files can be manually copied the required location. This procedure is the least convenient of the Extension Library deployment scenarios to maintain and is not really recommended over the automatic server deployment methods mentioned previously. However, it is included here so that the user can understand how an Extension Library is deployed on a server in the rare event that the administrator needs to remove it under certain circumstances.

NOTE

If you are using the 8.5.3 method for automatic server deployment, no physical files are deployed to the server, so you don't need to manually remove old versions.

The file **updateSite.zip**, which is contained in the download from the ExtLib release downloaded from OpenNTF, is copied into a temporary directory or folder in the server machine.

The user should locate and open the Domino server's **Eclipse Workspace** directory. This is normally found in the **Domino\Workspace** directory under the Domino server's **Data** folder. Inside this folder is the **applications\eclipse** folder, which contains both a **features** and a **plugins** folder, as shown in Figure 2.21.

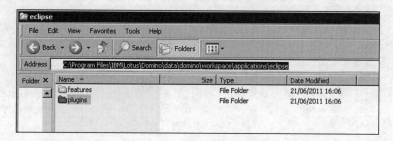

Figure 2.21   Default location for a manual installation of the ExtLib on a Domino server.

The files are then unpacked from the **updateSite.zip** into the relevant folders. You can delete the file **site.xml** after it is unpacked. You don't need that file for manual deployments.

Once the files have been transferred, the administrator needs to restart the HTTP task on the Domino server by issuing the **Restart Task HTTP** command on the console. It might be tempting to use the command **Tell HTTP Restart**, but that does not restart the JVM that the XPages runtime uses.

To verify that the ExtLib has been installed on the server, issue the command **Tell http osgi ss com.ibm.xsp.extlib**. It reports to the console, as shown in Figure 2.22.

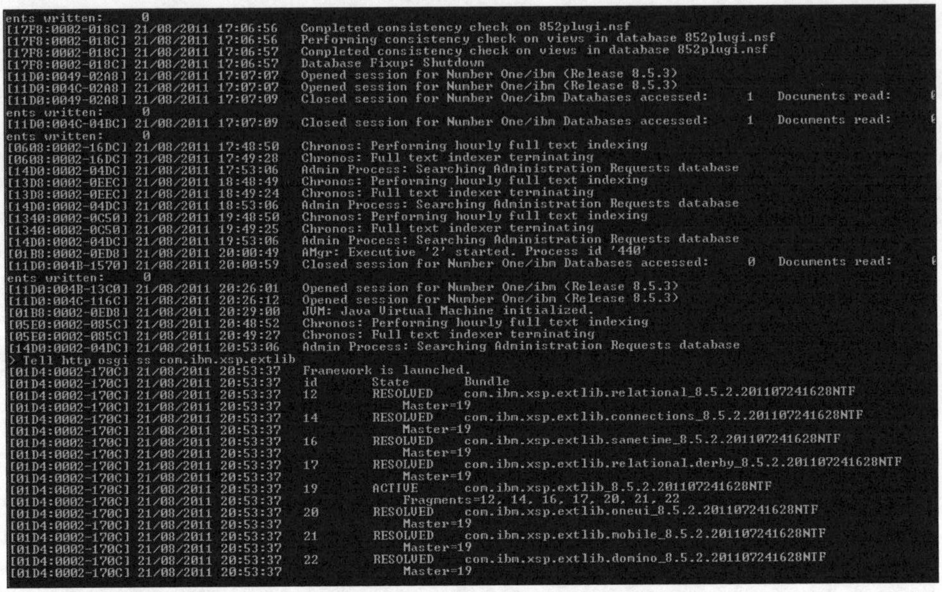

Figure 2.22   Server console command and output.

The output to the server console is from the version of the Extension Library from the 8.5.2.201102282303 release. It changes depending on the version of the ExtLib deployed. The Domino server also makes sure that two different versions of ExtLib deployed at any one time can run at the same time. If you upgrade the ExtLib by copying the files from a newer release to the directories mentioned earlier and restart the HTTP task, the Domino server activates only the newer version.

Deploying the Extension Library to End Users

If the developer is planning to create XPiNC applications that use the new ExtLib controls, it's necessary to deploy these controls to the end users of Lotus Notes Client. Again, this depends on the original of the Extension Library. The Upgrade Pack has its own add-on installer for the Notes Client. This installs the ExtLib runtime to exist alongside XPages runtime in the Notes Client. Using releases from OpenNTF of the ExtLib requires a completely different deployment method. This section shows you how to automatically deploy ExtLib to these users.

Automatic end user deployment of ExtLib involves the use of update sites, widget catalogs, and policies. Although this book covers the basics of how to set up ExtLib for deployment, it is advised that Domino administrators familiarize themselves with these topics before continuing, because some of the explanations are beyond the scope of this book.

Widget Catalog Setup

Most modern servers contain a widget catalog application, which is a vital resource for publishing and provisioning widgets, tools, and services. The catalog increases individual and team productivity within an organization.

If the administrator has yet to create a widget catalog for the server, here is an opportunity to do so. If there isn't a widget catalog on the server, creating a new database based on the widget catalog template is relatively easy. As highlighted in Figure 2.23, the **toolbox.ntf** template is used to create this application.

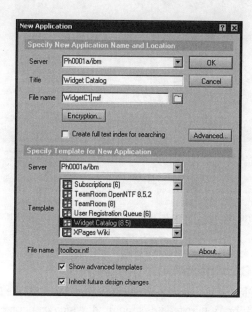

Figure 2.23 The New Application dialog box for the widget catalog.

If the server already has a widget catalog database, the administrator must ensure that whoever has the rights to provision the Extension Library as a widget has the access to do so. The **Admins** and **WidgetAuthor** roles need to be selected for this person in the database's ACL.

To use this widget catalog on the Notes Client, you need to enable it in the **Preferences**, as shown in Figure 2.24. This is a necessary setting for the administrator, but end users could use a widget category to install.

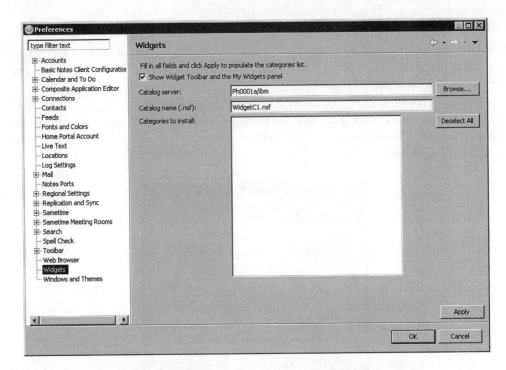

Figure 2.24   Enabling the Notes Client to use widgets via the Preferences dialog.

Creating a Widget Configuration

Now that the widget catalog is available, you can create a widget for the Extension Library. First, however, the Extension Library update site is required, which can come from two sources. One source can be from unpacking the **updateSite.zip** file from the Extension Library download. The other source can be the update site document created for automatic server deployment, as explained in the earlier section, "Automatic Server Deployment in Domino 8.5.3." The update site document on the server's update site application might be the preferable method to use here because it leads to a certain amount of control for the server administrator over the version of the Extension Library used in the organization.

The next step is to return to the server administrator's Notes Client and navigate to the **My Widgets** panel on the right pull-out. Here, if no other widgets are installed on the end user's Notes Client, there will be a link to **Start Creating Your Own Widgets**; otherwise, the administrator can start creating widgets by selecting from the **Get Started** drop-down menu. Selecting this launches the **Start Configuring Widgets** dialog, as in Figure 2.25. Select the radio button beside **Features and Plugins**, and then click **Next**.

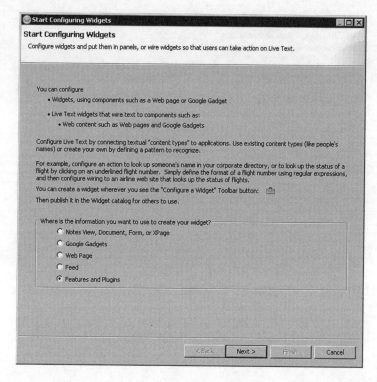

Figure 2.25   The Features and Plugins radio button selected on the Start Configuring Widgets dialog.

The next dialog along the wizard allows the user to put in either the location of an update site **site.xml** file in the system or a URL to an update site application located on a trusted server, as in Figure 2.26. Selecting the **Load** button to the right of the URL displays the available plugins and features at that location. If loading is successful, the user can select from the list the associated plugin and features from a particular download of the Extension Library. Selecting **Next** moves the wizard onto the next dialog.

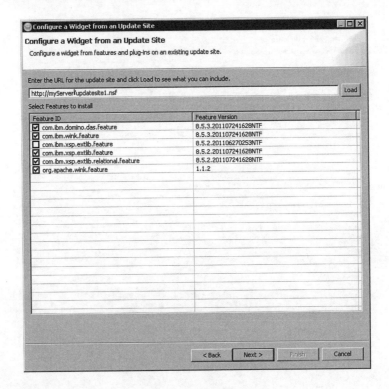

Figure 2.26   Add the URL to the update site database on the server.

As shown in Figure 2.27, the administrator then gives this widget a unique name and confirms the description. Click **Next**.

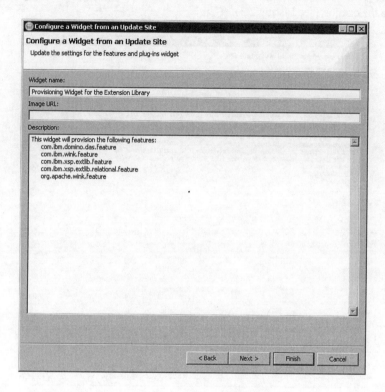

Figure 2.27 Give the widget a unique name, and then click Next.

The wizard moves on to a more important window, one that shouldn't be ignored, in Figure 2.28. It's an opportunity to modify the install manifest, which becomes the **extension.xml** when published to the catalog (see Listing 2.3).

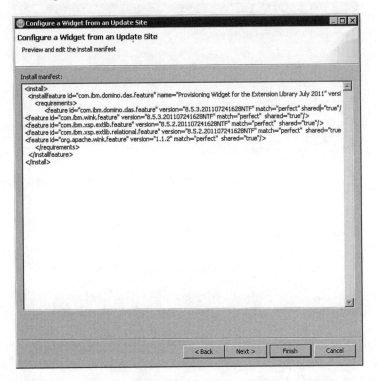

Figure 2.28   Here the install manifest can be previewed and edited.

It's worth noting the various properties:

- **url=""**—This can be either a **http/nrpc/file** URL that points to **updateSite.nsf** or a local **site.xml** file.
- **hideThumbnail="true"**—Set this flag to tell the widget to hide in **My Widgets** sidebar pane. It will only be shown if the user chooses **Show All** in the **My Widgets** sidebar.
- **match="perfect"**—Guarantees that the provisioning engine will attempt to install the exact version that has been specified in the install manifest.

- **shared="true"**—Provided that **shared="true"** is set in the install manifest snippet, as below, the plugin is installed to **Notes_install_dir\framework\shared\eclipse**. If there is no write access to that directory, the plugin is installed to **Notes_install_dir\data\workspace\applications**. This property is also important for multiuser Notes Clients. If this property is set to "false," the widget and the Extension Library are installed only for the one user, as with the example in Listing 2.3. The example in Figure 2.28 shows this property set to "true," which means it is installed to all multiusers.

Listing 2.3 Sample Source of XML with Features Highlighted

```
<webcontextConfiguration version="1.1">
<palleteItem title="OpenNTF ExtLib"
url="http://yourserver/admin/update/extlib.nsf/site.xml"
providerId="com.ibm.rcp.toolbox.prov.provider.ToolboxProvisioning"
imageUrl="" id="com.ibm.xsp.extlib">
<preferences />
<data>
<installManifest>
 <![CDATA[ <install>
<installfeature description="OpenNTF ExtLib" id="com.ibm.xsp.extlib"
name="OpenNTF ExtLib">
<requirements>
<feature id="com.ibm.xsp.extlib.feature" match="perfect" shared="false"
action="install" version="8.5.2.201102282303NTF"/>
</requirements>
</installfeature>
</install> ]]>
</installManifest>
</data>
</palleteItem>
</webcontextConfiguration>
```

Selecting **Next** on the wizard brings the user to the final dialog, shown in Figure 2.29. After selecting **Finish**, the user must restart the Notes Client.

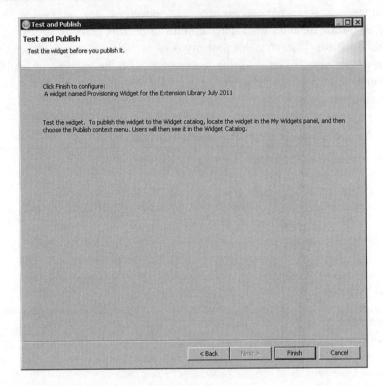

Figure 2.29   The widget for the ExtLib is complete. Review and click Finish.

Once the Notes Client has restarted, the administrator can publish the newly installed Extension Library widget to the widget catalog by selecting this option shown in Figure 2.30.

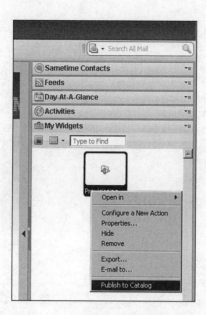

Figure 2.30   Right-click on the ExtLib widget in My Widgets and select Publish to Catalog.

This action creates a new document in the widget catalog and imports the **extension.xml** file, as shown in Figure 2.31. Here the administrator specifies a category for the widget so the widget can be deployed to end users when this category is specified. The administrator also specifies the platform and checks the box for **Plugin and Features**.

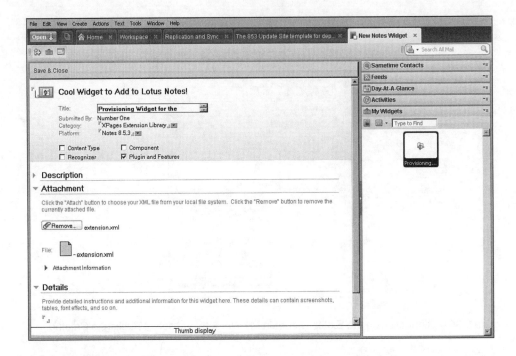

Figure 2.31   Composing the widget document in the widget catalog.

Now the widget containing the ExtLib is ready to be deployed to other Notes Client users.

Provisioning the Extension Library Widget to Other Users

Provisioning the ExtLib widget to end users on the Notes Client can be done in two ways: manually and automatically with a desktop policy.

Manual Deployment

The administrator can make available the details of the widget catalog application and server to connect to for the end user. Then end users can enable widgets on the Notes Client by selecting **File → Preferences → Widgets**. Figure 2.32 shows the check box selected, the server and the catalog selected, and, more importantly, the category selected. Selecting **Apply** installs the widget and the Extension Library. Restarting Notes makes this feature functional.

Alternatively, an administrator can send the end user an XML definition—install manifest—by email, which can then be dragged to the **My Widgets** sidebar.

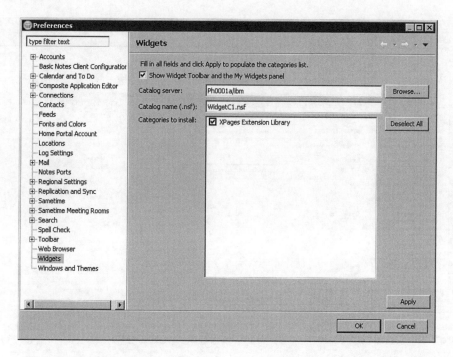

Figure 2.32 Manually installing the Extension Library widget on an end user's Notes Client.

Automatic Deployment with Policies

Desktop policies control a user's workspace, so the administrator can use them to force the end user to use the Extension Library and a particular version on the client machine. All the administrator must do is point the desktop policy to a widget catalog and a certain category contained within that application. These policies can be used to update the settings of the Notes workspace.

Desktop policies are created through the Domino administrator. On the **People & Groups** tab, select **Policies** and then **Add Policy**. Enter a name for the policy.

In the row for the **Desktop** field, click the **New** button, which creates a new Desktop Settings policy. Enter a name for the Desktop Settings policy, and then switch to the **Widgets** tab. As shown in Figure 2.33, the important fields are the **Widget Catalog Server**, the **Widget Catalog Application Name**, and the **Widget Catalog Categories**. After that, it is up to the server administrator to decide how to enforce the widget policy for the desktop. For example, by leaving the default setting for **How to Apply This Setting** on the widget catalog server and application of **Set Value and Prevent Changes**, the end user cannot change the values in the Widgets preference panel.

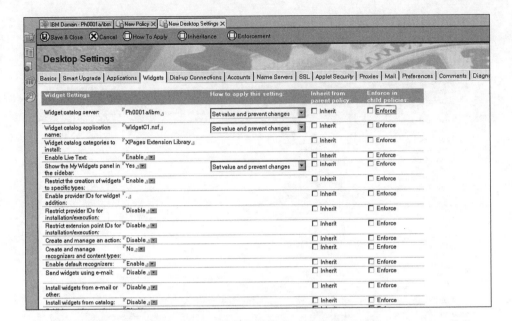

Figure 2.33   Creating a desktop policy for the widget catalog category.

Server administrators compose the policies based on the organization's requirements. They can set in the outer policy to whom the policy is to be assigned, users, or groups. For more information on Domino policies and how they are configured, go to the Lotus Domino Administration Help. (It is available from the Domino Administrator client by selecting **Help** → **Help Topics**. You can also find the documentation online at http://publib.boulder.ibm.com/infocenter/ domhelp/v8r0/index.jsp; select the **Domino 8 Administrator** link.)

The next time the user starts Notes, the library is installed automatically.

Conclusion

This chapter explored the various ways to install and deploy the ExtLib. Initially, deployment to the Domino server was time-consuming and labor intensive, which posed a real barrier to the adoption of the Extension Library as a platform to base production applications upon. This has been overcome with the ability to deploy NSF-based plugins to the server.

With the IBM supported version of the XPages Extension Library in the Upgrade Pack, installation, deployment, and adoption can be accomplished without too much fuss. With no excuses, it's time to play with the XPages ExtLib.

CHAPTER **3**

TeamRoom Template Tour

The previous two chapters introduced the XPages Extension Library and the various ways to install and deploy the library. The next logical step is to view the library in action—to see the controls used in a tangible way in a live application.

The application of choice will be the TeamRoom template, which has been modernized to use not only XPages but the Extension Library as well. The TeamRoom is a Lotus Notes application designed to support processes that help people work together. It is one of the original social and collaboration tools. It is no wonder that the TeamRoom is one of the most widely used templates in businesses across the world. Businesses are constantly evolving with varying business needs that revolve around new technologies as well as a modern look and feel. What better application to modernize?

Modernizing a Lotus Notes template using XPages is straightforward. Given enough time, resources, and skill, a team can transform an application to be something special. However, specialness was not the goal of the team that undertook this task. IBM's XPages development team developed the template by transforming the XPages Extension Library and then brought these developments back into the template. When a feature, a technology, or a control needed in the template was generic in nature, the team would develop it first in the Extension Library and then bring it into the template. This basic strategy meant that the template development time would be longer, but the payback is that these same techniques could be reused by the consumers of the Extension Library and dramatically reduce the time and effort needed to develop their own applications.

This chapter will demonstrate this methodology and show these Extension Library controls in action. It will illustrate how these controls are configured and why. This information will enable developers to learn about the Extension Library and be enlightened about how empowering it can be.

Where to Get the TeamRoom Template and How to Get Started

This template, besides being a fully functional (or full function) team collaboration environment, is the perfect showcase for the XPages Extension Library. It will enable developers to learn how some of the controls from the Extension Library can be used in a real-life application and make it a great learning resource on how to leverage the XPages Extension Library.

There are two versions of the TeamRoom template. The first version comes with the IBM Lotus Notes Domino Upgrade Pack 1 release for IBM Lotus Notes Domino 8.5.3 and is designed only for use with the IBM-supported version and the 8.5.3 OpenNTF versions of the XPages Extension Library.

The second version of the template is available from OpenNTF in the TeamRoom Open-NTF 8.5.2 project, which will not work with the 8.5.3 XPages Extension Library. The main difference between the two versions is that the IBM-supported version for Domino 8.5.3 supports mobile devices (see Chapter 10, "XPages Goes Mobile"), making it easier to access TeamRoom data via mobile web browsers while on the road. Although the new TeamRoom template has the same traditional Notes Client features as before, the web experience is completely different.

The TeamRoom template from the Upgrade Pack is signed with the ID "Lotus Notes Template Development" just like any other IBM Lotus Notes Domino product template, so applications created from this template will run on any server. The server's administrator needs to sign the TeamRoom obtained from OpenNTF. Once this is done, the XPages TeamRoom is ready to go. Users can get their first look at the XPages TeamRoom in Figure 3.1.

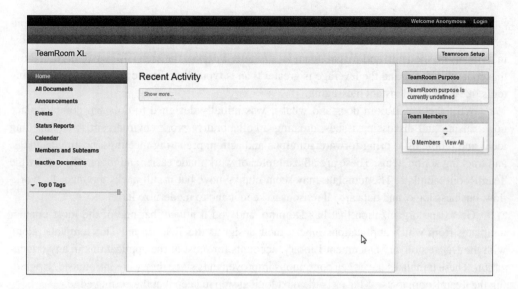

Figure 3.1   How the TeamRoom first appears on a browser.

Configuration of the XPages TeamRoom is similar to the original version of the template. Most, if not all, of the administration of the TeamRoom is done by the end user of the application, and it is documented within the application itself. Administration of the TeamRoom won't be covered here, because that isn't the objective of this chapter. The aim in this chapter is to explore the XPages components of the TeamRoom and to learn how to use the Extension Library.

The TeamRoom Template and Why It Was a Good Candidate for Modernization

The Lotus Notes TeamRoom was introduced as a regular template into Lotus Notes Domino R6 in 2002. In a way, it was one of the first real social collaboration tools supplied out of the box with IBM Lotus Domino. Wherever you find an IBM Notes Domino server, there will be many applications deployed that were created from the TeamRoom template, because it's popular. The application is designed to support processes that help people work together. The TeamRoom facilitates the creation and ongoing development of processes and practices common to high-performance teams.

TeamRoom is a tool for information sharing and collaboration. By creating a shared context for teamwork, TeamRoom does what many good tools do: It creates leverage, both for the individuals on the team and for the team as a whole. Because the technology is built on Notes, this context is richer and the leverage is greater than is typically possible with simple messaging tools like e-mail and instant messaging.

What the TeamRoom does and what it was initially designed to do seem commonplace now: raising and discussing issues, creating a collaborative work environment, brainstorming ideas and problems to bring forward solutions and action, preparing meetings, posting agendas, and tracking action items. These are all examples of work made easier and more efficient by the TeamRoom template. The template may seem clunky now, but it still packs a punch. Its workflow, business logic, and data are all reasons to keep it and to modernize it.

Go to any organization that has Domino, and you'll notice that one of the most popular templates from which applications inherit their design is the TeamRoom. This template, along with the Discussion and Document Library, accounts for most of the applications in any organization. These templates have seen continuous improvements since they were introduced. Upgrading the TeamRoom to use XPages is the next logical step to keep it at the cutting edge.

TeamRoom Redesign Brief and Features

When the template designers at IBM first sat down together to discuss how they should modernize the TeamRoom template, they decided that they needed to update the application to enhance its usability by using the most up-to-date UI design methodologies and adopting design concepts from other IBM Software web products.

The designers also examined the current version of the XPages Extension Library at the time and decided that, where possible, they should build reusable controls that could be delivered as extended controls as part of a future version of the XPages Extension Library. This would allow them and customers to build further XPages-based applications using the same design practices at a much quicker rate. Indeed, it is because of this decision that the XPages Extension Library contains many of the features described in this chapter.

Application Layout

The update to the look and feel of the TeamRoom application is probably the biggest change that the end user of the application will see. To ensure that they were following design concepts from other IBM Software web applications, the template development team decided to move to the OneUI application layout. Rather than having to rebuild the layout for each page within the application, the development team built the Application Layout control for ExtLib, which is described in Chapter 9, "The Application's Layout."

Open the same TeamRoom in Designer, and you can see how this control is configured. The **layout.xsp** Custom Control is where the Application Layout control (`xe:application-Layout`) is put together (see Listing 3.1). Observe the markup, and notice how few properties are set. Yet when this Custom Control is added to an XPage, the power of this control is evident. The layout control is configured here first to use the *OneUI Application Configuration*. From this several properties are then used to set this control further, like the Banner, Legal Text, Navigation, Placebar, and Searchbar. Then there is an Editable Area control, xp:callback, to allow developers to add content when the **layout** Custom Control is added to an XPage. It's easy to control the layout within the TeamRoom template.

Listing 3.1   The Configured Application Layout Control in layout.xsp

```
<xe:applicationLayout id="oneUILayout1">
    <xe:this.configuration>
      <xe:oneuiApplication legalText="(c) Copyright IBM Corporation
      2011"
        navigationPath="${javascript:compositeData.navigationPath}"
        defaultNavigationPath="/home"
          footer="false"
          banner="true">
        <xe:this.placeBarActions>
          <xe:pageTreeNode
            page="setup">            </xe:pageTreeNode>
        </xe:this.placeBarActions>
        <xe:this.searchBar>
          <xe:appSearchBar
            pageName="search.xsp">
          </xe:appSearchBar>
        </xe:this.searchBar>
        <xe:this.bannerUtilityLinks>
          <xe:userTreeNode>
            <xe:this.label>
...

          </xe:userTreeNode>
          <xe:loginTreeNode></xe:loginTreeNode>
        </xe:this.bannerUtilityLinks>
        <xe:this.placeBarName>
 <![CDATA[${javascript:var teamname =
strings.getString("teamroom.name");
...
 return teamname;}]]>
        </xe:this.placeBarName>
      </xe:oneuiApplication>
    </xe:this.configuration>
    <xe:this.facets>
      <xp:div
```

Listing 3.1   (Continued)

```
                xp:key="LeftColumn">
         <xe:navigator
            id="outline"
            expandable="true">
          <xe:this.treeNodes>
            <xe:pageTreeNode .
                page="home"
              selection="/home" />
...
          </xe:this.treeNodes>
         </xe:navigator>
         <xc:tagCloud
             id="tagCloud">
          </xc:tagCloud>
         <xp:callback
            id="left"
            facetName="LeftColumn">
            </xp:callback>
      </xp:div>
      <xp:callback
          id="right"
          xp:key="RightColumn"
          facetName="RightColumn">        </xp:callback>
     </xe:this.facets>
     <xp:callback
         id="c"
         xp:key="MiddleColumn">
</xp:callback>
   </xe:applicationLayout>
```

The **layout** Custom Control also contains the contents of the left column: navigation and tag cloud. The navigator (xe:navigator) is a new control that is detailed in Chapter 8, "Outlines and Navigation." In the TeamRoom, the navigator is placed on the layout not only to control the navigation throughout the application but to provide users with a visual indicator of where they are in the application as they browse from page to page. The Left Column also contains the **Tag Cloud** Custom Control (xc:tagCloud), which contains the control (xe:tagCloud). This is for easier identification of the most-used categories of documents within the application. The **Tag Cloud** control originated in the XPages Discussion template, where it was implemented as a custom control; however, for the TeamRoom template, the template design team rewrote it and added it to ExtLib for easier reuse.

Recent Activities: The Home Page

The application home XPage (**home.xsp**) shows a **Recent Activities** stream modeled on more up-to-date design concepts. The **home.xsp** XPage pulls in the data from the **xvwRecentActivity** view that displays the document activity by modified date descending. This is then represented on the **home** page in an extended control called the **Data View** (`xe:dataView`). This control is described in Chapter 7, "Views." The **Data View** control is another of the most widely used controls for displaying data collections from the Extension Library. The **Data View**'s real power lies in how it can present this data, as in Figure 3.2.

In the right column are two widgets (`xe:widgetContainer`) that are contained within the **homeTeamRoomPurpose.xsp** and **homeMembersView.xsp** Custom Controls. These widgets only appear in the home XPage. The **homeMembersView.xsp** Custom Control is the more interesting of the two. Here the control uses a conventional XPages **Repeat** control (`xp:repeat`) but uses a Java bean to populate the fields within. Coding in Java isn't directly connected to XPages Extension Library, but it is important to know when the developer wants to manipulate the XPages Extensions API and develop with Java in general. Chapter 14, "Java Development in XPages," will take developers by the hand and let them work with Java in XPages.

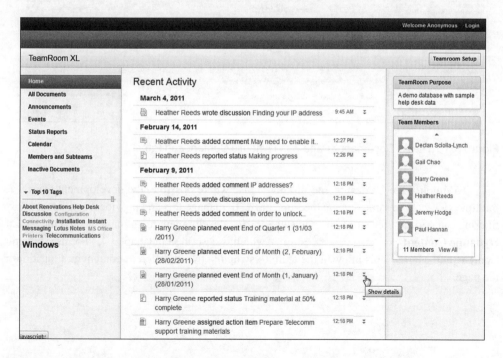

Figure 3.2 The home page highlighting the Data View control in the right column.

All Documents

In the All Documents XPage (**allDocuments.xsp**) of the application, the template development team improved on the code for the standard XPages **View** controls and **Pager** controls. This allowed them to show abstracts of the main text directly in the view and have the pager (`xe:pagerSaveState`) remember what page it was on when the user went into a document and then back out to the view (see Figure 3.3). An example of this page control can be found in the **allDocsAllTab** Custom Control.

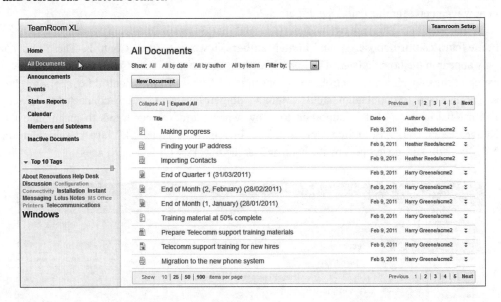

Figure 3.3   The All Document XPage with Dynamic Content and Page.

To simplify the UI design and promote reuse where possible, the development team uses multiple views of the same data on the same page. To manage this and provide a consistent UI for filtering categorized views to a specific category, the development team implemented the ExtLib **Dynamic Content** (`xe:dynamicContent`), which is described in Chapter 4, "Forms, Dynamic Content, and More!" This allowed the team to switch between different content at a location in the page.

The **Dynamic Content** is a very powerful control to learn and master. It makes for a slicker application and reduces the number of XPages needed. The example from Listing 3.2 is taken from the All Documents XPage. Here the **Dynamic Content** control displays the default facet: namely, the allDocsAllTab, or a selected document. Depending on an action that drives a key, this control displays a different Custom Control with partial refresh.

Listing 3.2   Dynamic Content Control Example

```
<xe:dynamicContent id="dynamicView"
  defaultFacet="#{javascript: sessionScope.allDocsSelectedTab ||
'tabAll';}"
  useHash="false"
  partialEvents="true">
  <xe:this.facets>
    <xc:allDocsAllTab id="tabAll"
    xp:key="tabAll" />
    <xc:allDocsAllByDateTab id="tabByDate"
     xp:key="tabAllByDate" />
    <xc:allDocsAllByAuthorTab id="tabByAuthor" xp:key="tabAllByAuthor"
/>
    <xc:allDocsAllByTeamTab id="tabByTeam"
    xp:key="tabAllByTeam" />
    <xc:allDocsAllByTagTab id="tabByTag"
    xp:key="tabAllByTag" />
  </xe:this.facets>
</xe:dynamicContent>
```

The Document Form

The template team also reexamined document creating, reading, and updating and incorporated those lessons learned into the Extension Library. The results are illustrated in Figure 3.4. The Custom Control **homeMainTopic** handles this for the TeamRoom template. A new control **Form Table** (xe:formTable) does all the heavy lifting because it provides a quick and easy way to create a OneUI-based form without having to worry about styling or consistency. This control and others described in this section are detailed in Chapter 4.

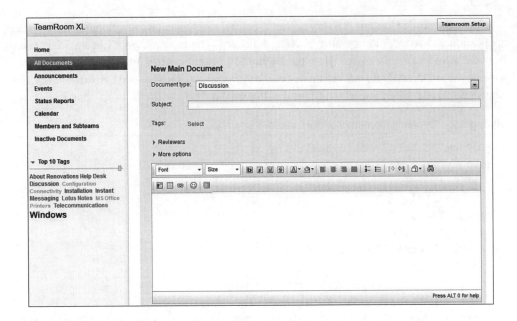

Figure 3.4   The new document form.

Inside a document within the application, the team examined how comments on the document were shown. They redesigned them to use a OneUI design feature called Comments In A Forum, which, again, they extracted as a control within ExtLib for easier reuse. You can see how this is put together in the **topicThreadForum** Custom Control and in Figure 3.5.

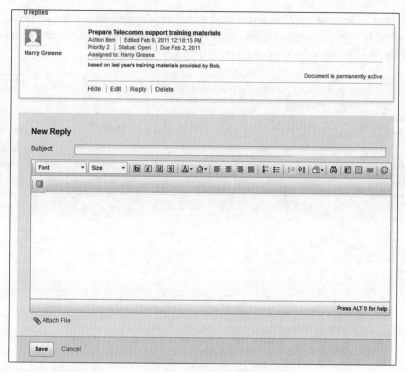

Figure 3.5   The response form with an abstract from the parent.

As part of the modernization of the application, the team also wanted to include a number of Web 2.0 style features, which you can see implemented in the application through the use of in-context editing in the threaded view, including response creation and editing.

The simplification of the New/Edit Main Document UI required that the input of new data into the application be presented in a standard format, in which required fields and the most commonly used fields would be more prominent. To do this, the development team once again turned to the OneUI layout and implemented a standard form design that was created as a new ExtLib control for easier reuse.

Calendar

The original TeamRoom template contained a calendar that is still popular in its current implementations. The development team knew that the calendar for the new template had to be equally modern to the rest of the design changes that they were making. Rather than design a new calendar, the team looked to the iNotes® team within IBM and decided that it would be best to reuse the calendar from iNotes. Working with that team, they implemented the **iNotes Calendar** (`xe:calendarView`) as a reusable control in ExtLib, as shown in Figure 3.6. This is a great addition to ExtLib because it makes it much easier for developers to add calendar functionality to their applications with in-calendar editing and single-click switching to different calendar modes. The calendar control is described in much more detail in Chapter 7.

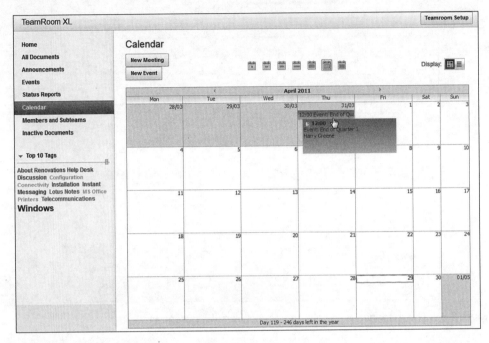

Figure 3.6   The calendar view.

The **calendarView** Custom Control contains the calendar view that is used on the Calendar XPage (**calendar.xsp**). It also contains an example of a REST service (xe:restService). XPages Extension Library includes a new set of RESTful services collectively called Domino Data Services, which are described further in Chapters 7 and 11, "REST Services."

Members

The member handling within the application was given a complete overhaul to make it even easier for the end user. Adding members to the review section of a new document, which uses the **controlSectionCombineNames** Custom Control, is done using the **Value Picker** control (xe:valuePicker), which the team created for ExtLib and is shown in Figure 3.7. This control is fully integrated with the Domino Directory or, as in the case of subteams, can be pointed to a view within the application. This is described in Chapter 6, "Pop-Ups: Tooltips, Dialogs, and Pickers."

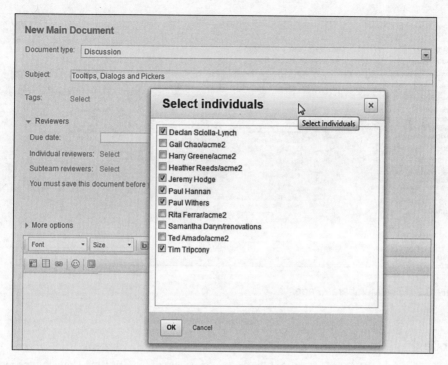

Figure 3.7   The Value Picker control on the document form.

The members view within the TeamRoom template uses an attribute that the development team created for ExtLib. This attribute allows a single column to be displayed as a multiple column view. The **multiColumnCount** attribute on the Data View control is set to 2, and the results of its use are shown in Figure 3.8. The attribute displays the details for each member and their profile photo in two columns. The member details are composed using a unified User API that the ExtLib provides. It can show the thumbnail photos for each member in the columns. The photos are stored within the NSF. These features are described in Chapters 7 and 14.

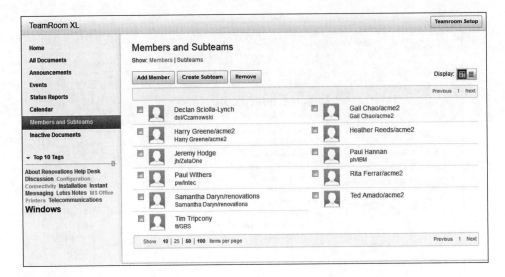

Figure 3.8 The Members XPage.

Mobile

The version of the XPages Extension Library that is compatible with IBM Lotus Notes Domino 8.5.3 includes a new set of mobile controls and capabilities. They make existing XPages application display and function in the mobiles' web browser with the same look and feel as native applications. Figure 3.9 shows these controls in the newer versions of the TeamRoom. The mobile features are described further in Chapter 10.

Figure 3.9 How the TeamRoom looks on a mobile device.

Lessons Learned and Best Practices

The template design team for the TeamRoom template learned a number of things as they built the redesigned TeamRoom template. The most important of these was that ExtLib allowed them to modernize the design of the template much faster than if they had decided to build all the controls themselves. The Discussion template, which had already been modernized using XPages in the Lotus Notes Domino 8.5 release, has been updated again using the ExtLib. The Discussion XL template, available from the Lotus Notes Domino 8.5.3 Upgrade Pack 1, was quickly brought up to date by the lessons learned from modernizing the TeamRoom. This is likely to be the trend for future development and modernization of popular Notes Domino templates like the Document Library.

The team also learned that source control is essential when numerous people are working on related areas within a template at the same time. Although source control is not covered in this book, it is recommended that any team of developers working on a Domino application investigate it.

Conclusion

This chapter examined the TeamRoom template as moderized using XPages that we will be looking at throughout this book and showed where the different aspects of ExtLib have been used within the application.

It also showed the design process the template development team at IBM took while redesigning this application. Although there was an overhead associated with extracting many of the controls that the team designed, the long-term benefits of implementing them as reusable controls in ExtLib far outweigh those costs. Implementing the controls into ExtLib has allowed the template development team at IBM to reuse the controls in numerous standard templates. More importantly, it has allowed other Domino developers to use them in their own applications.

PART II

The Basics:
The Application's
Infrastructure

CHAPTER 4

Forms, Dynamic Content, and More!

One of the major benefits of the Extension Library is the number of prebuilt and preformatted components that allow the developer to quickly and easily deploy complex layouts and design patterns. Components such as the Form Layout controls (`xe:formTable`, `xe:formRow`, and `xe:formColumn`) along with the controls like Forum Post (`xe:forumPost`) enable developers to create rich user interfaces without spending time worrying about designing the layout. Coupled with components that enable the capability to extend AJAX into the application with dynamic content controls such as the Switch (`xe:switchFacet`) and the In Place Form (`xe:inPlaceForm`), the Extension Library will instill modern design patterns and best practices into Lotus Domino applications with simple drag-and-drop ease. As the application is extended with additional controls, such as the Dojo widgets described in Chapter 5, "Dojo Made Easy," and the name and value pickers described in Chapter 6, "Pop-Ups: Tooltips, Dialogs, and Pickers," it's possible, with little effort, to create a truly rich Internet application with an exceptional user experience.

Form Layout Components

The Form Layout components provide a quick and easy way to create a OneUI-based form without having to worry about styling or consistency. Each component creates a theme-based control that allows developers to focus on the content of the control rather than layout. Each component fits in with the overall OneUI theme, extending a common look and feel to all aspects of the application.

Form Table (`xe:formTable`, `xe:formRow`, `xe:formColumn`)

The Form Table (`xe:formTable`), Form Layout Row (`xe:formRow`), and Form Layout Column (`xe:formColumn`) controls provide an easy and efficient way to lay out a OneUI-based form without having to worry about formatting the table. The `xe:formTable` defines the container for the layout and provides default settings for the layout, the form title and description, and more. Within the table, the optional `xe:formColumn` component is used to split the form into a multicolumn layout, with `xe:formRow` components defining each row of the table. Each `xe:formRow` component is usually associated with a single field. When using the `xe:formColumn` components, `xe:formRow` components are placed within their respective `xe:formColumn` components. The `xe:formTable` has facets for the `header` and `footer` to place content above or below the form body. The header facet is placed below the form title and form description. Table 4.1 describes each of the `xe:formTable` properties, and Tables 4.2 and 4.3 describe the `xe:formColumn` and `xe:formRow` properties, respectively.

Table 4.1   `xe:formTable` Properties

Property	Description
legend	Specifies the fieldset legend for nested form controls. Equivalent to the HTML element's legend attribute on a fieldset tag.
disableErrorSummary	Provides a summary of all failed Server-Side field validations at the top of the form, above the form name and description. To disable this summary, set this property to true.
disableRowError	Displays a message above the field with the validation error message when a field fails Server-Side validation. To disable this error message, set this property to true.
errorSummaryText	Allows customization of the first line of the error summary's text, which defaults to "Please check the following:".
fieldHelp	Specifies whether fields with an identifying **helpId** property should render the field help icon. Built-in field help has not been fully implemented as of the August 22, 2011 release of the Extension Library.
formDescription	Specifies the text that describes the form. The description is placed below the form title at the top of the form.
formTitle	Specifies the text of the form title displayed at the top of the form.
labelWidth	Sets the default width for the label cell on all form rows. The default can be overridden on a subsequent **formRow** component. The overridden value will apply to all field labels within the same column.
disableRequiredMarks	By default displays an asterisk next to all required field labels. Normally false; when true, the asterisks are not displayed.
labelPosition	Sets the default position for the field label on field row components. Can be above, left, or none. When set to none, a field label (and the containing cell) is not rendered.

Table 4.2   xe:formColumn Properties

Property	Description
colSpan	Allows the **formColumn** to stretch across multiple columns of the parent **formTable**. Because of the current rendering of the columns, use this property with caution, or better yet, just avoid it.

Table 4.3   xe:formRow Properties

Property	Description
for	An optional identifier to connect the label to a specific field within the form row. If omitted, the **formRow** defaults to the first editable field in the row. If the row contains more than one field, use the **for** property to identify which field should be used for the association. The **for** property also controls the field that will be used to compute whether the required field indicator will be displayed.
helpId	Identifies the specific field help associated with this row. Built-in field help as of the August 22, 2011 release is not fully implemented, and this property currently has no effect (except for making the runtime render a question mark icon next to the field row that does absolutely nothing).
Label	Specifies the label text for the row.
labelWidth	Specifies the row-specific label width. Note that all field label widths within the same column are in the same HTML table and share the width values in the same manner that cells in the same HTML table share cell widths.
labelPosition	Sets the position for the field label on field row components. Can be above, left, or none. When set to none, a field label (and the containing cell) is not rendered.

Listing 4.1 shows a simple sample layout with a single column. The results of the code are displayed in Figure 4.1.

Listing 4.1   A Simple xe:formTable with a Form Row and a Footer Facet

```
<?xml version="1.0" encoding="UTF-8"?>
<xp:view
  xmlns:xp="http://www.ibm.com/xsp/core"
  xmlns:xe="http://www.ibm.com/xsp/coreex">

  <xe:formTable
    id="formTable1"
```

Listing 4.1   (Continued)

```
    formTitle="Form Title"
    formDescription="Form Description"
    labelWidth="100px">

    <xe:this.facets>
      <xp:div
        xp:key="footer">
        <xp:button
          value="Label"
          id="button1">
          <xp:eventHandler
            event="onclick"
            submit="true"
            refreshMode="complete">
          </xp:eventHandler>
        </xp:button>
      </xp:div>
    </xe:this.facets>

    <xe:formRow
      id="formRow1"
      label="Field Label"
      labelWidth="100px"
      labelPosition="left">
      <xp:inputText
        id="sampleInput">
        <xp:this.validators>
          <xp:validateRequired
            message="Please provide a field value">
          </xp:validateRequired>
        </xp:this.validators>
      </xp:inputText>
    </xe:formRow>

  </xe:formTable>

</xp:view>
```

Figure 4.1 The rendered output from Listing 4.1.

Listing 4.2 generates a similar layout to Figure 4.1, except with two columns instead of one single table column, as shown in Figure 4.2.

Listing 4.2 A Simple `xe:formTable` with Two Columns

```
<?xml version="1.0" encoding="UTF-8"?>
<xp:view
  xmlns:xp="http://www.ibm.com/xsp/core"
  xmlns:xe="http://www.ibm.com/xsp/coreex">

  <xe:formTable
    id="formTable1"
    formTitle="Form Title"
    formDescription="Form Description"
    labelWidth="100px"
    disableErrorSummary="false"
    disableRowError="false"
    fieldHelp="true"
    disableRequiredMarks="false"
    labelPosition="left">

    <xe:this.facets>
      <xp:div
        xp:key="footer">
        <xp:button
          value="Label"
          id="button1">
          <xp:eventHandler
            event="onclick"
            submit="true"
            refreshMode="complete">
```

Listing 4.2   (Continued)

```
            </xp:eventHandler>
          </xp:button>
        </xp:div>
      </xe:this.facets>

      <xe:formColumn>
        <xe:formRow
          id="formRow1"
          labelWidth="100px"
          labelPosition="left"
          helpId="#{id:tooltip1}"
          label="label">
          <xp:inputText
            id="sampleInput">
            <xp:this.validators>
              <xp:validateRequired
                message="Please provide a field value">
              </xp:validateRequired>
            </xp:this.validators>
          </xp:inputText>

        </xe:formRow>
      </xe:formColumn>

      <xe:formColumn>
        <xe:formRow
          id="formRow3"
          labelWidth="100px"
          labelPosition="left"
          helpId="#{id:tooltip1}"
          label="label">
          <xp:inputText
            id="inputText2">
            <xp:this.validators>
              <xp:validateRequired
                message="Please provide a field value">
              </xp:validateRequired>
            </xp:this.validators>
          </xp:inputText>
```

```
    </xe:formRow>
  </xe:formColumn>

  </xe:formTable>
</xp:view>
```

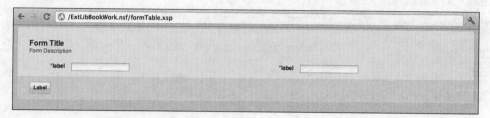

Figure 4.2   The rendered output from Listing 4.2.

The `xe:formRow` also has two facets that can be used instead of their associated properties. The `label` and `help` facets allow you to place complex objects in place of the rendered objects to allow full control of those sections. Under the current release, the `help` facet is the recommended way to add `fieldHelp` to an `xe:formRow` control.

The Team Room template makes extensive use of the form table and related components. An example of them in action can be seen in the Main Document in Figure 4.3.

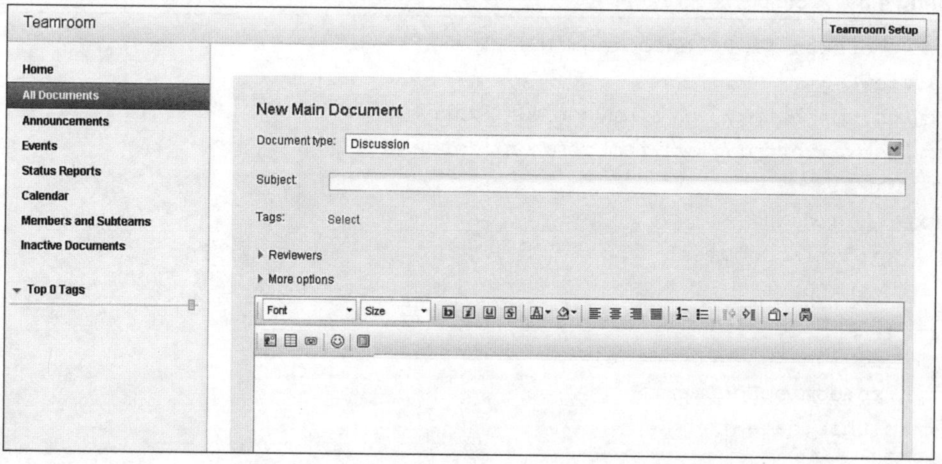

Figure 4.3   The Main Document XPage utilizing the `xe:formTable` components.

Forum Post (`xe:forumPost`)

The `xe:forumPost` control is a simple OneUI-styled control that creates a pre-formatted forum-post style user interface. The control contains seven callbacks where predefined content can be placed. The callbacks and their purposes are detailed in Table 4.4.

Table 4.4   Callbacks for the `xe:forumPost` Component

Callback	Description
authorAvatar	This callback is used to place the user's avatar
authorName	The author's name
authorMeta	Additional information about the author
postTitle	The title for the post if applicable
postMeta	Additional information about the post, such as date/time and location
postDetails	The body or content of the post
postActions	The action bar for the post for actions such as reply to or report

Listing 4.3 shows the XSP code required to generate a simple example of the forum post user interface.

Listing 4.3   A Simple `xe:forumPost`

```
<?xml version="1.0" encoding="UTF-8"?>
<xp:view
  xmlns:xp="http://www.ibm.com/xsp/core"
  xmlns:xe="http://www.ibm.com/xsp/coreex">

  <xp:this.data>
    <xp:dominoDocument
      var="post"
      formName="forumPost"
      action="openDocument">
    </xp:dominoDocument>
  </xp:this.data>

  <xe:forumPost
    id="forumPost1">
    <xp:this.facets>
      <xp:span
```

```
    xp:key="postActions">
    <xp:link
      escape="true"
      text="respond"
      id="link1">
    </xp:link>
  </xp:span>
<xp:span
  xp:key="postDetails">
  <xp:text
    value="#{post.messageBody}" />
</xp:span>
<xp:span
  xp:key="postMeta">
  <xp:text
    value="#{post.postDate}">
    <xp:this.converter>
      <xp:convertDateTime
        dateStyle="long">
      </xp:convertDateTime>
    </xp:this.converter>
  </xp:text>
</xp:span>
<xp:span
  xp:key="postTitle">
  <xp:text
    value="#{post.subject}" />
</xp:span>
<xp:span
  xp:key="authorMeta">
  <xp:text
    value="#{post.contactInfo}" />
</xp:span>
<xp:span
  xp:key="authorName">
  <xp:text
    value="#{post.authorName}" />
</xp:span>
<xp:span
  xp:key="authorAvatar">
```

Listing 4.3   (Continued)

```
        <xp:image
           id="image1"
           disableTheme="true"
           url="#{post.authorAvatarURL}">
        </xp:image>
      </xp:span>
    </xp:this.facets>
  </xe:forumPost>


</xp:view>
```

Figure 4.4 shows two `xe:forumPost` components, the first with the callbacks identified by name, and the second with a sample populated forum post.

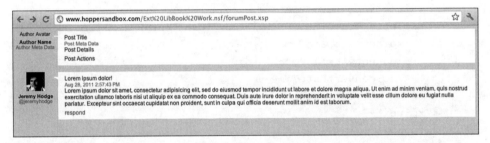

Figure 4.4   The `xe:forumPost` callbacks identified and an implemented `xe:forumPost`.

Dynamic Content

One of the design patterns that has become commonplace and is often expected in modern applications is the ability to dynamically switch content without changing the overall context. This concept is what AJAX technologies are built around. Through the use of partial refreshes, content can be dynamically inserted, removed, or changed from a read-only to an editable state. Many components within the Extension Library enable this capability, and this section will review three of them: the In Place Form, (`xe:inPlaceForm`), the Dynamic Content control (`xe:dynamic-Content`), and the Switch (`xe:switch`).

In Place Form Control (`xe:inPlaceForm`)

The `xe:inPlaceForm` control dynamically shows or hides content on a form for in-context editing. In-context editing is a design pattern wherein a portion of the read-only contents of a document are replaced with an inline editable version of the content, allowing the user to update the data without leaving the context of the page. The editable, normally hidden content is enclosed within the component's `<xe:inPlaceForm>`...`</xe:inPlaceForm>` tags. When the content's display state should change, a handle to the In Place Form component is retrieved using the `getComponent()` method, and one of the `show()`, `hide()`, or `toggle()` methods are called to update the displayed state.

When the XPage is created, the `xe:inPlaceForm` control is created within the JSF component tree; however, the descendant controls and data sources are not. When the component's `show()` and `toggle()` methods are called to display the content, the controls are dynamically created and added to the tree. When the component's `hide()` and `toggle()` methods are called to hide the content, they are removed from the tree and discarded. This keeps the impact of the component on the XPages application to a minimum because the overhead is minimal. The additional components and data sources needed to display the editable contents of the In Place Form are only used when needed.

As seen in Figure 4.5, the In Place Form has three properties beyond the standard set that most components have. The first is the **partialEvents** property. This property controls whether partial refresh and partial execute should be automatically applied to any events that originate from within the In Place Form's tree. Set to false by default, when this property is true, the component prevents a full refresh from being triggered for the entire page by any object within the In Place Form. Instead, the event will be converted to a partial refresh with partial execution and will be restricted to the component tree below the In Place Form.

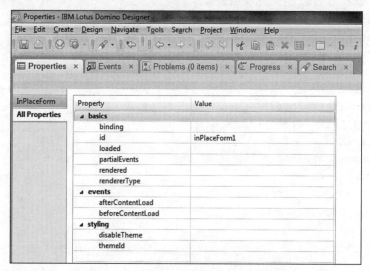

Figure 4.5 The properties of the `<xe:inPlaceForm>` component.

The other two properties, **beforeContentLoad** and **afterContentLoad**, are Server-Side JavaScript (SSJS) events that are triggered before and after the content of the In Place Form is loaded. The events are triggered the first time the XPage is created and then on each call to `show()` or `toggle()` when the content of the In Place Form is displayed.

Listing 4.4 lists an XPage created with an In Place Form that displays a simple Hello World statement with the current time. The always-displayed **Full Refresh** button toggles the display of the content within the In Place Form. The **Restricted Full** button inside the In Place Form is set to perform a full refresh, but when clicked, it is restricted to only partially refreshing the contents of the In Place Form, because the **partialEvents** property is set to `"true"` on the In Place Form component.

Listing 4.4　An XPage with an In Place Form Component

```
<?xml version="1.0" encoding="UTF-8"?>
<xp:view
  xmlns:xp="http://www.ibm.com/xsp/core"
  xmlns:xe="http://www.ibm.com/xsp/coreex">

  <xe:inPlaceForm
    id="inPlaceForm1"
    partialEvents="true">
    <xe:this.afterContentLoad><![CDATA[#{javascript:
      print("afterContentLoad");
    }]]></xe:this.afterContentLoad>
    <xe:this.beforeContentLoad><![CDATA[#{javascript:
      print("beforeContentLoad");
    }]]></xe:this.beforeContentLoad>

    <xp:button
      id="fullrefreshtest"
      value="Restricted Full">
      <xp:eventHandler
        event="onclick"
        submit="true"
        refreshMode="complete" />
    </xp:button>

    Hello World

    <xp:text
      value="#{javascript:return (new Date()).toLocaleString()}" />

  </xe:inPlaceForm>

  <xp:button value="Full Refresh" id="button1">
```

```
<xp:eventHandler event="onclick" submit="true"
  refreshMode="complete">
  <xp:this.action><![CDATA[#{javascript:
    var c = getComponent("inPlaceForm1");
    c.toggle();
  }]]></xp:this.action>
</xp:eventHandler>
</xp:button>

<xp:text value="#{javascript:return (new Date()).toLocaleString()}"
/>

</xp:view>
```

The results of setting the partialEvents property to `"true"` as done in Listing 4.4 are seen in Figure 4.6, where the results of the rendered XPage is displayed. The **Full Refresh** button was clicked displaying the contents of the In Place Form. Because the **Full Refresh** button does a full refresh, the time next to both buttons is the same. However, when the **Restricted Full** button is clicked, only the time next to it is updated, even though the button is set to execute a full refresh.

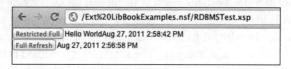

Figure 4.6   The XPage output by Listing 4.4 showing a full refresh restricted to a partial refresh.

Dynamic Content (`xe:dynamicContent`)

The Dynamic Content (`xe:dynamicContent`) component is similar to the In Place Form component (`xe:inPlaceForm`) in that it is used to dynamically show content; however, it is different in that it can switch between any number of facets containing different content, rather than just showing or hiding a single piece. Each piece of dynamic content is placed within a facet of the component and given a unique name. Table 4.5 lists the properties for the Dynamic Content component.

Table 4.5   Properties of the Dynamic Content Component

Property	Description
defaultFacet	Specifies the facet that will be displayed when no other facet has been specifically loaded or when the currently selected facet does not exist. Defaults to the first facet if empty. Set to `-empty-` to not load a facet by default.
partialEvents	When true, restricts the full refresh events generated by controls within this component to partial refreshes within the component.
useHash	When true, the component appends a hash tag to the end of the URL to save the state of the dynamic component's selected facet. Only one dynamic content control can append the hash to the end of the URL.
afterContentLoad	Method binding for an SSJS event that is triggered after the content of the dynamic content control is loaded. Executes during page load and on each content change.
beforeContentLoad	Method binding for an SSJS event that is triggered before the content of the dynamic content control is loaded. Executes during page load and on each content change.

To display a piece of dynamic content, the component is retrieved using the `get Component()` method in SSJS. Then the `show()` method of the component is called, passing the name of the facet that is to be displayed. When called, the currently displayed facet is removed from the tree, and the newly selected facet is added and subsequently displayed. To retrieve the name of the currently selected facet, the `getCurrentFacet()` method is called. Alternatively, instead of retrieving a handle to the component and calling the `show()` method, a new simple action called **changeDynamicContentAction** has been added and is selected in the **Add Action** button on any event handler, as seen in Figure 4.7. In this figure, the **allDocuments** XPage from the TeamRoom template contains a **New Document** button. This button, when clicked, instructs the dynamic content component with the id **dynamicContent** to load the facet with the name **newDocumentContent**.

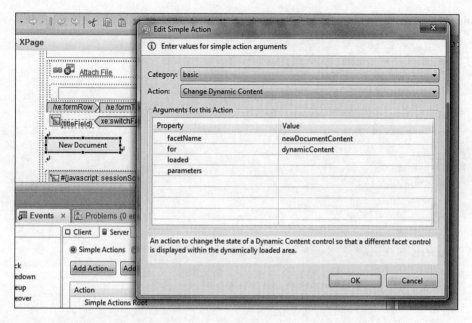

Figure 4.7 The allDocuments XPage from the Team Room using the changeDynamicContentAction.

In Listing 4.5, a dynamic content control is added with three facets. Below the facet, a button for each facet is added. When clicked, each button acquires the dynamic content component and calls the `show()` method to display its appropriate facet. The line below the buttons contains a combo box with the name of each facet, storing its value in a view scoped variable named `selectedFacet`.

Listing 4.5 An XPage with a Dynamic Content Control

```
<?xml version="1.0" encoding="UTF-8"?>
<xp:view
  xmlns:xp="http://www.ibm.com/xsp/core"
  xmlns:xe="http://www.ibm.com/xsp/coreex">

  <xe:dynamicContent
    id="dynamicContent1"
    partialEvents="true"
    useHash="true">
    <xp:this.facets>
      <xp:div
        xp:key="facet1">Facet 1</xp:div>
```

Listing 4.5   (Continued)

```
    <xp:div
      xp:key="facet2">Facet 2</xp:div>
    <xp:div
      xp:key="facet3">Facet 3</xp:div>
  </xp:this.facets>
</xe:dynamicContent>

<xp:button
  id="showFacet1"
  value="Facet 1">
  <xp:eventHandler
    event="onclick"
    submit="true"
    refreshMode="complete">
    <xp:this.action><![CDATA[#{javascript:
      var c = getComponent("dynamicContent1");
      c.show("facet1");
     }]]></xp:this.action>
  </xp:eventHandler>
</xp:button>

<xp:button
  id="button1"
  value="Facet 2">
  <xp:eventHandler
    event="onclick"
    submit="true"
    refreshMode="complete">
    <xp:this.action><![CDATA[#{javascript:
      var c = getComponent("dynamicContent1");
      c.show("facet2");
     }]]></xp:this.action>
  </xp:eventHandler>
</xp:button>

<xp:button
  id="button2"
  value="Facet 3">
  <xp:eventHandler
    event="onclick"
```

```
    submit="true"
    refreshMode="complete">
    <xp:this.action><![CDATA[#{javascript:
      var c = getComponent("dynamicContent1");
      c.show("facet3");
    }]]></xp:this.action>
  </xp:eventHandler>
</xp:button>


<br />

<xp:comboBox
  id="comboBox1"
  value="#{viewScope.selectedFacet}">
  <xp:selectItem
    itemLabel="facet1"></xp:selectItem>
  <xp:selectItem
    itemLabel="facet2"></xp:selectItem>
  <xp:selectItem
    itemLabel="facet3"></xp:selectItem>
</xp:comboBox>

<xp:button
  id="button7"
  value="Show Selected Facet">
  <xp:eventHandler
    event="onclick"
    submit="true"
    refreshMode="complete">
    <xp:this.action>
      <xe:changeDynamicContentAction
        facetName="#{javascript:viewScope.selectedFacet}"
        for="dynamicContent1">
      </xe:changeDynamicContentAction>
    </xp:this.action>
  </xp:eventHandler>
</xp:button>


</xp:view>
```

The results of Listing 4.5 are shown in Figure 4.8. When the **Show Selected Facet** button is clicked, the `changeDynamicContentAction` changes the contents of the dynamic content control. The **facetName** property of the action is computed using the `viewScope.selectedFacet` value to determine which facet to display.

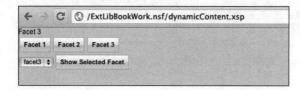

Figure 4.8   The XPage output by Listing 4.5 showing a Dynamic Content control.

Switch (`xe:switchFacet`)

The Switch (`xe:switchFacet`) component works like the Dynamic Content component with a few exceptions. It is not necessary to change the currently displayed facet programmatically; instead, the **selectedFacet** property is used to determine the currently displayed facet. To change the displayed facet, compute the value and return the name of the facet to be selected. Because the selection of the displayed facet is automatic, there is no `show()` method or equivalent to the simple action `changeDynamicContentAction`.

Listing 4.6 is an XPage that shows the Switch component in action. The selected facet is controlled by the value selected in the combo box, which stores its value in the `viewScope.selectedFacet` scoped variable. The Switch's **selectedFacet** property is then computed using an Expression Language statement that resolves to `viewScope.selected-Facet`. When the **Show Selected Facet** button is clicked, it simply performs a full refresh, forcing the switch to recompute and display the selected facet.

Listing 4.6   An XPage with a Switch Control

```
<?xml version="1.0" encoding="UTF-8"?>
<xp:view
  xmlns:xp="http://www.ibm.com/xsp/core"
  xmlns:xe="http://www.ibm.com/xsp/coreex">

  <xe:switchFacet
    id="dynamicContent1"
    defaultFacet="facet3"
    selectedFacet="#{javascript:viewScope.selectedFacet}">
    <xp:this.facets>
      <xp:div xp:key="facet1">Facet 1</xp:div>
```

```
      <xp:div xp:key="facet2">Facet 2</xp:div>
      <xp:div xp:key="facet3">Facet 3</xp:div>
   </xp:this.facets>

</xe:switchFacet>

<xp:comboBox
   id="comboBox1"
   value="#{viewScope.selectedFacet}">
   <xp:selectItem
     itemLabel="facet1"></xp:selectItem>
   <xp:selectItem
     itemLabel="facet2"></xp:selectItem>
   <xp:selectItem
     itemLabel="facet3"></xp:selectItem>
</xp:comboBox>

<xp:button
   id="button7"
   value="Show Selected Facet">
   <xp:eventHandler
     event="onclick"
     submit="true"
     refreshMode="complete">
   </xp:eventHandler>
</xp:button>

</xp:view>
```

Miscellaneous Controls

Among the many controls provided in the Extension Library, several are used to perform functions from data entry to session control and more. Most of these controls are described in other chapters of the book because they fit into specific categories of controls. A few controls do not fit into a category. Those components are reviewed in this section.

Multi-Image (`xe:multiImage`)

The multi-image component adds an image to an XPage. The component contains a named list of images that can be selected based on a data value or by a computed expression. The control has all the properties required to properly display the image, such as **alt**, **longdesc**, and **usemap**, and have a full set of user-driven events. The icons are defined by the **icons complex** property, which contains several iconEntry subcomponents.

Each iconEntry has its own tag for **alt**, **loaded**, **style**, **styleClass**, and the URL to the individual image. The selected image for display is controlled by either the **selected** or **selectedValue** property of the iconEntry. The **selectedValue** property is matched against the multi-image component's **value** property, and if they match, that image is displayed. The **value** property is a value binding that can connect to a data source or be computed using SSJS or Expression Language. If the **selectedValue** of an iconEntry is not set, the computed expression contained in the selected property decides if the image is selected for display.

Listing 4.7 displays the code for a sample XPage that contains a combo box bound to the viewScope variable selectedImage. When the combo box value changes, the page is refreshed, and the multi-image, which is also bound to the selectedImage viewScope variable, is updated.

Listing 4.7 An XPage with a Multi-Image Component

```
<?xml version="1.0" encoding="UTF-8"?>
<xp:view
  xmlns:xp="http://www.ibm.com/xsp/core"
  xmlns:xe="http://www.ibm.com/xsp/coreex">

  <xp:comboBox
    id="comboBox1"
    value="#{viewScope.selectedImage}">
    <xp:selectItem itemLabel="accept"></xp:selectItem>
    <xp:selectItem itemLabel="add"></xp:selectItem>
    <xp:selectItem itemLabel="anchor"></xp:selectItem>
    <xp:selectItem itemLabel="bomb"></xp:selectItem>
    <xp:selectItem itemLabel="help"></xp:selectItem>
    <xp:eventHandler
      event="onchange"
      submit="true"
      refreshMode="complete">
    </xp:eventHandler>
  </xp:comboBox>

  <xe:multiImage
    id="multiImage1"
    value="#{viewScope.selectedImage}">
    <xe:this.icons>
      <xe:iconEntry
```

```
        url="/accept.png"
        selectedValue="accept">
      </xe:iconEntry>
      <xe:iconEntry
        url="/add.png"
        selectedValue="add">
      </xe:iconEntry>
      <xe:iconEntry
        url="/bomb.png"
        selectedValue="bomb">
      </xe:iconEntry>
      <xe:iconEntry
        selectedValue="anchor"
        url="/anchor.png">
      </xe:iconEntry>
      <xe:iconEntry
        selectedValue="help"
        url="/help.png">
      </xe:iconEntry>
    </xe:this.icons>
  </xe:multiImage>

</xp:view>
```

List Container (`xe:list`)

The List Container component, `<xe:list>`, creates an HTML unordered list (`<ul>...</ul>`). The control generates the `<ul>` tag set and then wraps each of its immediate child components in list item tags (`<li>...</li>`). The component provides additional functionality to style the list itself through the **style** and **styleClass** properties, the first and last list items with the **firstItemStyle** and **firstItemStyleClass**, and the **lastItemStyle** and **lastItemStyleClass** properties. Every item in the list (including the first and last item) can also be styled using the **itemStyle** and **itemStyleClass** properties. Listing 4.8 shows how the `xe:list` component creates a list out of five text components, with the results displayed in Figure 4.9.

Listing 4.8 An XPage with the `xe:list` Component

```
<?xml version="1.0" encoding="UTF-8"?>
<xp:view
  xmlns:xp="http://www.ibm.com/xsp/core"
  xmlns:xe="http://www.ibm.com/xsp/coreex">
```

Listing 4.8   (Continued)

```
<xe:list id="list1">
  <xp:text
    id="bullet1"
    value="Bullet 1" />
  <xp:text
    id="bullet2"
    value="Bullet 2" />
  <xp:text
    id="bullet3"
    value="Bullet 3" />
  <xp:text
    id="bullet4"
    value="Bullet 4" />
</xe:list>

</xp:view>
```

Figure 4.9   The XPage output by Listing 4.8 showing an HTML list.

Keep Session Alive (`xe:keepSessionAlive`)

The Keep Session Alive component is a handy control that will prevent a user's session from timing out. The component continually pings the server from the rendered page, resetting the idle timeout that would eventually cause the user's session to time out and the current state of the application to be discarded. To use the component, just drag and drop the control from the Extension Library tool palette onto the page and set the **delay interval** property in seconds. The delay should be shorter than the shortest timeout specified in your configuration (typically 30 minutes).

The control should be used with reserve, however. The longer a session is open on the server, the more resources the server consumes, which can limit the scalability and performance of your applications. The Keep Session Alive component also has a limited effect on servers with Single Sign On for multiple servers configured for their web environment. Single Sign On for multiple servers operates by installing a cookie in the browser with a token that indicates the authenticated zone; when the authentication expires, the user's session is no longer valid, and the user must reauthenticate. Although the Keep Session Alive in this case will prevent the user's

XPage session from expiring because of time out, if the user's authentication expires, the new generated session identification issued when the user re-authenticates will be different from the previous session, and the old session is effectively terminated. To see an example of the xe:keepSessionAlive component in use, look at the layout custom control in the OpenNTF TeamRoom application.

Conclusion

The Extension Library components for form layout and dynamic content enable an XPages application developer to easily deploy advanced and modern AJAX applications with ease, instilling best practices and common UI patterns. When combined with other Extension Library components such as the Application Layout and the various view components described in the next few chapters, XPages application development becomes considerably easier.

CHAPTER 5

Dojo Made Easy

Ever since IBM Lotus Domino Release 8.5.0, the Dojo toolkit has been IBM's JavaScript frame-work of choice. It comes preinstalled with the Domino server and is intrinsically linked with the XPages runtime. Much of the standard XPages functionality extends the standard Dojo toolkit. Developers have been integrating Dojo with XPages since its introduction into Domino, taking advantage of the prebuilt code libraries to enhance their XPages applications. Subsequent releases have specifically targeted making it easier to combine XPages and Dojo. To this end, the Extension Library Dojo controls are designed to make it easier still to implement some of the more frequently used modules, whether for novice developers or seasoned developers making extensive use of the Dojo modules and attributes available.

Developers already familiar with Dojo might want to jump to the section "Dojo Modules and Dojo in the Extension Library." For those who have never or rarely used Dojo, the following sections will give some background and walk through a couple of examples of Dojo modules in XPages.

What Is Dojo?

Dojo is an open source JavaScript framework, a free collection of cross-browser-compatible functions and widgets, first released in 2006. Each JavaScript file is an object with various attributes and functions, referred to as a Dojo module. For example, `dijit.form.TextBox` is a Dojo module that converts an HTML input tag to a Dojo-styled text box. Modules can also extend other Dojo modules, so `dijit.form.ValidationTextBox` and `dijit.form.Number-TextBox` both extend `dijit.form.TextBox`. This allows developers to add functionality by creating their own extensions without needing to modify the preinstalled files. One of the strengths of these Dojo modules is that they are specifically designed to support developers in addressing accessibility requirements.

95

All the XPages Client-Side JavaScript functionality can be found in script libraries in the Dojo root folders; most either extend or mimic standard Dojo modules. For example, any partial refresh calls `dojo.xhrGet()` or `dojo.xhrPost()`, the standard Dojo AJAX requests to the server. The XPages DateTimeHelper extends a number of Dojo modules, including `dijit.form.Button`, `dojo.date`, and `dijit._widget`. Client-Side validation also mimics the format of Dojo functions. Consequently, the core Dojo libraries are loaded in an XPage by default, so even a blank XPage in which you are not explicitly including Client-Side JavaScript libraries will include the following Dojo JavaScript libraries, as shown in Figure 5.1:

/xsp/.ibmxspres/dojoroot-1.6.1/dojo/dojo.js

/xsp/.ibmxspres/.mini/dojo/.en-gb/@Iq.js (for English)

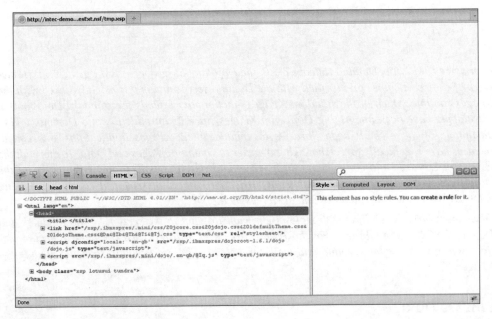

Figure 5.1   Dojo libraries loaded.

Default Dojo Libraries Using Dojo Modules in XPages

Before Domino 8.5.2, incorporating Dojo modules into XPages was challenging because many controls did not have a dojoType attribute. The only way to implement Dojo on an EditBox, for example, was to apply it programmatically. So in addition to the core control client side,

JavaScript was required to trigger on load. Listing 5.1 demonstrates this programmatic implementation of the `dijit.form.ValidationTextBox`. Lines 1 to 4 show the core Edit Box control. Line 6 then begins an Output Script control, triggering `XSP.addOnLoad()` in line 16. The `addOnLoad()` calls a function that generates a new `dijit.form.ValidationTextBox` on line 9 adding various attributes. Line 13 adds the parameter to the new function, which applies the Dojo module to the Edit Box control.

Listing 5.1 Programmatic Implementation of `dijit.form.ValidationTextBox`

```
1   <xp:inputText
2       id="response"
3       value="#{ansDoc.response}">
4   </xp:inputText>
5
6   <xp:scriptBlock
7       id="scriptBlock1">
8       <xp:this.value><![CDATA[var convertInput = function() {
9       new dijit.form.ValidationTextBox(
10          {name:"#{id:response}",
11              required: true,
12              promptMessage: "Please complete the field"},
13          XSP.getElementById("#{id:response}")
14          );
15      };
16      XSP.addOnLoad(convertInput);
17      ]]></xp:this.value>
18  </xp:scriptBlock>
```

There is no reason you cannot use programmatic conversion of a core control to a Dojo module, if applicable. But with Domino 8.5.2, it became possible to declaratively convert the control thanks to the addition of the dojoType attribute to a variety of core controls. So for the Edit Box control, for example, in Domino 8.5.2 a Dojo panel was added and **dojoType** and **dojoAttributes** properties appeared on the All Properties panel, as shown in Figure 5.2. Not only is this easier to implement, but text strings entered as Dojo attribute values are picked up if localization is required and turned on for an application.

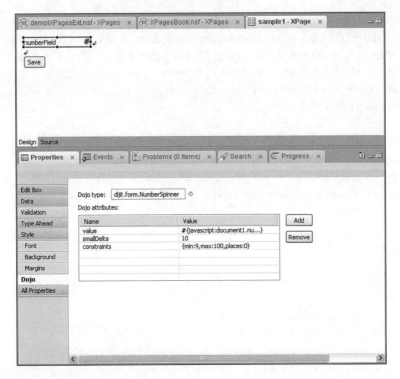

Figure 5.2   Dojo panel on Edit Box control.

Before digging into the Extension Library, let's review several examples of implementing Dojo in XPages. Any developer who has used Dojo modules in XPages is aware of the steps required, ingrained quite probably by forgetting one of the steps at one time or another. The first critical step is to set `dojoParseOnLoad` and `dojoTheme` attributes to `"true"`, as shown in lines 4 and 5 of Listing 5.2. The former tells the browser that after loading it needs to convert all content with a **dojoType** property; the latter tells the browser to load the relevant theme for styling all Dojo widgets (or *dijits*). The final step is to add as resources on the XPage any Dojo modules referenced on the page in a **dojoType** property.

Listing 5.2   `dojoParseOnLoad` and `dojoTheme`

```
1   <?xml version="1.0" encoding="UTF-8"?>
2   <xp:view
3       xmlns:xp="http://www.ibm.com/xsp/core"
4       dojoParseOnLoad="true"
5       dojoTheme="true">
6
7   </xp:view>
```

Of course, you can perform all this on either an XPage or a Custom Control, but for simplicity, the reference will only be made to XPages. To provide a more appropriate comparison with the Extension Library controls, the examples in the sections that follow focus on declarative implementations of Dojo modules.

Simple Dojo Example: `dijit.form.ValidationTextBox`

The Dojo modules applied to an Edit Box are among the simplest implementations of Dojo. The `dijit.form.ValidationTextBox` is a simple extension to the Edit Box, which adds Client-Side validation with a styling consistent with other dijits to offer immediate validation and a prompt message. It has a number of Dojo attributes, some of which you can see in Listing 5.3. Figure 5.3 shows the resulting output. There is a host of printed and online documentation of Dojo (for examples, see the Dojo Toolkit website http://dojotoolkit.org/reference-guide/index.html). This book will not seek to exhaustively reproduce a glossary of the Dojo attributes and what they do.

Listing 5.3 `dijit.form.ValidationTextBox`

```
<xp:this.resources>
   <xp:dojoModule
      name="dijit.form.ValidationTextBox">
   </xp:dojoModule>
</xp:this.resources>
<xp:inputText
   id="inputText1"
   value="#{viewScope.validationBox}"
   dojoType="dijit.form.ValidationTextBox">
   <xp:this.dojoAttributes>
      <xp:dojoAttribute
         name="required"
         value="true">
      </xp:dojoAttribute>
      <xp:dojoAttribute
         name="promptMessage"
         value="Please complete this field">
      </xp:dojoAttribute>
   </xp:this.dojoAttributes>
</xp:inputText>
```

Figure 5.3 `dijit.form.ValidationTextBox.`

Defining Dojo modules and attributes is made a little challenging because there is no type-ahead or other context-sensitive help to advise on the Dojo modules available for use. There is also no validation of the correct naming conventions for the modules or validation of additional resources that need to be included. But this is to provide developers with the flexibility to take advantage of new releases of Dojo at the earliest opportunity and develop their own Dojo modules. For developers who are comfortable with the attributes available, this is not a problem; however, novice developers might find the size of the Dojo toolkit daunting.

Dojo Example for Slider

Some dijits are more involved than just setting a Dojo type and attributes to a Core control. A good example of this is the slider. There are actually two types of sliders: `dijit.form.HorizontalSlider` and `dijit.form.VerticalSlider`. The implementations are similar, so we shall just cover the `HorizontalSlider`.

As with `dijit.form.ValidationTextBox`, the slider is an input control, so you need to store the value in an Edit Box control (or, in most implementations, a Hidden Input control). However, you cannot directly attach the slider to the Edit Box. Instead, you apply the Dojo styling to a div and add an onchange event to pass the value to the Edit Box. Although the XPages Div control has **dojoType** and **dojoAttributes** properties, it does not have an onchange event, so it is easier to use an HTML div.

Further code is required to apply labels to the horizontal slider. You must apply an additional Dojo module to an HTML ordered list, `dijit.form.HorizontalRuleLabels`. Listing 5.4 shows the combination of XPage and HTML markup used to create a horizontal slider, which allows the user to select a value (in multiples of 10) within a range of 0 and 100, showing labels at increments of 20. The code required is rather extensive for a simple slider. Figure 5.4 shows the resulting output.

Listing 5.4   `dijit.form.HorizontalSlider`

```
<xp:this.resources>
   <xp:dojoModule
      name="dijit.form.HorizontalSlider">
   </xp:dojoModule>
   <xp:dojoModule
      name="dijit.form.HorizontalRuleLabels">   </xp:dojoModule>
</xp:this.resources>

<div
   id="horizontalSlider"
   dojoType="dijit.form.HorizontalSlider"
   value="50"
   minimum="0"
   maximum="100"
   discreteValues="11"    style="width:500px"
   showButtons="false"
   onChange="dojo.byId('#{id:horizontalHolder}').value =
dijit.byId('horizontalSlider').value">
   <ol
      dojoType="dijit.form.HorizontalRuleLabels"
      container="bottomDecoration">
      <li>0</li>
      <li>20</li>
      <li>40</li>
      <li>60</li>
      <li>80</li>
      <li>100</li>
   </ol>
</div>
<br />
<xp:inputText
   id="horizontalHolder"
   value="#{viewScope.horizontalSlider}"
   defaultValue="50">
</xp:inputText>
```

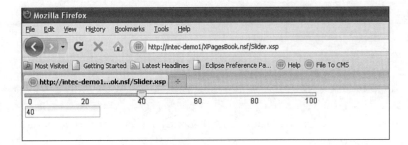

Figure 5.4 `dijit.form.HorizontalSlider.`

Dojo Themes

All the dijits are styled according to a theme. The theme is defined on the **XPages** tab in the **Application Properties**, accessed from **designer**, using the **Application Theme** dialog list, as in Figure 5.5. The OneUI and Server Default themes use tundra by default. If the property **Use runtime optimized JavaScript and CSS resources** at the bottom of this tab is checked, a single aggregated stylesheet is delivered to the browser. This includes the following stylesheet:

/xsp/.ibmxspres/dojoroot-1.6.1/dijit/themes/tundra/tundra.css

In addition, the tundra theme is applied to the body tag, so the output HTML is `<body class="xsp lotusui tundra">`.

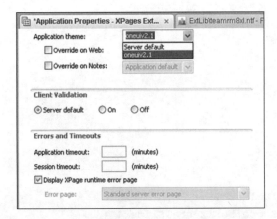

Figure 5.5   XPages tab of Application Properties in Domino Designer.

Dojo provides three other themes: nihilo, soria and, since Dojo 1.5.0, claro. Implementing these themes is just a matter of including the relevant stylesheets and applying the style to the body tag. The former is straightforward in XPages, the latter a little more involved. Within an XPage, you are limited on the attributes you can manipulate. However, via a custom theme, you can apply the Dojo theme to the body tag and reference the relevant stylesheets. If an application is not currently using a theme, just create a new Theme design element, found under the **Resources** category in the **Application** pane.

You can insert the code in Listing 5.5 between the theme tags. Lines 1 through 5 include the Dojo-themed stylesheet. Lines 8 through 14 apply the Dojo theme to the `ViewRoot` control, which becomes the body tag when the web page is loaded. Note in particular the inclusion in lines 2 and 8 of `dojoTheme="true"`. By adding this, the logic checks whether the developer has set dojoTheme to `"true"` on the XPage or CustomControl. If the developer has set `dojoTheme` to `"true"`, the stylesheet is loaded and the class is applied. If not, the stylesheet is not loaded and the class is not applied. To use soria or claro, just replace the three instances of `nihilo` with the relevant theme name.

Listing 5.5   Applying a Dojo Theme

```
1   <!-- Include Dojo stylesheet -->
2   <resource dojoTheme="true">
3       <content-type>text/css</content-type>
4       <href>/.ibmxspres/dojoroot/dijit/themes/nihilo/nihilo.css</href>
5   </resource>
6
7   <!-- Add style to body element -->
8   <control dojoTheme="true">
9       <name>ViewRoot</name>
10      <property mode="concat">
11          <name>styleClass</name>
12          <value>nihilo</value>
13      </property>
14  </control>
```

Dojo Modules and Dojo in the Extension Library

As the examples in the preceding sections demonstrate, some Dojo modules are easy to implement into XPages, but others are more convoluted. Even for a confident developer already accustomed to using dijits in applications, it could get annoying to have to keep adding dojoTypes and dojoAttributes to all core controls, which was one of the driving forces behind implementing the Dojo controls in the Extension Library. Using native controls offered several other benefits:

- Easier to implement drag-and-drop functionality
- Promoting some of the more common Dojo modules available for use within XPages
- Validating and manipulating values
- Limiting the number of controls that need to be dropped onto the XPage or Custom Control

That is not to say that the Extension Library precludes the need to implement Dojo manually within XPages. It does not, nor is it intended to. Some Dojo modules, such as the `dojox.image.Lightbox` control, are not available in the Extension Library controls. Equally, there might be instances in which developers have created their own Dojo extensions that they still intend to use but do not have the skills or are not ready to componentize.

Benefits and Differences of Dojo Extension Library Components

By componentizing the Dojo modules as extended controls, the Extension Library offers several benefits. Performance is one aspect. Another is that if a Dojo control from the Extension Library is used, `dojoParseOnLoad` or `dojoTheme` does not need to be set and the relevant Dojo module(s) does not need to be added to an XPage. Whether accustomed or not to adding the gamut of dojo attributes to Dojo controls, the extended controls also avoid the need to remember (and indeed avoid mistyping!) dojo attributes. This also means that it is quicker to implement the extended controls than just setting a Dojo type and attributes, whether dragging and dropping and using the "pretty panels" or typing directly into the Source pane. And for developers who are integrating with Java beans, controls also allow options for integration with backend Java classes, whether with valueChangeListeners or for controlling return types of, for example, the Dojo Number Text Box or Dojo Number Spinner.

However, for dijits to use a Dojo theme other than tundra, the code outlined in Listing 5.5 for a Theme design element is still required to apply the relevant Dojo theme to the body tag. There is nothing within the Extension Library to short-circuit that requirement.

In the examples that follow, properties of the Extension Library are hard-coded, for ease of explanation. But remember that, as with any other property in XPages, the value of all the properties of the Extension Library controls can be programmatically calculated, either using on page load or dynamically.

Without further ado, let's start looking at the Dojo form controls from the Extension Library that add to the form controls we covered in the previous chapter. Other Dojo controls are covered in subsequent chapters. For example, the Dojo Data Grid control is covered in Chapter 7, "Views."

Dojo Extensions to the Edit Box Control

Many controls extend the Edit Box control, whether for storing text values, number values, or date/time values. These controls are not used in the TeamRoom database, so we will review the Extension Library demo database, which is available from OpenNTF. Specifically, we will review the **Core_DojoFormControls.xsp** XPage.

Dojo Text Box (`xe:djTextBox`)

The Dojo Text Box control is an excellent example of a control that appears to be simple but can provide functionality not available in the core Edit Box control. In most implementations, all that is required is to drag and drop it onto the XPage or custom control.

When you look at the properties available and compare them to the core Edit Box control, some differences become apparent. Table 5.1 describes the main properties that are standard across the Dojo widgets.

Table 5.1 Dojo Widget Properties

Property	Description
alt	Holds alternate text if the browser cannot display the control; uncommon for form controls.
waiRole	Defines the WAI-ARIA role for the control. For more information on WAI-ARIA, see http://www.w3.org/WAI/.
waiState	Defines the WAI-ARIA state of the control. For more information on WAI-ARIA, see http://www.w3.org/WAI/.
trim	Removes leading or trailing spaces, but not duplicate spaces within the field's value.
dragRestriction	If true, prevents the field from being draggable.
intermediateChanges	If true, triggers the onChange event for each value change.
tooltip	For most controls, such as Dojo Text Box, the title property is used to add hover text. Some controls, such as the Dojo Tab Pane, use the title property for the tab label. For those controls, this tooltip property is used instead to add hover text.

Table 5.2 describes the properties specific for the Dojo Text Box controls. On the All Properties panel of the Dojo Text Box, the data category contains the same properties as the Edit Box (xp:inputText) control. But a smaller subset of properties is listed under the basics category. Some of the options, including **autocomplete**, **password**, **htmlFilterIn,** and **htmlFilter**— visible on an Edit Box control—are not available for this control. Note that some properties like **readonly** and **maxlength** are camel case for the Dojo controls and become **readOnly** and **maxLength** on the Dojo Text Box control.

Table 5.2 xe:djTextBox Properties

Property	Description
lowercase	If true, the field's value is converted to lowercase when the user exits the field.
propercase	If true, the field's value is converted to propercase when the user exits the field.
uppercase	If true, the field's value is converted to uppercase when the user exits the field.

The Dojo Text Box also offers some additional properties. Some properties, such as **alt**, **tabIndex**, **title**, **waiRole**, and **waiState**, are standard for the Dojo extended controls, always appearing under the accessibility category. WAI might be unfamiliar to some Domino developers who are not used to web development. WAI is an initiative by the World Wide Web Consortium (W3C) to ensure that websites follow accessibility guidelines. This has been extended for applications by Web Accessibility Initiative—Accessible Rich Internet Applications (WAI-ARIA), which differentiates applications from static web pages. It is not yet standard, but it is good practice. A full taxonomy of roles (http://www.w3.org/WAI/PF/GUI/roleTaxonomy-20060508.html) and states (http://www.w3.org/WAI/PF/adaptable/StatesAndProperties-20051106.html) is available on the W3C site. The good news is that even if you do not define the **waiRole** and **waiState** properties on the Dojo extended controls, default roles and states are added. But, if required, the properties are exposed to allow you to override the defaults.

Other properties are exposed that offer additional functionality over the Edit Box control or even the standard TextBox control in the Dojo toolkit. In the basics category, the **maxLength** property enables developers to ensure that users are restricted to a certain number of characters. This is triggered on key press, so rather than alerting users after they have left the field, the user physically cannot type more characters than you allow. However, bear in mind that if the field should include punctuation, decimal separators, and so on, each counts as one character. You can use the **trim** property to remove any leading or trailing spaces. It does not remove duplicate spaces within the string.

The dojo category is expanded from the Edit Box control with some additional Dojo properties: **dragRestriction**, **intermediateChanges,** and **tooltip**. These properties are standard for the Dojo widgets and may not be appropriate for all controls. For example, the **tooltip** property is used only for controls such as the Dojo Tab Pane, where the **title** property has a different function than applying hover text. The format category provides boolean properties **lowercase**, **uppercase,** and **propercase** to force case conversion. The formatting takes effect as soon as the user exits the field.

Some of the differences in the events category between the Edit Box control and the Dojo Text Box control are just minor. Properties like **onfocus**, **onblur**, **onchange**, and **onclick** become **onFocus**, **onBlur**, **onChange,** and **onClick**. It's not a major difference, and indeed there is no difference in implementation. But there are a few additions. The mousing events are supplemented by **onMouseEnter** and **onMouseLeave**, ostensibly no different from **onMouseOver** and **onMouseOut**. A simple alert statement will show that the onMouseOver event is triggered before the onMouseEnter event. Likewise, onMouseOut is triggered before onMouseLeave.

Dojo Validation Text Box (`xe:djValidationTextBox`)

There are no prizes for guessing that the Dojo Validation Text Box control is similar to the Dojo Text Box control, except that it adds validation. All the properties we outlined on the Dojo Text Box control are available, including those for dynamically setting the value to lowercase, uppercase, or propercase and trimming the value.

However, the Dojo Validation Text Box is not, by default, mandatory. Initially, this sounds incomprehensible. What's the point of the Dojo Validation Text Box if it's not validated? But if we investigate a little further, we will come across the **promptMessage** property. This enables the developer to add a message for the user. At runtime, this is delivered to the user by default as a tooltip, as in Figure 5.6.

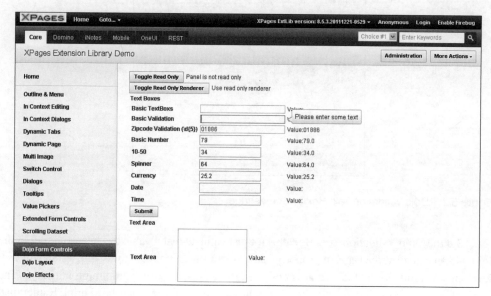

Figure 5.6 Dojo Validation Text Box promptMessage.

Basic validation is managed in the same way as for any other input control: by using the **required** property. But validation for the traditional Edit Box control is handled on the client or the server, as determined by the developer in the **Application Properties** or the administrator in the **Server Settings**. In the Dojo Validation Text Box, validation is always handled Client-Side, even if client validation is switched off in the **Application Properties**. That is because the Dojo Validation Text Box is a Dojo control, and Dojo validation runs Client-Side (because Dojo is a set of Client-Side JavaScript libraries). So as soon as the user tabs out of the field, the validation is triggered and the field is highlighted, as in Figure 5.7. As with the `dijit.form.ValidationTextBox` Dojo module, an error message in the **invalidMessage** property has no effect if the control just has the **required** property set to `"true"` but no other validation applied.

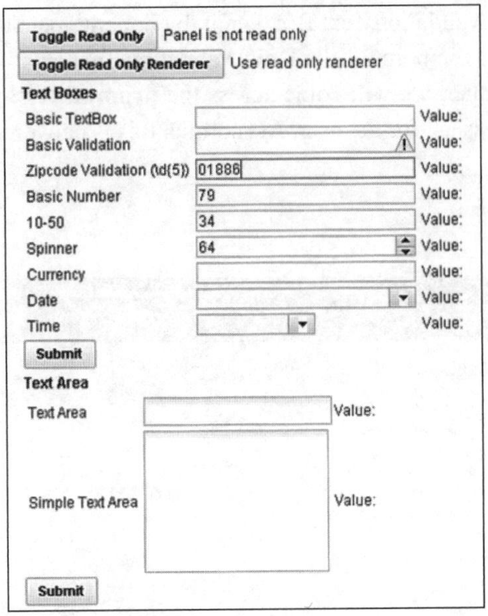

Figure 5.7   Dojo Validation Text Box error message.

But the Dojo Validation Text Box doesn't just validate that a value has been entered. In the dojo-widget category, the **regExp** property takes as its value a regular expression, a standard web development validation notation that is designed to be agnostic of programming language. The **regExpGen** property can generate a regular expression using Client-Side JavaScript. Rather than researching and typing a regular expression, Dojo provides some prebuilt objects for validating standard regular expressions, such as **dojo.regexp.realNumber** and **dojo.regexp.ipAddress**. These can be found in files like **dojo.number** and **dojox.validate**, all of which extend **dojo.regexp**, the object that defines the function to validate against regular expressions. For example, Listing 5.6 takes the ipAddress function in **dojox.validate.regexp.js**, amending it only to expect no parameters. As a function in the **regExpGen** property, this code will validate that the user enters a valid IP address, without the need to work out or type in the relevant regular expression. As with traditional XPages validation, there is a default, but developers can also provide their own message, using the **invalidMessage** property.

Listing 5.6   Validating an IP Address

```
<xe:djValidationTextBox
    value="#{sessionScope.djValidationTextBox1}"
    invalidMessage="Please enter a valid ip address">
    <xe:this.regExpGen><![CDATA[// summary: Builds an RE that matches an
IP address
```

```
//
// description:
//   Supports five formats for IPv4: dotted decimal, dotted hex, dotted
octal, decimal, and hexadecimal.
//   Supports two formats for Ipv6.
//
// flags  An object. All flags are boolean with default = true.
//     flags.allowDottedDecimal  Example, 207.142.131.235. No zero
padding.
//     flags.allowDottedHex  Example, 0x18.0x11.0x9b.0x28. Case
insensitive. Zero padding allowed.
//     flags.allowDottedOctal  Example, 0030.0021.0233.0050. Zero
padding allowed.
//     flags.allowDecimal  Example, 3482223595. A decimal number between
0-4294967295.
//     flags.allowHex  Example, 0xCF8E83EB. Hexadecimal number between
0x0-0xFFFFFFFF.
//       Case insensitive. Zero padding allowed.
//     flags.allowIPv6   IPv6 address written as eight groups of four
hexadecimal digits.
//     FIXME: ipv6 can be written multiple ways IIRC
//     flags.allowHybrid   IPv6 address written as six groups of four
hexadecimal digits
//       followed by the usual four dotted decimal digit notation of
IPv4. x:x:x:x:x:x:d.d.d.d

// assign default values to missing parameters
flags = {};
if(typeof flags.allowDottedDecimal != "boolean"){
flags.allowDottedDecimal = true; }
if(typeof flags.allowDottedHex != "boolean"){ flags.allowDottedHex =
true; }
if(typeof flags.allowDottedOctal != "boolean"){ flags.allowDottedOctal
= true; }
if(typeof flags.allowDecimal != "boolean"){ flags.allowDecimal = true;
}
if(typeof flags.allowHex != "boolean"){ flags.allowHex = true; }
if(typeof flags.allowIPv6 != "boolean"){ flags.allowIPv6 = true; }
if(typeof flags.allowHybrid != "boolean"){ flags.allowHybrid = true; }
// decimal-dotted IP address RE.
var dottedDecimalRE =
// Each number is between 0-255. Zero padding is not allowed.
```

Listing 5.6   (Continued)

```
    "((\\d|[1-9]\\d|1\\d\\d|2[0-4]\\d|25[0-5])\\.){3}(\\d|[1-
9]\\d|1\\d\\d|2[0-4]\\d|25[0-5])";

// dotted hex IP address RE. Each number is between 0x0-0xff. Zero
padding is allowed, e.g. 0x00.
var dottedHexRE = "(0[xX]0*[\\da-fA-F]?[\\da-fA-F]\\.){3}0[xX]0*[\\da-
fA-F]?[\\da-fA-F]";

// dotted octal IP address RE. Each number is between 0000-0377.
// Zero padding is allowed, but each number must have at least four
characters.
var dottedOctalRE = "(0+[0-3][0-7][0-7]\\.){3}0+[0-3][0-7][0-7]";

// decimal IP address RE. A decimal number between 0-4294967295.
var decimalRE =  "(0|[1-9]\\d{0,8}|[1-3]\\d{9}|4[01]\\d{8}|42[0-
8]\\d{7}|429[0-3]\\d{6}|" +
    "4294[0-8]\\d{5}|42949[0-5]\\d{4}|429496[0-
6]\\d{3}|4294967[01]\\d{2}|42949672[0-8]\\d|429496729[0-5])";

// hexadecimal IP address RE.
// A hexadecimal number between 0x0-0xFFFFFFFF. Case insensitive. Zero
padding is allowed.
var hexRE = "0[xX]0*[\\da-fA-F]{1,8}";

// IPv6 address RE.
// The format is written as eight groups of four hexadecimal digits,
x:x:x:x:x:x:x:x,
// where x is between 0000-ffff. Zero padding is optional. Case
insensitive.
var ipv6RE = "([\\da-fA-F]{1,4}\\:){7}[\\da-fA-F]{1,4}";

// IPv6/IPv4 Hybrid address RE.
// The format is written as six groups of four hexadecimal digits,
// followed by the 4 dotted decimal IPv4 format. x:x:x:x:x:x:d.d.d.d
var hybridRE = "([\\da-fA-F]{1,4}\\:){6}" +
    "((\\d|[1-9]\\d|1\\d\\d|2[0-4]\\d|25[0-5])\\.){3}(\\d|[1-
9]\\d|1\\d\\d|2[0-4]\\d|25[0-5])";

// Build IP Address RE
var a = [];
if(flags.allowDottedDecimal){ a.push(dottedDecimalRE); }
```

```
if(flags.allowDottedHex){ a.push(dottedHexRE); }
if(flags.allowDottedOctal){ a.push(dottedOctalRE); }
if(flags.allowDecimal){ a.push(decimalRE); }
if(flags.allowHex){ a.push(hexRE); }
if(flags.allowIPv6){ a.push(ipv6RE); }
if(flags.allowHybrid){ a.push(hybridRE); }
var ipAddressRE = "";
if(a.length > 0){
    ipAddressRE = "(" + a.join("|") + ")";
}
return ipAddressRE; // String]]></xe:this.regExpGen>
</xe:djValidationTextBox>
```

Alternatively, if developers already have a prexisting Client-Side JavaScript function to validate the value entered, the **validatorExt** property in the dojo-widget category provides an extension point to call the function. The beauty of this is that developers only need to enter a Client-Side JavaScript object that is a function; the XPage runs the validation in all the events that are appropriate. This speeds up development and minimizes the effort of refactoring.

By default, your validation triggers only when the user has finished editing the field. To trigger validation or other events with each key press, you can set **intermediateChanges** to true. (By default, it is false.)

On top of all this, the **validator** and **validators** properties still exist for core XPages validation. Overall, the Dojo Validation Text Box provides an extremely flexible mechanism for validating the control while maintaining the Dojo look and feel.

Two additional formatting properties are available: **displayMessageExt** and **tooltipPosition**. The **tooltipPosition** property defines the position relative to the field in which any tooltip messages will appear. With the **displayMessageExt** property, a developer can write a Client-Side JavaScript function to override the appearance of the prompts and validation error messages.

WHAT ARE REGULAR EXPRESSIONS?

For those who are not familiar with the notation, there are websites that can provide standard regular expressions and help you build and test your own. A good starting point is http://www.regular-expressions.info. The zipcode field is a good example of a regular expression in action. \d{5} means the field must consist of five characters, all of which are digits. Regular expressions can be simple, as in this example, or extremely complex. The UK postcode is a good example of a particularly complex regular expression, where specific combinations of letters and numbers are allowed:

```
(GIR 0AA)|(((A[BL]|B[ABDHLNRSTX]?|C[ABFHMORTVW]|D[ADEGHLNTY]
|E[HNX]?|F[KY]|G[LUY]?|H[ADGPRSUX]|I[GMPV]|JE|K[ATWY]
|L[ADELNSU]?|M[EKL]?|N[EGNPRW]?|O[LX]|P[AEHLOR]|R[GHM]|S[AEGKL
MNOPRSTY]?|T[ADFNQRSW]|UB|W[ADFNRSV]|YO|ZE)[1-
9]?[0-9]|((E|N|NW|SE|SW|W)1|EC[1-4]|WC[12])[A-HJKMNPR-
Y]|(SW|W)([2-9]|[1-9][0-9])|EC[1-9][0-9])  [0-9][ABD-
HJLNP-UW-Z]{2})
```

If you have a specific format of entry, there's usually a regular expression to validate it.

Table 5.3 summarizes the additional properties of the Dojo Validation Text Box, extending those already covered under the Dojo Text Box.

Table 5.3 xe:djValidationTextBox Properties

Property	Description
promptMessage	Enables developers to add a field hint to users when they enter the field.
invalidMessage	Enables a developer to add an error message if any field validation fails. The message will not appear if the only validation applied is required="true".
validatorExt	Holds a Client-Side JavaScript function to extend validation.
regExp	Holds a regular expression with which to validate the value the user entered.
regExpGen	Holds Client-Side JavaScript, which returns a regular expression with which to validate the value the user entered.
displayMessageExt	Holds Client-Side JavaScript to customize the display of Dojo prompt or validation messages.
tooltipPosition	The position relative to the field with which to display any prompt or validation messages.

Dojo Number Text Box, Dojo Currency Text Box (`xe:djNumberTextBox` and `xe:djCurrencyTextBox`)

The Dojo Number Text Box and Dojo Currency Text Box controls extend the Dojo Validation Text Box still further in relation to validating numeric values. All the validation methods we have covered are already available, although the **required** property is virtually redundant, because a blank value is translated to 0 on save. But the power of the Dojo Number Text Box lies in the `xe:djNumberConstraints` extension. It is a complex property comprising a variety of child properties, as can be seen in Figure 5.8. The significant property, as shown, is **type**. This determines the output format from the control, but because of an issue with Dojo, **scientific** is not yet supported. Similarly, the value **currency** and the related properties **currency** and **symbol** are only applicable for the Dojo Currency Text Box.

Figure 5.8 `xe:djNumberConstraints`.

The main strength of the `xe:djNumberConstraints` extension, whose properties are shown in Table 5.4, is enforcing appropriate data entry by the user. Percentages can be messy to enforce, handling the percentage sign if users do or do not enter it, manipulating the value for subsequent calculations, and so on. Setting type to **percent** gets around this by ensuring the user enters a number followed by the percentage sign, such as "50%", which the control then converts to the decimal value "0.5". Likewise, specifying a pattern or places can translate the value entered by the user into an expected format, such as with a certain number of leading zeros or decimal places. With use of **min** and **max,** the entered value can be validated against a range, with an appropriate message defined in the **rangeMessage** property, specific for these controls. See Figure 5.9.

Table 5.4 `xe:djNumberConstraints` Properties

Property	Description
currency	Defines the relevant currency symbol to be applied to the field. The value should be a three-character ISO 4217 currency code, such as GBP. This property relates only to the Dojo Currency Text Box.
fractional	Defines whether to include the fractional portion, for Dojo Currency Text Box only.
locale	The locale to be applied to determine formatting rules for the field's value, one of the extraLocale values loaded in the Dojo config.
max	Defines the maximum value allowed for the field.
min	Defines the minimum value allowed for the field.
pattern	Defines the formatting rule for the field's value, to override any locale-specific formatting.
places	The number of digits to force entry of after the decimal place.
strict	Defines the degree of tolerance allowed to user input; it is false by default. This is more applicable to date/time constraints.
symbol	Defines the currency symbol to be applied to the field, overriding the default currency symbol for the ISO 4217 currency code defined in the currency property. This property relates only to the Dojo Currency Text Box.
type	Defines the type applied to the field: decimal, scientific (not supported), percent, currency (Dojo Currency Text Box only).

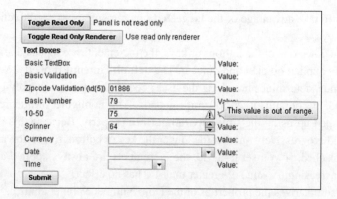

Figure 5.9 Dojo Number Text Box, Dojo Number Spinner, and Dojo Currency Text Box.

The Dojo Number Text Box has one further property that is of particular benefit if the entered value is passed to a managed bean or another Java object. This is the **javaType** property. Anyone who has worked with managed beans will be aware that the value is sometimes handled as a java.util.Long, sometimes as a java.util.Double, but never consistently. It all depends on the value the user enters, which can be annoying. The **javaType** property enables developers to override the type of the value passed to your underlying Java object and ensure it is always an int, always a double, always a float, and so on. Table 5.5 summarizes these additional properties available for the Dojo Number Text Box and Dojo Currency Text Box.

Table 5.5 `xe:djNumberTextBox` and `xe:djCurrencyTextBox` Properties

Property	Description
javaType	Defines the Java number type of the Server-Side value; by default, it is double.
rangeMessage	Defines the validation message to show if the value entered is outside the minimum and maximum bounds.

Dojo Number Spinner (`xe:djNumberSpinner`)

The Dojo Number Spinner allows the user to either type in a number or scroll up and down through the range with the keyboard or the buttons provided on the right edge of the control. This control is an implementation of `dijit.form.NumberSpinner` and an extension of the Dojo Number Text Box with all the properties applicable to that control (so currency-related properties of the `xe:djNumberConstraints` extension are not applicable). The control provides two properties for managing the incremental steps of the spinner: **smallDelta** and **largeDelta**. By default, the implicit increments are 1 and 10 respectively, but this can be overridden as required. The **smallDelta** increment is used when the user clicks the buttons provided or uses the cursor up and down keys. To take advantage of the **largeDelta** increment, users need to click the **Page Up** or **Page Down** keys.

If you hold down one of the buttons or keys, the increments are repeated after half a second and subsequently applied quicker and quicker. The **defaultTimeout** property, expecting an integer in milliseconds, determines how long the user needs to hold down the key before the increment is repeated; by default, it is 500 milliseconds. You configure the degree to which the increments are sped up using the **timeoutChangeRate** property. Because this is 0.9, the increments are applied progressively quicker the longer the key or button is held down, until the maximum speed is reached. If you set it at 1.0, the increments are always applied at the same time interval, never increasing. A value of greater than 1.0 has no effect.

Table 5.6 summarizes the properties of the Dojo Number Spinner control.

Table 5.6 `xe:djNumberSpinner` Properties

Property	Description
defaultTimeout	Allows the developer to control the number of milliseconds the user needs to hold down the key before it becomes typematic, or auto-incrementing.
timeoutChangeRate	Defines how much quicker each typematic event occurs.
largeDelta	Defines the increment when the Page Up and Page Down buttons are pressed.
smallDelta	Defines the increment when the cursor Up and Down buttons are pressed.

Dojo Date Text Box and Dojo Time Text Box (`xe:djDateTextBox` and `xe:djTimeTextBox`)

The Dojo Date Text Box and Dojo Time Text Box controls extend the Dojo Validation Text Box control. However, like the Dojo Number Text Box, Dojo Currency Text Box, and Dojo Number Spinner, they have their own **constraints complex** property. For the Dojo Date Text Box and Dojo Time Text Box, the **constraints complex** property implements the `xe:djDateTime-Constraints` extension, as detailed in Table 5.7 and illustrated in Figure 5.10.

Table 5.7 `xe:djDateTimeConstraints` Properties

Property	Description
am	Allows the developer to override the "am" abbreviation for A.M. times. This is only applicable to the Dojo Time Text Box and only where **timePattern** is specified and uses the AM/PM portion (for example, **timePattern** is "h:mm a").
clickableIncrement	Defines the clickable increment of the Time Picker and is applicable only to the Dojo Time Text Box. The value is entered in the format Thh:mm:ss.
datePattern	Defines the date pattern and overrides any setting in the **formatLength** property. Date patterns are in accordance with Unicode Technical Standard 35 Date Format Patterns, such as dd-MM-yy.
formatLength	Defines the date or time format. Available options are long, short, medium, and full.
locale	The locale to be applied to determine formatting rules for the field's value, one of the **extraLocale** values loaded in the Dojo config.
pm	Allows the developer to override the "pm" abbreviation for P.M. times. This is only applicable to the Dojo Time Text Box and only where **timePattern** is specified and uses the AM/PM portion (for example, **timePattern** is "h:mm a").
selector	Defines the selector, either date or time.
strict	Defines the degree of tolerance allowed to user input; it is false by default.
timePattern	Defines the time pattern and overrides any setting in the **formatLength** property. Time patterns are in accordance with Unicode Technical Standard 35 Date Format Patterns, such as hh:mm a.
visibleIncrement	Defines the visible increment of the Time Picker and is applicable only to the Dojo Time Text Box. The value is entered in format Thh:mm:ss.
visibleRange	Defines the visible range of the Time Picker and is applicable only to the Dojo Time Text Box. The value is entered in the format Thh:mm:ss.

The main one for the Dojo Date Text Box is the **datePattern** property, which allows developers to define the format of the date presented to the user in the Dojo Date Text Box. For example, dd-MM-yyyy overrides the locale format to show 16th June 2011 as 16-06-2011, and dd MMM yyyy shows as 16 Jun 2011. Alternatively, the **formatLength** property can be used to choose one of four predefined date or time formats. If both are used, the **datePattern** property takes precedence.

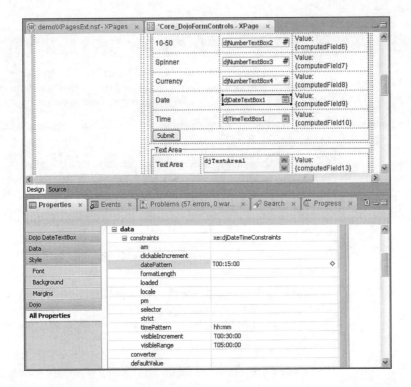

Figure 5.10   `xe:djDateTimeConstraints`.

The Dojo Time Text Box control also uses the **xe:djDateTimeConstraints** property. But unlike the Dojo Date Text Box, properties are surfaced to allow the developer to manage the display of the control. To control how many hours are shown, you can define the **visibleRange** property. The **visibleIncrement** property defines the labels presented to the user, and the **clickableIncrement** property defines the increment for each value the user can select. You define each property using the format THH:mm:ss, so a **visibleIncrement** of 30 minutes is T00:30:00, as in Figure 5.11. With **datePattern** for the Dojo Date Text Box, the **timePattern** property defines the format for the times displayed to the user and presented in the field. Therefore, a format of h:mm presents, for example, 9:00, 9:30, and so on.

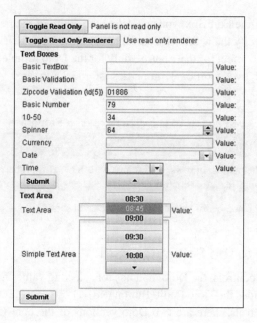

Figure 5.11 Time Picker.

Dojo Extensions to the Multiline Edit Box Control

There are two Dojo controls in the Extension Library that extend the Multiline Edit Box: the Dojo Text Area (`xe:djTextarea`) and the Dojo Simple Text Area (`xe:djSimpleTextarea`). One of the advantages of these controls is that they also have some of the string manipulation properties familiar from the Dojo extensions that are based on the Edit Box controls. So **trim**, **propercase**, **lowercase,** and **uppercase** are implemented, which makes it easy to manipulate the content as soon as the user leaves the field. There is no built-in Dojo functionality to validate the Dojo Text Area control, but you can utilize all the core XPages validation techniques.

One of the strengths of XPages is that you can present and edit a collection of documents in the same web page. However, the challenge for a developer is that, unless the user is editing a small document such as a Comments document, the editable form can take up a large amount of real estate. If that includes the Multiline Edit Box as well, it takes up even more real estate when **rows** and **cols** properties are defined. But the beauty of the Dojo Text Area control is that it is auto-expanding. This means it takes up less screen real estate while still expanding as much as is required to show the user all the content. The Dojo Simple Text Area control, however, is fixed size. Of course, size attributes can be computed using Server-Side JavaScript, just as they can for any other XPages properties.

As with the Multiline Edit Box, you can define the width of the field using the **rows** property or using CSS to specify the width. Of course, because the Dojo Text Area is auto-expanding, the **rows** property has no effect for that control, only for the Dojo Simple Text Area control.

Table 5.8 details two additional properties of the Dojo Text Area and Dojo Simple Text Area.

Table 5.8 `xe:djTextArea` and `xe:djSimpleTextArea` Properties

Property	Description
rows	Defines the number of rows the text area will show. This property is applicable only to the Dojo Simple Text Area control.
cols	Defines the number of columns the text area will show.

Dojo Extensions to the Select Control

As with the other input controls, the Dojo modules for selecting values have been included in the Extension Library. Besides the Dojo Radio Button (`xe:djRadioButton`) and Dojo Check Box (`xe:djCheckBox`) controls, there are two Dojo versions of the core Combo Box control: the Dojo Combo Box (`xe:djComboBox`) and Dojo Filtering Select (`xe:djFilteringSelect`).

The core Combo Box control is good for ensuring that users select from a restricted list of options, but it does not allow type-ahead. The Edit Box control offers this kind of type-ahead functionality, but it does not force the user to select one of the options provided. The benefit of the Dojo Combo Box and Dojo Filtering Select controls in the Extension Library is that they combine the type-ahead and restrict the user to just the options available. The sole difference between the two is that the Dojo Combo Box control holds a list only of values, whereas the Dojo Filtering Select control holds a list of label/value pairs.

Dojo Combo Box and Dojo Filtering Select (`xe:djComboBox` and `xe:djFilteringSelect`)

Developers who are more familior with dojo.data stores such as the ItemFileReadStore can take advantage of the **store** property and reference a JavaScript store. This is just a JSON object returning a collection of items that could be returned by an XAgent or some other API to return a JSON object. However, if the source data has been provided by a third party, it might not return a name attribute for the Dojo Combo Box to search. In this situation, the **searchAttr** property can be used to specify a different attribute in the JSON object on which to search. By default, any search, whether against defined items or against a dojo.data store, is case insensitive, but you can enforce case sensitivity by setting the **ignoreCase** property to true.

By default, whether querying a coded list of options or a dojo.data store, a **starts with** query will be performed. That is, the only results returned will be those that start with the letter or letters. Sometimes developers might prefer to query the store differently; Dojo provides this functionality. There are three expressions to be used for **starts with** searches, **contains** searches, and **exact match** searches. However, the expressions use the phrase `"${"`, which has a specific meaning to the XSP Command Manager, so the easiest method of entering the expressions is using Server-Side JavaScript. The three variants are included in Listing 5.7, Listing 5.8, and Listing 5.9.

Listing 5.7 Contains Search Expression

```
<xe:djComboBox
   id="djComboBox2"
   value="#{sessionScope.djComboBox1}"
   tooltipPosition="before"
   title="This is a comboBox" pageSize="2">

<xe:this.queryExpr><![CDATA[${javascript:"*$\{0}*"}]]></xe:this.queryEx
pr>
   <xp:selectItem
      itemLabel="Ford"
      itemValue="ford">
   </xp:selectItem>
   <xp:selectItem
      itemLabel="Toyota"
      itemValue="toyota">
   </xp:selectItem>
   <xp:selectItem
      itemLabel="Renault"
      itemValue="renault">
   </xp:selectItem>
   <xp:selectItem
      itemLabel="Mercedes"
      itemValue="mercedes">
   </xp:selectItem>
</xe:djComboBox>
```

Listing 5.8 Exact Match Search Expression

```
<xe:djComboBox
   id="djComboBox2"
   value="#{sessionScope.djComboBox1}"
   tooltipPosition="before"
   title="This is a comboBox"
   pageSize="2">
```

Listing 5.8   (Continued)

```
<xe:this.queryExpr><![CDATA[${javascript:"$\{0}"}]]></xe:this.queryExpr
>
   <xp:selectItem
      itemLabel="Ford"
      itemValue="ford">
   </xp:selectItem>
   <xp:selectItem
      itemLabel="Toyota"
      itemValue="toyota">
   </xp:selectItem>
   <xp:selectItem
      itemLabel="Renault"
      itemValue="renault">
</xp:selectItem>
   <xp:selectItem
      itemLabel="Mercedes"
      itemValue="mercedes">
   </xp:selectItem>
</xe:djComboBox>
```

Listing 5.9   Starts with Search Expression

```
<xe:djComboBox
   id-"djComboBox2"
   value="#{sessionScope.djComboBox1}"
   tooltipPosition="before"
   title="This is a comboBox" pageSize="2">

<xe:this.queryExpr><![CDATA[${javascript:"*$\{0}"}]]></xe:this.queryExp
r>
   <xp:selectItem
      itemLabel="Ford"
      itemValue="ford">
   </xp:selectItem>
   <xp:selectItem
      itemLabel="Toyota"
      itemValue="toyota">
   </xp:selectItem>
   <xp:selectItem
      itemLabel="Renault"
```

```
      itemValue="renault">
   </xp:selectItem>
   <xp:selectItem
      itemLabel="Mercedes"
      itemValue="mercedes">
   </xp:selectItem>
</xe:djComboBox>
```

To ease selection, a number of properties are available. The **pageSize** property allows you to define some entries that the drop-down box should show. If the query returns more entries, a link is added to allow the user to page down and page up through the available options, as shown in Figure 5.12 and Figure 5.13. This property doesn't enhance performance by minimizing the number of options delivered to the browser, but you can use it to enhance presentation. As with the Dojo Number Spinner control, it is also possible to manage the response to the selection. In this case, the **searchDelay** property allows you to set the number of milliseconds delay before matching results are returned.

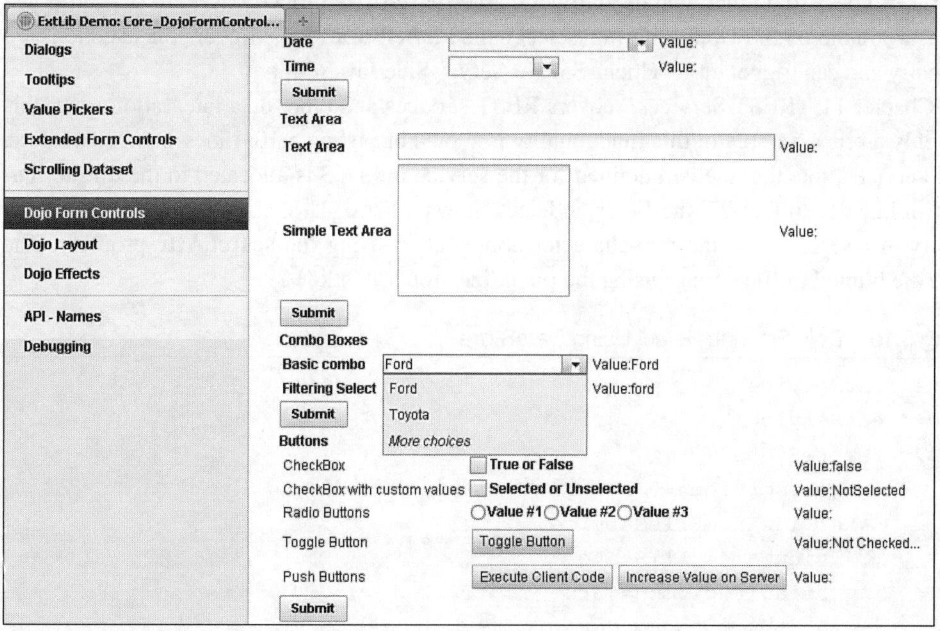

Figure 5.12   More choices on Dojo Combo Box.

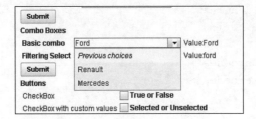

Figure 5.13 Previous choices on Dojo Combo Box.

Because the Dojo Filtering Select uses label/value pairs and the Dojo Combo Box uses just a list of values, Dojo Filtering Select takes advantage of two additional properties and an event to handle the labels displayed. The first is **labelType**. By default, the labels are treated as plain text, but by setting this property to **html,** the labels are treated as HTML. The second is **labelAttr**, applicable for developers using a datastore. As with the **searchAttr** property, you can use this with a Dojo datastore to tell the Dojo Filtering Select to display labels from the store based on an attribute other than name. This does not affect the attribute from the store that is used to search on as the user types. To do that, you need to define the **searchAttr** property as well. An additional event is available on the Dojo Filtering Select called **labelFunc**. This triggers on selection of a valid entry and can trigger either Client-Side or Server-Side JavaScript.

Chapter 11, "REST Services," covers REST services and other data integration, so at this point only a brief example of this functionality is shown in Listing 5.10. Lines 1 to 22 cover the REST service. Note that the jsId defined for the service in line 3 is allocated to the djFilteringSelect in line 26. In line 27, the FilteringSelect shows a list of U.S. states using the **labelAttr** property, but searches on the two-character abbreviation using the **searchAttr** property. The results are limited to 10 per page using the **pageSize** property in line 29.

Listing 5.10 Dojo Filtering Select Using DataStore

```
1   <xe:restService
2   id="restService1"
3   jsId="stateStore">
4      <xe:this.service>
5         <xe:viewItemFileService
6           viewName="AllStates"
7           defaultColumns="true"
8           dojoType="dojo.data.ItemFileReadStore"
9           count="400">
10          <xe:this.columns>
11            <xe:restViewColumn
12               columnName="Name"
13               name="Name">
14            </xe:restViewColumn>
15            <xe:restViewColumn
```

```
16                    columnName="Key"
17                    name="Key">
18              </xe:restViewColumn>
19          </xe:this.columns>
20       </xe:viewItemFileService>
21    </xe:this.service>
22 </xe:restService>
23 <xe:djFilteringSelect
24    id="djComboBox3"
25    value="#{sessionScope.djComboBox2}"
26    store="stateStore"
27    labelAttr="Name"
28    searchAttr="Key"
29    pageSize="10">
30 </xe:djFilteringSelect>
```

Table 5.9 details the noteworthy properties of the Dojo Combo Box and Dojo Filtering Select.

Table 5.9 `xe:djComboBox` and `xe:djFilteringSelect` Properties

Property	Description
hasArrow	Defines whether a drop-down arrow appears beside the field, to show selections.
ignoreCase	Defines whether the search of the store is case-sensitive.
queryExpr	Defines a query for the way the store is searched, as a "starts with", "contains", or "exact match". For terminology, see Listing 5.7, Listing 5.8, and Listing 5.9.
searchAttr	Defines the attribute in the Dojo datastore to search on; by default, it is `name`.
searchDelay	Defines the number of milliseconds to delay before beginning the search.
pageSize	Allows the developer to specify the number of entries to show on each page of the search results.
store	Allows the developer to define a Dojo datastore from which to take the options for the Dojo Combo Box or Dojo Filtering Select.
labelAttr	Defines the attribute in the Dojo datastore from which to retrieve the label. If no property is defined, the attribute in the **searchAttr** property is used. This property is available only for the Dojo Filtering Select.
labelFunc	Defines an event handler to be called when the label changes, returning the label to be displayed. This property is available only for the Dojo Filtering Select.
labelType	Defines whether the label is plain text or HTML. This property is available only for the Dojo Filtering Select.

Dojo Check Box and Dojo Radio Button

The primary intention of the Dojo Check Box and Dojo Radio Button controls is to style the controls appropriate for other Dojo controls. Both controls support the same functionality as the core control versions, so you can assign them to a group with custom values defined. The main difference with the Radio Button Group or Check Box Group is that the core controls for groups display their options in a table within a fieldset. The Dojo Check Box and Dojo Radio Button controls display options inline. In addition to this standard functionality and similarity to the other Dojo controls, the Dojo Check Box and Dojo Radio Button are enabled for accessibility. So the **title** property and the WAI-related properties can be defined, as can any of the other Dojo controls.

Dojo Extensions to Buttons

There are two Dojo Extensions to Buttons: the Dojo Button control and the Dojo Toggle Button control. Like the Dojo Check Box and Dojo Radio Button controls, the Dojo Button is not appreciably different from the core control version. Again, the main differences are the Dojo styling and the inclusion of properties for accessibility, the same ones covered earlier. Just like the core Button control, the Dojo Button control can have a label, show an icon, or both. The **label** property allows the developer to control the text to show, but the **showLabel** property can suppress the label from appearing. However, showing an icon is not merely a case of selecting an image. CSS handles the icon, with the relevant class defined as a string in the **iconClass** property. Dojo has some built-in icons for various editing functions, defined in the **<dojoroot>\dijit\themes** folder and shown in Listing 5.11. Line 4 shows the Dojo theme classes `dijitEditorIcon` and `dijitEditorIconCut` applied to the button. The former loads a sprite (a collection of images, held in a single file to minimize calls to the server), and the latter positions the sprite to show a specific image—in this case, the **Cut** icon. Line 15 applies an icon to a second button, this time using a CSS class. Listing 5.12 shows the stylesheet that loads an image from the **icons** folder on the server. Note that because this is a stylesheet, it is loaded using the HTTP server, not the XSP Command Manager, so standard Domino web URL syntax applies rather than */.ibmxspres/....* You can see the buttons produced in Figure 5.14. If multiple images from the **icons** folder are to be included in the application, using a sprite would be the recommended approach.

Listing 5.11 Dojo Button Icons

```
1  <xe:djButton
2  id="djButton2"
3  label="Execute Client Code"
4     iconClass="dijitEditorIcon dijitEditorIconCut">
```

```
5      <xp:eventHandler
6          event="onClick"
7          submit="false">
8          <xp:this.script><![CDATA[alert("You clicked me,
#{javascript:@UserName()}!")]]></xp:this.script>
9      </xp:eventHandler>
10 </xe:djButton>
11 <xe:djButton
12     id="djButton3"
13     showLabel="false"
14     label="Increase Value on Server"
15     iconClass="testIcon">
16     <xp:eventHandler
17         event="onClick"
18         submit="true"
19         refreshMode="partial"
20         refreshId="computedField19">
21         <xp:this.action><![CDATA[#{javascript:if
(sessionScope.djButton4) {
22     sessionScope.djButton4+=1
23 } else {
24     sessionScope.djButton4 = 1
25 }}]]></xp:this.action>
26     </xp:eventHandler>
27 </xe:djButton>
```

Listing 5.12 testIcon Class

```
.testIcon {
   background-image: url(/icons/actn010.gif); /* editor icons sprite
image */
   background-repeat: no-repeat;
   width: 18px;
   height: 18px;
   text-align: center;
}
```

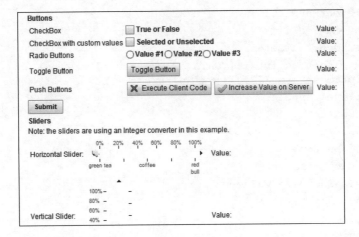

Figure 5.14 Dojo buttons.

Dojo Toggle Button Control

The Dojo Toggle Button is a control that is new to developers who are not familiar with Dojo. The control is similar to the Dojo Check Box control but is styled like the Button control. Like the Dojo Check Box, it can be bound to a datasource, with a value set when the button is unclicked and a different value set when the button is clicked. From inspecting the source HTML produced for the Dojo Toggle Button control, it becomes apparent that the Dojo Toggle Button consists of a button with a dojoType and a hidden input field, as shown in Figure 5.15—a similar technique to the way developers have built the kind of functionality the Dojo Toggle Button provides. Not surprisingly, when the user clicks the Dojo Toggle Button, a value is set into the hidden field. The toggle effect runs Client-Side, although Server-Side events can also be triggered. The hidden field has the same ID as the button, except that it is suffixed with **_field**. The value of the hidden field is not the **checkedValue** or **uncheckedValue** properties, but an empty string if unchecked or **on** if checked.

Figure 5.15   Dojo Button HTML.

By default, as with the Dojo Check Box, the values are false when unclicked and true when clicked. But you can override these values by defining the **checkedValue** and **uncheckedValue** properties, the property names highlighting that this is an extension of the Dojo Check Box control. The only downside is that the styling of the toggle button does not change depending on whether the button is clicked or unclicked. But with the understanding of the HTML produced by the control, it is a simple matter to add that functionality as in Listing 5.13. Lines 8 to 20 add an onChange `xp:eventHandler_`to the control. Note that this has to be defined as an `xp:eventHandler` rather than the default `xe:eventHandler`, which does not exist. Line 11 loads the Client-Side ID of the button into a variable. Line 12 gets the button itself using `dojo.byId()` because of the classneeds setting, not a dojoAttribute. Lines 13 and 14 get the field and test whether the value is **on**. Lines 15 and 17 then set the class of the button.

Listing 5.13   Styling the ToggleButton Control

```
1   <xe:djToggleButton
2       id="djToggleButton1"
3       title="Toggle Button"
4       value="#{sessionScope.djButton3}"
```

Listing 5.13   (Continued)

```
5       label="Toggle Button"
6       checkedValue="Checked..."
7       uncheckedValue="Not Checked...">
8       <xp:eventHandler
9          event="onChange"
10         submit="false">
11         <xe:this.script><![CDATA[var id="#{id:djToggleButton1}";
12 var btn=dojo.byId(id);
13 var field = dojo.byId(id+"_field");
14 if (field.value == "on") {
15    btn.setAttribute("class","btnRed");
16 } else {
17    btn.setAttribute("class","btnGreen");
18 }
19 ]]></xe:this.script>
20     </xp:eventHandler>
21 </xe:djToggleButton>
```

Listing 5.14 shows the CSS for the classes.

Listing 5.14   btnRed and btnGreen Classes

```
.btnRed {
   color: rgb(255,0,0);
}

.btnGreen {
   color: rgb(0,255,0);
}
```

Composite Dojo Extensions

Some extension controls are available under the Dojo category that do not fit into the previous categories. Rather than extending core controls available, these controls add new functionality not previously available as controls in XPages.

As Listing 5.3 shows, the dijit.form.HorizontalSlider requires multiple HTML elements. In the same way, some of the Dojo controls are more complex. Sliders comprise multiple components for their implementation, whereas the Dojo Link Select and Dojo Image Select controls have complex properties to define the values.

Sliders

The beginning of this chapter covered adding a slider with traditional Dojo. The code was covered in Listing 5.4, where the slider comprised a div with an ordered list of labels and an onchange event passing the value to a hidden field via Client-Side JavaScript. The sliders in the Extension Library remove the necessity to use a div with an onChange event to store the value. Rather, the sliders themselves are bound directly to the field.

There are two types of sliders, the **Dojo Horizontal Slider** (xe:djHorizontalSlider) and the **Dojo Vertical Slider** (xe:djVerticalSlider), as Figure 5.16 shows. Although the properties for both are identical and shown in Table 5.10, you need to choose the relevant slider at development time.

Table 5.10   xe:djHorizontalSlider and xe:djVerticalSlider Properties

Property	Description
clickSelect	Defines whether the user can change the value by clicking on a position on the bar in addition to dragging the slider.
discreteValues	Defines the number of discrete values between the minimum and maximum values.
maximum	Defines the maximum value for the slider.
minimum	Defines the minimum value for the slider.
pageIncrement	Defines the number of increments applied to the slider when the user clicks the Page Up or Page Down button.
showButtons	Defines whether buttons are shown to move the slider.
slideDuration	Defines the number of milliseconds it takes to move the slider from 0% to 100%; it is 1000 milliseconds by default.

The values of the slider are controlled by four properties: **defaultValue** defines the initial starting value (if the field the control is bound to does not already have a value), whereas **minimum** and **maximum** define the bounds of the slider, and **discreteValues** defines the number of steps between the minimum and maximum. By default, whenever the user clicks on a part of the slider, that value is selected, and this is controlled by the **clickSelect** property. If set to false, this functionality is suppressed. Also, by default, there are buttons on either end of the slider for moving the current position. Again, these can be suppressed by setting the **showButtons** property to false.

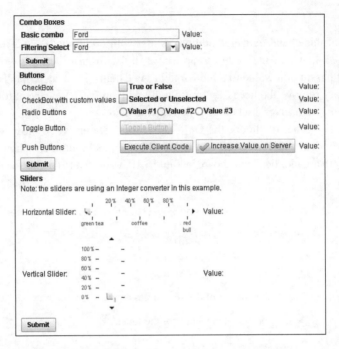

Figure 5.16   Sliders.

Besides clicking on a position of the slider or using the buttons, you can use keyboard shortcuts to control the movement, like you did for the spinner controls. All four cursor keys can be used for both sliders: left (←) and down (↓) moving in one direction, right (→) and up (↑) moving in the other direction. Although the cursor keys can be used to increment in small amounts, **Page Up** and **Page Down** increment in larger amounts. The smaller increment is always one step on the slider, but the developer can override the larger increment—by default 2 steps—using the **pageIncrement** property. Furthermore, because the speed of increment could be controlled for the spinners, it can also be controlled for the sliders, by means of the **slideDuration** property. This is a value in milliseconds that the slider will take to move from one end of the slider to the other; by default, it is one second.

As with the traditional Dojo implementation, you can add labels. This comprises two further controls: the **Dojo Slider Rule** (xe:djSliderRule) for the markers and the **Dojo Slider Rule Labels** (xe:djSliderRuleLabels) for the actual labels. For both controls, two properties determine how many and where the rules appear: **count** and **container**. The **container** provides a ComboBox list of options, with all four options available regardless: topDecoration, leftDecoration, bottomDecoration, and rightDecoration. Obviously, you must choose the relevant container for the relevant slider; rightDecoration and leftDecoration are not applicable for the Dojo Horizontal Slider.

You can map styling to CSS classes for both controls. You can style the markers by using the **ruleStyle** property on the Dojo Slider Rule, whereas you can style the labels by using the **labelStyle** property on the Dojo Slider Rule Labels.

You can set a number of additional properties for the Dojo Slider Rule Labels. The **minimum** and **maximum** properties set the top and bottom level for the labels, and **numericMargin** can define how many labels to omit at either end of the label list. So setting the value to 1 omits 0% and 100% from a default Dojo Slider Rule Labels control. As this suggests, the default labels are percentages, running from 0% to 100%. But you can override this in two ways. You can pass an array of labels into the **labels** property or use the **labelList** property, as shown in Listing 5.15. This method is recommended over <li> tags because it supports localization.

Listing 5.15   Dojo Horizontal Slider

```
<xe:djHorizontalSlider
   id="djHorizontalSlider2"
   value="#{sessionScope.djSlider1}"
   maximum="100"
   minimum="0"
   style="margin: 5px;width:200px; height: 20px;"
   discreteValues="10"
   pageIncrement="3">
   <xp:this.converter>
      <xp:convertNumber
         integerOnly="true">
      </xp:convertNumber>
   </xp:this.converter>
   <xe:djSliderRuleLabels
      id="djSliderRuleLabels2"
      container="topDecoration"
      style="height:10px;font-size:75%;color:gray;"
      count="6"
      numericMargin="1">
   </xe:djSliderRuleLabels>
   <xe:djSliderRule
      id="djSliderRule5"
      container="topDecoration"
      style="height:5px;" count="6">
   </xe:djSliderRule>
   <xe:djSliderRule
      id="djSliderRule6"
      style="height:5px;"
      count="5"
      container="bottomDecoration">
```

Listing 5.15   (Continued)

```
   </xe:djSliderRule>
   <xe:djSliderRuleLabels
      id="djSliderRuleLabels5"
      container="bottomDecoration"
      style="height:10px;font-size:75%;color:gray;">
<xe:this.labelsList>
         <xe:djSliderRuleLabel
            label="green tea">
         </xe:djSliderRuleLabel>
         <xe:djSliderRuleLabel
            label="coffee">
         </xe:djSliderRuleLabel>
         <xe:djSliderRuleLabel
            label="red bull">
         </xe:djSliderRuleLabel>
      </xe:this.labelsList>      </xe:djSliderRuleLabels>
</xe:djHorizontalSlider>
```

Table 5.11 shows the properties for the Dojo Slider Rule and Dojo Slider Rule Labels.

Table 5.11   `xe:djSliderRule` and `xe:djSliderRuleLabels` Properties

Property	Description
count	Defines how many markers or labels should appear.
labels	Allows the developer to write a Client-Side JavaScript expression to define the labels. This property is available only for the Dojo Slider Rule Labels.
labelsList	Allows the developer to define a localizable set of labels. This property is available only for the Dojo Slider Rule Labels.
maximum	Defines the maximum position for the labels. This property is available only for the Dojo Slider Rule Labels.
minimum	Defines the minimum position for the labels. This property is available only for the Dojo Slider Rule Labels.
numericMargin	Defines the number of labels to omit from either end of the label list. This property is available only for the Dojo Slider Rule Labels.
container	Defines where in relation to the slider line the markers or labels should appear.
ruleStyle	Defines the styling for the markers.
labelStyle	Defines the styling for the labels and is available only for Dojo Slider Rule Labels.

Dojo Link Select (`xe:djLinkSelect`)

The Dojo Link Select control allows developers to group link options so that when one link is selected, the others are deselected. You can see this in action with the filter area of the All Documents page on the TeamRoom database. Here, for example, selecting All by Date not only selects that entry but deselects the default All link. Unlike the traditional link functionality, you can bind the Link Select to a field or scoped variable. In addition, you can trigger a wealth of events from the Link Select.

Despite having properties **multipleTrim** and **multipleSeparator**, the control allows only one value to be selected at any one time. You can define the available options in a number of ways. The All Documents page (**allDocumentsFilter.xsp** custom control) uses **selectItem** controls, but you can also use a selectItems control. As with the ComboBox and FilteringSelect controls covered earlier, there is currently no mechanism to add an `xp:selectItem` or `xp:selectItems` control from the palette. So you can use the core ComboBox or ListBox control to define the values; then you can cut and paste the code across from the core control to the Dojo control.

Alternatively, there are three dataProviders available. Those who are comfortable with Java may choose to use the beanValuePicker. The other options are the simpleValuePicker and the dominoViewValuePicker. The simpleValuePicker allows a developer to define a list of options as a string of label value pairs. The label values themselves are defined in the **valueList** property. You can define the separator between the label and the value using the **labelSeparator** property, and you can define the separator between values using the **valueListSeparator** property. The dominoViewValuePicker allows you to select the options from a view, by defining the **databaseName** and **viewName** properties. The **labelColumn** property defines the column from which the values will be picked. The value set when the label is clicked is pulled from the first column in the view. So Listing 5.16 shows a Dojo Link Select where the options are pulled from the AllStates view, showing the Names column. Figure 5.17 shows the resulting output. As you can see, the onChange event refreshes the computed field with the value whenever you select a new link.

Listing 5.16 Link Select Control with `dominoViewValuePicker`

```
<xe:djextLinkSelect
   id="djextLinkSelect2"
   defaultValue="MA"
   value="#{viewScope.link3}">
   <xe:this.dataProvider>
      <xe:dominoViewValuePicker
         viewName="AllStates"
         labelColumn="Name">
      </xe:dominoViewValuePicker>
   </xe:this.dataProvider>
   <xp:eventHandler
```

Listing 5.16   (Continued)

```
        event="onChange"
        submit="true"
        refreshMode="partial"
        refreshId="computedField3">
    </xp:eventHandler>
</xe:djextLinkSelect>
```

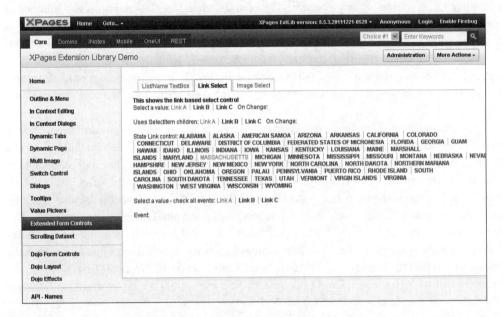

Figure 5.17   Link Select with `dominoViewValuePicker`.

Table 5.12 shows the pertinent properties for the Dojo Link Select control.

Table 5.12 `xe:djLinkSelect` Properties

Property	Description
dataProvider	Provides the options for the Dojo Link Select as an `xe:simpleValue-Picker`, `xe:dominoViewValuePicker`, or `xe:beanValuePicker`.
firstItemStyle	Defines styling for the first link.
firstItemStyleClass	Defines the class to be applied to the first link.
itemStyle	Defines styling for the intermediate links.
itemStyleClass	Defines the class to be applied to the intermediate links.
lastItemStyle	Defines styling for the last link.
lastItemStyleClass	Defines the class to be applied to the last link.

Dojo Image Select

The Dojo Image Select control is similar to the Link Select in that it provides a group of links, or in this case images, only one of which can be selected. Again, it is bound to a field or scoped variable, with a default value that can be set. The images are defined using **selectImage** child controls of the **imageValues** property. Each **selectImage** has **image** and **selectedImage** properties, to define the images that appear when the link is deselected or selected. The **selectedValue** property defines the value that will be set when the image is clicked. In addition, properties are available for styling each image, both in its deselected state and its selected state. The example on the **Core_FormControl.xsp** XPage in the Extension Library Demo database, reproduced in Listing 5.17 and shown in Figure 5.18, shows buttons appropriate for a Calendar View control, although, as will be shown in Chapter 7, a slightly different method is used for the calendar view in the TeamRoom database.

Listing 5.17 Dojo Image Select for Calendar Picker

```
<xe:djextImageSelect
    id="djextImageSelect1"
    title="Select a value default is two days"
    value="#{viewScope.image1}"
    defaultValue="T">
    <xe:this.imageValues>
        <xe:selectImage
            selectedValue="D"

selectedImage="/.ibmxspres/.extlib/icons/calendar/1_Day_selected_24.
gif"

image="/.ibmxspres/.extlib/icons/calendar/1_Day_deselected_24.gif"
```

Listing 5.17   (Continued)

```
            imageAlt="One Day">
        </xe:selectImage>
        <xe:selectImage
            selectedValue="T"

selectedImage="/.ibmxspres/.extlib/icons/calendar/2_Days_selected_24.
gif"

image="/.ibmxspres/.extlib/icons/calendar/2_Days_deselected_24.gif"
            imageAlt="Two Days">
        </xe:selectImage>
        <xe:selectImage
            selectedValue="F"

selectedImage="/.ibmxspres/.extlib/icons/calendar/1_Work_Week_selected_
24.gif"

image="/.ibmxspres/.extlib/icons/calendar/1_Work_Week_deselected_24.gif"
            imageAlt="One Work Week">
        </xe:selectImage>
        <xe:selectImage
            selectedValue="W"

selectedImage="/.ibmxspres/.extlib/icons/calendar/1_Week_selected_24.
gif"

image-"/.ibmxspres/.extlib/icons/calendar/1_Week_deselected_24.gif"
            imageAlt="One Week">
        </xe:selectImage>
        <xe:selectImage
            selectedValue="2"

selectedImage="/.ibmxspres/.extlib/icons/calendar/2_Weeks_selected_24.
gif"

image="/.ibmxspres/.extlib/icons/calendar/2_Weeks_deselected_24.gif"
            imageAlt="Two Weeks">
        </xe:selectImage>
        <xe:selectImage
            selectedValue="M"

selectedImage="/.ibmxspres/.extlib/icons/calendar/Month_selected_24.
gif"
```

```
image="/.ibmxspres/.extlib/icons/calendar/Month_deselected_24.gif"
        imageAlt="One Month">
    </xe:selectImage>
    <xe:selectImage
        selectedValue="Y"

selectedImage="/.ibmxspres/.extlib/icons/calendar/All_Entries_selected_
24.gif"

image="/.ibmxspres/.extlib/icons/calendar/All_Entries_deselected_24.gif
"
        imageAlt="All Entries">
    </xe:selectImage>
  </xe:this.imageValues>
  <xp:eventHandler
    event="onClick"
    submit="true"
    refreshMode="partial"
    refreshId="computedField3">
  </xp:eventHandler>
</xe:djextImageSelect>
```

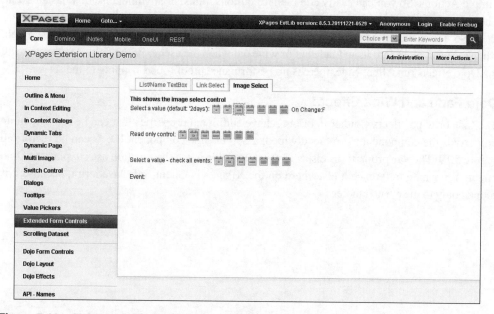

Figure 5.18   Dojo Link Select for Calendar Picker.

Table 5.13 details the additional properties available for the Dojo Image Select control.

Table 5.13   `xe:djImageSelect` Properties

Property	Description
image	Defines the image shown when this image is not selected.
imageAlt	Defines the alt text to appear when the user hovers over the image.
selectedImage	Defines the image shown when this image is selected.
selectedStyle	Defines styling to be applied when this image is selected.
selectedStyleClass	Defines the class to be applied when this image is selected.
selectedValue	Defines the value to pass when this image is selected.
style	Defines styling to be applied when this image is not selected.
styleClass	Defines the class to be applied when this image is not selected.

Dojo Effects Simple Actions

The inclusion of Dojo within the Extension Library extends beyond controls for storing user-entered content. Some commonly used Dojo effects have also been added, implemented as Simple Actions. So you can easily add them to buttons, links, or anything else that has an event. These simple actions add animations to a form, to enhance the user experience.

So, for example, you can use a Dojo effect to fade in or wipe in helper text beside a field when the user clicks into it, and fade out or wipe out when the user exits the field. And because all the Dojo effects run Client-Side, there is no performance hit of round-tripping to the server.

Dojo Fade and Wipe Effects

The fade or wipe effects—either in or out—have additional properties that can be set. The **node** property is the component to be faded/wiped, a Server-Side component ID, as can be seen from Figure 5.19. The **var** property, as elsewhere, is a variable name the function uses to play the Dojo effect. You cannot reference it elsewhere on the XPage via Client-Side JavaScript, because it is scoped only to the eventHandler.

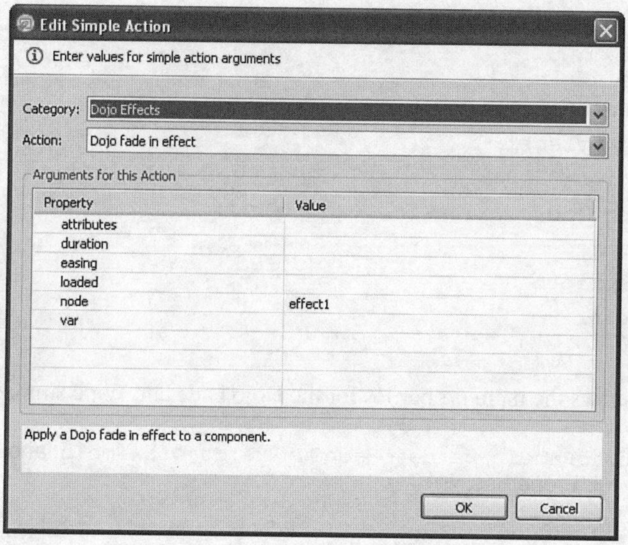

Figure 5.19 Dojo Fade In Effect.

The **duration** property defines how long in milliseconds the effect takes to run, whereas the **easing** property takes a function that will handle how the effect runs, such as accelerating the rate with which the node fades in. You can write this function from scratch, as on the **Core_ DojoEffects.xsp** XPages Extension Library Demo database, or as a predefined function, such as those in the dojo.fx.easing object (see Listing 5.18).

Listing 5.18 Dojo Fade Out with dojo.fx.easing

```
<xp:this.resources>
  <xp:dojoModule
     name="dojo.fx.easing">
  </xp:dojoModule>
</xp:this.resources>

<xp:button
   value="Fade Out - Duration 2s"
   id="button3">
  <xp:eventHandler
     event="onclick"
     submit="false">
```

Listing 5.18   (Continued)

```
    <xp:this.script>
        <xe:dojoFadeOut
        node="effect1"
        duration="200"
        easing="dojo.fx.easing.expoInOut">
        </xe:dojoFadeOut>
    </xp:this.script>
</xp:eventHandler>
```

Table 5.14 shows the main properties for the Dojo Fade and Wipe simple actions.

Table 5.14   `xe:dojoFadeIn`, `xe:dojoFadeOut`, `xe:dojofxWipeIn`, and `xe:dojofxWipeOut` **Properties**

Property	Description
duration	Defines the duration the animation should take.
easing	Requires a Client-Side JavaScript function to define the rate of acceleration of the animation.
node	Defines the node to which the animation should be applied.
var	Defines a variable name under which the animation runs.

Dojo Slide To Effect

The slide effect has all the properties of the fade and wipe effects but also two additional properties, **top** and **left**, for defining how far relative to the top and left of the screen the relevant node should be slid. You can set all the properties available with a specific value or calculate them via Server-Side JavaScript. The slide effect in Listing 5.19 shows how or why to use the **attributes** property: namely, to enable the developer to set any of the effects via Client-Side JavaScript. Why not just type `dojo.coords(_id).t` directly into the **top** property? First, because _id has a specific meaning to the XSP Command Manager, so it throws an error. Second, because the **top** property must be a number, not a string. So you must use the **attributes** property to pass the function, which sets top to the node's current **top** property, to the browser. This function also shows how to retrieve a node's current position to slide a node relative to that current position.

Listing 5.19   Slide Effect with attributes Property

```
<xp:button
    value="Slide left"
    id="button8">
    <xp:eventHandler
        event="onclick"
        submit="false">
        <xp:this.script>
            <xe:dojofxSlideTo
                node="effect1"
                left="0">
                <xp:this.attributes>
                    <xp:parameter
                        name="top"
                        value="dojo.coords(_id).t">
                    </xp:parameter>
                </xp:this.attributes>
            </xe:dojofxSlideTo>
        </xp:this.script>
    </xp:eventHandler>
</xp:button>
```

Table 5.15 shows the significant properties of the Dojo Slide To Effect.

Table 5.15   `xe:dojofxSlideTo` Properties

Property	Description
left	Defines how far relative to the left of the screen the node should be slid.
top	Defines how far relative to the top of the screen the node should be slid.

Dojo Animation

The Dojo animation effect implements the dojo.animateProperty object within a simple action. The effect has all the properties already covered in the other Dojo effect simple actions. In addition, there are some specific properties. You can use the **delay** property to add a delay in milliseconds before the effect should start. You can use the **rate** property to change the number of frames per second at which the animation runs; by default, it is 100 frames per second, which is rather quick. The value of the **rate** property is a number in milliseconds, so to change it to 5 frames per second, the value would be 200 (200 × 5 = 1000 milliseconds = 1 second). You can use the **repeat** property to repeat the animation a certain number of times. But the most important property is the **properties** property, allowing one or more xe:dojoAnimationProps objects to be added. These handle what animation runs and its varying settings.

Table 5.16 shows the main properties for the Dojo animation effect.

Table 5.16   xe:dojoDojoAnimateProperty Properties

Property	Description
delay	Defines the delay before the animation begins.
duration	Defines the duration of the animation.
easing	Requires a Client-Side JavaScript function to define the rate of acceleration of the animation.
node	Defines the node to which the animation should be applied.
properties	Defines the animation properties.
rate	Defines the rate per second, taking a value in milliseconds.
repeat	Defines the number of times the animation should repeat.
var	Defines a variable name under which the animation runs.

In addition to the **loaded** property, the xe:dojoAnimationProps object has four properties shown in Table 5.17. The Extension Library demo database has an example of this on the **Core_DojoEffects.xsp** XPage, for increasing the size of a box, shown in Listing 5.20. Line 9 sets the animation to run on the bluebox component. Lines 14 and 15 define the starting and ending width and height of the box.

Table 5.17   xe:dojoDojoAnimationProps Properties

Property	Description
end	Defines the ending value of the attribute this animation applies to.
name	Defines the attribute this animation applies to, such as "width" or "height".
start	Defines the starting value for the attribute this animation applies to.
unit	Defines the unit for the values in start and end.

Listing 5.20 `Core_DojoEffect.xsp` Dojo Animation Simple Action

```
1   <xp:button
2       value="Grow the box"
3       id="button5">
4       <xp:eventHandler
5           event="onclick"
6           submit="false">
7           <xp:this.script>
8                   <xe:dojoAnimateProperty
9                   node="bluebox"
10                  duration="3000">
11                  <xp:this.properties>
12                      <xe:dojoAnimationProps
13                          name="width"
14                          start="200"
15                          end="400">
16                      </xe:dojoAnimationProps>
17                      <xe:dojoAnimationProps
18                          name="height"
19                          start="200"
20                          end="400">
21                      </xe:dojoAnimationProps>
22                  </xp:this.properties>
23              </xe:dojoAnimateProperty>
24          </xp:this.script>
25      </xp:eventHandler>
26  </xp:button>
```

Earlier in this chapter, code was provided to style the ToggleButton control. At this point, it is appropriate to revisit that code, shown in Listing 5.13. Listing 5.21 shows alternate code for the ToggleButton using a Dojo animation simple action, with the output shown in Figure 5.20. To revisit the functionality, the animation should change the font color of the ToggleButton, alternating between red and green. However, the properties of the `xe:dojoAnimationProps` object can only accept literal values or Server-Side JavaScript returning a literal value. It is not possible to add Client-Side JavaScript code to ensure the end color alternates. As a result, you must use the **attributes** property to compute the properties object in Client-Side JavaScript, in lines 16 to 29. Line 18 creates the color object (the **name** property of an `xe:dojoAnimationProps` object). Line 19 sets the start attribute of the color object, although `_id.style.color` is not set when the page is loaded. Lines 20 to 26 set the end attribute to a function that sets the color to red if it is initially green, otherwise red.

Listing 5.21   Using Dojo Animation Simple Action to Style the ToggleButton

```
1   <xe:djToggleButton
2   id="djToggleButton2"
3      value="#{sessionScope.djButton3}"
4      label="Toggle Button"
5      checkedValue="Checked..."
6      uncheckedValue="Not Checked..."
7      style="color:rgb(255,0,0)">
8      <xp:eventHandler
9         event="onclick"
10        submit="false">
11        <xp:this.script>
12           <xe:dojoAnimateProperty
13              node="djToggleButton2"
14              duration="500">
15              <xe:this.attributes>
16                 <xp:parameter
17                    name="properties">
18                    <xp:this.value><![CDATA[{"color":
19  {"start":_id.style.color,
20  "end":function() {
21     if (_id.style.color=="rgb(0, 255, 0)") {
22           return "rgb(255,0,0)";
23     } else {
24           return "rgb(0,255,0)";
25     }
26  }
27}
28}]]></xp:this.value>
29                 </xp:parameter>
30              </xe:this.attributes>
31           </xe:dojoAnimateProperty>
32        </xp:this.script>
33     </xp:eventHandler>
34  </xe:djToggleButton>
```

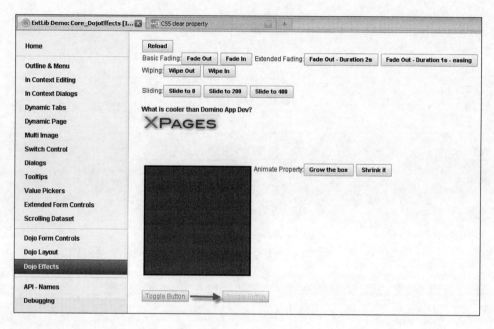

Figure 5.20 Dojo Fade In Effect.

Conclusion

This chapter covered many of the Dojo controls provided by the Extension Library to add to the content controls covered in the previous chapter. These Dojo controls offer little additional functionality to the traditional Dojo controls, but they do make it easier to implement the controls and minimize the risk of mistyping or misremembering Dojo attributes.

CHAPTER 6

Pop-Ups: Tooltips, Dialogs, and Pickers

The previous two chapters have covered the controls in the Extension Library for managing and presenting content for users and handling events. For many input forms, that will suffice. But as part of the Web 2.0 experience that AJAX provides to users, dynamic management of larger areas of content, whether via dialogs, tooltips, or pickers, is a key component. This is where the Extension Library offers a variety of options with pop-ups.

These pop-ups are part of the current web page, so they are not intercepted by pop-up blockers, providing a much more user-friendly experience. The Extension Library contributes tooltips for displaying additional content, dialogs for displaying or managing content, and pickers for facilitating selection of values. The Extension Library again makes this easier for developers by overcoming some of the challenges of integrating Dojo and XPages.

Tooltip (`xe:tooltip`)

The Tooltip is a useful control for maximizing screen real estate and unobtrusively providing additional information for users. As with many of the other Dojo controls, the Tooltip control—an implementation of the **dijit.Tooltip** widget—has been added to the Extension Library to make it quicker and easier to implement. You can see the properties in Table 6.1.

Table 6.1 `xe:tooltip` Properties

Property	Description
dynamicContent	Determines whether the content should be loaded dynamically via an AJAX request or retrieved at page load. This is required if the content to be displayed is not within the **label** property.
for	Defines the control ID that triggers the tooltip.
label	Can hold textual content for the tooltip. Alternatively, you can add controls within the tooltip.
showDelay	Determines the number of milliseconds before the tooltip is displayed; by default, it is 400 milliseconds.
afterContentLoad	Can be used to trigger Server-Side JavaScript (SSJS) before the tooltip is displayed. This code runs only if **dynamicContent** is `true`.
beforeContentLoad	Can be used to trigger SSJS after the tooltip is displayed. This code runs only if **dynamicContent** is `true`.
position	Defines where the tooltip is displayed in relation to the control the tooltip is for.

The main property for the Tooltip control is **for**. Like the **for** property of the Label control, this is the ID of the component the tooltip relates to. The **position** property allows the developer to define where the tooltip should appear in relation to the component the tooltip is attached to. The options are `above`, `below`, `before`, and `after`. However, use caution when changing the default; if there is not enough screen real estate available for the tooltip to appear, it doesn't show.

You can manage the content in one of two ways. First, you can use the **label** property to display simple textual content, whether a string or a computed value. See Listing 6.1 and Figure 6.1.

Listing 6.1 Basic Tooltip

```
<xe:tooltip
    id="tooltip1"
    for="computedField1"
    label="#{row.City}">
</xe:tooltip>
```

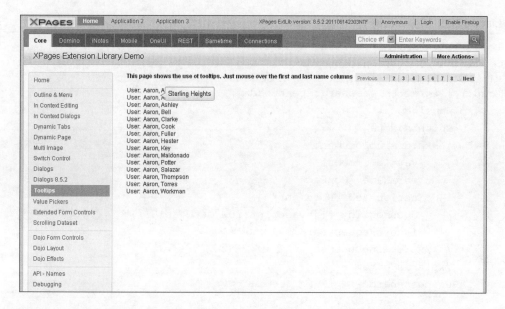

Figure 6.1 Basic Tooltip.

Second, you can place other controls between the `xe:tooltip` tags to build up the content. This can be just individual controls but can also include data components, as in Listing 6.2, which shows part of the code for a Tooltip control from the **Core_Tooltip.xsp** XPage in the Extension Library Demo database, shown in Figure 6.2. Note particularly the inclusion of the **dynamicContent** property. This is required if the you are not using the **label** property for the content of the tooltip. Don't confuse this with the Dynamic Content control in the Extension Library. Instead, it means that the data content within the tooltip should be calculated dynamically when the tooltip is shown triggering an AJAX GET request made to the server. Because the tooltip is within a repeat control and the **documentId** is based on the current row of the repeat, dynamicContent is set to `"true"` to ensure the **documentId** property is recalculated at runtime and the correct dominoDocument datasource is returned.

Listing 6.2 Complex Tooltip

```
<xe:tooltip
    id="tooltip2"
    for="computedField2"
    dynamicContent="true"
    showDelay="1000">
    <xe:this.beforeContentLoad>
<![CDATA[#{javascript:print("DynamicTooltip: Before Content
```

Listing 6.2   (Continued)

```
Load")}]]></xe:this.beforeContentLoad>
   <xe:this.afterContentLoad>
<![CDATA[#{javascript:print("DynamicTooltip: After Content
Load")}]]></xe:this.afterContentLoad>
   <xp:panel>
      <xp:this.data>
         <xp:dominoDocument
            var="document1"
            formName="Contact"
            action="editDocument"
            documentId="#{javascript:row.getNoteID()}"
            ignoreRequestParams="true">
         </xp:dominoDocument>
      </xp:this.data>
      Business card
```

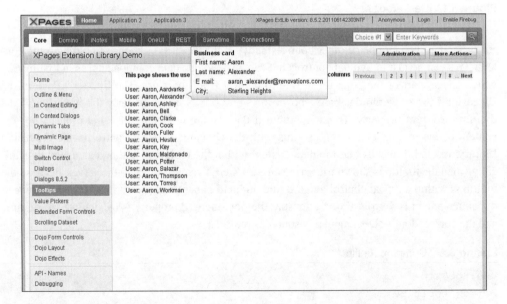

Figure 6.2   Complex Tooltip.

This raises a particular performance issue with the Tooltip control. Because an AJAX request is being made whenever the user mouses over the component that the tooltip is attached to, it can impact the user experience. There will be a short delay of 400 milliseconds before the tooltip is shown, but the **showDelay** property can add a more specific delay, in milliseconds, before the request is made and the content is retrieved. Listing 6.2 shows the code for the **showDelay** property. If the user accidentally hovers on a control that has a tooltip applied to it, the tooltip does not interfere with the user experience. The **showDelay** property is more important if **dynamicContent** is set to `"true"`, because it also delays the AJAX call to the server, thereby reducing unnecessary accidental calls to the server. However, the larger the **showDelay** value is, the longer the user has to wait before the AJAX call is made and the content is retrieved.

The **beforeContentLoad** and **afterContentLoad** events can trigger SSJS, but only if the **dynamicContent** property is set to `"true"`. That is because there needs to be a call to the server to trigger the SSJS, which only happens for dynamic content calls. If **dynamicContent** is `"false"`, the content has already been passed to the browser, so no call is made to the server. The examples in Listing 6.2 merely print to the server console, but you can use more complex code. However, you can only modify controls inside the `xe:tooltip` tags, because that context is being partially refreshed.

Dialogs

The Extension Library contributes two dialog controls: one modal and the other nonmodal. This means that one locks the rest of the screen to prevent further editing, whereas the other closes the dialog if the user clicks outside it. It is associated with a particular component.

Both dialog controls are based on Dojo modules. The Dialog control is modal and is based on the **dijit.Dialog** Dojo module. The Tooltip Dialog control is nonmodal and is based on the **dijit.TooltipDialog** module. The Extension Library controls make it easier for developers to implement them within XPages, both by means of avoiding workarounds and providing appropriate properties to remove the need to know the Dojo attributes. Moreover, as part of the implementation, additional functionality is provided.

Dialog (`xe:dialog`)

Among the core XPages controls, there was no control to allow developers to launch a modal dialog to users. Dojo provided a widget—**dijit.Dialog**—but implementation was not simple because of a conflict in functionality between XPages and Dojo. XPages, and JSF on which XPages is based, creates a Server-Side map in memory of the XPage components, all collated under a Form tag. When content is posted back from the browser via a partial or full refresh, the content within the Form tag posted back to the browser is evaluated, the Server-Side map is updated, and any changes relevant to the browser are passed back.

However, when the Dojo parser converts an HTML div to a **dijit.Dialog**, it moves the entire content outside the Form tag. This means the modal dialog content is not passed back from the browser to the server, so no Server-Side updates are made and no Server-Side script is triggered. There are resources available on the Web to work around this limitation, the most effective of which moves the content back inside the Form tag. However, this requires additional code to be stored either on the server (and any clients using XPiNC) or within each NSF. It also requires adding the module and a div with the relevant dojoType to each XPage. The Extension Library provides the Dialog control not only to avoid the need for this workaround but to enhance the functionality of the dialog.

The Setup area of the TeamRoom database, **setup.xsp**, gives a good demonstration of the modal dialogs. First of reference is the second tab **Tags (Categories)**, specifically the **Map Categories** functionality, shown in Figure 6.3. Developers who have used the Dojo dialog in the past will know that it is opened via Client-Side JavaScript using the show() function and closed using the hide() function. The Map Categories functionality shows that the Extension Library Dialog control can be launched via Client-Side JavaScript. But this doesn't happen by using the traditional functions for the Dojo dialog. Instead, the control extends the XSP object used for other Client-Side JavaScript in XPages, adding an openDialog() function, as shown in Listing 6.3, from the **setupTags.xsp** Custom Control. The parameter passed to this function is the Client-Side ID of the dialog to open, the dialog that is held in the **setupMapTags.xsp** Custom Control.

Listing 6.3   Opening a Dialog (Client-Side JavaScript)

```
<xp:button
    id="mapCategoriesButton"
    themeId="Button.Cancel">
    <xp:this.value><![CDATA[#{javascript:return
I18n.format(strings.getString("setup.tags.mapcategories"));}]]>
</xp:this.value>
    <xp:eventHandler
          event="onclick"
          submit="false">
       <xp:this.script>
<![CDATA[XSP.openDialog("#{id:dialogMapTags}");]]></xp:this.script>
    </xp:eventHandler>
</xp:button>
```

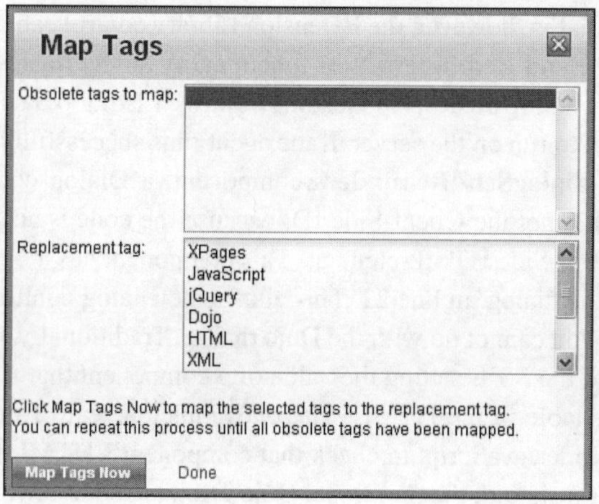

Figure 6.3   Map Categories dialog.

Similarly, you can close the dialog via Client-Side JavaScript, intuitively using the `XSP.closeDialog()` function. Listing 6.4 shows an implementation. The function again takes as its parameter the Client-Side ID of the dialog to close. But the `XSP.closeDialog()` function also has an optional second parameter, not shown in Listing 6.3. This is the Client-Side ID of a component to be partially refreshed after you close the dialog.

Listing 6.4   Closing a Dialog (Client-Side JavaScript)

```
<xp:link
    escape="true"
    id="link1">
    <xp:this.text><![CDATA[#{javascript:return
I18n.format(strings.getString("setup.tags.dialog.button2"));}]]>
</xp:this.text>
    <xp:eventHandler
        event="onclick"
        submit="false">
        <xp:this.script>
<![CDATA[XSP.closeDialog('#{id:dialogMapTags}')]]></xp:this.script>
    </xp:eventHandler>
</xp:link>
```

Unlike the Dojo dialog, however, the Extension Library control can be launched with SSJS. This can be seen by the **Send Reminders Now** functionality on the **Basics** tab of the **Setup** area, in Domino Designer the **setupBasics.xsp** Custom Control. Listing 6.5 shows a button that runs SSJS to trigger an agent to run on the server. If the agent runs successfully, line 16 creates a variable that accesses the **dialogSendReminders** component, a Dialog control. Note that this is using the Server-Side ID, not the Client-Side ID, because the code is accessing the Server-Side component, not the Client-Side HTML element. This component has a `show()` method exposed to SSJS, which opens the dialog, in line 22. This allows the Dialog control to be opened directly from SSJS, something you cannot do with the Dojo dialog. Traditionally, this kind of functionality would have required the SSJS setting the value of a component that is partially refreshed, so the value becomes available in the HTML. The onComplete event of the eventHandler would then have used Client-Side JavaScript to check that component's HTML to see whether the dialog should be shown. If it should, the traditional Dojo `show()` method would have been used.

Listing 6.5   Opening a Dialog (SSJS)

```
1   <xp:button
2       id="sendRemindersNow"
3       themeId="Button.Cancel">
4           <xp:this.value><![CDATA[#{javascript:return
I18n.format(strings.getString("setup.basics.sendremindersnow"));}]]></x
p:this.value>
5           <xp:eventHandler
6               event="onclick"
7               submit="true"
8               refreshMode="partial"
9               refreshId="dialogSendReminders">
10              <xp:this.action><![CDATA[#{javascript:var
thisDatabase:NotesDatabase = session.getCurrentDatabase();
11 var thisAgent:NotesAgent = thisDatabase.getAgent("SendReminder");
12 if (thisAgent!=null)
13 {
14      var doc:NotesDocument =
database.getProfileDocument("TempVars","");
15      doc.replaceItemValue('useXPageUrl', 'true');
16      var result = thisAgent.runOnServer();
17      doc.replaceItemValue('useXPageUrl', '');
18
19      if (result==0)
20      {
21              var dialog = getComponent("dialogSendReminders");
```

```
22              dialog.show();
23       }
24 }}]]></xp:this.action>
25       </xp:eventHandler>
26 </xp:button>
```

Closing the dialog from SSJS can be done the same way as closing a Dojo dialog from SSJS. A refresh of the page closes the dialog. But just as the Dialog control exposes a show() method to SSJS, it exposes a hide() method to SSJS. Compare Listing 6.4 to Listing 6.6. Listing 6.4 is the code from the TeamRoom database in the **setupMapTags.xsp** Custom Control. Listing 6.6 shows that same link rewritten to close the dialog in SSJS. Also, like its Client-Side counterpart, the SSJS hide() method can take a parameter of the component to partially refresh. Note that unlike its Client-Side counterpart, the hide() method takes the component's Server-Side ID, not the Client-Side ID rendered to the browser, because it is being triggered from SSJS. For the Done link on the Map Tags dialog in the TeamRoom, Client-Side JavaScript is more appropriate for performance and ease of coding. But the code in Listing 6.6 is a useful addition for scenarios in which SSJS needs to be triggered and, based on its success, the dialog closes or not.

Listing 6.6 Closing a Dialog (SSJS)

```
<xp:link
escape="true"
id="link1">
   <xp:this.text><![CDATA[#{javascript:return
I18n.format(strings.getString("setup.tags.dialog.button2"));}]]>
</xp:this.text>
      <xp:eventHandler
      event="onclick"
      submit="true"
      refreshId="mapTags"
      refreshMode="partial">
         <xp:this.action><![CDATA[#{javascript:var dialog =
getComponent("dialogMapTags");
dialog.hide();}]]></xp:this.action>
      </xp:eventHandler>
</xp:link>
```

The **setupSendReminders.xsp** and **setupMapTags.xsp** Custom Controls contain the modal dialogs for these two tabs. As you can see, the content can be very basic or quite complex. But from a development point of view, the control is not particularly dissimilar to a Panel or Div from the core controls. The whole process is designed to be intuitive and build on the skills already developed from XPages development. Other controls are just placed between the `xe:dialog` tags to build up the look and feel and functionality of the modal dialog. Business logic is triggered from Link or Button controls (whether the buttons are core or extended versions). An additional control is available for highlighting the button area, the **Dialog Button Bar**. This adds a styling to that specific area, as you can see in Figure 6.4 from the dialogs page of the Extension Library Demo database.

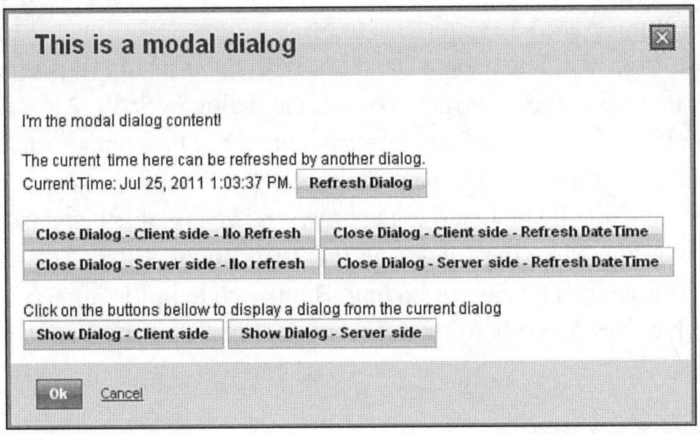

Figure 6.4   Dialog Button Bar.

Moreover, other modal dialogs can trigger modal dialogs, as in Figure 6.5, as can value pickers and name pickers. This provides a wealth of flexibility for the content of modal dialogs.

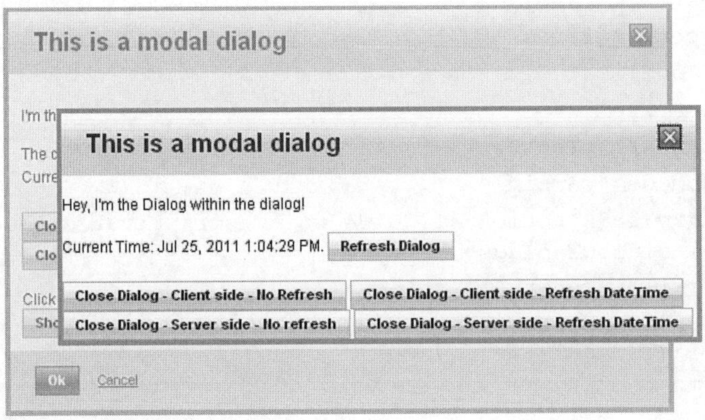

Figure 6.5   Embedded dialogs.

The modal dialogs in the TeamRoom do not take advantage of many of the available properties. Only those in the **announcementConfirmDelete.xsp** and **controlSelectionSelect-Tags.xsp** Custom Controls use the **title** property, a property that has become familiar from the other Dojo-related controls. No other properties are used. Some of the properties are designed for performance, such as **parseOnLoad** and **preload**. You can use the **preload** property to ensure the dialog's content is loaded with the web page instead of when the request is made to show the dialog. This ensures better performance on presenting the dialog, but it affects the performance of the initial load time. By default, the contents are then cached, and the cached dialog is shown each time. The **preventCache** property can prevent this. The **refreshOnShow** parameter ensures that the contents are reloaded every time the dialog is shown.

Besides comprising controls, the dialog can show external content by using the **href** property. In this case, the content might take time to load, if indeed the target URL is available. To enhance the user experience, you can define the **loadingMessage** property to alert the user, and you can define the **errorMessage** property to provide a meaningful message if the URL cannot be loaded. The **onContentError** event allows Client-Side JavaScript to be computed to return a string in place of **errorMessage**.

The control also provides events that are specific for dialogs. The **beforeContentLoad** and **afterContentLoad** events allow SSJS to be triggered before or after the dialog is shown to the user. The **onShow** and **onHide** events trigger Client-Side JavaScript before the dialog is shown or before the dialog is closed. The **onDownloadStart**, **onDownloadEnd,** and **onDownloadError** events are specifically used if the **href** property has been defined, allowing Client-Side JavaScript to be triggered before and after the source is loaded and if there's an error loading the relevant page.

Table 6.2 outlines the main properties for the Dialog and Tooltip Dialog controls.

Table 6.2 `xe:dialog` and `xe:tooltipDialog` Properties

Property	Description
title	Defines the label to display as the title of the dialog.
errorMessage	Defines the error message if the content of the dialog cannot be loaded, primarily of use if the content is loaded from the **href** property.
extractContent	Is relevant if **href** property is defined. Instead of including the full response of the AJAX call, only the content between the \<BODY\> tags will be used; the \<HTML\> and \<HEAD\> tags will be stripped off.
href	Defines a URL from which to load the content for the dialog.
keepComponents	Determines whether the components should be retained in the Server-Side tree of the page after the dialog is closed.
loadingMessage	Defines the loading message while the content of the dialog is being loaded, primarily of use if the content is loaded from the **href** property.

Table 6.2   Continued

Property	Description
preload	Defines whether the content of the dialog should be preloaded before the user launches the dialog.
preventCache	Defines whether the dialog content should be cached. The property adds an additional parameter to the AJAX call to ensure that the URL is always unique. This property is relevant if **href** is defined.
refreshOnShow	Defines whether the dialog content should be refreshed every time the dialog is launched.
parseOnLoad	Defines whether Dojo controls are automatically displayed.
afterContentLoad	Can be used to trigger SSJS before the dialog's contents are loaded.
beforeContentLoad	Can be used to trigger SSJS after the dialog's contents are loaded.
onContentError	Can be used to run Client-Side JavaScript when an error occurs in the content of the dialog.
onDownloadEnd	Can be used to run Client-Side JavaScript after the URL in the **href** property has been loaded.
onDownloadError	Can be used to run Client-Side JavaScript if the URL in the **href** property cannot be loaded.
onDownloadStart	Can be used to run Client-Side JavaScript before the URL in the **href** property is loaded.
onHide	Can be used to run Client-Side JavaScript each time the dialog is closed.
onShow	Can be used to run Client-Side JavaScript each time the dialog is displayed.

Tooltip Dialog (`xe:tooltipDialog`)

The Tooltip Dialog control, as its name suggests, is a combination of the Tooltip and the Dialog controls. It is not found in the TeamRoom database, but you can see it in action in the Extension Library Demo database, on **Core_Tooltip.xsp**. An investigation of the underlying implemented Java class shows that it extends the Dialog's Java class, UIDialog. No additional properties are surfaced through the All Properties panel, so Table 6.2 is relevant for this control. It presents a dialog with all the same functionality as the Dialog control, except that it is not modal and directly attached to another component, as seen in Figure 6.6, like the tooltip. This means you cannot drag the ToolTip Dialog control around the screen; it is fixed relative to the component it is attached to. Therefore, much of the functionality between the Tooltip Dialog and the Dialog controls is identical.

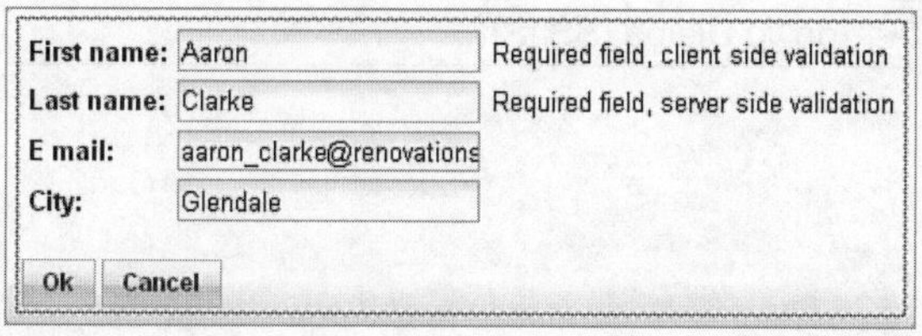

Figure 6.6   Tooltip dialog.

No **for** property is exposed in the **All Properties** panel. Instead, you need to set it when the dialog is opened. For the Client-Side JavaScript function to open the Tooltip Dialog, XSP.open-TooltipDialog() consequently takes two parameters. As with the openDialog() function, the first parameter is the Client-Side ID of the tooltip dialog to be opened. The second parameter is completely understandable—namely, the Client-Side ID of the component to which the tooltip is attached. For SSJS, the component exposes another method, setFor(), taking as its parameter the Server-Side ID of the component to which the tooltip dialog should be attached. After you have set this, you can use the show() method to launch the dialog.

Closing the Tooltip Dialog follows the same premise as closing the modal dialog. The Client-Side JavaScript code XSP.closeTooltipDialog('#{id:tooltipDialog1}') closes the dialog opened in Listing 6.7.

Listing 6.7   Opening the Tooltip Dialog (Client-Side JavaScript)

```
<xp:link
   escape="true"
   id="link2"
   text="Edit - Tooltip">
   <xp:eventHandler
      event="onclick"
      submit="false">
      <xp:this.script>
<![CDATA[XSP.openTooltipDialog('#{id:tooltipDialog1}',
'#{id:computedField2}')]]></xp:this.script>
   </xp:eventHandler>
</xp:link>
```

If SSJS is the preference, the code in Listing 6.8—in syntax identical to that of the modal dialog—closes the same Tooltip Dialog.

Listing 6.8   Closing the Tooltip Dialog (SSJS)

```
<xp:button
   value="Cancel"
   id="button4">
   <xp:eventHandler
      event="onclick"
      submit="true"
      immediate="true">
         <xp:this.action>
              <xp:actionGroup>
                   <xp:executeScript>
                        <xp:this.script> <![CDATA[#{javascript:var c
= getComponent("tooltipDialog1")
c.hide()}]]></xp:this.script>
                   </xp:executeScript>
              </xp:actionGroup>
         </xp:this.action>
   </xp:eventHandler>
</xp:button>
```

Value Picker (xe:valuePicker)

So far, this chapter has covered two dialogs whose content the developer defines. The Value Picker and Name Value Picker are controls that open a dialog whereby the content is an automatically formatted list of values to select from. This is similar functionality to the Dialog List or an Address Book Dialog in the Notes Client. You can store the selected value in a field or, in the Extension Library Demo database and the Create SubTeam area of the TeamRoom database, in a List TextBox or Name List TextBox.

The dataProvider for the Value Picker control is one of three options, the same providers described in Chapter 5, "Dojo Made Easy," when covering the Link Select control: **simpleValuePicker**, **dominoViewValuePicker,** and **beanValuePicker**. You can see a simpleValuePicker in the Main Topic in the **homeMainTopic.xsp** Custom Control for selecting tags. Look at the code in Listing 6.9 and the picker in Figure 6.7. The tagOptions scoped variable is just a @DbLookup to the MissionLookup view, which returns just a comma-separated list of values, without a separate label. Consequently, the **labelSeparator** and **valueListSeparator** properties are both a comma. That is why a **simpleValuePicker** was used instead of a **dominoViewValuePicker**; the **dominoViewValuePicker** maps to a column of labels while pulling the value from the first column in the relevant view.

Listing 6.9 Tags Value Picker

```
<xe:valuePicker
    id="tagsPicker"
    pickerText="Select"
    for="tagsField"
    listWidth="300">
    <xe:this.dataProvider>
        <xe:simpleValuePicker
            caseInsensitive="true"
            labelSeparator=","
            valueListSeparator=","
            valueList="#{javascript: requestScope.tagOptions }">
        </xe:simpleValuePicker>
    </xe:this.dataProvider>
</xe:valuePicker>
```

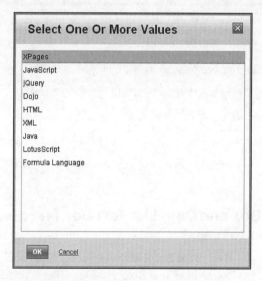

Figure 6.7 Tags Select on homeMainTopic.xsp.

The styling of the link and dialog are handled using properties of the Value Picker control. By default, a magnifying glass icon serves as the link to open the Picker dialog, but you can override this with a different image using the **pickerIcon** property or replace it with text, as in Listing 6.9, using the **pickerText** property. To override the default title of the picker dialog, shown in Figure 6.7, set the **dialogTitle** property, and manage the size of the picker dialog using the **listHeight** and **listWidth** properties. These two properties expect a value in the same format as a

CSS height or width attribute, (1.5em, 50px, and so on). The picker itself is bound to a field by using the **for** property, like a Label control.

By default, the Value Picker provides just a list of values. There are two additional Extension Library styles you can use in the **dojoType** property to alter this. **extlib.dijit.PickerCheck-box** adds a CheckBox beside each value, making it easier to select multiple values while ensuring that only one value is selected, if the control for the picker does not accept multiple values. **extlib.dijit.PickerListSearch** adds a search box, but bear in mind that this searches against the values, not the labels shown in the Value Picker dialog.

Table 6.3 details the key properties for the Value Picker control.

Table 6.3   `xe:valuePicker` Properties

Property	Description
dataProvider	Provides the values for the Picker. The options are • `xe:simpleValuePicker` to define a set of options hard-coded or computed with SSJS • `xe:dominoViewValuePicker` to pull options from a view • `xe:beanValuePicker` to pull options from a bean
dialogTitle	Defines the title for the Picker dialog.
for	Defines the control to which the value picked should be passed.
listHeight	Defines the height of the pane holding the list values.
listWidth	Defines the width of the pane holding the list values.
pickerIcon	Overrides the icon the user clicks on to launch the Picker.
pickerText	Defines the text the user clicks on to launch the Picker.

Dojo Name Text Box and Dojo List Text Box (`xe:djextNameTextBox` and `xe:djextListTextBox`)

The values selected in the picker on the **homeMainTopic.xsp** Custom Control, shown in Figure 6.8, are displayed using the Dojo Name Text Box. The Dojo Name Text Box and Dojo List Text Box controls are similar, both extending the same underlying Java class, `Abstract DojoExtListTextBox`. This Value Picker allows multiple values, defined not on the picker but on the Dojo Name Text Box. Because that control has the **multipleSeparator** property set, it allows multiple values; therefore, the Value Picker automatically allows multiple values to be selected.

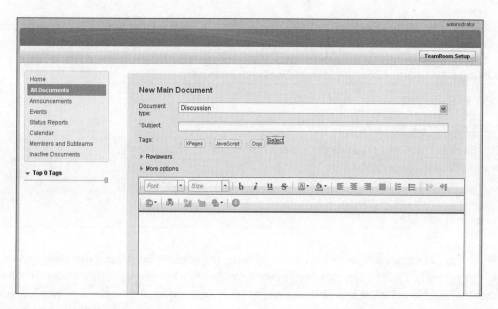

Figure 6.8   Dojo Name Text Box.

These two controls provide a visual representation of the values selected and remove the need for validation on the control that's bound to the underlying data element. Users cannot type a value in, and they can't accidentally delete part of a value. Instead, users see each value shown separately with a cross by the side to remove the whole value with a single click.

The Dojo Name Text Box has no specific additional properties other than the accessibility and dojo categories of properties encountered for the Dojo controls in Chapter 5. The main reason for using the Dojo List Text Box instead of its sibling is its ability to display the label instead of the value stored in the field the control is bound to by setting the **displayLabel** property.

Name Picker (xe:namePicker)

The Name Picker control is a Value Picker that allows the user to select from address books. The Name Picker has all the same properties already covered for the Value Picker. Apart from the default image for the picker, the difference is with the available dataProviders. The implementation in the TeamRoom database is on the Add Member page: **addMember.xsp** Custom Control. It uses a dominoNABNameProvider. By default, this is already set up to point to the server's Domino Directory, which means that no additional properties need to be added to allow the user to pick from the Domino Directory, as in Listing 6.10. If multiple address books are required, you can use the **addressBookSel** property to define which address book or books should be shown. Alternatively, you can define the location of a specific address book in the **addressBookDb** property, with **addressBookSel** set to db-name. You can set two other properties—**groups** and **people**—to define which users within the address book(s) should be shown for selection.

Listing 6.10   Name Picker with dominoNABNameProvider

```
<xe:namePicker
   id="namePicker"
   for="fldWho"
   pickerText="#{javascript: strings.picker_valueEmpty_select }">
   <xe:this.dataProvider>
      <xe:dominoNABNamePicker></xe:dominoNABNamePicker>
   </xe:this.dataProvider>
</xe:namePicker>
```

You can show multiple address books by using the **namePickerAggregator** dataProvider, which is simply a mechanism that enables the developer to add multiple dataProviders. When a **dominoNABNamePicker** is added to a **namePickerAggregator**, it provides a comboBox for the user to pick from any address books in Directory Assistance to be selected, along with any other dataProviders defined, as in Figure 6.9.

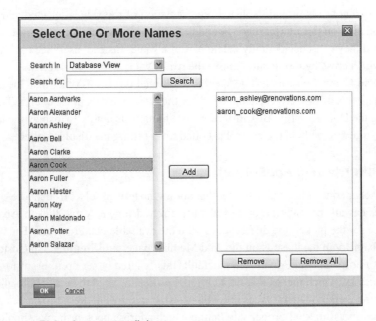

Figure 6.9   namePickerAggregator dialog.

Those who are comfortable with Java may choose to use the **beanNamePicker**. The currently selected address book in Figure 6.9 shows the final dataProvider available: the **dominoViewNamePicker**. This is analogous to the **dominoViewValuePicker** dataProvider that is available for the Value Picker. Again, there are three key properties: **databaseName**, **viewName**, and **labelColumn**. In addition, a **label** property defines the title that will appear in the comboBox of address books.

As Figure 6.9 shows, the dialog allows you to search a view in the current database. You can move values from one field to the other by double-clicking. You can add a single name by using the **Add** button. If the Name Value Picker is mapped to a control that does not allow multiple values, the **Add** button replaces any previously selected name with the newly selected name. The **Remove** button is no longer provided because only one value can be selected at any one time. Regardless of whether the Name Value Picker control is mapped to allow multiple values, all values are removed by using the **Remove All** button.

Validating a Picker

In the pickers in the TeamRoom database, the selected value is not put into an editable control where the user could type a value. But if it were, it would be important to validate that the value the user typed was also available from the picker. Historically, this would be done with SSJS in the **Submit** button or a validator that reproduced the lookup performed by the Value Picker. The pickerValidator is a new Extension Library validator that allows a control to be validated against the Value Picker provided for the user. It is not utilized in the TeamRoom database, but you can see it in action in the Extension Library Demo database.

The first part of any validation is to add typeahead. As with the validation, historically this occurs by making another lookup to the underlying database or calling on a dataContext and performing validation via SSJS. The Value Picker and Name Value Picker components have a new method exposed to SSJS that makes this easier. Line 19 of Listing 6.11 shows the method, `get-TypeAheadValue()`. One key property in the typeahead here is **valueMarkup**. When set to `true`, as here, the value is prefixed with the label in the typeahead store. If valueMarkup was not set to `true`, users would need to type an e-mail address to find a match instead of a name. However, it is the value that is put in the field when the user selects a value from the typeahead, not the full label/value pair.

Validation is done using the pickerValidator on lines 4 through 12. The **message** property on the validator, as with other validators, defines the error message to be presented to the user. There are two ways of performing the validation. The first is to set the **for** property and map it back to the Value Picker or Name Value Picker for the current control. The other is to add a dataProvider, as used in Listing 6.11 on lines 6 through 11.

Listing 6.11   Picker Validation

```
1   <xp:inputText
2       id="inputText3">
3       <xp:this.validators>
4           <xe:pickerValidator
5               message="The value is invalid">
6               <xe:this.dataProvider>
7                   <xe:dominoViewValuePicker
8                       viewName="AllEMails"
9                       labelColumn="Name">
10                  </xe:dominoViewValuePicker>
11              </xe:this.dataProvider>
12          </xe:pickerValidator>
13      </xp:this.validators>
14      <xp:typeAhead
15          mode="full"
16          minChars="1"
17          preventFiltering="true"
18          valueMarkup="true">
19          <xp:this.valueList>
20              <![CDATA[#{javascript:
getComponent("valuePicker1").getTypeAheadValue(this)}]]>
21          </xp:this.valueList>
22      </xp:typeAhead>
23  </xp:inputText>
```

But just as there is a method of the component exposed to SSJS for enabling the typeahead, there is a method exposed for validation. Line 6 of Listing 6.12 shows the method, isValid-Value(). Here the code verifies whether the current value is valid, checking against the picker. If it's not, an error message is presented, including the invalid value, as shown in Figure 6.10.

Listing 6.12   Custom Validator for Picker Validation

```
1   <xp:inputText
2       id="inputText21">
3       <xp:this.validators>
4           <xp:customValidator>
5               <xp:this.validate><![CDATA[#{javascript:var picker =
getComponent('namePicker11')
6   if(!picker.isValidValue(value)) {
```

```
7            return "Invalid value: "+value
8  }}]]></xp:this.validate>
9          </xp:customValidator>
10     </xp:this.validators>
11     <xp:typeAhead
12         mode="full"
13         minChars="1"
14         preventFiltering="true">
15         <xp:this.valueList>
16             <![CDATA[#{javascript:
getComponent("namePicker11").getTypeAheadValue(this)}]]>
17         </xp:this.valueList>
18     </xp:typeAhead>
19 </xp:inputText>
```

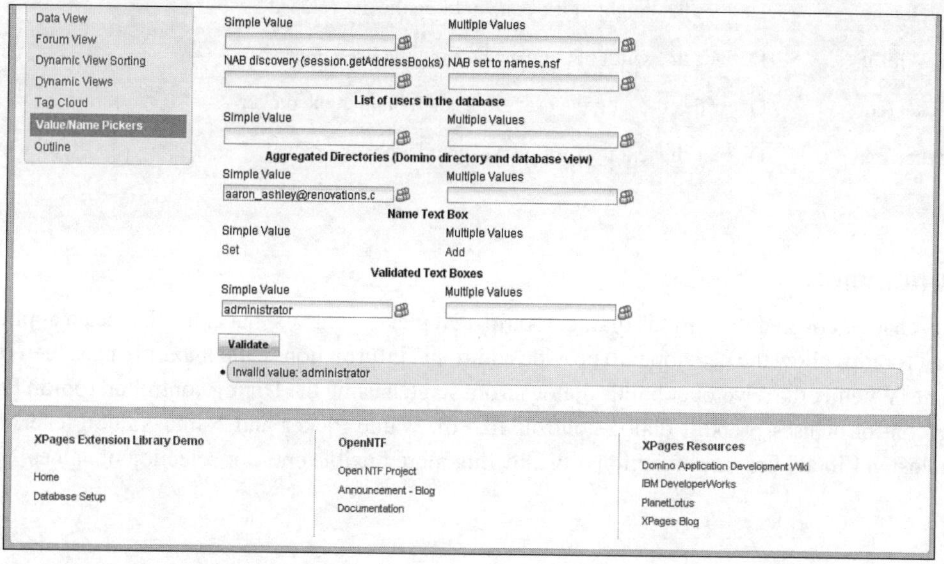

Figure 6.10   Name Picker validation.

Table 6.4 defines the main properties for the Name Picker control.

Table 6.4   `xe:namePicker` Properties

Property	Description
dataProvider	Provides the values for the picker. The options are • `xe:dominoNABNamePicker` to pull options from a Domino Directory database. • `xe:dominoViewNamePicker` to pull options from a View. • `xe:namePickerAggregator` to add multiple dataProviders. One or more of these four dataProviders can be added as child controls. • `xe:beanValuePicker` to pull options from a bean.
dialogTitle	Defines the title for the picker dialog.
for	Defines the control to which the value picked should be passed.
listHeight	Defines the height of the pane holding the list values.
listWidth	Defines the width of the pane holding the list values.
pickerIcon	Overrides the icon the user clicks on to launch the picker.
pickerText	Defines the text the user clicks on to launch the picker.

Conclusion

This chapter covered the various dialog, tooltip, and picker controls that can enhance an application. Tooltips allow the developer to provide additional information while maximizing screen real estate. Whether the developer builds dialogs from scratch using the Dialog control or Tooltip Dialog control or uses prebuilt dialog controls like the Value Picker and Name Value Picker, the Extension Library provides functionality allowing more flexible entry or selection of values.

CHAPTER 7

Views

The previous three chapters have covered the various controls in the Extension Library designed for creating and editing content. The next step is to present documents in a view. Before the Extension Library, three core container controls were available for displaying a collection of documents: the View Panel, the Data Table, and the Repeat. The Extension Library provides several new controls, ranging from those designed to reproduce Notes Client views, those designed to maximize data sources, and those to view layout controls. Also included are new pager controls for enhancing navigation.

Dynamic View Panel (`xe:dynamicViewPanel`)

Just as the View Panel was the simplest core container control for displaying a Domino View or Folder, the Dynamic View Panel is the simplest Extension Library control for displaying a Domino View or Folder. As the name suggests, the Dynamic View Panel generates the same kind of tabular display that the View Panel provides. However, it is more tightly bound to the DominoView datasource, the underlying View design element. Whereas the View Panel allows the developer to select a subset of the columns from the dominoView datasource as well as add content, the Dynamic View Panel simply renders the underlying View design element in an XPage.

To see this in action, take the core TeamRoom database design and apply the Dynamic View Panel. For developers who are familiar with the database, this example will showcase the strengths of the Dynamic View Panel.

First, create an XPage called **TeamroomViews.xsp**. Listing 7.1 shows the code to add to the XPage. Lines 2 through 22 add a ComboBox control bound to a `viewScope` variable called `viewName`. The options for the ComboBox control are all the views in the database. Lines 25 through 54 add a second ComboBox bound to the same `viewScope` variable. But this one accesses the `"OtherVOutline"` NotesOutline on line 32. Lines 36 through 45 loop through the entries in the NotesOutline and, if the outline points to a Named Element that is a View design element, it builds an array where the label is the entry's label and the alias is the view name. Finally, lines 56 through 67 add a Dynamic View Panel to the page. This is the target for a partial refresh when the value of the ComboBox is changed. Because the Dynamic View Panel renders all the columns that are in the underlying View design element, you can add a DominoView data-source whose `viewName` variable is `#{javascript:viewScope.get("viewName")}`.

Listing 7.1   TeamroomViews.xsp

```
1   All Views 
2   <xp:comboBox
3       id="comboBox1"
4       value="#{viewScope.viewName}">
5       <xp:selectItem
6           itemLabel="--Select--"
7           itemValue=""></xp:selectItem>
8       <xp:selectItems>
9           <xp:this.value><![CDATA[#{javascript:var v =
database.getViews();
10 var a = []
11 for(var i=0; i<v.size(); i++) {
12          a[i] = v[i].getName()
13 }
14 return a}]]></xp:this.value>
15      </xp:selectItems>
16      <xp:eventHandler
17          event="onchange"
18          submit="true"
19          refreshMode="partial"
20          refreshId="dynamicViewPanel1">
21      </xp:eventHandler>
22 </xp:comboBox>
23 <xp:br></xp:br>
24 Main Outline Views 
25 <xp:comboBox
26      id="comboBox2"
27      value="#{viewScope.viewName}">
28      <xp:selectItem
29          itemLabel="--Select--"
30          itemValue=""></xp:selectItem>
```

```
31     <xp:selectItems>
32        <xp:this.value><![CDATA[#{javascript:var
outline:NotesOutline=database.getOutline("OtherVOutline");
33 var entry:NotesOutlineEntry=outline.getFirst();
34 var i=0;
35 var a=[];
36 while (entry != null) {
37    // If it's a named element pointing to a view
38    if (entry.getEntryClass() == 2191 && entry.getType() == 2187) {
39       a[i]=entry.getLabel() + "|" + entry.getNamedElement();
40       i = i+1;
41    }
42    var tmpEntry:NotesOutlineEntry=outline.getNext(entry);
43    entry.recycle();
44    entry=tmpEntry;
45 }
46 return a;}]]></xp:this.value>
47     </xp:selectItems>
48     <xp:eventHandler
49        event="onchange"
50        submit="true"
51        refreshMode="partial"
52        refreshId="dynamicViewPanel1">
53     </xp:eventHandler>
54 </xp:comboBox>
55 <xp:br></xp:br>
56 <xe:dynamicViewPanel
57    rows="30"
58    id="dynamicViewPanel1"
59    showCheckbox="true"
60    showHeaderCheckbox="true">
61    <xe:this.data>
62       <xp:dominoView
63          var="viewEnt">
64          <xp:this.viewName><![CDATA[#{javascript:
viewScope.get("viewName")}]]></xp:this.viewName>
65       </xp:dominoView>
66    </xe:this.data>
67 </xe:dynamicViewPanel>
```

When this XPage is previewed, which should look like Figure 7.1, the output is extremely powerful. Not only does it allow access to any of the views in the database and display the documents from the view, it reproduces functionality that will be familiar to Domino developers who have developed applications for the Notes Client. If a column in the corresponding View design element is set to display view icons, the icons are faithfully reproduced. If columns are sortable in the corresponding View design element, they are sortable in the Dynamic View Panel using the same functionality familiar to developers who have used the View Panel control. The only aspect of the View design element that the Dynamic View Panel does not reproduce is the Calendar display style.

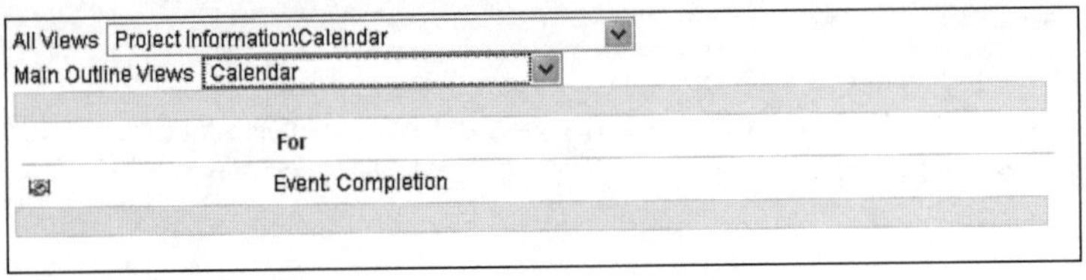

Figure 7.1 Dynamic View Panel.

As with the View Panel, you can allow the user to select entries from the view via the **show-Checkbox** and **showHeaderCheckbox** properties. See Listing 7.1. Although they are not visibly exposed, you can add header and footer facets to the Dynamic View Panel, as you can for the core View Controls. The queryOpenView and postOpenView events are available, as they are for other DominoView datasources. You can also add events when a column is clicked via the onColumnClick event; because you are not adding columns directly to the Dynamic View Panel control, unlike the core View Controls, there is a single event for the whole control.

Like the View Panel, the Dynamic View Panel allows developers to quickly and easily reproduce the View design element. However, the only way to customize the presentation of the underlying View design element is via the **customizerBean** property, which allows column values to be modified via Java. But if the View design element contains all the functionality you need, the Dynamic View Panel is a good option to reproduce it in an XPage.

Table 7.1 outlines the main properties for the Dynamic View Panel control.

Table 7.1 `xe:dynamicViewPanel` Properties

Property	Description
caption	Defines a caption to be displayed above the View Panel
summary	Defines a description of the view to be displayed to users as part of accessibility
attrs	Can provide extra attributes for the View Panel
customizerBean	Defines the managed bean or class name to be used to convert the output of columns in the view
rowAttrs	Can provide extra attributes for each row of the View Panel
pageName	Defines the XPage to open when users open a document
onColumnClick	Can trigger Client-Side JavaScript when the user clicks on a column
showCheckbox	Defines whether a check box should be added to each row to allow the user to select documents
showColumnHeader	Defines whether column headers should be shown
showHeaderCheckbox	Defines whether a check box should be added to the header row to allow the user to select all documents in the view
showUnreadMarks	Defines whether unread marks should be shown

Data Grid

The Dojo DataGrid is a view control with a fully functioning scrollbar that offers a rich user experience similar to that of the Notes Client, as Figure 7.2 shows. Like the View Panel in the core controls, the Dojo DataGrid is presented as a flat table of columns, usually with just one row per document, although content other than just the columns in the underlying View design element can be shown.

A rich set of functionality is implemented. Columns can be re-sorted or reordered, and contents can be edited in place. Entries in the view can also be selected for bulk processing. There is no pager, but instead a scrollbar. As the user scrolls through the view, additional contents are retrieved from the server via AJAX calls and presented to the user. Using AJAX calls optimizes initial page load and performance.

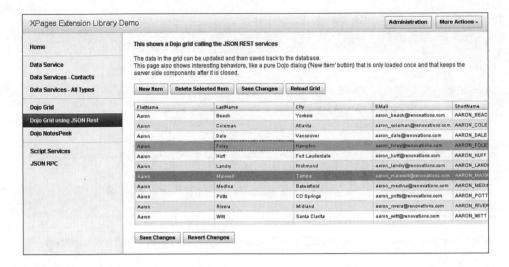

Figure 7.2   Dojo DataGrid.

REST Service

The Dynamic View control, as with the View Panel core control, uses a dominoView datasource. But XPages is about separating the presentation layer from the data layer. So the Extension Library controls covered in the rest of this chapter use data stores. This might be a new concept to XPages developers coming from a Notes Client development background, but not to developers from a web development background. Effectively, data stores allow uniform methods of access to the data layer. This chapter does not go into more detail than is necessary about the various data stores, concentrating on the presentation layer. Chapter 11, "REST Services," and Chapter 12, "XPages Gets Relational," cover the data stores in more detail, whether they are REST services or RDBMS data stores, retrieving information from Domino or non-Domino databases.

Listing 7.2 generates a viewJsonService REST service. You will investigate the code later, but the output is effectively a collection of objects, each of which contains items composed of name-value pairs, as shown in Figure 7.3.

Listing 7.2   viewJsonService REST Service Control

```
1   <xe:restService
2     id="restService1">
3     <xe:this.service>
4       <xe:viewJsonService
5         viewName="AllContacts"
6         var="entry"
7         formName="Contact">
```

```
8          defaultColumns="true"
9          contentType="application/json"
10         <xe:this.columns>
11            <xe:restViewColumn
12               name="ShortName">
13                  <xp:this.value><![CDATA[#{javascript:var e =
entry.getColumnValue("EMail")
14 if(e) {
15    var p = @UpperCase(@Left(e,"@"))
16    return p
17 }
18 return ""}]]></xp:this.value>
19            </xe:restViewColumn>
20         </xe:this.columns>
21      </xe:viewJsonService>
22    </xe:this.service>
23 </xe:restService>
```

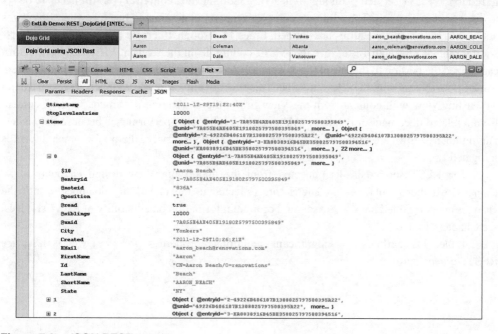

Figure 7.3   JSON REST output.

The REST Service control displayed here is also the most familiar type available: the **viewJsonService**. It is similar to the `?ReadViewEntries` URL command. For this type of REST service, each object relates to a View Entry in an underlying View design element. The REST Service is similar to the **viewItemFileService**, except that the **viewItemFileService** is read-write, whereas the **viewJsonService** is read only. Unless editability (including deletion of the underlying documents) is required, the **viewJsonService** is recommended as a more robust implementation.

Some of the items are specific to the View Entries, such as **@entryid**, **@unid,** and **@noteid**. These items are automatically generated and the naming convention is consistent for any REST service based on a View. Others are columns from the View, such as **Id**, **Firstname,** and **Created**. The naming convention for these items is generated from the programmatic name of the column. Of particular note is the **ShortName** item, whose value is AARON_BEACH. This will not be found in the underlying View design element, but it has been defined programmatically on the REST service. This is one of the benefits of the REST service.

Understanding the output makes it easier to deconstruct the REST service to create it. Returning to Listing 7.2, the properties **viewName**, **formName,** and **var** will be familiar from any other dominoView datasource. The unfamiliar properties are on lines 8 and 9. The **defaultColumns** property ensures that all the columns in the underlying View design elements are transferred to the REST service. Although it is a **viewJsonService**, **contentType** still needs to be set to `application/json`. The column's complex property beginning on line 6 is where any items not in the relevant View Entries are defined. Lines 11 through 19 create a column called **ShortName**. Lines 13 through 18 retrieve the EMail column from the relevant View Entry and return capitalized the portion to the left of the @ symbol. As can be seen in Figure 7.3, this adds an item named **ShortName** with the relevant value. This functionality allows developers to easily extend an existing view with content from the View Entry, the underlying document, or even content from a related document or database. Although this influences performance because only a certain number of rows are returned for each call to the REST service, the performance impact is mitigated.

The REST service is disconnected from the underlying View design element, so no changes, whether as updates or deletes, are reflected in the underlying documents until the changes are committed back to the server. For more information on editability of REST services, see Chapters 11 and 12.

Table 7.2 outlines the significant additional properties for the viewJsonService RESTService control.

Table 7.2 `xe:viewJsonService` Properties (Omitting Properties Generic for Datasources)

Property	Description
columns	Allows the developer to create additional columns on the fly
compact	Defines whether the JSON stream should be compacted
contentType	Defines the content type of the AJAX response
count	Defines the number of view entries to be returned by the service
defaultColumns	Defines whether the columns in the underlying View design element should be passed in the REST service
expandLevel	Defines whether responses should be expanded or collapsed
globalValues	Defines what generic values should be passed for the view
systemColumns	Defines which generic attributes should be passed for each view entry

Dojo Data Grid Control (`xe:djxDataGrid`)

The main container component is the Dojo Data Grid control, shown in Listing 7.3. The Dojo Data Grid is bound to a REST service by the **storeComponentId** property, the ID of the REST Service control on the XPage. Alternatively, if the store is created in Client-Side JavaScript, you can use the **store** property, the value being the JavaScript variable name. If the store needs to be accessed from Client-Side JavaScript, for example in the Client-Side JavaScript events covered later in this section, you must also set the **jsId** property. Three properties of the Dojo Data Grid control are relevant to the REST service. Two relate to messages presented to the user: **loadingMessage**, which defines the message presented to users as the data is being retrieved from the store, and **errorMessage**, which defines the message presented to users if an error occurs while retrieving the data. The third is **updateDelay**, which defines the number of milliseconds before loading more content to the Dojo Data Grid.

By default, the size of the Dojo Data Grid is six rows high and 100% width, but you can modify this easily by using Cascading Style Sheets (CSS) height and width on the Dojo Data Grid control. However, these settings are overridden by using properties of the Dojo Data Grid control. You can set the height by using the **autoHeight** property, set to the number of rows to show. The width is slightly harder to change. You can set it in the **initialWidth** property, but this takes effect only if **autoWidth** is set to true. However, this Dojo attribute is not exposed in the **All Properties** panel, so you need to set it using the **dojoAttributes** property, in the same way you set Dojo attributes on core controls. So in Listing 7.3, although a height and width are defined using CSS in line 7, the number of rows in the **autoHeight** property in line 4 and the width in the **initialWidth** property in line 8 are used when the Dojo Data Grid is drawn.

Listing 7.3   Dojo Data Grid Part One: Dojo Data Grid Control

```
1   <xe:djxDataGrid
2       id="djxDataGrid1"
3       storeComponentId="restService1"
4       autoHeight="10"
5       jsId="restService1"
6       rowSelector="2em"
7       style="width:85em; height: 25em;"
8       initialWidth="500px"
9       selectionMode="multiple">
10      <xe:this.dojoAttributes>
11        <xp:dojoAttribute
12            name="updateDelay"
13            value="0">
14        </xp:dojoAttribute>
15        <xp:dojoAttribute
16            name="autoWidth"
17            value="true">
18        </xp:dojoAttribute>
19      </xe:this.dojoAttributes>
```

Listing 7.3 and Figure 7.4 also demonstrate an implementation of the **rowSelector** property in line 6. This adds an additional column whose width is the value of the **rowSelector** property, inserted to the left of the Dojo Data Grid. This is not required to enable row selection, but it does provide a column with no other single-click event designed to make selection easier. However, this will have no effect if the **selectionMode** property is set to none. The default setting for **selectionMode** is extended, which allows multiple rows to be selected but also allows a range of rows to be selected by holding down the Shift key. The multiple option allows rows to be toggled as selected or deselected, but it does not allow the use of the **Shift** key to select a range of rows. The final option, single, allows only one row to be selected; as soon as another row is selected, the previously selected row is deselected.

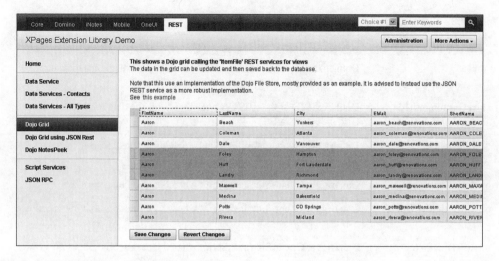

Figure 7.4 Dojo Data Grid rowSelector.

Two other properties are worthy of comment. The first property, **selectable**, allows text within each cell to be selected and the text to be copied and pasted. The second property is **escapeHTMLInData**. By default, any HTML in any content in the cells is escaped, but if set to false, the columns show HTML. However, because this can be used to run malicious code, it is recommended that you only change the default setting with caution.

Table 7.3 outlines the main properties for the Dojo Data Grid control.

Table 7.3 `xe:djxDataGrid` Properties

Property	Description
autoHeight	Defines the number of rows to show in the Dojo Data Grid and overrides any CSS settings
errorMessage	Defines an error message to display if the view contents could not be loaded
escapeHTMLInData	Defines whether HTML in the column data should be escaped when the cell contents are displayed
headerMenu	Defines a headerMenu to be used by the Dojo Data Grid
loadingMessage	Defines a message to display while the contents of the view are being loaded
rowsPerPage	Defines the number of rows to be retrieved in each AJAX query
selectable	Defines whether text is selectable within the Dojo Data Grid
selectionMode	Defines settings for how the user can select rows of the Dojo Data Grid
singleClickEdit	Allows cells to be edited by single-clicking rather than double-clicking

Table 7.3   Continued

Property	Description
store	Defines the Client-Side JavaScript variable name that holds the data for the Dojo Data Grid
storeComponentId	Defines the ID of the REST service that holds the data for the Dojo Data Grid
updateDelay	Defines the number of milliseconds to delay before updating the control after receiving updates from the store
onRowClick	Can trigger Client-Side JavaScript when the user clicks on a row
onRowContextMenu	Can trigger Client-Side JavaScript when the user accesses a row's context menu
onRowDblClick	Can trigger Client-Side JavaScript when the user double-clicks on a row
onStyleRow	Can style the row in response to mouse events on the row or row index properties
initialWidth	Defines the width of the Dojo Data Grid and overrides any CSS settings
rowSelector	Defines the width of the row selector column, which appears to the left of the view

Dojo Data Grid Contents

The Dojo Data Grid is effectively a table, so the content is added by means of Dojo Data Grid Row controls and Dojo Data Grid Column controls. Listing 7.4 continues the Dojo Data Grid from line 18 of Listing 7.3. However, unlike a normal table, there is no requirement to explicitly add a Dojo Data Grid Row control if the columns will be in the same row. There are no properties of note for the Dojo Data Grid Row control.

The Dojo Data Grid Column control has three important properties. The **field** property defines which item's value from the REST service should be displayed and holds the item's name. The **label** property can override the column header, which, by default, will be the item name. The **width** property specifies the width of the column and can be a specific width or `Auto`. In most cases, the Dojo Data Grid Column is shown, but if the column should be accessible to Client-Side JavaScript but not shown to the user, you can set the **hidden** property to `false`.

Sometimes the REST service provided cannot be modified or has been provided via a JavaScript function. However, you still might need to modify the output. The **formatter** property allows you to do this by specifying the name of a Client-Side JavaScript function that takes the value and returns a modified output. This can be seen in line 45 and lines 52 through 55 in Listing 7.4, where the `formatEmail()` function reproduces the ShortName item from the REST service.

In addition, the **get** property enables the developer to call a function instead of using the **field** property. The function takes two parameters—`colIndex` and `item`—both populated automatically by the Dojo Data Grid. The `getShortName` function called in line 38 and shown in lines 56 through 58 in Listing 7.4 simulated the previous column that uses `field="ShortName"` to get the same content.

Listing 7.4   Dojo Data Grid Part Two: Dojo Data Grid Columns and Formatter

```
1    <xe:djxDataGridColumn
2        id="djxDataGridColumn6"
3        field="FirstName"
4        width="auto"
5        editable="true">
6    </xe:djxDataGridColumn>
7    <xe:djxDataGridColumn
8        id="djxDataGridColumn7"
9        field="LastName"
10       width="auto"
11       editable="true">
12   </xe:djxDataGridColumn>
13   <xe:djxDataGridColumn
14       id="djxDataGridColumn8"
15       field="City"
16       width="auto">
17   </xe:djxDataGridColumn>
18   <xe:djxDataGridColumn
19       id="djxDataGridColumn2"
20       field="State"
21       width="auto"
22       editable="true"
23       cellType="dojox.grid.cells.Select">
24       <xe:this.options><![CDATA[#{javascript:
@DbColumn(@DbName(),"AllStates",1)}]]></xe:this.options>
25   </xe:djxDataGridColumn>
26   <xe:djxDataGridColumn
27       id="djxDataGridColumn9"
28       field="EMail"
29       width="auto">
30   </xe:djxDataGridColumn>
31   <xe:djxDataGridColumn
32       id="djxDataGridColumn10"
```

Listing 7.4   (Continued)

```
33      field="ShortName"
34      width="auto">
35   </xe:djxDataGridColumn>
36   <xe:djxDataGridColumn
37      id="djxDataGridColumn1"
38      get="getShortName"
39      label="Get Short Name"
40      width="auto">
41   </xe:djxDataGridColumn>
42   <xe:djxDataGridColumn
43      id="djxDataGridColumn11"
44      field="EMail"
45      formatter="formatEmail"
46      label="ShortName"
47      width="auto">
48   </xe:djxDataGridColumn>
49 </xe:djxDataGrid>
50 <xp:scriptBlock
51    id="scriptBlock1">
52    <xp:this.value><![CDATA[function formatEmail(value) {
53    var val=value.substr(0,value.indexOf("@"));
54    return val.toUpperCase();
55 }
56 function getShortName(colIndex,item) {
57    if (item) return item.ShortName;
58 }]]></xp:this.value>
59 </xp:scriptBlock>
```

InViewEditing

Editability is provided by setting the **editable** property on a Dojo Data Grid Column control to `true`. On double-clicking a cell in that column (or single-clicking it if the Dojo Data Grid control's **singleClickEdit** property is set to `true`), it becomes editable to free-type a new textual value. But by changing the **cellType** property on the Dojo Data Grid Column control, different editors can be provided. The other settings are `dojox.grid.cells.Bool`, which provides a check box, and `dojox.grid.cells.Select`, which provides a drop-down list of options. For `dojox.grid.cells.Select`, the **options** property allows the developer to define the values the user can select from as a comma-separated list or array. Listing 7.4 shows an example of this for the Dojo Data Grid Column control on lines 23 and 24.

Table 7.4 shows the key properties available for the Dojo Data Grid Column control.

Table 7.4 `xe:djxDataGridColumn` Properties

Property	Description
cellType	Defines the editor to be used when editing the column property
editable	Defines whether the column is editable
label	Defines the column header label
field	Defines the name of the field from the data store to be displayed
formatter	Defines a Client-Side JavaScript function or function name to be used to format the content
get	Defines a Client-Side JavaScript function or function name to be used to generate the content
width	Defines the width of the column

Although this will enable editability of a column, Client-Side JavaScript needs to be run to pass the changes back to the REST service. This is shown in Listing 7.5. Line 10 saves the Dojo store, whereas line 21 cancels any changes.

Listing 7.5 Saving Dojo Data Grid Edits

```
1  <xp:button
2     value="Save Changes"
3     id="button1">
4     <xp:eventHandler
5        event="onclick"
6        submit="false">
7        <xp:this.script><![CDATA[var args = {
8     onError: function() { alert('Update error'); }
9  }
10 restService1.save(args)
11 ]]></xp:this.script>
12    </xp:eventHandler>
13 </xp:button>
14 <xp:button
15    value="Revert Changes"
16    id="button2">
17    <xp:eventHandler
18       event="onclick"
```

Listing 7.5   (Continued)

```
19        submit="false">
20        <xp:this.script><![CDATA[var ds = eval('restService1')
21 ds.revert()
22 ]]></xp:this.script>
23    </xp:eventHandler>
24 </xp:button>
```

View Events

There are additional events available for the Dojo Data Grid control, such as **onRowClick** and **onRowDblClick**, detailed in Table 7.3. These are Client-Side JavaScript events, but the event has arguments including **grid**, **rowIndex**, **rowNode**, **cell**, **cellIndex,** and **cellNode**. Listing 7.6 shows code for the onRowClick event, which triggers an alert. Line 1 creates a CDATA block because quotes are used, but because this is Client-Side JavaScript, the content is a literal string. Line 1 gets the rowIndex attribute of the arguments. Line 2 uses that index to retrieve the relevant row from the REST service and pull the @unid attribute.

Listing 7.6   onRowClick Event

```
1   <xe:this.onRowClick><![CDATA[var idx=arguments[0].rowIndex;
2        var unid=restService1._items[idx].attributes["@unid"];
3        alert("Row is " + idx + \n + "UNID is " + unid);]]>
4   </xe:this.onRowClick>
```

Line 3 issues an alert with both pieces of information, as in Figure 7.5. Note that this is referencing the **jsId** property of the service, because it is accessing the REST service via Client-Side JavaScript. The onRowContextMenu allows Client-Side JavaScript to be triggered when right-clicking on a row.

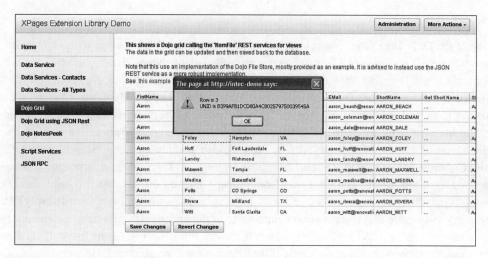

Figure 7.5   Dojo Data Grid Events.

There is an **onStyleRow** event that triggers when the Dojo Data Grid is drawn and as the cursor moves over each row. You can use this to manipulate the styling of the content within the cell based on the arguments that are passed in, which include **index**, **selected**, **odd**, **over**, **customClasses,** and **customStyles**. Whether changing the style of a row using **customStyles** or a CSS class in **customClasses**, this allows you to set a variety of styling depending on row position or user activity. For example, you can use Listing 7.7 to add a yellow background based on the over argument (that is, if the mouse hovers over the row, as seen in Figure 7.5).

Listing 7.7   onStyleRow Event

```
<xe:this.onStyleRow><![CDATA[var arg=arguments[0];
    if (arg.over) arg.customStyles+="background-color:#FFFF00";]]>
</xe:this.onStyleRow>
```

iNotes ListView (xe:listView)

The iNotes ListView control is a rich view component based on the view widgets in the iNotes Mail template. In styling, it looks similar to the Dojo Data Grid control, but there is different and additional functionality available, such as showing icons, image resizing, and a variety of events.

The iNotes ListView also uses a REST service. For a Notes View, you can use a **viewJson-Service** REST service for the Data Grid control, employing the default columns from the view or adding columns.

Dynamic ListView

Unlike the Dojo Data Grid, you can implement the iNotes ListView control without including any columns. If no ListView Column controls are added to the iNotes ListView control, it works similarly to the Dynamic View Panel control, as can be seen in Figure 7.6. Namely, it creates a view with all the columns from the underlying View design element. Moreover, columns set to display icons will be reproduced, showing the icons instead of the numbers that are the actual values in the view. Any columns enabled for sorting in the underlying View design element also allow sorting on the XPage. By default, any hidden columns are still shown, unless the **hideColumns** property on the iNotes ListView is set to `true`. Then hidden columns are also suppressed from the XPage. The **alternateRows** property enables the developer to have alternate rows styled differently to help readability of a large view. The **showColumnName4EmptyTitle** property can ensure that if there is no column title in the underlying View design element, the item name from the REST service is used as the column title. This can ensure that column titles always appear, but it should be used only if the item name will be meaningful to users.

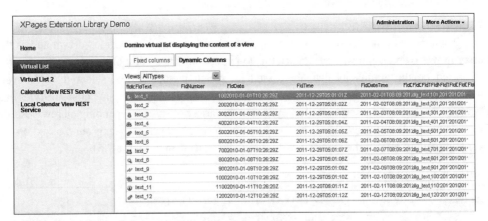

Figure 7.6   iNotes ListView.

To compare the output of the iNotes ListView with the Dynamic View Panel, create an XPage called **TeamroomiNotesListView.xsp** in the core TeamRoom database used for the Dynamic View Panel. Insert the code in Listing 7.8. Much of the code will look similar to the **TeamroomViews.xsp** XPage. But instead of the Dynamic View Panel, there is a **viewJsonService** REST Service control and an iNotes ListView control.

Listing 7.8   TeamroomiNotesListView.xsp

```
1   All Views 
2   <xp:this.resources>
3     <xp:script
4        src="/OpenLogXPages.jss"
5        clientSide="false">
6     </xp:script>
7   </xp:this.resources>
8   <xp:comboBox
9     id="comboBox1"
10    value="#{viewScope.viewName}">
11    <xp:selectItem
12       itemLabel="--Select--"
13       itemValue="">
14    </xp:selectItem>
15    <xp:selectItems>
16       <xp:this.value><![CDATA[#{javascript:var v =
database.getViews();
17 var a = []
18 for(var i=0; i<v.size(); i++) {
19    a[i] = v[i].getName()
20 }
21 return a}]]></xp:this.value>
22    </xp:selectItems>
23    <xp:eventHandler
24       event="onchange"
25       submit="true"
26       refreshMode="partial"
27       refreshId="listView1">
28    </xp:eventHandler>
29  </xp:comboBox>
30  <xp:br></xp:br>
31  Main Outline Views 
32  <xp:comboBox
33    id="comboBox2"
34    value="#{viewScope.viewName}">
35    <xp:selectItem
36       itemLabel="--Select--"
37       itemValue="">
38    </xp:selectItem>
39    <xp:selectItems>
```

Listing 7.8   (Continued)

```
40        <xp:this.value><![CDATA[#{javascript:var
outline:NotesOutline=database.getOutline("OtherVOutline");
41 var entry:NotesOutlineEntry=outline.getFirst();
42 var i=0;
43 var a=[];
44 while (entry != null) {
45    // If it's a named element pointing to a view
46    if (entry.getEntryClass() == 2191 && entry.getType() == 2187) {
47       a[i]=entry.getLabel() + "|" + entry.getNamedElement();
48       i = i+1;
49    }
50    var tmpEntry:NotesOutlineEntry=outline.getNext(entry);
51    entry.recycle();
52    entry=tmpEntry;
53 }
54 return a;}]]></xp:this.value>
55    </xp:selectItems>
56    <xp:eventHandler
57       event="onchange"
58       submit="true"
59       refreshMode="partial"
60       refreshId="listView1">
61    </xp:eventHandler>
62 </xp:comboBox>
63 <xp:br></xp:br>
64 <xe:restService id="restService1">
65    <xe:this.service>
66       <xe:viewJsonService
67          defaultColumns="true"
68          viewName="#{viewScope.viewName}">
69       </xe:viewJsonService>
70    </xe:this.service>
71 </xe:restService>
72 <xe:listView
73    id="listView1"
74    style="height:250.0px;width:800.0px"
75    storeComponentId="restService1"
76    alternateRows="true"
77    showColumnName4EmptyTitle="true"
78    autoResize="true">
79 </xe:listView>
```

The iNotes ListView has numerous events, all of which support only Client-Side JavaScript. This is because the control and its functionality are an extension of what is available in iNotes, which, because it is not built on XPages, does not have access to Server-Side JavaScript (SSJS). The events **onCellClick** and **onCellDblClick**, not surprisingly, reproduce the onRowClick and onRowDblClick events of the Data Grid. However, the underlying content is accessed differently. For both events, there is an object available, `ext`, that gives access to all the necessary elements. The `ext.tumbler` attribute gives access to the row number, but note that this starts with the first row as 1, not 0. For greater ease than the **onRowClick** and **onRowDblClick** events, there is actually an `ext.item` object that gives direct access to the item from the store with all the properties from the underlying View design element, as well as the other automatically generated attributes from the store. The `ext` object also gives access to the row and cell that were clicked.

Some of the other events, such as **onContextMenu**, **onDeleteEntry**, **onNewEntry**, **onOpenEntry,** and **onSelectEntry,** are covered in the "iNotes Calendar" section. The events work identically for both, with the same arguments available. One additional event available for iNotes ListView is **onSortChanged**. This event is triggered when a sortable column is clicked. No arguments are available for this event.

Table 7.5 defines the main properties for the iNotes ListView control.

Table 7.5   `xe:listView` Properties

Property	Description
jsId	Defines the Client-Side JavaScript ID for the view.
storeComponentId	Defines the ID of the REST service that holds the data for the Data Grid.
structureComponentId	Defines the ID of a Design Store to define the structure of the REST service.
onCellClick	Can trigger Client-Side JavaScript when the user clicks on a cell.
onCellDblClick	Can trigger Client-Side JavaScript when the user double-clicks on a column.
onContextMenu	Can trigger Client-Side JavaScript when the user accesses a row's context menu.
onDeleteEntry	Can trigger Client-Side JavaScript when the user deletes an entry.
onNewEntry	Can trigger Client-Side JavaScript when the user creates an entry.
onOpenEntry	Can trigger Client-Side JavaScript when the user opens an entry.
onSelectEntry	Can trigger Client-Side JavaScript when the user selects an entry.
onSortChanged	Can trigger Client-Side JavaScript when the sort order of the view is changed.
alternateRows	Defines the styling for alternate rows.

Table 7.5 Continued

Property	Description
canBeNarrowMode	Defines whether the view can be viewed in Narrow Mode. Only applicable if ListView Columns are defined.
hideColumns	Defines whether columns hidden in the underlying View design element should also be hidden from the iNotes ListView. Only applicable if no ListView Columns are defined.
showColumnName ForEmptyTitle	Defines whether the column name should be displayed if the underlying View design element does not have a column title.

ListView Column

When ListView Column controls are added to the iNotes ListView, the process is more analogous to the Dojo Data Grid control. The output is specifically the columns chosen—nothing more, nothing less. Consequently, the **hideColumn** property is ignored. The assumption is that if you choose to add the column to the iNotes ListView, you want it to show.

The two properties under the **dojo-widget** category—**columnName** and **title**—define the content of the column. The **columnName** property defines the item's attribute name to be shown, and the **title** property defines the column header title to appear for the user. Note that if the content for the column is an array, it does not currently show. The **gradient** property can add a gradient for the whole column. Bear in mind that if **gradient** is set, alternate row colors have no effect for this column.

Reviewing the properties of the ListView Column, it is evident it will support all the Notes Client functionality available in view columns. If the column should show an icon, you should set the **icon** property. If response documents should show, you can define the **response** property. If the column is categorized, you can use the **twistie** property to ensure that a twistie appears. If the column should extend to take up the remaining width of the view, you can set the **extendable** property; otherwise, the final column spans the remaining view width defined on the iNotes ListView control. The **fixedWidth** property allows you to fix the column to a specific width. The **sort** property allows you to define a sort order: 1 for descending, or 2 for ascending.

Because the **hideColumn** property is applicable only if no ListView Columns are defined, the **canBeNarrowMode** property is only applicable if ListView Columns *are* defined. This becomes apparent when ListView Columns are added and the properties for them are inspected. However, this does not need to be set to `true` to take advantage of the narrow mode functionality. But what is this narrow mode functionality? It occurs when the iNotes ListView goes far beyond the Dynamic View Panel or Dojo DataGrid controls. The narrow mode functionality enables a multirow layout, with contents for a single entry spanning multiple rows, as in Figure 7.7.

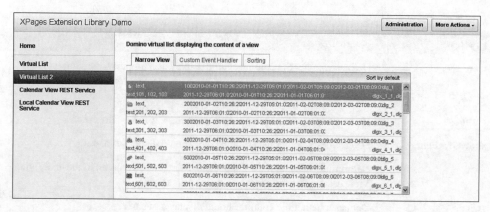

Figure 7.7   Narrow Mode.

In Narrow Mode, the **columnTitle** property of the ListView Column has no effect. The column headings are not displayed, because the header does not support multiple rows. But as is apparent, the alternate row colors affect each item in the store. Narrow Mode supports three additional properties. The first property is **narrowDisplay**, which determines how the column displays (or not). The available options for **narrowDisplay** are **top** (appearing on the first row), **wrap** (appearing on the second row) or **hide**. The second property is **beginWrapUnder**, which determines which column the wrapping starts under; it does not necessarily have to start under the first column. The final property is **sequenceNumber**, which determines the column order and provides a rich view layout.

Table 7.6 summarizes the properties for the ListView Column control.

Table 7.6   xe:listViewColumn Properties

Property	Description
columnName	Defines the name of the attribute from each JSON object for which to display a value. This corresponds to a column in the underlying View design element.
columnTitle	Defines the title to appear above the column.
beginWrapUnder	Defines under which column wrapping should start in narrow mode.
narrowDisplay	Determines how the column should show in narrow mode, whether it should appear on the first row, appear on the second wrapped row, or be hidden.
sequenceNumber	Defines the column order.
extendable	Determines whether the column should extend to take up remaining space for the view's panel.
fixedWidth	Defines whether the column width is fixed to a size defined by the developer.

Table 7.6   Continued

Property	Description
icon	Defines whether the column should display as a property, the same as the setting on the properties of the View design element for the Notes Client. The number corresponds to a view icon in the **icons** folder on the server.
response	Determines whether the column should show response documents.
showGradient	Determines whether the column color should display as a gradient.
sort	Determines whether the column can be sorted. The column in the underlying View design element must also be marked as sortable.
twistie	Defines whether the column should display a twistie.
width	Defines a width for the column.

iNotes Calendar (`xe:calendarView`)

One of the common requests of developers using XPages was for a Calendar view control. Although jQuery provided a plugin and some developers used Repeat Controls to generate a calendar-style layout and display content, there were still calls for a standard XPages control for displaying content in a calendar layout.

Considerable effort had already been spent in developing a fully functioning web-based calendar layout control for iNotes, so the approach taken was to package the iNotes functionality within an XPages control in the Extension Library. This approach provides a wealth of functionality but does mean some peculiarities in event handling.

Calendar Views in the Notes Client

For XPages developers who have never developed for the Notes Client, it will be useful to outline the process of creating a Calendar View for display in the Notes Client. This is because many of the columns required by a Notes Calendar View are also required by the iNotes Calendar Control.

The most important step when creating a Calendar View for the Notes Client is to set the **Style** property on the first tab of the View's properties panel to **Calendar** instead of the default **Standard Outline** setting, as shown in Figure 7.8. This is the **($Calendar)** view in a database based on the Mail template that comes with the Lotus Notes install.

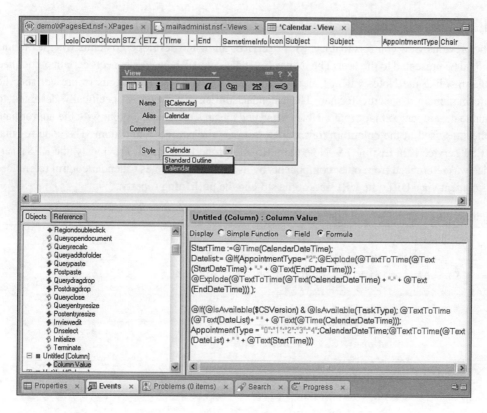

Figure 7.8   Notes Calendar View in Domino Designer.

The first column of the Calendar View must be a Notes Date/Time. This is the output of the formula shown in Figure 7.8. There are some additional settings to be defined in the first Column's Properties box. The column needs to be sorted on the second tab of the Column's properties panel in ascending order. On the fourth tab of the Column's properties, the column must be set to display a Date/Time with both **Display Date** and **Display Time** checked. The second column must be the duration in minutes of the event. There are a variety of other settings you can apply to the View's properties panel for display purposes, but the refinements available are unnecessary for the purposes of comparison with the iNotes Calendar View control. If further information is required, it is best to consult the Domino Designer Help database page titled **"Creating a Calendar View."**

In Figure 7.8, a number of additional columns are shown that bear further comment. There is an icon used to determine the calendar entry type. The **Time** and **End** columns hold the start and end time for the calendar entry. The **Subject** column holds the title for the calendar entry, and the **Chair** column holds the chair of the meeting or person who originated the calendar entry.

REST Service: calendarJsonLegacyService

The previous view controls that use REST services allow the developer to define which columns should be presented to the user. The iNotes Calendar control, however, expects certain predefined columns, like the Notes Client Calendar view, so the REST service needs to present specific information in a specific format. The calendarJsonLegacyService is specifically designed to enable developers to map from a Notes View and ensures the data is output with the appropriate labels, as used in the **calendarView.xsp** Custom Control in the TeamRoom. The code for that REST service is in Listing 7.9. Note the **pathInfo** property in line 3. Previously, the REST service was referenced from other components by its ID. But the iNotes Calendar control references its content via a URL, the URL set for the store in the **pathInfo** property.

Listing 7.9   calendarJsonLegacyService

```
1   <xe:restService
2      id="restService2"
3      pathInfo="/inoteslegacyjson"
4      preventDojoStore="false">
5      <xe:this.service>
6         <xe:calendarJsonLegacyService
7            viewName="calendarOutline"
8            var="entry"
9            contentType="text/plain"
10           colCalendarDate="CalDateTime"
11           colEntryIcon="Icon"
12           colStartTime="StartDateTime"
13           colEndTime="EndDateTime"
14           colSubject="For"
15           colChair="Chair">
16              <xe:this.compact><![CDATA[#{javascript:
sessionScope.CompactJson2=="true"}]]></xe:this.compact>
17         </xe:calendarJsonLegacyService>
18      </xe:this.service>
19   </xe:restService>
```

The other significant difference with the previous REST services is the value of the **contentType** property on the service. Previously, the JSON was output with the setting **application/ json**, meaning that each column was output as another item within the entry object. For the iNotes Calendar control, the property's value must be **text/plain**. The difference in the output can be seen by comparing Figure 7.3 and Figure 7.9. The latter shows a single viewentry, with all the usual system columns such as **@unid** and **@noteid**. However, there is one item called **entrydata** for all the other mapped rows. This contains an object with other objects within it, one for each of the relevant columns. Note also that instead of the property names defined in the REST service, programmatic names like **$134** are output. This is another of the benefits of the calendarJson LegacyService: that those programmatic names are automatically generated, with the mapping done against human-readable property names.

Figure 7.9   calendarJsonLegacyService REST output.

The **compact** property of the calendarJsonLegacyService enables the JSON data to be compacted when it's pushed out to the browser. This is managed in the TeamRoom database with a `sessionScope` variable.

REST Service: Notes Calendar Store

The other option for utilizing a Notes Calendar view is to use the Notes Calendar Store control. This takes a REST service with appropriately named columns and converts it into a store that the iNotes Calendar Control can understand.

The first step is to set up a REST service. Note that the REST service needs to provide columns with the specific names seen in Figure 7.9. This can be seen in Listing 7.10, which shows the **CalendarStoreCustomRestService.xsp** in the XPages Extension Library Demo database. The default columns existing in the underlying View design element are suppressed by setting the **defaultColumns** property to `"false"` in line 8. Then the specific columns required from lines 11 through 65, each with programmatic names mapping to the relevant columns in the **($Calendar)** view of the Notes Mail Template, are added to the **columns** property. In this scenario, all the required columns exist in the underlying View design element because the REST service is actually pointing to the **($Calendar)** view in a Notes Mail Template, so defaultColumns could be set to `"true"`, and the **columns** property could be omitted. But it is a useful example to show the columns required for the REST service and the specific names the columns must have.

The **pathInfo**, **contentType,** and **compact** properties have the same values for the viewJsonLegacyService as the calendarJsonLegacyService.

Listing 7.10 viewJsonLegacyService

```
1   <xe:restService
2       id="restService2"
3       pathInfo="inoteslegacyjson">
4       <xe:this.service>
5           <xe:viewJsonLegacyService
6               databaseName="${compositeData.databaseName}"
7               viewName="${compositeData.viewName}"
8               defaultColumns="false"
9               var="entry"
10              contentType="text/plain">
11              <xp:this.columns>
12                  <!-- Cal Date -->
13                  <xe:restViewColumn
14                      name="$134" columnName="$134">
15                  </xe:restViewColumn>
16                  <!-- Icon -->
17                  <xe:restViewColumn
18                      name="$149"
19                      columnName="$149">
20                  </xe:restViewColumn>
21                  <!-- Start Date -->
22                  <xe:restViewColumn
23                      name="$144"
24                      columnName="$144">
25                  </xe:restViewColumn>
26                  <!-- End Date -->
27                  <xe:restViewColumn
28                      name="$146"
29                      columnName="$146">
30                  </xe:restViewColumn>
31                  <!- Description -->
32                  <xe:restViewColumn
33                      name="$147"
34                      columnName="$147">
35                  </xe:restViewColumn>
36                  <!- Alt Description -->
```

```
37              <xe:restViewColumn
38                name="$151"
39                columnName="$151">
40              </xe:restViewColumn>
41              <!-- Type -->
42              <xe:restViewColumn
43                name="$152"
44                columnName="$152">
45              </xe:restViewColumn>
46              <!-- Chair -->
47              <xe:restViewColumn
48                name="$153"
49                columnName="$153">
50              </xe:restViewColumn>
51              <!-- Confidential -->
52              <xe:restViewColumn
53                name="$154"
54                columnName="$154">
55              </xe:restViewColumn>
56              <!-- Status -->
57              <xe:restViewColumn
58                name="$160"
59                columnName="$160">
60              </xe:restViewColumn>
61              <xe:restViewColumn
62                name="$UserData"
63                columnName="$UserData">
64              </xe:restViewColumn>
65          </xp:this.columns>
66          <xe:this.compact>
67
<![CDATA[#{javascript:sessionScope.CompactJson2=="true"}]]>
68          </xe:this.compact>
69        </xe:viewJsonLegacyService>
70     </xe:this.service>
71</xe:restService>
```

Once the REST service has been provided, the final step is to add a Notes Calendar Store control to the XPage, as in Listing 7.11. Note the setting of the **dojoType** and the **dojoAttribute** properties. The xpagesext.CalendarStore Dojo type will not be found among the other

Dojo files on the Domino server or Notes Client. The control takes advantage of Dojo-style properties to add a **pathInfo** attribute that maps to the same **pathInfo** property set on the REST service.

Listing 7.11   Notes Calendar Store

```
<xe:notesCalendarStore
    id="${compositeData.storeComponentId}"
    jsId="nstore1"
    dojoType="xpagesext.CalendarStore">
    <xe:this.dojoAttributes>
        <xp:dojoAttribute
            name="pathInfo"
            value="/inoteslegacyjson">
        </xp:dojoAttribute>
    </xe:this.dojoAttributes>
</xe:notesCalendarStore>
```

Notes Calendar Control

Once the REST service has been set up and, if necessary, a Notes Calendar Store control or iCal Store control added, the final step is to add an iNotes Calendar control. This is the control that actually adds the calendar to the XPage, providing the same functionality available in the Notes Client or on iNotes. Listing 7.12 shows the Notes Calendar control settings from the **calendarView.xsp** Custom Control in the TeamRoom database. Because this is mapping directly to a calendarJsonLegacyStore REST service, the **storeComponentId** property is set to that REST service's ID, restService2. If a Notes Calendar Store or iCal Store is used, the **storeComponentId** will be the ID of the relevant intermediary store rather than the REST service that actually provides the data.

Listing 7.12   Notes Calendar Control

```
<xe:calendarView
    id="calendarView1"
    jsId="cview1"
    type="#{javascript:sessionScope.dateRangeActions_selectedValue}"
    storeComponentId="restService2"
    style="width:100%">
    <xe:this.summarize>
        <![CDATA[#{javascript:summarize =
sessionScope.calendarFormatActions_selectedValue == "true";}]]>
    </xe:this.summarize>
</xe:calendarView>
```

The **summarize** property is a boolean. If `false`, the full range of date or time slots is shown regardless of whether there is a calendar slot for that date or time, as in Figure 7.10. If `true`, a list of calendar entries grouped under the date or time slots used is shown instead, as in Figure 7.11.

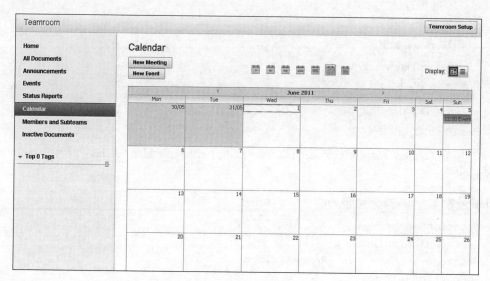

Figure 7.10   Calendar—summarize=`"false"`.

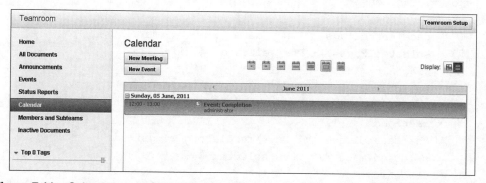

Figure 7.11   Calendar—summarize=`"true"`.

The **type** property determines the range for the calendar. In the TeamRoom, it maps to an instance of the **actionManager.xsp** Custom Control shown in Listing 7.13, although an Image Select control, covered in Chapter 5, "Dojo Made Easy," could have been used instead. This Custom Control allows a set of action buttons to be added to the XPage to provide a single-select style group of buttons. As one button is selected, the others are deselected, and the group's value is set from the **selectedValue** of the currently selected button. This shows that the **defaultSelectedValue** for the groups of actions is M, but the available options that can be provided are as follows:

> One day: D
>
> Two days: T
>
> Work week: F
>
> Seven-Day Week: W
>
> Two Weeks: 2
>
> Month: M
>
> Year: Y

Not all options must be provided to set the range for the calendar, but this shows all options available.

Listing 7.13   dateRangeActions

```
<xc:actionManager
    refreshId="mainPanel"
    actionGroupName="dateRangeActions"
    padActions="true"
    defaultSelectedValue="M">
    <xc:this.actions>
        <xc:actions
            deselectedImage="/1_Day_deselected_24.gif"
            selectedImage="/1_Day_selected_24.gif"
            imageAlt=""
            selectedValue="D">
        </xc:actions>
        <xc:actions
            deselectedImage="/2_Days_deselected_24.gif"
            selectedImage="/2_Days_selected_24.gif"
            imageAlt=""
            selectedValue="T">
        </xc:actions>
        <xc:actions
            deselectedImage="/1_Work_Week_deselected_24.gif"
            selectedImage="/1_Work_Week_selected_24.gif"
            imageAlt=""
            selectedValue="F">
```

```
            </xc:actions>
            <xc:actions
                deselectedImage="/1_Week_deselected_24.gif"
                selectedImage="/1_Week_selected_24.gif"
                imageAlt=""
                selectedValue="W">
            </xc:actions>
            <xc:actions
                deselectedImage="/2_Weeks_deselected_24.gif"
                selectedImage="/2_Weeks_selected_24.gif"
                imageAlt=""
                selectedValue="2">
            </xc:actions>
            <xc:actions
                deselectedImage="/Month_deselected_24.gif"
                selectedImage="/Month_selected_24.gif"
                imageAlt=""
                selectedValue="M">
            </xc:actions>
            <xc:actions
                deselectedImage="/All_Entries_deselected_24.gif"
                selectedImage="/All_Entries_selected_24.gif"
                imageAlt=""
                selectedValue="Y">
            </xc:actions>
        </xc:this.actions>
</xc:actionManager>
```

View Events

The Notes Calendar control also supports some events specifically for calendars. As with the iNotes ListView and for the same reason, all these events support only Client-Side JavaScript.

The **onNewEntry** events allow the developer to intercept a click and capture the relevant date or time slot clicked. Listing 7.14 shows the **onNewEntry** event in the TeamRoom calendar. Line 2 verifies that the user has access to create documents. Because the event supports only Client-Side JavaScript, the code is wrapped in the #{javascript:} syntax to run SSJS through the XSP Command Manager when the XPage is parsed. It also verifies that the user can write the result to the Client-Side JavaScript function printed on the rendered web page. Line 4 uses the getDate() function of the **calendar** object to access the JavaScript date for the clicked slot. The calendar object is passed as an argument into the function. If there's any doubt, a review of the HTML generated by the event will show those arguments, as demonstrated in the HTML that's produced: `<script language="JavaScript" event="newEntryAction" type="dojo/connect" args="calendar">`. The date is manipulated into *yyyymmdd* format in lines 6 through 13 and in line 25 is appended as a query string parameter to the URL to which the user will be redirected. The final parameter added in lines 28 and 29 is a calendar type of **Meeting**, held in a properties file. The browser is then redirected to the complete URL, and the **calendarEntry.xsp** XPage populates the relevant fields from the query string parameters.

Listing 7.14   onNewEntry Event

```
1   <xe:this.onNewEntry><![CDATA[
2   if(#{javascript:(userBean.accessLevel >=
lotus.domino.ACL.LEVEL_AUTHOR) && userBean.canCreateDocs}){
3      var yyyymmdd = null;
4      var calDate = calendar.getDate();
5      // if we have a calendar date, format it as a yyyymmdd string
6      if (calDate != null) {
7         var yyyy = new String(calDate.getFullYear());
8         var month = calDate.getMonth() + 1;
9         var mm = month < 10 ? new String('0' + month) : month;
10        var day = calDate.getDate();
11        var dd = day < 10 ? new String('0' + day) : day;
12        yyyymmdd = yyyy + mm + dd;
13 }
14
15     var path = "";
16     if(dojo.isMozilla || dojo.isWebKit){
17        path = #{javascript:"\"" + @FullUrl('/') + "\""};
18     }
19
20     // append the XPage to create a calendar entry
21     path += "calendarEntry.xsp";
22
23     // add a parameter value for the selected date if available
24     if (yyyymmdd != null) {
25        path += "?date=" + yyyymmdd;
26     }
27     // Add a docType=Meeting parameter so meetings are selected by
default;
28     var sDocTypeParam =
("#{javascript:strings.getString('defaultdoctype3')}");
```

```
29      path += "&docType=" + sDocTypeParam;
30
31      //change the current URL
32      document.location.href = path;
33 }]]>
34 </xe:this.onNewEntry>
```

The **onRescheduleEntry** event receives the calendar argument in addition to an item argument. This is the calendar entry that's being rescheduled, enabling the developer to access the Notes Universal ID of the calendar entry by using item.unid. The **onOpenEntry** and **onDeleteEntry** events receive only a single argument—**items**—an array of the calendar entry or entries selected. There are also events for **onSelectEntry**, **onChangeView** (for when the view type is being changed), and **onContextMenu**.

Table 7.7 summarizes the main properties for the iNotes Calendar control.

Table 7.7 xe:calendarView Properties

Property	Description
jsId	Defines Client-Side JavaScript ID for the view.
storeComponentId	Defines the ID of the REST service that holds the data for the Data Grid.
summarize	Defines the format in which entries are displayed. If true, the entries are summarized, showing only the dates for which there are entries. If false, a full calendar is shown with boxes for the display period.
type	Defines the number of days displayed at a time.
onChangeView	Can trigger Client-Side JavaScript when the user changes the display type of the view.
onContextMenu	Can trigger Client-Side JavaScript when the user accesses a row's context menu.
onDeleteEntry	Can trigger Client-Side JavaScript when the user deletes an entry.
onNewEntry	Can trigger Client-Side JavaScript when the user creates an entry.
onOpenEntry	Can trigger Client-Side JavaScript when the user opens an entry.
onRescheduleEntry	Can trigger Client-Side JavaScript when the user reschedules the date of an entry by dragging it to a different cell in the calendar.
onSelectEntry	Can trigger Client-Side JavaScript when the user selects an entry.

Data View (xe:dataView)

The Data View is the main view component used in the TeamRoom database. It is a rich view component with several similarities to the core view controls but greater flexibility in layout. Indeed, the **repeatControls** and **removeRepeat** properties show the control's relationship to the Repeat control. Similarly, alternate row coloring has to be done in the same way it would be done for Repeat Controls, because just a single **rowClass** property is applied to all rows rather than a **rowClasses** property found on the View Panel or Data Table. But beyond the core controls, the Data View allows properties and facets for categorization, expandable sections, sorting, multiple column layouts, images, and navigation, either by means of pagers or an AJAX request to the server to add more rows—a means of navigation becoming more and more prevalent on the web but until now not easily implemented in XPages.

The data properties for the Data View will be familiar. It has the traditional properties of **var**, **indexVar**, **rows**, **first**, and **openDocAsReadonly**. When it comes to the source for the data, there are similarities but even greater flexibility. You can set the **data** property to any of the three datasources now available to XPages: the core dominoView datasource, available for a View Panel or Data Table; and the core dominoDocument or the new Extension Library objectData datasource, both available for the Data Table control. But the Data View provides even greater flexibility, because the **value** property can be used instead and set to any type of collection, just as developers have always done for Repeat controls. This provides total flexibility in defining the data.

Like the View Panel, the Data View control is built to manage document selection via the **showCheckbox** and **showHeaderCheckbox**. Indeed, the control uses the same SSJS method to access the documents: `getSelectedIds()`.

Table 7.8 outlines the main properties for the Data View control.

Table 7.8   `xe:dataView` Properties

Property	Description
detailsOnClient	Defines whether expand and collapse actions should be processed on the browser/Notes client. If `false`, expand and collapse actions make a call to the server.
expandedDetail	Defines whether the Detail area should be expanded by default. If `false`, this property can still be overridden by using the **disableHideRows** property.
pageName	Defines the XPage to open when users open a document.
categoryColumn	Defines columns for the Category area of the Data View. See the properties of `xe:viewCategoryColumn` in Table 7.14 for more details. You can also develop the Category area using the facet names `categoryRow`, `category-Row1`, `categoryRow2`, and so on.
collapsibleCategory	Defines whether the **Category** area is collapsible.

Property	Description
collapsibleDetail	Defines whether the **Detail** area is collapsible.
collapsibleRows	Defines whether rows for response documents are collapsible.
disableHideRow	Defines whether the **Detail** area is expanded and not collapsible.
extraColumns	Defines columns for the **Extra Columns** area of the Data View. See the properties of the xe:viewExtraColumn in Table 7.14 for more details. The **Extra Columns** area can also be developed using the facet names extra0, extra1, extra2, and so on.
iconColumn	Defines a column for the **Icon** area of the Data View. See the properties of the xe:viewIconColumn in Table 7.15 for more details. You can also develop the **Icon** area using the facet name icon.
multiColumnCount	Defines how many documents should be displayed on each row.
showCheckbox	Defines whether a check box should be added to each row to allow the user to select documents.
showHeaderCheckbox	Defines whether a check box should be added to the header row to allow the user to select all documents in the Data View.
showItemsFlat	Defines whether response documents should be shown in a hierarchy. It is the opposite of the **Show Response Documents in a Hierarchy** setting on a View design element.
summaryColumn	Defines a column for the **Summary** area of the Data View. See the properties of the xe:viewSummaryColumn in Table 7.14 for more details. The Summary area can also be developed using the facet name summary.
rowStyle	Defines styles for displaying the rows.
rowStyleClass	Defines classes for displaying the rows.

Pagers

The Data View control itself is a framework providing a layout with facets, or customizable areas of the control. Like the core view controls—the Data Table, the View Panel, and the Repeat control—the Data View control has a header and a footer area, each divided into three areas: one left-aligned, one center-aligned, and one right-aligned. These are nominally called **pagerTopLeft**, **pagerTop,** and **pagerTopRight** for the header and **pagerBottomLeft**, **pagerBottom,** and **pagerBottomRight** for the footer.

You'll see new areas for adding functionality. That's deliberate. The Extension Library also adds new pager controls to the core Pager control, which allows the user to move from one page to the next. These pager controls allow developers to quickly and easily implement view manipulation functionality that developers have until now had to code manually. Because the additional content is not initially passed to the browser, the new pager controls do a round-trip to the server for all events.

The **Pager Expand/Collapse** control (xe:pagerExpand) is appropriate for categorized content, providing the facility to expand and collapse the categories. This can be found on many of the views in the TeamRoom database, most notably the **All Documents** page in Figure 7.12, shown working when showing by date, by author, or by team. As with the core Pager control, for this and the other Pager controls added by the Extension Library, there are properties to determine partial refresh and the component to attach the Pager Expand/Collapse to, unless it is already within a View control. The default textual labels are "Expand All" and "Collapse All", but you can override these with the **expandText** and **collapseText** properties.

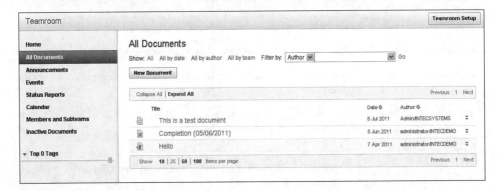

Figure 7.12 Pager controls 1.

Table 7.9 defines the main properties for the Pager Expand/Collapse control.

Table 7.9 xe:pagerExpand Properties

Property	Description
collapseText	Defines the label for collapsing all entries—by default, **Collapse All**
expandText	Defines the label for expanding all entries—by default, **Expand All**
for	Defines to which control the pager applies

Figure 7.13 shows the **Pager Show/Hide Details** (xe:pagerDetail) control in action on the Events page (the **eventView.xsp** Custom Control). If the Data View has a details row, this pager allows all details to be shown or hidden at a single click. For this control, the text, defaulting to **Show Details** and **Hide Details**, is managed by the **showText** and **hideText** properties.

Table 7.10 defines the main properties for the Pager Show/Hide Details control.

Table 7.10 xe:pagerDetail Properties

Property	Description
for	Defines to which control the pager applies
hideText	Defines the label for hiding entries—by default, **Hide Details**
showText	Defines the label for showing entries—by default, **Show Details**

The **Pager Sizes** (xe:pagerSizes) control allows the user to determine how many documents show per page, although the initial value is still controlled by the developer on the relevant view control. The **sizes** property allows the developer to define the options to allow the user to select from. A comboBox provides some options to select from. Any values can be entered, but non-numeric options are ignored. The **text** property enables the developer to define the text to appear. As with the Group Pager Child control, using {0} inserts the first parameter of the pager—in this case, the **sizes** property. So, the code in Listing 7.15 produces a pager saying Please select from 10 | 20 | 50. The Pager Sizes control is visible on most pages in the TeamRoom database, as Figure 7.13 shows.

Listing 7.15 Pager Sizes Control Code

```
<xe:pagerSizes
    id="pagerSizes1"
    sizes="10|20|50"
    text="Please select from {0}">
</xe:pagerSizes>
```

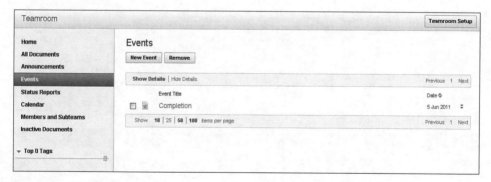

Figure 7.13 Pager controls 2.

Table 7.11 outlines the key properties for the Pager Sizes control.

Table 7.11   `xe:pagerSizes` Properties

Property	Description
for	Defines to which control the pager applies.
sizes	Defines the number of entries per page the user can show, delimited by |. Entries should be numbers or `all`.
text	Defines the label for the pager, including `{0}`, where the **sizes** property should be added.

Figure 7.14 shows the final pager control, the **Pager Add Rows** control (`xe:pager-AddRows`). This control can be found on the Home page of the TeamRoom application. Although the core Pager control replaces the current content with the next page of content, this control still shows the current page content while appending additional content. This control would usually be used instead of the core Pager. That control adds the same number of rows as currently displayed to the user, and the Pager Add Rows control adds the number of rows defined by the **rowCount** property of the Pager Add Rows control. As with the other pager controls, the developer can override the default text, this time using the **text** property. An additional property, the **store** property, is available for this control. It enables the developer to define whether the view's state in terms of the additional rows should be stored on the server. If the property is set to `false`, when the user returns to the view, it shows only the number of rows defined in the Data View control, not any additional rows the user has added.

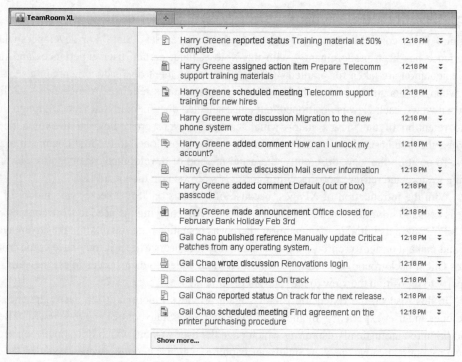

Figure 7.14   Pager controls 3.

Table 7.12 summarizes the main properties of the Pager Add Rows control.

Table 7.12   xe:pagerAddRows Properties

Property	Description
for	Defines to which control the pager applies.
refreshPage	Defines whether a partial/full refresh should be triggered when the user clicks on the link. If false, an AJAX request populates the rows.
rowCount	Defines the number of rows to be added each time the user clicks on the link.
state	Defines whether the state should be updated on the server to store the updated total number of rows displayed. If `false`, whenever the user returns to this page, the default number of rows is shown.
text	Defines the label for the pager.
disabledFormat	Defines how the pager should appear when the display contains all documents in the view.

PagerSaveState (`xe:pagerSaveState`) /View State Beans

One new Pager control has not yet been covered: the Pager Save State. For developers whose experience has been predominantly with the Notes Client, certain user experiences and their implementation are taken for granted. Because the Notes Client opens documents in a separate tab, when the document is closed, the view's original state is retained. Also, when switching between views, each view is positioned to the last selected document in that view, although there is no retention of the view's state—which categories were opened/closed to which depth. Because the web is stateless, by default a view is always positioned to the first document in that view. To position the view differently, the usual method of development has been to add more coding to store and retrieve cookies within the user's browser on the local PC.

With the introduction of XPages, because of its basis on JSF, a server-side model of the page is kept and `sessionScope` variables can be stored, removing the need to store cookies on a user's PC. But in its initial implementation, there was no native functionality to take advantage of this and make it easier to reproduce the functionality that users expect if they have come from a Notes Client background. So coding still needed to be added to datasources to set the **startKey** property to reposition the view to the relevant document.

In this respect, the Extension Library again provides functionality to easily enhance the developer and user experience, by means of the Pager Save State control and the viewStateBean. In addition to automatically capturing which page the user was on, which developers can reproduce programmatically, the viewStateBean captures which categories were expanded or collapsed, so the user can be returned to the view in that state.

Table 7.13 defines the properties for the Pager Save State control.

Table 7.13   `xe:pagerSaveState` Properties

Property	Description
for	Defines to which control the pager applies
globalRows	Defines whether the number of rows stored for the user should be all views or just the current view

The functionality is implemented in the TeamRoom database, as evidenced on the All Documents page. It comprises two parts: a Pager Save State control to manage storing the state of the view, and an additional SSJS call to tell the server to restore the view's state.

As Listing 7.16 shows, the first part is done on the XPage or Custom Control, which holds the viewpart of the code for the **allDocsAllTab.xsp** Custom Control in the TeamRoom. A Pager Save State control is added to the XPage or Custom Control in lines 1 through 5. The **for** property is set in line 2 to ID of the Data View or other repeating control for which the view's state should be saved. The **globalRows** property is used in line 3 to store the state globally across all views of the application. Otherwise, the view state is stored specifically for the view provided for the user.

The Data View or other repeating control also needs to be bound to the viewStateBean's data Iterator, as shown in line 10. Other than these additions, the Data View is created as normal.

Listing 7.16 Pager Save State and viewStateBean Binding

```
1   <xe:pagerSaveState
2       for="allDocumentsDataView"
3       globalRows="true"
4       id="pagerSaveState1">
5   </xe:pagerSaveState>
6   <xe:dataView
7       xp:key="tabAll"
8       id="allDocumentsDataView"
9       var="viewEntry"
10      binding="#{viewStateBean.dataIterator}"
11      collapsibleRows="true"
12      pageName="/topicThread.xsp"
13      collapsibleDetail="true"
14      columnTitles="true"
15      rowStyleClass="xspHtmlTrView"
16      rows="25"
17      detailsOnClient="true">
18      <xe:this.data>
19        <xp:dominoView var="view1" viewName="xvwDocsByActiveDate"
20  ...
```

The second part is done on the document when closing and returning to the relevant view. The **restoreState** property of the viewStateBean is set to true using SSJS, as shown in line 10 of Listing 7.17. Then when the view is opened, its state is restored, with the view positioned at the relevant row and any expanded or collapsed categories also restored.

Listing 7.17 Restoring the viewStateBean

```
1   <xp:link
2       id="backLink">
3       <xp:eventHandler
4           event="onclick"
5           submit="true"
6           refreshMode="complete"
7           immediate="false"
8           save="false">
```

Listing 7.17   (Continued)

```
9           <xp:this.action><![CDATA[#{javascript://
10 viewStateBean.restoreState = true;
11 return sessionScope.topicThreadPreviousXPage;
12 }]]></xp:this.action>
13    </xp:eventHandler>
14 </xp:link>
```

Columns

The pagers are added to the Data View control via the specific facets. You can add the columns in two ways. There are properties on the Data View control for **categoryColumn**, **extraColumns**, **iconColumn,** and **summaryColumn,** where you can enter various column properties. But you can manage the data for those areas via optional facets whose names are displayed in the visual representation of the Data View control, Figure 7.15. The **categoryColumn** and **extraColumns** areas can hold multiple facets, as previously detailed in Table 7.6. This is part of the flexibility of the Data View control: that it is effectively a rich content layout control that allows data or a datasource to be bound to it.

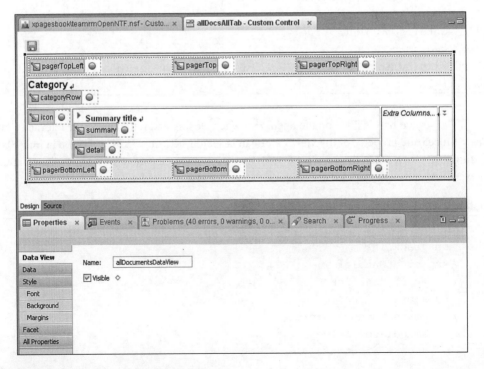

Figure 7.15   Data View control.

Adding content to a facet might be a process that XPages developers will be very familiar with. The various column components that can be added will be more unfamiliar. The following sections run through both methods of defining the column content.

Category Column (xe:viewCategoryColumn)

The outermost area of the data within the Data View is the Category area. Because the Data View control is basically just a layout control, so is the category row. This can be either values from a column in the underlying view or content placed into the categoryRow facet, as in the **home.xsp** XPage. For the Home page of the TeamRoom database, it is the date(s) of the view entries, as in Listing 7.18. You can see the output in Figure 7.16. Here the value shown is the date of the entry and, if it is today or yesterday, it is prefixed with the relevant string. Because this is using view-Entry, even though the content of the categoryRow facet is more than just a column from the view, the Data View will respect the categorization and put entries under the relevant category heading.

Listing 7.18   categoryRow Facet on home.xsp

```
<xp:span
    style="font-weight:bold">
    <xp:text
        disableTheme="true">
        <xp:this.value><![CDATA[#{javascript:var date =
@Date(viewEntry.getColumnValue("ActivityDate"));
if(@Today().equals(date)){
    return strings.getString("today") + "   ";
}
if(@Yesterday().equals(date)){
    return strings.getString("yesterday") + "   ";
}
return "";}]]></xp:this.value>
    </xp:text>
    <xp:text
        value="#{javascript:viewEntry.getColumnValue('ActivityDate')}"
        disableTheme="true"
        id="dateCategoryField"
        escape="true">
        <xp:this.converter>
            <xp:convertDateTime
                pattern="MMMM d, yyyy">
            </xp:convertDateTime>
        </xp:this.converter>
    </xp:text>
</xp:span>
```

Figure 7.16   home.xsp category row.

There is nothing stopping the facet from having content that bears no relationship to the data held by the Data View, in which case it appears just as a heading above the data.

The other method of applying content to the categoryRow facet is to use the **categoryColumn** property on the Data View to add a **viewCategoryColumn** component. Figure 7.17 shows all the properties available for the **viewCategoryColumn** component. Only one **viewCategoryColumn** can be added to the **categoryColumn** property, so it is not possible with the Data View to have multilevel categorization. The **viewCategoryColumn**, **viewSummaryColumn**, and **viewExtraColumn** components have the same properties. The most important category is the **columnName** property, which maps the column to a column in the underlying datasource. If the column value should be a link, the **href** property can determine the URL to redirect to. There are some properties for managing styling, the **contentType** can be set as HTML, and a converter can be applied to the result. The **columnTitle** property is not applicable to a **viewCategoryColumn** component.

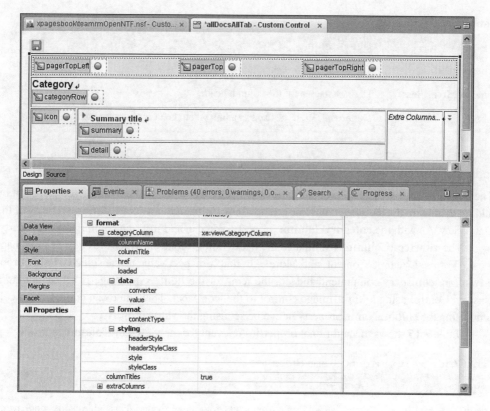

Figure 7.17   viewCategoryColumn properties.

The whole row (or rows if the category provides multiple values relating to the data in the Data View) can be made collapsible by setting the **collapsibleCategory** property on the Data View.

Table 7.14 summarizes the key properties for the viewCategoryColumn, viewSummary-Column, and viewExtraColumn controls.

Table 7.14   xe:viewCategoryColumn, xe:viewSummaryColumn, xe:viewExtraColumn
Properties

Property	Description
columnName	Defines the column from which to retrieve a value
columnTitle	Defines a title to display at the top of the column
contentType	Defines whether the column values should be treated as plain text or HTML
converter	Defines a converter to be used to convert the underlying data type to a String

Table 7.14 Continued

Property	Description
headerStyle	Defines styles for the column header
headerStyleClass	Defines classes for the column header
href	Defines a URL to be used as a link when the user clicks on the column value

Icon Column (`xe:viewIconColumn`)

The icon area appears as the first column for each entry. As with the other areas, you can set it by adding content to the **icon** facet or adding a **viewIconColumn** to the **iconColumn** property of the Data View. As with the **categoryColumn** property, you can add just one column to the property.

The **viewIconColumn** is similar to the **Multi-image** control, which was covered in Chapter 4, "Forms, Dynamic Content, and More!," in that it maps a value to the **selectedValue** property of an **iconEntry** component. Indeed, the icon for the **home.xsp** XPage is set by adding a Custom Control using a Multi-Image control to the icon facet. That value can come from a column using the **columnName** property or can be set using the **value** property.

Table 7.15 shows the additional properties relevant for the **viewIconColumn** control.

Table 7.15 `xe:viewIconColumn` Properties

Property	Description
columnName	Defines the column from which to retrieve a value. This column does not have to contain an icon.
icons	Defines a list of icons that might appear, depending on the column value.

Summary Column and Extra Columns (`xe:viewSummaryColumn` and `xe:viewExtraColumn`)

The next column shown, in a more prominent format than the other columns, is set by adding a **viewSummaryColumn** to the **summaryColumn** property or adding content to the **summary** facet on the Data View. Again, only one **viewSummaryColumn** can be added. Therefore, if additional content is required, the summary facet might be preferable, as on the **home.xsp** XPage. All the properties for the **viewSummaryColumn** are the same as for the **viewCategoryColumn**.

You cannot define the subsequent columns using a facet. You must use the **extraColumns** property on the Data View. This can take one or more **viewExtraColumn** components, which again have the same properties as the **viewCategoryColumn**.

Column titles for the summary column and extra columns show only if the **columnTitles** property is `true`. If column titles show, any columns in the underlying View design element that are sortable are also sortable in the Data View without additional properties being set.

Detail

So far, the Data View shows only a single row per entry. But the Data View provides functionality to add additional detail, appearing below the summary column. You cannot manage the content for the detail using columns; only the **detail** facet allows you to manage the content. This allows great flexibility in building the look and feel of the detail area.

Some additional properties on the Data View affect how the detail shows. The **collapsibleDetail** property handles whether the detail can be expanded or collapsed. The **expandedDetail** determines whether the detail row is expanded by default. You can ensure that detail shows by setting **collapsibleDetail** to `false` and setting **expandedDetail** to `true`, but it's easier to set **disableHideRow** to `true`. Setting **disableHideRow** forces the detail to show and prevents the detail from being hidden. As with almost any other property of an XPage, the setting can be computed as well as hard-coded to `true` or `false`.

One more property is applicable only for the Notes Client. For the browser, the detail content is only passed to the browser if it should be visible, to maximize performance of initial page load. You can set the **detailsOnClient** property to ensure detail is passed to the XULRunner within the Notes Client when the page is first loaded to prevent an additional call to the server when showing and hiding detail. This is because server connection speeds are predominantly better for XPiNC, whereas calls to the server currently take longer than they do from a browser.

Multiple Columns

As if the flexibility so far seen for the Data View control was not enough, there is more, as shown in the **Members** area in the **membersMembersTileView.xsp** Custom Control, shown in Figure 7.18. On initial viewing, this looks quite different from the Data View. But this has the **showCheckbox** property set to `true` and has a summary column—details that always show.

The only real difference in implementation is that the **multiColumnCount** property of the Data View control is set to `2`. This means that the whole Data View is shown tiled with two entries per row. If the content will not take up much space in the width of the screen, such as in a business card format, developers can maximize the screen real estate available with greater ease of development.

Figure 7.18   Members Tile View.

Forum View

The Forum View is similar to the Data View, but the Forum View does not include the **category-Row**, **icon**, and **extraColumn** areas. Instead, the **Data** area includes just the **Summary** and **Detail** areas. Other than this, all the properties and implementation are the same as the Data View control.

The Forum View control is found in the TeamRoom database on the **topicThread.xsp** XPage in the **topicThreadForum.xsp** Custom Control. Figure 7.19 is a screenshot of that XPage, demonstrating how it can show threads and allow the user to expand and collapse the content as required. This again showcases the flexibility of the Data View and Forum View controls, in that the Custom Control displayed in the Forum View—**topicPost.xsp**—is the same one used to show the main topic above the Forum View.

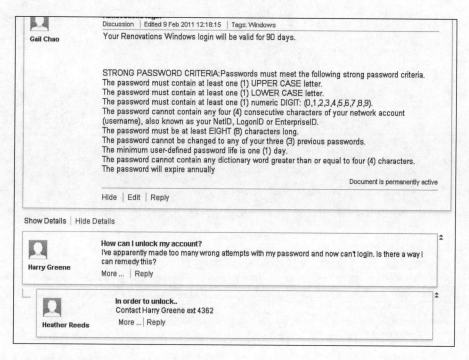

Figure 7.19   Forum View in topic thread.

Conclusion

The preceding chapters have covered displaying content for editing and viewing an individual document. The Extension Library provides a wealth of new view components from controls that reproduce Notes Client styling, enable developers to easily take advantage of the Dojo Data Grid, reproduce iNotes functionality, and add flexible layouts.

CHAPTER 8

Outlines and Navigation

Chapter 7, "Views," covered how to display the data in your applications using one of the new view controls in the XPages Extension Library. For the end user to be able to switch between the different views in the application, the developer needs to create an application layout and navigation. This chapter covers both the Dojo layout controls and the navigation controls that have been added to the XPages Extension Library.

The Dojo Layout Controls

As covered in Chapter 3, "TeamRoom Template Tour," the XPages-based TeamRoom application uses a special control in the XPages Extension Library for its application layout. This control is described in full detail in Chapter 9, "The Application's Layout." Developers, however, do not have to use this control in their XPages design, especially if they won't be using the OneUI look and feel for their application. To allow developers full control over their application layout, the XPages Extension Library provides several Dojo layout controls that can be used instead.

Neither the XPages TeamRoom application nor the XPages Extension Library Demonstration application uses these Dojo layout controls; however, another Open Source application on OpenNTF called XPages Help Application does. You can download the application from http://xhelp.openntf.org. It makes a great learning resource for developers who want to use the Dojo layout controls in their own applications.

The Content Pane

The basis of any Dojo layout is the Dojo Content Pane (`xe:djContentPane`). Although there are specific controls—the Border Pane control (`xe:djBorderPane`) for the Border Container control (`xe:djBorderContainer`), the Tab Pane control (`xe:djTabPane`) for the Tab Container control (`xe:djTabContainer`), the Stack Pane for the Stack Container (`xe:djStackPane`), and the Accordion Pane (`xe:djAccordionPane`) for the Accordion Container (xe:djAccordionContainer)—all of these are analogous to the Content Pane control. In fact, another implementation of the Content Pane control was already covered in Chapter 6, "Pop-Ups: Tooltips, Dialogs, and Pickers." There are additional properties for some of the other pane controls, but they are only extensions to the Content Pane.

The Content Pane, as its name suggests, is just an area to contain content, similar to a div or a panel. The benefit is that there are performance-related properties to allow flexible loading of data. Figure 8.1 shows content panes loaded through partial refresh. Whereas the rest of the content on the page is loaded along with the XPage, the two content panes with the **partialRefresh** property set to `true` are loaded via AJAX calls. This means the content is loaded after the rest of the page and, potentially in the scenario of a Tab Pane or Accordion Pane, only as and when the user can see the pane. This can be useful with complex pages across a connection suffering from latency issues.

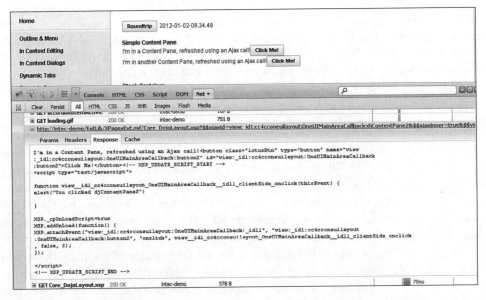

Figure 8.1   Content Pane from XPages Extension Library Demo database, loaded via partial refresh.

The other performance-related properties—**parseOnLoad**, **preload**, **preventCache**, and **refreshOnShow**—also start to become more appropriate and more powerful. Table 8.1 lists the notable properties for the Content Pane control.

Table 8.1 `xe:djContentPane` Properties

Property	Description
errorMessage	Defines an error message to display if the contents of the pane cannot be loaded
extractContent	Defines whether the pane should only display whatever is between the BODY tags if the contents are loaded using the **href** property
href	Can define a URL from which to load the contents of the pane
loadingMessage	Defines a message to display to the user while the contents of the pane are being loaded
partialRefresh	Defines whether the contents of the pane are loaded inline with the rest of the page or separately via an AJAX call
preload	Defines whether the contents of the pane are loaded even if it is not visible
preventCache	Can ensure that AJAX calls to load the contents are not cached
refreshOnShow	Defines whether the contents should be reloaded each time the pane goes from a hidden to a visible state
onContentError	Can run Client-Side JavaScript when an error occurs in the content of the dialog
onDownloadEnd	Can run Client-Side JavaScript after the URL in the **href** property has been loaded
onDownloadError	Can run Client-Side JavaScript if the URL in the **href** property cannot be loaded
onDownloadStart	Can run Client-Side JavaScript before the URL in the **href** property is loaded
onHide	Can run Client-Side JavaScript each time the pane is closed
onShow	Can run Client-Side JavaScript each time the pane is displayed

The Border Container and Border Pane

The Border Container (`xe:djBorderContainer`) provides a clean, simple, but flexible layout for the whole application, as shown in Figure 8.2. The layout comprises panes for content within specific regions of the page. As with many of the other Dojo controls, the Border Container supports keyboard events. The Tab key cycles through the splitters. You can change the size of the pane by using the cursor keys: left / right for a vertical pane, and up / down for a horizontal pane.

The main control is the Border Container control. The key setting for the Border Container is to set a **height** via Cascading Style Sheets (CSS) in either the **style** or **styleClass** properties. The **width** setting is optional. But if no height is set, the Border Container is not displayed.

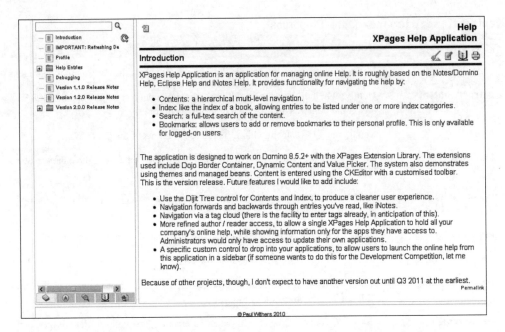

Figure 8.2   Border Container in the XPages Help Application from OpenNTF.

The Border Container can comprise up to five **Border Pane** controls. The order in which the panes appear in the source is irrelevant. It is the **region** property on each Border Pane that defines where in the Border Container each pane appears. The five options are displayed in Figure 8.3, although not all five have to be used (see Figure 8.2). In combination with the panes, the **Design** property on the Border Container handles how the panes are laid out. Figure 8.2 uses the default design option, `headline`, where the top and bottom panes extend the whole width of the Border Container. The other option is `sidebar`, where the right and left panes extend the whole height of the Border Container.

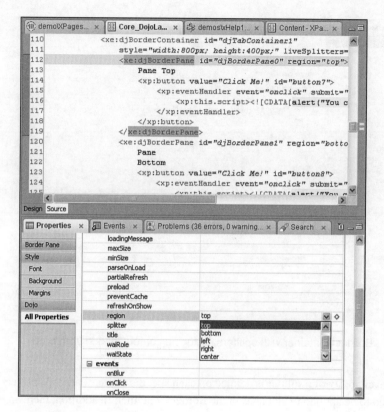

Figure 8.3 Border Pane region property.

The other piece of functionality relating to the panes is splitters. Panes are, by default, fixed to a specific height or width, either handled automatically by the Border Container or overridden by CSS. However, when you define splitters, users are permitted to change the height or width of the panes, as shown in Figure 8.4.

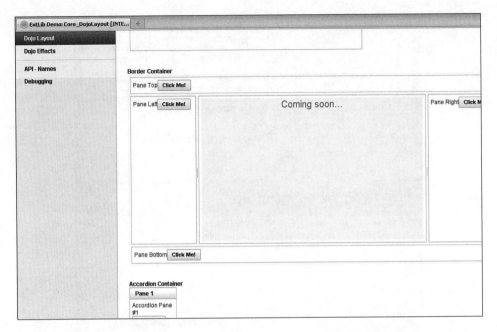

Figure 8.4   Border Container with splitters, including content loaded from href.

The availability of a splitter is defined on each specific Border Pane, so splitters do not necessarily need to be applied to all panes in the Border Container. In addition, there are two properties on the Border Container to control the behavior of the splitters. The **liveSplitters** property controls whether the panes are dynamically resized as the user drags the splitter or on the onmouseup event. The other property is **persist**. By default, this property is set to `false`; when the page is refreshed, the panes revert to their default height and width. If set to `true`, the resized height and width are stored in cookies in the user's browser, so a page refresh renders the Border Container with the preferred height and width of each pane, as changed by the user. These and other prominent properties are detailed in Table 8.2.

Table 8.2   `xe:djBorderContainer` Properties

Property	Description
design	Defines the layout of the Border Container. If `headline`, the top and bottom panes span the full width of the container. If `sidebar`, the left and right panes span the full height of the container.
gutters	Defines whether the panes should have a border and margin.
liveSplitters	Specifies whether panes resize as the splitter is dragged or only when dropped.
persist	Defines whether pane sizes are stored in cookies.
height	Must be specified via CSS, or the Border Container does not show.

Even with splitters enabled, the developer can maintain some control of the content display by setting the **minSize** and **maxSize** properties of a specific Border Pane. These properties take a numeric value controlling the height for top or bottom panes and controlling the width for others. However, the **minSize** and **maxSize** properties only take effect when the user tries to resize the pane, so the height or width of the pane should always be set by default as well.

The content of the Border Pane does not necessarily have to be coded on the XPage. With the Border Pane, unlike the normal Content Pane, you can load the content from an external URL in the same trusted domain, using the **href** property. This can be useful, for example, with a header stored centrally or for content from an existing web application. Figure 8.4 shows **soon.xsp** loaded into the central pane of the Border Container. However, if you're loading an XPage using the **href** property, you should set the **extractContent** property to `true` to avoid issues caused by the HTML headers from both pages.

When you load external content into a Border Pane control, additional properties are relevant. You can use the **loadingMessage** and **errorMessage** properties to customize the messages displayed to the user. Three additional Client-Side JavaScript events are available: **onDownloadStart**, **onDownloadEnd,** and **onDownloadError**. These are triggered before the relevant URL is loaded, after it's loaded, and if there's an error.

Table 8.3 details more properties of the Border Pane that help with the appearance and sizing of the pane. These properties extend those of the Content Pane; see Table 8.1.

Table 8.3 `xe:djBorderPane` Properties

Property	Description
maxSize	Defines the maximum size for the pane, in pixels
minSize	Defines the minimum size for the pane, in pixels
splitter	Defines whether splitters appear on the edge of the pane, to allow users to resize the pane
layoutPriority	Defines how close to the center the pane should appear
region	Defines where the pane should appear in relation to the Border Container

Accordion Container and Accordion Pane

The Border Container gives a framework for laying out content. Within that framework, navigation can be managed by using the **Accordion Container**. The Accordion Container is a vertical container of content panes, one of which shows at any one time, as in Figure 8.5. Clicking on the title for a pane expands that pane. You can also use keyboard shortcuts. The cursor keys navigate through the panes. Right (→) or down (↓) navigates one way, and left (←) or up (↑) navigates the other. The Tab key then navigates into the content.

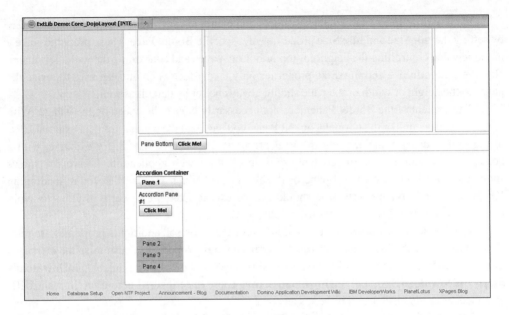

Figure 8.5   Accordion Container.

As with the Border Container, the Accordion Container needs to have a height specified, or it will not show. There are only two additional properties for the Accordion Container. The **selectedTab** property defines which pane is expanded. The value is the ID of the Accordion Pane control that should be expanded. The other property of note is **duration**, which defines the number of milliseconds for the transition between one pane and the other. Other properties used for the Accordion Container are detailed in Table 8.4.

Table 8.4   `xe:djAccordionContainer` Properties

Property	Description
duration	Defines the number of milliseconds for transitioning between panes
selectedTab	Defines the ID of the pane that has focus
height	Height must be specified via CSS, or the Accordion Container does not show

The Accordion Container comprises multiple **Accordion Pane** controls—multiple, because what would be the point in having just one pane? There are no additional properties provided over the Content Pane, but the **title** property defines the label for the pane. As with the Content Pane, the Accordion Pane can be built up from any other controls, or it can use the **href** property to load its content from an external source from the same trusted domain. You can use this to load an XPage containing navigation from another application.

The Tab Container and the Tab Pane

The Tab Container is the Dojo equivalent of the core Tabbed Panel that has been familiar to XPages developers since Release 8.5.0. However, there is one significant difference: Only the first tab is loaded initially. Clicking on the second tab makes an AJAX call to load the additional content, as Figure 8.6 shows. Similar to the other Dojo controls, the Tab Container supports keyboard shortcuts at the basic level using cursor keys to move between tabs. Tab Containers can be nested within one another, giving a flexibility of layout. Also, similar to the other Dojo container controls, the height must be specified for the Tab Container to display as expected.

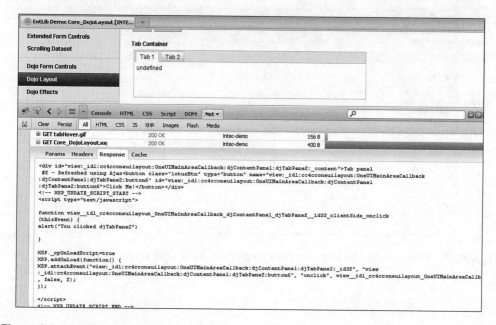

Figure 8.6   AJAX call for Tab Pane content.

The Tab Container has numerous properties for managing its look and feel and behavior. The **doLayout** property overrides the default height set for the Tab Container, expanding and collapsing the height of the Tab Container depending on the contents of the selected tab. You can position tabs on any side of the container by using the **tabPosition** property. The default setting is `top`, but Figure 8.7 shows the other options. You can use the **tabStrip** property, `false` by default, to add a background behind the tabs.

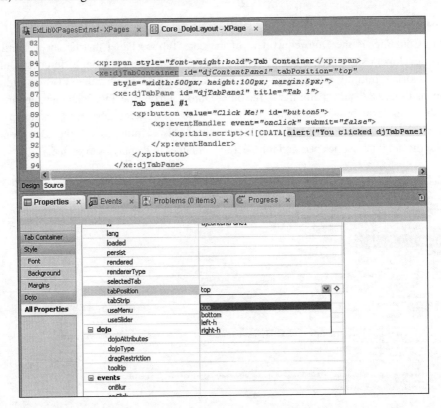

Figure 8.7   Tab Container tabPosition, tabStrip property, and other properties.

As Figure 8.8 shows, `tabStrip="true"` adds a class to the main div called **dijitTabContainerTopStrip**, which you can use to manipulate the styling.

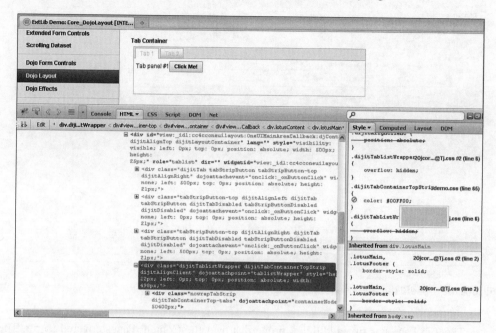

Figure 8.8 tabStrip property as `true`.

If there are too many tabs to fit into the space, you can add slider buttons at either end of the Tab Container to scroll through the tabs, and add a menu to select tabs, as Figure 8.9 shows. The **useSlider** and **useMenu** options, defaulting to `true`, control these settings. Just like the Tabbed Panel, the **selectedTab** property enables you to define the initial tab by referencing the ID of the relevant tab, such as `djTabPanel`. However, unlike the Tabbed Panel, the **persist** property allows the currently selected tab to be stored in a cookie so it can persist across sessions.

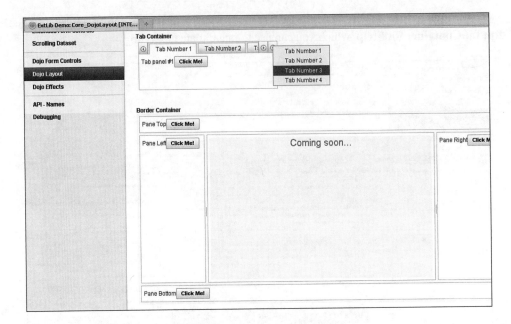

Figure 8.9   useSlider and useMenu.

The Tab Pane has two additional properties over the Content Panes covered so far. The **tabUniqueKey** property allows a unique key to be assigned to each tab, used when programmatically selecting the tab. The **closable** property, defaulting to `false`, determines whether you can delete the tab (see Figure 8.10).

You can also use the Tab Container to create dynamic tabs by taking advantage of its methods. As with many of the other methods of the Dojo Extension Library controls, you can do this via Client-Side JavaScript or Server-Side JavaScript (SSJS). Line 3 of Listing 8.1 shows the Client-Side JavaScript method `createTab()`. In SSJS, the same method exists, but there is an additional method, `createTab(Map<String,String>)`, to create a tab passing parameters, such as the tabUniqueKey and title properties of the Tab Pane, as shown on line 8 of Listing 8.1.

Listing 8.1   `createTab` Methods

```
1   <xp:button
2      value="New Contact - Client Side"
3      id="button4">
4      <xp:eventHandler event="onclick" submit="false">
5         <xp:this.script>
<![CDATA[dijit.byId('#{id:djTabContainer1}').createTab()]]>
</xp:this.script>
6      </xp:eventHandler>
```

```
7  </xp:button>
8  <xp:button
9     value="New Contact - Server Side"
10    id="button6">
11    <xp:eventHandler
12       event="onclick"
13       submit="true"
14       refreshMode="partial"
15       refreshId="tabs">
16       <xp:this.action><![CDATA[#{javascript:
getComponent("djTabContainer1").createTab({tabUniqueKey:@Unique(),
tabTitle:"New Tab"})}]]></xp:this.action>
17    </xp:eventHandler>
18 </xp:button>
```

Figure 8.10 shows the output when the Server-Side and Client-Side buttons are clicked. Note specifically the tab titles.

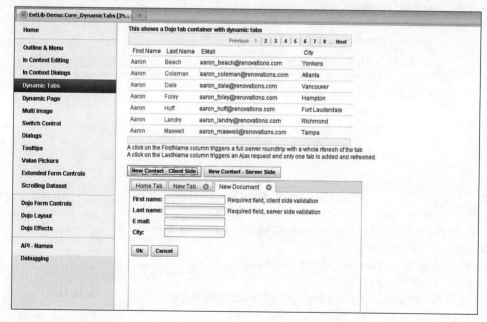

Figure 8.10   New tabs.

Buttons are available to create the tabs. The content of the tabs is handled through the **default-TabContent** property of the Tab Container, which contains a variable name relating to a facet key (see Listing 8.2). Line 5 shows the **defaultTabContent** property set to doc. Line 6 creates a facet, and Lines 7 onward show the start of the code for the TabPane template that should be used to create the new tab. Note that some default property settings are defined, such as closable and title, but you can override these either in a postOpenDocument setting or in the SSJS createTab(Map<String,String>) method. The tab created with Client-Side JavaScript in Figure 8.10 has the default title "New Document," whereas the tab created in SSJS has the "New Tab" title passed through the method.

Listing 8.2   defaultTabContent

```
1   <xe:djTabContainer
2       id="djTabContainer1"
3       tabPosition="top"
4       style="width:500px; height:300px; margin:5px;"
5       defaultTabContent="doc">
6       <xp:this.facets>
7           <xe:djTabPane
8               xp:key="doc"
9               id="djTabPane2"
10              title="New Document"
11              closable="true"
12              partialEvents="true">
13              <xp:panel>
14                  <xp:this.data>
15                      <xp:dominoDocument
16                          var="document1"
17                          formName="Contact">
18                          <xp:this.postOpenDocument> <![CDATA[#{javascript:var
fn = document1.getItemValueString("FirstName")
19 var ln = document1.getItemValueString("LastName")
20 var title = fn + " " + ln
21 var pane = getComponent("djTabPane2")
22 pane.setTitle(title)
23 pane.setTabUniqueKey(document1.getNoteID())
24 }]]></xp:this.postOpenDocument>
25                      </xp:dominoDocument>
26                  </xp:this.data>
27                  <xp:table>
28                      <xp:tr>
```

```
29                            <xp:td>
30                               <xp:label
31                                  value="First name:"
32                                  id="firstName_Label1"
33                                  for="firstName1">
34                               </xp:label>
35                            </xp:td>
36                            <xp:td>
37                               <xp:inputText
38                                  value="#{document1.FirstName}"
     id="firstName1"
39                                  required="true">
40                               </xp:inputText>
41                            </xp:td>
```

Two other methods are worthy of mention. Just like the Dojo method for creating a tab in Client-Side JavaScript, there is another method for switching to a tab, namely `selectChild()`, taking the Client-Side ID of the tab to open. SSJS provides a similar method, `setSelectedTab()`, taking the ID of the tab to open.

Table 8.5 details more properties of the Dojo Tab Container.

Table 8.5   `xe:djTabContainer` Properties

Property	Description
defaultTabContent	Defines a facet ID that contains default content to display when creating a new tab.
doLayout	Defines whether the size of the currently displayed tab should be changed to match the size of the Tab Container.
persist	Defines whether the selected tab is stored in a cookie.
selectedTab	Defines the ID of the pane that has focus.
tabPosition	Defines where the tabs appear in relation to the tab panes.
tabStrip	Defines whether a tab strip should appear behind the tabs.
useMenu	Defines whether menus should be available to allow tab selection. The menu is shown only if the tabs exceed the width of the Tab Container.
useSlider	Defines whether buttons should be available to move to adjacent tabs. The buttons are shown only if the tabs exceed the width of the Tab Container.
height	Must be specified via CSS, or the Accordion Container does not show.

The Stack Container and the Stack Pane

The Stack Container is similar to the Tab Container, except that only one Content Pane is shown at any one time. There are no new properties over the Tab Container, so all the properties in Table 8.5 are relevant for the Stack Container. Indeed, the Tab Container Java class, `UIDojoTabContainer`, actually extends the Stack Container Java class, `UIDojoStack-Container`. Like the Tab Container, the **selectedTab** and **persist** properties can be defined to handle Stack Pane behavior. However, unlike the other containers, it's not necessary to define a height on the Stack Container. If it is defined, that height is used across all Stack Panes.

The Stack Pane control works the same as the basic Content Pane, and indeed it adds no additional properties to the Content Pane class. As a summary, Figure 8.11 shows the hierarchy of the various Layout Containers, and Figure 8.12 shows the hierarchy of the various Content Panes, including their Java classes.

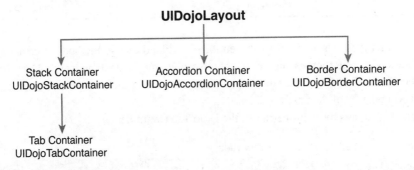

Figure 8.11   Layout Container hierarchy.

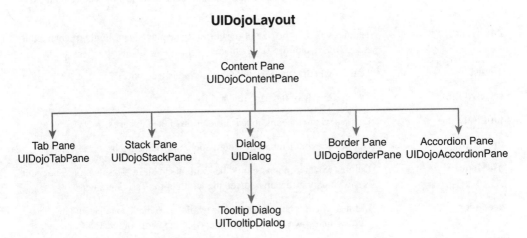

Figure 8.12   Content Pane hierarchy.

Understanding the Tree Node Concept

Also included in the XPages Extension Library are controls that give the developer further navigation techniques. Most of these controls are designed for use within the Application Layout control described in the next chapter, but they can also be used within an application to provide navigation for the end user. These controls allow the developer to provide breadcrumbs, pop-up menus, toolbars, generic outlines, lists of links, and tag clouds. Apart from the tag cloud, each of these controls uses a concept of tree nodes to define contents of the control. Listing 8.3 shows a basic navigator control with three basicLeafNode children.

Listing 8.3   Basic Navigator Control with Nodes

```
<xe:navigator
  id="navigator1">
  <xe:this.treeNodes>
    <xe:basicLeafNode
      onClick="option1"
      label="This is option 1" />
    <xe:basicLeafNode
      onClick="option2"
      label="This is option 2" />
    <xe:basicLeafNode
      onClick="option3"
      label="This is option 3" />
  </xe:this.treeNodes>
</xe:navigator>
```

Before developers can implement any of the navigation controls in the XPages Extension Library, they should understand the different tree nodes they can use within the controls. There are basic node types in which the developer can define the functionality of the node, and there are advanced node types in which the data for the node can come from Domino view resources and Java Beans.

Standard Node Types

The basicLeafNode (xe:basicLeafNode)

The basicLeafNode, as shown in Listing 8.4, is the standard node that all other tree nodes are modeled upon. With the exception of the separatorTreeNode, described later in this chapter, all the other tree nodes, both basic and advanced, contain the same general properties as the basicLeafNode.

Listing 8.4   Simple basicLeafNode Examples

```
<xe:basicLeafNode
  label="Home"
  selected="true"
  href="/">
</xe:basicLeafNode>
...
<xe:basicLeafNode
  style="color:rgb(128,128,128)">
  <xe:this.label><![CDATA[#{javascript:var v =
com.ibm.xsp.extlib.util.ExtLibUtil.getExtLibVersion();
return "XPages ExtLib version: "+v}]]></xe:this.label>
</xe:basicLeafNode>
...
<xe:basicLeafNode
  label="Go to Mobile App"
  href="http://myServer/home.nsf/mobileApp.xsp">
</xe:basicLeafNode>
```

As with most of the standard XPages controls, the basicLeafNode contains both **loaded** and **rendered** properties. The developer can compute these properties to determine if the node should be loaded or shown to the end user.

To manage the look and feel of the node, the developer can set the CSS or style class of the node using the **style** and **styleClass** properties. The text that is rendered to the web browser is set with the **label** property, and the developer can specify an image using the **image, imageAlt, imageHeight**, and **imageWidth** properties if required. The **selected** property is a Boolean value. If it is set or computed to `true`, an additional CSS style class of `lotusSelected` is added to the node when it is rendered to the web browser.

The developer has different options to determine what happens when a node is clicked in the web browser. The **href** property renders the node as a standard link to the specified URL. This could be a URL within the application or a link to a different application or website. The **onClick** property allows the developer to execute a piece of Client-Side JavaScript code, and the **submitValue** property allows the developer to specify a value that is passed back to the server. This value is accessed from the **onItemClick** event of the control that contains the tree nodes and is described in more detail later in this chapter.

The basicContainerNode (`xe:basicContainerNode`)

As its name suggests, the basicContainerNode, as demonstrated in Listing 8.5, is a container; as such, it can have its own subset of child nodes. It's like a branch on a tree that can contain its own leaves and branches. In addition to all the properties that can be found on the basicLeafNode, the **basicContainerNode** has two more properties called **children** and **transparent**.

Listing 8.5   A basicContainerNode Example

```
<xe:basicContainerNode
  label="More Actions">
  <xe:this.children>
    <xe:pageTreeNode
      page="Core_Home"
      label="Goto Home">
    </xe:pageTreeNode>
    <xe:pageTreeNode
      page="Domino_Home"
      label="Goto Domino">
    </xe:pageTreeNode>
    <xe:separatorTreeNode></xe:separatorTreeNode>
    <xe:basicContainerNode
      label="Server side redirect">
      <xe:this.children>
        <xe:basicLeafNode
          label="Goto Home"
          submitValue="home">
        </xe:basicLeafNode>
        <xe:basicLeafNode
          label="Goto Domino"
          submitValue="domino">
        </xe:basicLeafNode>
      </xe:this.children>
    </xe:basicContainerNode>
  </xe:this.children>
</xe:basicContainerNode>
```

The **children** property is where developers can add in any number of other nodes in the same way that they would add nodes directly to the treeNode root. Any of the treeNode types can be added to the children node of a basicContainerNode, and multiple levels can be achieved by adding basicContainerNode entries that can in turn contain other nodes and container nodes.

The **transparent** property is a Boolean value that defaults to `false`. When it is set or computed to `true`, the container node is not rendered as part of the tree; however, the child nodes still render. One suggested use for this is allowing the developer to create a single tree that contains two sets of nodes and then using the **loaded** or **rendered** properties to display only one set of child nodes to the end user rather than have to use the **loaded** or **rendered** properties on each of the leaf nodes.

The separatorTreeNode (xe:separatorTreeNode)

The separatorTreeNode is used when it's necessary to add a visual separator to the tree. This is the most basic of all the tree node types and only contains, in addition to the standard styling properties, a **loaded** and **rendered** property that allows the developer to define if and when to display this node.

The loginTreeNode (xe:loginTreeNode)

The loginTreeNode in its most basic form when there are no properties set automatically produces a tree node that contains a link to log the user into the database using the standard *?open-database&login* URL format.

If the Domino server is configured for session-based login, this control will not be rendered if the user is already authenticated. It has been discovered that this functionality does not work so these lines should be removed to avoid confusion.

The userTreeNode (xe:userTreeNode)

Normally used in conjunction with the loginTreeNode, the userTreeNode simplifies the display of the currently logged in user. In its simplest form, when added to the page with no properties set, it either displays Anonymous if there is no logged in user, or displays the user's common name if the user is authenticated with the server. If the **label** property is set or to be used, the developer needs to compute what is displayed in both cases.

You can use the **userField** property here to display the user data. This property is usually left blank, so by default it displays the displayName value from the data provider. For Domino, the user's abbreviatedName, commonName, canonicalName, and so on can be used, as shown in Listing 8.6.

Listing 8.6   A userTreeNode Example

```
<xe:userTreeNode
    userField="abbreviatedName"
    style="font-weight:bold">
</xe:userTreeNode>
```

The Advanced Node Types

The pageTreeNode (xe:pageTreeNode)

The pageTreeNode gives the developer an easy way to link to another page within the application. In addition to the properties found on the basicLeafNode, the pageTreeNode provides three extra properties.

The **page** property is a drop-down list of all the XPages within the application. The developer can select a page from the list or compute the page if desired. This property replaces the **href** property in the basicLeafNode. In addition to the **page** property, there is a **queryString** property. When a developer uses this property, the text specified here is added to the page selected in the **page** property.

The last of the additional properties in the pageTreeNode is the **selection** property, as demonstrated in Listing 8.7. It is used in conjunction with the **navigationPath** property in the application-Layout control described in the next chapter. If the **selection** property matches the **navigationPath** property, the `lotusSelected` CSS class is automatically added to the node when it is rendered to the web browser. The XPages Extension Library Demo Application uses this control extensively, and the markup in Listing 8.7 is from this application. Figure 8.13 displays this example, rendered as tabs above the placebar for Core, Domino, iNotes, Mobile, and REST.

Listing 8.7   A pageTreeNode Example with the Selection Property

```
<xe:this.titleBarTabs>
  <xe:pageTreeNode
    page="Core_Home"
    selection="/Core/.*"
    label="Core">
  </xe:pageTreeNode>
  <xe:pageTreeNode
    page="Domino_Home"
    selection="/Domino/.*"
    label="Domino">
  </xe:pageTreeNode>
  <xe:pageTreeNode
    page="DWA_Home"
    selection="/DWA/.*"
    label="iNotes">
  </xe:pageTreeNode>
  <xe:pageTreeNode
    loaded="false"
    page="iWidget_Home"
    selection="/iWidget/.*"
    label="iWidget">
  </xe:pageTreeNode>
  <xe:pageTreeNode
    page="Mobile_Home"
    selection="/Mobile/.*"
    label="Mobile">
```

Listing 8.7   (Continued)

```
    </xe:pageTreeNode>
    <xe:pageTreeNode
      page="OneUI_Home"
      selection="/OneUI/.*"
      label="OneUI">
    </xe:pageTreeNode>
    <xe:pageTreeNode
      page="REST_Home"
      selection="/REST/.*"
      label="REST">
    </xe:pageTreeNode>
  </xe:this.titleBarTabs>
```

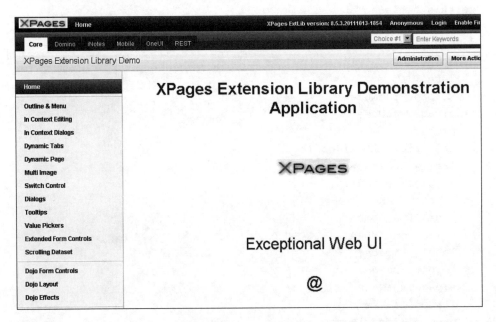

Figure 8.13   The selection property in action on the Demo application.

If you are not using the **selection** property but the current page matches the page listed in the **page** property, the lotusSelected CSS class is added to the node when it is rendered in the web browser. In this particular case, the **queryString** property is not considered. This may mean that if you have multiple pageTreeNode entries that point to the same page but have different **queryString** values, all the entries may show as being selected.

This control is used extensively throughout the Xpages Extension Library Demo application to manage and control the application's navigation.

The repeatTreeNode (xe:repeatTreeNode)

The repeatTreeNode is a cross between a core XPages repeat control and a basicContainerNode. Just like a standard repeat control, you set up a value for it to repeat in the **value** property. This could be a datasource attached to the XPage or just a simple JavaScript array. The values of the repeat are accessed using the variable name supplied in the **var** property. The current repeat index value is accessed in the variable name supplied in the **indexVar** property.

The items that are repeated are specified in the **children** property. Just like the basicContainerNode, this property can contain one or more tree nodes and can even contain other basicContainerNode or repeatTreeNode entries, as shown in Listing 8.8.

Unlike the basicContainerNode, however, the repeatTreeNode does not render its own entry in the tree, and the **children** are rendered at the same level as the repeatTreeNode.

Listing 8.8   A repeatTreeNode Example

```
<xe:repeatTreeNode
  var="val">
  <xe:this.children>
    <xe:basicLeafNode>
      <xe:this.submitValue><![CDATA[#{javascript:return
val[1]}]]></xe:this.submitValue>
      <xe:this.label><![CDATA[#{javascript:return
val[0]}]]></xe:this.label>
    </xe:basicLeafNode>
  </xe:this.children>
  <xe:this.value><![CDATA[#{javascript:return [
  ["Home","home"],
  ["Domino","domino"],
  ["OneUI","oneui"]
  ];}]]>
  </xe:this.value>
</xe:repeatTreeNode>
```

The beanTreeNode (xe:beanTreeNode)

The beanTreeNode contains only two properties: a **loaded** property that can specify whether the beanTreeNode should be loaded, and a **nodeBean** property that specifies which bean you should use to provide the tree items.

A **nodeBean** is a Java class bean that implements components of the ITreeNode interface. Listing 8.9 shows a basic **nodeBean** from the XPages Extension Library demo application. This bean creates three basicLeafNode entries. You can find more information on creating beans in Java in Chapter 14, "Java Development in XPages."

Listing 8.9   Sample nodeBean

```
package extlib.tree;
import com.ibm.xsp.extlib.tree.impl.BasicLeafTreeNode;
import com.ibm.xsp.extlib.tree.impl.BasicNodeList;
public class SimpleTreeNode extends BasicNodeList {
private static final long serialVersionUID = 1L;
public SimpleTreeNode() {
addLeaf("Node 1");
addLeaf("Node 2");
addLeaf("Node 3");
}

private void addLeaf(String label) {
BasicLeafTreeNode node = new
BasicLeafTreeNode();
node.setLabel(label);
addChild(node);
}
}
```

The dominoViewListTreeNode (xe:dominoViewListTreeNode)

The dominoViewListTreeNode creates a list of nodes based on the views and folders within an application. Additional properties are available for this node type, the first being the **database-Name** property. When it is blank, the database this node type uses is the current database; otherwise, it uses the database that you have specified. If you do specify an external database, the end user must have access to it via the Access Control List (ACL). Without access, an error occurs.

Similar to the repeatTreeNode is a **var** property that accesses the current entry in the list. You can then use this variable as part of the **onClick** or **submitValue** properties to pass the selected node back to the server.

The dominoViewListTreeNode also contains both **views** and **folders** properties, which allow the developer to decide if just the views or the folder or both should be displayed as node entries.

The dominoViewEntriesTreeNode (`xe:dominoViewEntriesTreeNode`)

The dominoViewEntriesTreeNode is a specialized version of the repeatTreeNode in that the developer can specify a Domino View datasource directly in the node's properties. As in the dominoViewListTreeNode, a **databaseName** property specifies which database to use. Also, a **viewName** property allows the developer to specify which view to use within that database.

Developers can pass in a key or array of keys similar to the Domino `getAllDocuments-ByKey` method using the **keys** property. In addition, they can specify that an exact match is made using the **keysExactMatch** property.

To set the label for each node that is rendered, developers can use the variable name set in the **var** property to access the returned document to extract a value or, if there is a column in the view they are accessing, they can use the **labelColumn** property to specify which column to use as the label.

Finally, like the dominoViewListTreeNode, the **onClick** and **submitValue** properties can detect which node the end user has clicked in the web browser, as shown in Listing 8.10.

Listing 8.10 Sample of the dominoViewEntriesTreeNode

```
<xe:dominoViewEntriesTreeNode
  var="viewEntry"
  viewName="AllStates"
  labelColumn="Name">
  <xe:this.submitValue><![CDATA[#{javascript:var v =
viewEntry.getColumnValues(); return v[0]}]]></xe:this.submitValue>
  </xe:dominoViewEntriesTreeNode>
```

Using the Navigator Controls

Now that the concept of the TreeNode has been explained, it is time to put it to use in the different navigation controls supplied by the XPages Extension Library. You can use each of these navigation controls within an XPages application to allow the user to move between different parts of the application.

The Navigator Control

The most standard control used in applications is the side menu. You normally use it to move between different sections of the application. For example, in the TeamRoom application, this control allows the user to move from the All Documents section to the Calendar section. Figure 8.14 shows the standard navigator menu from the TeamRoom application.

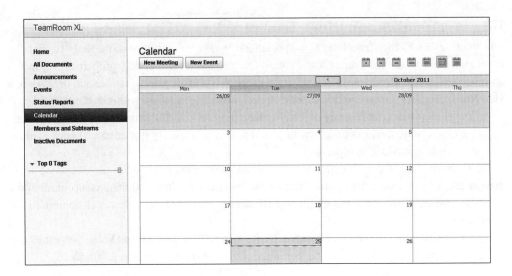

Figure 8.14   Standard TeamRoom navigator.

The `xe:navigator` control allows the developer to set up both flat and multi-level navigation menus depending on how the TreeNode has been set up. Also, three special properties define how the navigator handles multi-level menus. The **expandable** property, when set to `true`, renders a twisty arrow on all the basicContainerNode entries within the TreeNode. When rendered to the web browser, the end user can click on the twisty arrow to show or hide that level in the menu.

When the **expandable** property is set to `true`, the developer can also set the **expandEffect** property and the **expandLevel** property. The **expandEffect** property allows the developer to add a CSS-based user interface (UI) effect that shows to end users when they click the twisty arrow; currently, only a wipe effect is available. The **expandLevel** property allows the developer to decide which levels of the menu are automatically expanded when the menu is rendered to the web browser. Setting this to 0 makes the Navigator control show only the parent levels; setting it to 1 shows all the parents and expands them out one level.

As mentioned earlier, all the TreeNodes contain a property called **submitValue**. The counterpart to this property is **onItemClick**, which allows the developer to write a block of Client-Side JavaScript that can act upon the submitted value. On the Events tab of the property is an **onItemClick** event, which allows the developer to write Client-Side JavaScript or SSJS.

It is recommended that the onItemClick event be used to provide greater flexibility to the developer. Listing 8.11 shows a sample Navigator control with three basicLeafNodes that contain a **submitValue** property. The onItemClick event has been used to set a viewScope variable and then perform a partial refresh to display the selected value to the end user.

Listing 8.11   Navigator Control Using the onItemClick Event

```
<xe:navigator
   id="navigator1">
   <xe:this.treeNodes>
     <xe:basicLeafNode
       label="Option 1"
       submitValue="Option 1" />
     <xe:basicLeafNode
       label="Option 2"
       submitValue="Option 2" />
     <xe:basicLeafNode
       label="Option 3"
       submitValue="Option 3" />
   </xe:this.treeNodes>
   <xp:eventHandler
     event="onItemClick"
     submit="true"
     refreshMode="partial"
     refreshId="computedField1">
     <xp:this.action><![CDATA[#{javascript:viewScope.menuChoice =
context.getSubmittedValue()}]]></xp:this.action>
   </xp:eventHandler>
 </xe:navigator>
 <xp:br />
 Selected Value : 
 <xp:text
   escape="true"
   id="computedField1"
   value="#{javascript:viewScope.menuChoice}" />
```

The Bread Crumbs Control (xe:breadCrumbs)

When it comes to application design, the term *breadcrumbs* does not reflect the original meaning of the term, which is to lay a trail of breadcrumbs that allows users to retrace their steps. Modern UI design patterns define breadcrumbs as a way to show users where they are in relation to the application's hierarchy.

In the XPages Extension Library, the xe:breadCrumbs control, as shown in Listing 8.12, renders its list of TreeNodes as a single inline list with a > separating each entry. The **label** property allows the developer to define a label that appears before the first entry in the breadcrumb list. As with the Navigator control, the **onItemClick** property and the **onItemClick** events exist for this control and can be used in the same way.

Listing 8.12   Breadcrumbs Control Sample from the Demo App

```
<xe:breadCrumbs
  id="outline"
  label="You are in: ">
  <xe:this.treeNodes>
    <xe:pageTreeNode
      page="Domino_Home"
      label="Home">
    </xe:pageTreeNode>
    <xe:pageTreeNode
      page="Domino_UserBean"
      label="User Bean">
    </xe:pageTreeNode>
    <xe:pageTreeNode
      page="Domino_ViewState"
      label="View State">
    </xe:pageTreeNode>
  </xe:this.treeNodes>
</xe:breadCrumbs>
```

The List of Links Control (`xe:linkList`)

The `xe:linksList` control renders its TreeNodes as an unordered list using standard HTML. By default, the OneUI class of lotusInlineList is added to the rendered list. If you are using OneUI, the list renders as a single line with a separator between each item. Again, you can use the **onItemClick** property or event to determine what happens when the end user clicks one of the TreeNode entries in the list, as shown in Listing 8.13.

Listing 8.13   List of Links Sample from the ExtLib Demo App

```
<xe:linksList
  id="linksList1">
  <xe:this.treeNodes>
    <xe:basicLeafNode
      label="Hide"
      href="#list1"></xe:basicLeafNode>
    <xe:basicLeafNode
      label="Reply"
      href="#list2"></xe:basicLeafNode>
    <xe:basicLeafNode
```

```
            label="Edit"
            href="#list3"></xe:basicLeafNode>
      </xe:this.treeNodes>
   </xe:linksList>
```

The Sort Links Control (`xe:sortLinks`)

The `xe:sortLinks` control is the same as the `xe:listLinks` control except that it adds an additional CSS class of `lotusSort` to its container. If you are using OneUI, it changes the look of the list of links, making them slightly smaller.

The Link Container Controls

In addition to the `xe:linksList` and `xe:sortLinks` controls, the XPages Extension Library provides three controls that the developer can use to create and maintain lists. Unlike some of the other navigation type controls, the `xe:list` and `xe:listInline` controls do not use the TreeNode concept. Instead, they render any child controls as the list items. Listing 8.14 shows an example of both of these controls with a number of children that will be rendered as list entries.

Listing 8.14   Example of the `xe:list` and `xe:listInline` Controls

```
<xe:listInline
  id="listInline1">
  <xp:link
    escape="true"
    text="Link 1"
    id="link1" />
  <xp:link
    escape="true"
    text="Link 2"
    id="link2" />
  <xp:link
    escape="true"
    text="Link 3"
    id="link3" />
</xe:listInline>

  <xe:list
    id="list1">
    <xp:link
      escape="true"
```

Listing 8.14   (Continued)

```
        text="Link 1"
        id="link4" />
      <xp:link
        escape="true"
        text="Link 2"
        id="link5" />
      <xp:link
        escape="true"
        text="Link 3"
        id="link6" />
  </xe:list>
```

The Pop-up Menu Control (xe:popupMenu)

The xe:popupMenu control creates a list of menu options that can be hidden until you need them. You need to use this control in conjunction with any other control that can trigger an event to display the menu. Normally, this is either an xp:link control or an xp:button control, and the event is triggered on the Client-Side onClick event. Listing 8.15 shows a sample popupMenu control being triggered by a standard button control. It uses a Client-Side function called XSP.openMenu that is part of the XPages Extension Library.

Listing 8.15   popupMenu Control Bound to a Button

```
  <xp:button
    value="Display Popup Menu"
    id="button1">
    <xp:eventHandler
      event="onclick"
      submit="false">
      <xp:this.script>
 <![CDATA
 [XSP.openMenu(thisEvent,
 #{javascript:getComponent('popupMenu1').getMenuCtor()})
  ]]>
      </xp:this.script>
    </xp:eventHandler>
  </xp:button>
  <xe:popupMenu
```

```
   id="popupMenu1">
   <xe:this.treeNodes>
    ...
    <xe:basicContainerNode
      label="Hierarchical Choice 3">
      <xe:this.children>
        <xe:basicContainerNode
          label="SubChoice 1">
          <xe:this.children>
            <xe:basicLeafNode
              label="Menu 3-1-1"
              submitValue="Menu 311">
            </xe:basicLeafNode>
            <xe:basicLeafNode
              label="Menu 3-1-2"
              submitValue="Menu 312">
            </xe:basicLeafNode>
            <xe:basicLeafNode
              label="Menu 3-3-3"
              submitValue="Menu 313">
            </xe:basicLeafNode>
          </xe:this.children>
        </xe:basicContainerNode>
        ...
   </xe:this.treeNodes>
   <xp:eventHandler
     event="onItemClick"
     submit="true"
     refreshMode="partial"
     refreshId="computedField4">

<xp:this.action><![CDATA[#{javascript:viewScope.ppChoice=context.
getSubmittedValue()
}]]></xp:this.action>
   </xp:eventHandler>
 </xe:popupMenu>
```

Figure 8.15 illustrates how the pop-up menu example from Listing 8.15 appears in the XPages Extension Library Demo Application.

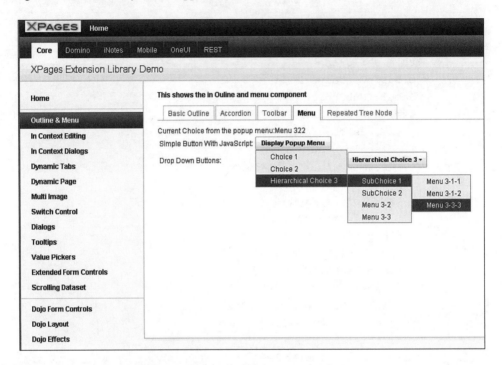

Figure 8.15   The Pop-Up Menu example.

Like the previous navigational controls that use the TreeNode concept, this control also contains both the **onItemClick** property and the onItemClick event that the developer can use to determine what happens when the end user clicks on one of the menu's entries.

The Toolbar Control (`xe:toolbar`)

Another common navigation design pattern is the toolbar, which has been implemented in the XPages Extension Library using the `xe:toolbar` control. The toolbar is normally displayed at the top of a document and gives the end users different actions they can perform on the document.

Similar to the other navigation controls, the toolbar uses the TreeNode concept to define the options that appear in the toolbar and fully supports the basicContainerNode to allow for dynamic drop-down menus in the toolbar. It also uses the same onItemClick events to define what happens when a menu option is selected. For the developer, there is also a **showButtonLabels** property that defaults to `true`. When this property is set to `true`, the labels defined in the Tree-Node objects are shown when the toolbar is rendered. When it's set to `false`, the labels are not shown, so each TreeNode object must have its **image** property defined for the node to appear, as shown in Listing 8.16.

Listing 8.16   Sample Toolbar Control

```
<xe:toolbar
  id="toolbar1">
  <xe:this.treeNodes>
    <xe:basicLeafNode
      label="Accept"
      image="/accept.png" />
    <xe:basicContainerNode
      image="/email.png"
      label="Email">
      <xe:this.children>
        <xe:basicLeafNode
          label="Email To Author" />
        <xe:basicLeafNode
          label="Email To Reviewers" />
      </xe:this.children>
    </xe:basicContainerNode>
    <xe:basicLeafNode
      label="Lock"
      image="/lock.png" />
  </xe:this.treeNodes>
</xe:toolbar>
```

The Outline Control (`xe:outline`)

The `xe:outline` control, as shown in Figure 8.16, is again similar to the other navigation controls insofar as it renders the TreeNodes as an unordered list. However, developers have access to an additional property called **TreeRenderer**, which allows them to select a custom rendering style to render the different nodes.

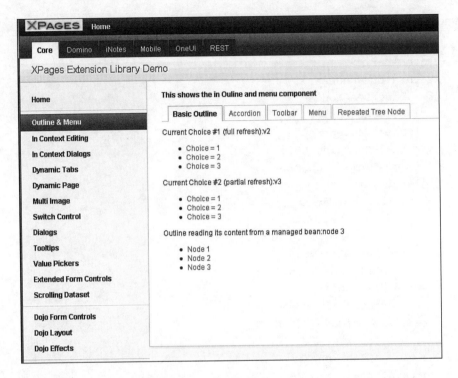

Figure 8.16   The Outline control sample on the Demo app.

By default the outline is rendered using the `xe:htmlDivSpanRenderer` using preset styles from the oneUI theme. However, if you explicitly set this as the TreeRenderer, you can optionally set your own css classes and styles for the container and for items in the outline.

You can also optionally select the TreeRenderer of `xe:htmlListRender` to produce a container with an HTML list of items; when developing for mobile devices, you can select the `xe:mobileAccordionMenu` renderer, which is covered in more detail in Chapter 10 "XPages Goes Mobile."

The Accordion Control (`xe:accordion`)

Earlier in this chapter, you learned how the developer can create an Accordion Container and Accordion Panes using the Dojo layout controls. The `xe:accordion` control produces the same code for rendering to the web browser but instead uses the TreeNodes to define the content of the Accordion Panes.

For the best results, the main TreeNodes should be based on the basicContainerNode node types. The label for the basicContainerNode will be used as the title for the Accordion Pane, and the child nodes will be rendered as an unordered list within the Accordion Pane, as shown in Figure 8.17.

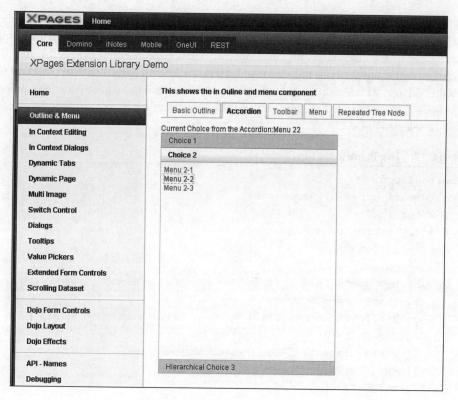

Figure 8.17   Accordion sample from the Extension Library Demo App.

Again, like the other controls that use the TreeNode concept, this control has an **onItem-Click** property and event that the developer can use to determine what happens when the end user selects one of the options within the Accordion Pane.

The Tag Cloud Control (`xe:tagCloud`)

Another common design pattern for web-based applications is the tag cloud. This normally shows the different tags that documents are listed under and uses a method of varying sizes and color shades to indicate which tags are more popular than others. In the XPages Extension Library, this design pattern has been implemented using the `xe:tagCloud` control.

In its simplest form, the tag cloud can be composed from any categorized Notes view. The control computes the number of documents per category, rendered as links, with links in a larger font size for the more numerous records in a certain category. This displays perfectly and performs functionally as expected, although the developer may want to do more to enable the links to navigate to another XPage or set a view filtering variable to only display documents by that selected category. For this case, further configuration of the view datasource and the control on XPage is recommended.

In the TeamRoom template, which has been enhanced using the XPages Extension Library, the tag cloud is configured using a Notes view, which is a single categorized column that displays the categories as separate entries for counting. This view, `"xpByCategory"`, is the view data-source used by the tag cloud, as in Listing 8.17. Here, too, the property `linkTargetPage` is set to another XPage, which instructs the link where to navigate. The request parameter property, `linkRequestParam`, is also set here so that the query string for `"categoryFilter"` equals that of the selected link.

Listing 8.17   The TeamRoom Tag Cloud

```
<xe:tagCloud
  alternateText="{0} documents"
  id="tagCloud1"
  sliderVisible="true">
  <xe:this.cloudData>
    <xe:dominoViewCloudData
      cacheMode="auto"
      viewName="xpByCategory"
      cacheRefreshInterval="120"
      maxTagLimit="30"
      linkTargetPage="/allDocumentsByTag.xsp"
      linkRequestParam="categoryFilter"
      sortTags="alphabet">
    </xe:dominoViewCloudData>
  </xe:this.cloudData>
</xe:tagCloud>
```

A basic configuration of the tag cloud needs only a few properties to be filled out. You can set other properties to enhance how the control functions in the application. Most of these are provided by the `xe:dominoViewCloudData` complex type control from the **cloudData** property.

The **categoryColumn** property, which is set to zero by default, is optional. If the categorized view column isn't the first column in that view, the developer must enter the number of the desired categorized column for the tag cloud to use.

The **sortTags** property is optional. By default, the tag cloud displays the tags alphabetically. But the developer can use weight for sorting by the occurrence count of that category.

The **maxTagLimit** property is useful for limiting the number of tags to be displayed in the cloud; otherwise, all the tags are displayed in the categorized view. You might consider this if there are concerns about the performance of this control.

The properties **cacheMode** and **cacheRefreshInterval** are linked. When the **cacheMode** property is set to `auto` (automatic), the cache refresh interval is dynamically computed based on the number of entries in the view. When it's set to Manual, the developer can specify the cache refresh interval in the **cacheRefreshInterval** property, which is set as a number in seconds. Valid values are Auto, Manual, and Off. Value defaults to Auto. It is not recommended that you apply the Off setting, thus disabling caching, except for debug purposes.

The **linkMetaSeparator** property is an optional character that acts as a delimiter between tag data and metadata, to be used in conjunction with the **linkRequestParam** value. Using a **linkMetaSeparator** character requires the backend categorized view column to output the data in the format xxx | yyy, where xxx is the tag name, | is the **linkMetaSeparator** character, and yyy is the metadata used as the request parameter. If no **linkMetaSeparator** is specified, the actual tag value is used for the request parameter value. Listing 8.18 shows an example of its use from the XPages Extension Library Demo App, and Figure 8.18 shows how this tag cloud renders in the browser.

Listing 8.18 Tag Cloud Sample from the Demo App

```
<xe:tagCloud
    alternateText="{0} Entries"
    sliderVisible="true">
    <xe:this.cloudData>
      <xe:dominoViewCloudData
        cacheMode="auto"
        cacheRefreshInterval="120"
        viewName="AuthorCloud"
        maxTagLimit="25"
        linkMetaSeparator="~"
        linkTargetPage="/Domino_ViewUserProfile.xsp"
        linkRequestParam="name"
        minEntryCount="3">

      </xe:dominoViewCloudData>
    </xe:this.cloudData>
  </xe:tagCloud>
```

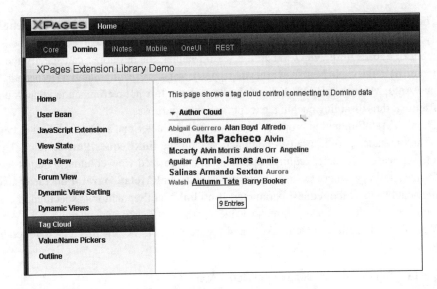

Figure 8.18   The Demo App Tag Cloud control.

The Widget Container Control (`xe:widgetContainer`)

The widget container is a simple container that displays content in a set box, as shown in Figure 8.19, with a few notable properties.

You can use the **titleBarText** and the **titleBarHref** together. The Title Bar text appears in the title bar at the top of the widget. When it's absent, no text is displayed. The **titleBarHref** turns this title into a link.

The **dropDownRendered** property defines the drop-down menu to be displayed on the title bar. It defaults to `true`, so the drop-down is displayed if any drop-down nodes are present. Then the complex type control `xe:dropDownNodes` displays a menu containing these actions. It can contain all the nodes that help developers build navigation into their applications.

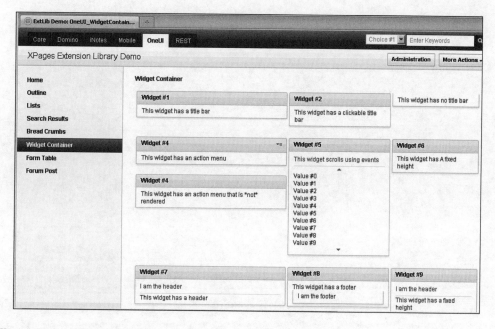

Figure 8.19 Widget Container samples.

Conclusion

The controls described in this chapter can help developers build complex navigation patterns into their applications without much effort. This chapter covered some basics of layout and placement of this navigation. It serves as grounding for the next chapter on the Application Layout control to complete a more rounded knowledge of the next generation of XPages controls.

CHAPTER 9

The Application's Layout

For many developers, one of the most challenging aspects of creating an application is designing the user interface. Not only must an effective application interface be aesthetically pleasing, but its layout must be intuitive and consistent, allowing users to predict what behaviors will produce the desired effect. Ideally, this consistency extends beyond each application to the overall software environment within which the user base operates.

When developing web applications, it is more difficult to design such interfaces than it is to design desktop applications because the developer lacks control over the execution environment. Each browser is unique in the way it renders the same markup. In some cases, a browser might render the same markup differently when accessing it from different operating systems. Additionally, a developer must often support multiple versions of each supported browser. The application must be, at a minimum, functional within each permutation of these factors. Ideally, it will be elegant, too.

In this chapter, you will learn how use of the Application Layout control can facilitate meeting this goal despite the difficulties presented when developing applications with the browser as your target platform.

History of OneUI

As the art of web development has matured in recent years, numerous web development frameworks have emerged. These frameworks attempt to ease the burden of developing rich web applications by solving common problems once so that developers need not repeat that effort each time they develop a new application. These frameworks are focused primarily on JavaScript. They compensate for differences in implementations of the language across different browsers—and different browser versions—and provide reusable widgets to both supplement and standardize the user interface (UI) features of a given web application, much like the Extension Library controls supplement the core controls of the XPages runtime. Dojo is one of many such JavaScript frameworks.

Unlike this category of framework, however, which typically only includes Cascading Style Sheets (CSS) and images directly related to providing reusable widgets, some web development frameworks are focused entirely upon CSS. IBM has created one such CSS framework, known as OneUI.

Many of the products in the IBM Collaboration Services platform are now able to integrate in various ways: IBM Connections, for example, provides an application programming interface (API) allowing data to be easily consumed from within a Domino application. In Chapter 13, "Get Social," the developer learns how the Extension Library makes such integration even easier. IBM Lotus Quickr has long allowed extensive integration with Domino. Until recently, however, providing a common look and feel across implementations of these products within the same organization was difficult at best. OneUI was developed to minimize this difficulty.

Aside from the core content of any given web page, the elements of the interface that surround that content are fairly predictable: site navigation, application or organization logo, copyright statement, and so on. The visual style of each of these elements, and even their location, is far less predictable. Often, even when navigating between applications developed by the same individual or team, the user must adjust to a different layout to learn—or remember—where to look to find the element they need to interact with.

IBM identified a core set of layout elements it considers to be universal. It chose a standard location for each and established base rules for how these elements look. Finally, it created a set of images to support construction of a layout that uses these standard elements, and it defined CSS rules that allow web content to define which layout role is provided by a given HTML element. Jointly, these images and CSS rules comprise the CSS framework known as OneUI.

This framework is included by default on every Domino server as of version 8.5.0. Because IBM Connections also uses the framework, any Domino application that leverages OneUI to define its layout will be visually compatible with any standard Connections implementation. Even if Domino is the only Lotus product in use at an organization, however, the OneUI framework can be used to provide visual standardization across all Domino applications within that organization. Such standardization often improves user productivity and satisfaction, besides lowering both time and cost for end user training.

Easy OneUI Development with the Application Layout Control

There's a downside to the extent to which OneUI standardizes application layout: the framework is rather complex. To specify positioning that all browsers will support, for example, some HTML elements must not only be assigned the correct CSS class, but be nested within a precise hierarchy of spans and divs that have been assigned a specific class. This complexity can create the illusion that adhering to the OneUI specification is more trouble than it is worth.

The Application Layout control in the Extension Library reduces this complexity by defining each portion of the OneUI related to layout as a property of the control. The XPages Team-Room application is an excellent example of how rapidly this control allows an entire application's layout to be designed.

First, let's look at the finished result, shown in Figure 9.1.

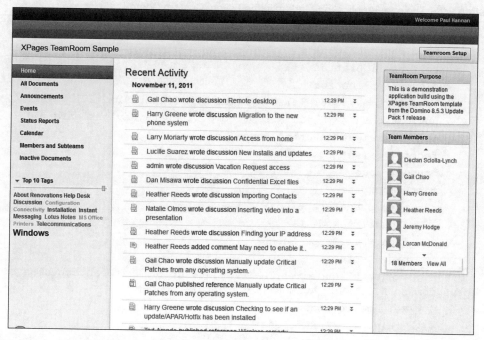

Figure 9.1   The OneUI Layout in the XPages TeamRoom template.

The TeamRoom template uses a single Custom Control called **layout** to define the layout for the entire application. This Custom Control contains an instance of the Application Layout control (xe:applicationLayout). This chapter first looks at the structure of its configuration property. Then it looks at the definition of its facets.

Unlike most controls in XPages, which support many properties for defining the nature and behavior of each instance of the control, the Application Layout control bundles nearly all its pertinent information about each instance into a single property, called **configuration**. The value of this property is known as a complex type, which means that the specified value can, in turn, support multiple properties. In the case of the configuration object of the Application Layout control, these values represent a hierarchy of properties that define the entire layout for an application.

The **configuration** property supports, as of the time of this writing, two possible layout configurations:

- xe:applicationConfiguration

- xe:oneuiApplication

The TeamRoom application uses the latter of these two types. The entirety of its definition is demonstrated in Listing 9.1.

Listing 9.1   The oneuiApplication Markup in the Layout Custom Control

```
<xe:applicationLayout
  id="applicationLayout1">
  <xe:this.configuration>
    <xe:oneuiApplication
      legalText="&#8206; (c) Copyright IBM Corporation 2012 &#x202C;"
      navigationPath="${javascript:compositeData.navigationPath}"
      defaultNavigationPath="/home"
      footer="false"
      banner="true"
      mastHeader="true">
      <xe:this.placeBarActions>
        <xe:pageTreeNode
          label="Teamroom Setup"
          page="setup">
          <xe:this.loaded><![CDATA[${javascript:userBean.accessLevel
> lotus.domino.ACL.LEVEL_AUTHOR}]]></xe:this.loaded>
        </xe:pageTreeNode>
      </xe:this.placeBarActions>
      <xe:this.searchBar>
        <xe:appSearchBar
          pageName="search.xsp"
          inactiveText="Search..."
          optionsParam="search"
          queryParam="search"
          loaded="${javascript:database.isFTIndexed()}"
          inputTitle="Enter a search value">
        </xe:appSearchBar>
      </xe:this.searchBar>
      <xe:this.bannerUtilityLinks>
        <xe:userTreeNode>
```

```
<xe:this.label><![CDATA[#{javascript:I18n.format(strings.getString
("welcome.x"), userBean.displayName)}]]></xe:this.label>
        </xe:userTreeNode>
        <xe:loginTreeNode></xe:loginTreeNode>
      </xe:this.bannerUtilityLinks>
        <xe:this.placeBarName><![CDATA[${javascript:var teamname =
strings.getString("teamroom.name");
var vw:NotesView = database.getView("MissionLookup");
var vc:NotesViewEntryCollection = vw.getAllEntries();
var ve:NotesViewEntry = vc.getFirstEntry();
if(null != ve){
 var v:java.util.Vector = ve.getColumnValues();
 if(!v.isEmpty()){
  // get the teamroom name
   teamname = v.get(1);
 }
}
return teamname;}]]></xe:this.placeBarName>
      </xe:oneuiApplication>

    </xe:this.configuration>
  </xe:applicationLayout>
```

Legal

The **legal** property determines whether the legal bar will display. By default, this property has a value of `true`. The legal bar displays the value specified in the **legalText** property. Any value entered in this property appears at the bottom of the application's layout, as shown in closer detail in Figure 9.2.

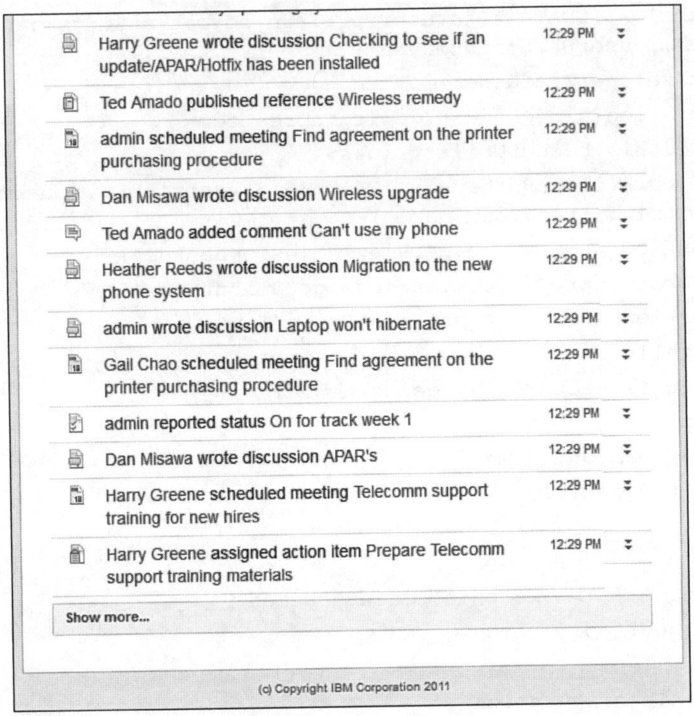

Harry Greene wrote discussion Checking to see if an update/APAR/Hotfix has been installed	12:29 PM	⇳
Ted Amado published reference Wireless remedy	12:29 PM	⇳
admin scheduled meeting Find agreement on the printer purchasing procedure	12:29 PM	⇳
Dan Misawa wrote discussion Wireless upgrade	12:29 PM	⇳
Ted Amado added comment Can't use my phone	12:29 PM	⇳
Heather Reeds wrote discussion Migration to the new phone system	12:29 PM	⇳
admin wrote discussion Laptop won't hibernate	12:29 PM	⇳
Gail Chao scheduled meeting Find agreement on the printer purchasing procedure	12:29 PM	⇳
admin reported status On for track week 1	12:29 PM	⇳
Dan Misawa wrote discussion APAR's	12:29 PM	⇳
Harry Greene scheduled meeting Telecomm support training for new hires	12:29 PM	⇳
Harry Greene assigned action item Prepare Telecomm support training materials	12:29 PM	⇳
Show more...		

(c) Copyright IBM Corporation 2011

Figure 9.2   Legal text on the Layout control.

A logo for the legal bar can be set by way of an image specified in the **legalLogo** property. This image can have its styling altered using **legalLogoHeight**, **legalLogoWidth**, **legalLogoStyle**, or even **LegalLogoClass**.

Navigation Path

The next two properties are directly related. The **navigationPath** property allows any page in the application to specify a contextual location representing where in the application the user currently is in the larger context of the entire application. This is most commonly expressed as a slash-delimited path, similar to a Linux filesystem path; an example might be **/teams/teamname**. Other portions of the layout configuration can reference this property value to determine whether they should be currently considered to be selected. The **defaultNavigationPath** property indicates what the value of the **navigationPath** property should be if none is provided.

In the case of the TeamRoom application, the **layout** Custom Control defines a custom property called **navigationPath**; any value passed to this property of the Custom Control is, in turn, passed to the Application Layout control's **navigationPath** property. Its **defaultNavigationPath** property has a value of /home, so if no **navigationPath** is specified, the current path is "/home".

The Footer

The footer bar is enabled by default by way of the **footer** property. Setting it to `false`, as with the TeamRoom, means it won't render. By default, a portion of the screen is reserved at the bottom of the layout for displaying useful links, specified via a separate **footerLinks** property. You can entirely suppress most portions of the layout by setting a corresponding property value to `false`; the TeamRoom application suppresses the footer section of the layout.

Figure 9.3 shows the footer being used in the XPages Extension Library Demo App (**XPages.Ext.nsf**). A portion of this footer is shown in Listing 9.2.

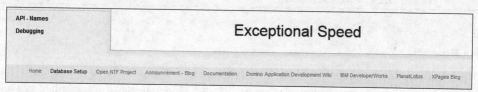

Figure 9.3   Footer links.

Listing 9.2   Footer Links in the ExtLib Demo App

```
    <xe:this.footerLinks>
    <xe:basicContainerNode
      label="XPages Extension Library Demo">
      <xe:this.children>
        <xe:basicLeafNode
          onClick=";"
          label="Home"
          href="/">
        </xe:basicLeafNode>
        ...
        ...
        ...
        <xe:basicLeafNode
          href="/Admin_Home.xsp"
          label="Database Setup">
        </xe:basicLeafNode>
      </xe:this.children>
    </xe:basicContainerNode>
    <xe:basicLeafNode
      label="PlanetLotus">
<xe:this.href><![CDATA[http://planetlotus.org/search.php?search=xpages&
sort=1]]></xe:this.href>
```

Listing 9.2   (Continued)

```
      </xe:basicLeafNode>
      <xe:basicLeafNode
        href="http://xpagesblog.com/"
        label="XPages Blog">
      </xe:basicLeafNode>
    </xe:this.children>
    </xe:basicContainerNode>
    </xe:this.footerLinks>
```

The Placebar

To fully understand the next property, let's briefly revisit a concept introduced in Chapter 8, "Outlines and Navigation." Many properties of an Application Layout instance are specified as a hierarchy of tree nodes, which are another complex type. The purpose each hierarchy serves differs based on which property it defines, but the use of tree nodes to specify each provides a flexible and standardized way to define the properties.

One of these properties is called **placeBarActions**. Any leaf nodes added to this property display as buttons in the upper-right portion of the layout—to be precise, in a horizontal section known as the placebar, which, like the footer, is one of the layout sections that can be suppressed by setting a corresponding property value to `false`. Any container nodes display as a drop-down menu; leaf nodes specified as children of such a container node provide the menu items for that drop-down menu. This use of a tree node hierarchy allows complex menu structures to be defined rapidly.

The TeamRoom application, however, specifies only a single leaf node in the form of a **pageTreeNode**. Because its **title** property has a value of `"TeamRoom Setup"`, the application displays a button with this value as its label, as shown in Figure 9.4.

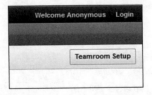

Figure 9.4   The TeamRoom Setup button on the placebar.

This pageTreeNode specifies a value of `"setup"` for its **page** property. As a result, when the node-generated button is clicked, the user is redirected to `"/setup.xsp"`, relative to the path of the application. Because an expression is specified for its **loaded** property—`userBean.accessLevel > lotus.domino.ACL.LEVEL_AUTHOR`—however, this button displays only if the current user's access level in the application is Editor or above. This expression refers to a concept known as the userBean, which is explained in detail in Chapter 14, "Java Development in XPages."

Another property used in this area of the TeamRoom application is **placeBarName**. Any value specified for this property displays in the left portion of the placebar, the same layout section that displays any **placeBarActions**. In the TeamRoom application, this property is an expression that attempts to retrieve the TeamRoom name from a setup document; if this value cannot be retrieved, it loads a default value from a file resource design element.

Search Bar

One particularly useful feature of the Application Layout control is the ease with which you can add a generic search bar to an application's layout. Because the TeamRoom application includes a value for the **searchBar** property, a fully functional search bar displays in the upper-right portion of the layout, as shown in Figure 9.5. This bar loads on the page only if the application is fully indexed for Full Text Search, as shown in the **loaded** property in Listing 9.3.

Figure 9.5   Search bar loaded on fully indexed app.

Listing 9.3   SearchBar Markup from the TeamRoom Layout

```
<xe:this.searchBar>
  <xe:appSearchBar
    pageName="search.xsp"
    inactiveText="Search..."
    optionsParam="search"
    queryParam="search"
    loaded="${javascript:database.isFTIndexed()}"
    inputTitle="Enter a search value">
  </xe:appSearchBar>
</xe:this.searchBar>
```

The TeamRoom application specifies a **pageName** of "search.xsp", so when users submit a search (either by clicking the displayed icon or pressing the Enter key), they are redirected to that page within the application. The **inactiveText** property is set to "Search...", so whenever no value is entered in the search field, that value is displayed as a low-opacity placeholder.

The next two properties also have a direct relationship. The **optionsParam** specifies the uniform resource locator (URL) parameter that should be included in the redirection if a search filter option is selected. The search bar supports a property called **options**, which can be specified as a list of leaf nodes; if specified, these display as a drop-down to the left of the search bar.

If, for example, the user selects **Blogs** from the Options drop-down and the **optionsParam** property has a value of `"category"`, the URL the user will be redirected to upon submitting the search will include a query string argument: `"category=Blogs"`. This allows the target search page to filter any relevant results to the specified subset. Because no options are specified in the TeamRoom layout, however, the **optionsParam** property is simply ignored.

The **queryParam** property is similar. Because this property has a value of `"search"`, if users search for "XPages", the URL they are redirected to includes a query string argument of `"search=XPages"`. If, instead, the property had a value of `"q"`, the argument would be `"q=XPages"`.

The **loaded** property for the search bar has been set to an expression that prevents the entire search bar from displaying if the current application instance has not been full-text indexed.

The Banner

The next configuration property, **bannerUtilityLinks**, is another example in which the value is specified as a hierarchy of tree nodes. All nodes listed for this property display in the top-right portion of the layout. The TeamRoom application includes two types of leaf nodes that have specific intelligence built in to their behavior: `xe:userTreeNode` and `xe:loginTreeNode`.

If the user has access to the application without authenticating and has not yet authenticated, the userTreeNode indicates that the user is anonymous, and the loginTreeNode displays a link to allow the user to authenticate, as shown in Figure 9.6.

Figure 9.6   The banner links display for an anonymous user.

If the user has authenticated, the userTreeNode displays the current user's name in common name format prefixed with **Welcome**, and the loginTreeNode is hidden, as shown in Figure 9.7.

Figure 9.7   The banner links display for an authenticated user.

NOTE

For the TeamRoom template, the string "Welcome", as used in previous example, can be changed by editing the value for "welcome.x" in the 'strings.properties' file.

Setting the **banner** property to `false` causes the banner bar not to render.

The Title Bar

The title bar is used in the TeamRoom to display the search bar. Setting the **titleBar** property to "false" causes this part of the layout not to render; this property is set to "true" by default. Other than that, the title bar can display text with the **titleBarName** property or display tabs with the complex property **titleBarTabs**. When both of these properties are set, the name is displayed before the tabs from left to right.

The XPages Extension Library Demo App contains a good example of the use of the **title-BarTabs** property. There it uses page tree nodes (xe:pageTreeNode) to populate the tabs and provide navigation to other XPages.

Product Logo

You can add a product or corporate logo to the layout by using the **productLogo** property. And, like the legal logo, this image styling can be controlled by the **productLogoWidth**, **productLogoHeight**, **productLogoStyle**, and **productLogoClass**.

Mast Header and Footer

Setting either of the properties **mastHeader** or **mastFooter** does nothing to the appearance in most cases. These are reserved facets for the Application Layout control, as shown in Listing 9.4 through xp:key.

Listing 9.4   Use of the mastHeader and mastFooter

```
<xe:applicationLayout
   id="applicationLayout1">
   <xp:this.facets>
     <xp:panel
       xp:key="MastFooter">
       <xp:label
         value="Overall Corporate Header: "
         id="label1"></xp:label>
       <xp:image
         url="/xpagesui-logo.jpg"
         id="image1"></xp:image>
     </xp:panel>
     <xp:panel
       xp:key="MastHeader">
       <xp:section
         id="section2"
         header="This is a section in the mastFooter"></xp:section>
     </xp:panel>
   </xp:this.facets>
```

Adding content to the **MastFooter** and **MastHeader** facets adds an extra footer and header to the layout. It is usually done to enclose the application in an overall corporate look and feel of which multiple applications might share.

The Layout Control Tooling in Designer

In 8.5.3 versions of the XPages Extension Library, extra plugins are available that provide tooling for a number of these new controls in Domino Designer. One of these is for the Layout control. This extra tooling helps the developer create layout even more quickly.

Upon selecting the Application Layout control from the palette in Designer and dropping it to the Design Pane on an XPage, developers see a message box informing them that it is best to add this control to a Custom Control for better reuse (see Figure 9.8).

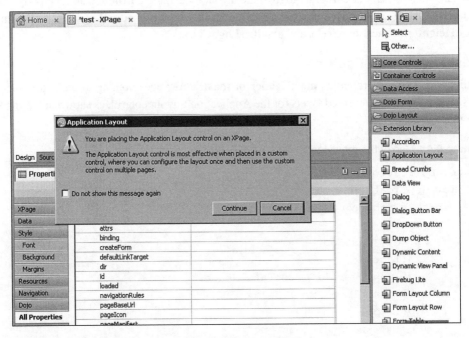

Figure 9.8   Reminder to use layout controls in Custom Controls.

Selecting to continue here brings the developer to a dialog to allow for the configuration of the layout control, as shown in Figure 9.9. Here the developer can quickly select the wanted items. These options were previously described in this chapter.

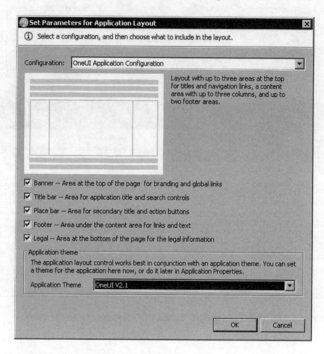

Figure 9.9   Application Layout Configuration dialog.

The application layout control markup is generated on the XPage when you select **OK** on the Configuration dialog, as shown in Figure 9.9. You can then carry out further configuration using the "pretty" panels, as with all other XPages controls in Designer, as shown on Figure 9.10.

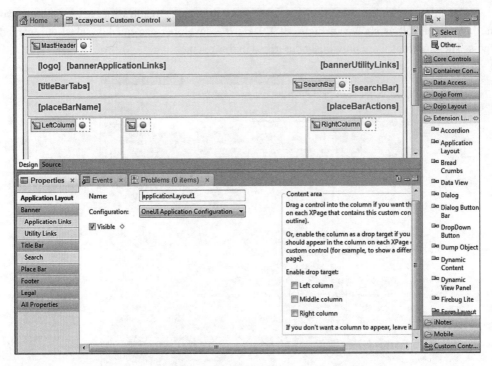

Figure 9.10   Basic configuration of the Layout Control on the Design Pane.

Using the Application Layout Within a Custom Control

In any XPage application, the primary resource for structural reusability is the Custom Control design element. By adding one or more individual controls to a Custom Control—and binding these control characteristics and behaviors to custom properties passed to their container—complex features can be implemented in numerous portions of an application with maximum flexibility and ease of maintenance. This holds particularly true in the case of the Application Layout control due to its use of facets.

Facets are a portion of the Java Server Faces specification that allows a component to easily locate specific contents by name. Any component in an XPage may contain zero or more children, but—with the exception of event handlers—rarely does a child component have discernible meaning to its container; each component serves an isolated purpose within the overall component tree. In contrast, a component that defines facets can easily determine whether a given facet has content, and, if it does, make specific use of that content based on which facet contains it.

You can observe the most frequently encountered use of facets when adding a standard View Panel to an XPage. In addition to inserting a viewColumn child component corresponding to each column selected from the source View, a Pager is automatically added to the View Panel's list of facets.

The Pager that is inserted in this scenario is given an attribute of `xp:key` with a value of `"headerPager"`. If the option to **Show Pager in Footer** is selected on the **Display** tab of the component properties for the View Panel, a new Pager instance is added to the View Panel's facets; this Pager's `xp:key` attribute is assigned a value of `"footerPager"`.

At runtime, this allows the View Panel to treat each Pager differently based on which facet has been specified. To be precise, the facet key determines where each Pager will be rendered.

The Application Layout control also defines several facets, and, like the facets used by Pager controls within a View Panel, each of these facets determines where the content is displayed:

- **MastHeader**—Content that displays at the top of the page
- **MastFooter**—Content that displays at the bottom of the page
- **SearchBar**—Content that displays to the left of the application's search bar, if specified; otherwise, it displays in place of it
- **LeftColumn**—Content that displays directly to the left of the main content area
- **RightColumn**—Content that displays directly to the right of the main content area

As with the View Panel Pager example, each of these facets is optional, but providing content for any causes that content to be rendered in the corresponding location on the page.

Although any of these facets may be contributed directly to a given instance of the Application Layout control, often the most effective approach is to define an Editable Area for each portion of the layout that you anticipate populating. An Editable Area is, itself, simply a way to define a facet for a Custom Control: When a Custom Control that defines an Editable Area is placed on an XPage, and content is added to its Editable Area, the Source XML indicates that the content of that area contributes to the Custom Control's facets. The TeamRoom application provides a demonstration of this relationship, as shown in Listing 9.5.

Listing 9.5   Application Layout Facets

```
<xp:this.facets>
  <xp:div
    xp:key="LeftColumn">
    <xe:navigator
      id="outline"
      expandable="true">
      <xe:this.treeNodes>
        <xe:pageTreeNode
          page="home"
          label="Home"
          selection="/home" />
        <xe:pageTreeNode
          page="allDocuments"
```

Listing 9.5   (Continued)

```
          label="All Documents"
          selection="/allDocuments" />
      <xe:pageTreeNode
        page="announcements"
        label="Announcements"
        selection="/announcements" />
      <xe:pageTreeNode
        page="events"
        label="Events"
        selection="/events" />
      <xe:pageTreeNode
        page="statusReports"
        label="Status Reports"
        selection="/statusReports" />
      <xe:pageTreeNode
        page="calendar"
        label="Calendar"
        selection="/calendar" />
      <xe:pageTreeNode
        page="members"
        label="Members and Subteams"
        selection="/members" />
      <xe:pageTreeNode
        page="inactiveDocuments"
        label="Inactive Documents"
        selection="/inactiveDocuments" />
    </xe:this.treeNodes>
  </xe:navigator>
  <xc:tagCloud
    id="tagCloud" />
  <xp:callback
    id="left"
    facetName="LeftColumn" />
</xp:div>
<xp:callback
  id="right"
  xp:key="RightColumn"
  facetName="RightColumn" />
</xp:div>
</xp:this.facets>
```

In the preceding XML, two approaches to specifying facet content for an Application Layout are shown. First, a div contributes to the `"LeftColumn"` facet of the control. As previously indicated, this ensures that the contents of the div display in the left column of the application's layout. In this case, a standard navigator is included, as well as a tag cloud. After these controls, however, a callback is provided, which specifies a **facetName** of `"LeftColumn"`. The `xp:callback` tag defines an Editable Area for this Custom Control.

Because the div that contributes to the `"LeftColumn"` facet of the Application Layout contains its own content—the navigator and tag cloud—and also includes a callback, each XPage that consumes this Custom Control automatically includes the content of the div but may also contribute its own content to that portion of the layout.

The other facet specified in the preceding example is `"RightColumn"`. Unlike the other facet, however, the only content of this facet is an Editable Area that specifies, again, the same **facetName**. As a result, this portion of the layout is always empty unless the XPage that consumes this Custom Control contributes to the facet. The example shown in Listing 9.6, excerpted from the **home.xsp** XPage from the TeamRoom application, demonstrates this in action.

Listing 9.6   Using Facets in the Layout Custom Control

```
<xc:layout
  navigationPath="/home">
  <xp:this.facets>
    <xp:panel
      xp:key="RightColumn">
      <xc:homeTeamRoomPurpose
        id="wgtTeamRoomPurpose"></xc:homeTeamRoomPurpose>
      <xc:homeMembersView
        id="members"></xc:homeMembersView>
    </xp:panel>
  </xp:this.facets>
```

The Panel defined in Listing 9.6 contributes to the Custom Control's `"RightColumn"` facet, which, in turn, causes its content to be contributed to the `"RightColumn"` facet of the Application Layout. Both of the Custom Controls defined inside the Panel display within the right column of the page—but only on this specific page. This use of chained facets allows each page in the application to define portions of the layout that are unique to that page.

The most important content of each page, of course, is what displays within the middle column. Because of the nature of the Application Layout control, this content need not specify a facet key. When this control is used within a Custom Control, and that Custom Control is added to an XPage, any content defined *within* that Custom Control displays within the middle column. The example in Listing 9.7, excerpted from the **events.xsp** XPage in the TeamRoom application, demonstrates this principle.

Listing 9.7   Main or MiddleColumn Facet in Action in the TeamRoom

```
<xc:layout
   navigationPath="/events">
   <xe:dynamicContent
      id="dynamicContent"
      useHash="false">
      <xe:this.defaultFacet>
<![CDATA[#{javascript:if (param.documentId || param.action){
return "eventFormContent";
}
return "eventViewContent";}]]>
      </xe:this.defaultFacet>
      <xp:this.facets>
         <xc:eventForm
            id="eventFormContent"
            xp:key="eventFormContent"></xc:eventForm>
         <xc:eventView
            id="eventViewContent"
            xp:key="eventViewContent"></xc:eventView>
      </xp:this.facets>
   </xe:dynamicContent>
</xc:layout>
```

Because the dynamicContent control is defined as a child of the layout Custom Control, in the case of the TeamRoom, all of its own content displays within the middle column of the layout. Although the dynamicContent defines its own facets to allow for other complex behaviors, it need not indicate that it contributes to a specific facet of the layout Custom Control; its location in the component tree is sufficient to indicate that it serves as the content for the middle column.

Conclusion

The Application Layout control is both complex and powerful, but its design facilitates easy, intuitive, and rapid standardization of layout content for an entire application. By populating each applicable property for a given instance of this control, an application's layout can typically be defined in a matter of minutes. This allows the developer to rapidly move beyond the tedious business of designing the peripheral portions of the user interface and focus, instead, on ensuring the application's functionality will meet the needs of its users, confident that its overall layout will be aesthetically pleasing, intuitive, and consistent, no matter what browser or operating system a given end user chooses to use.

PART III

Bell and Whistles: Mobile, REST, RDBMS, and Social

CHAPTER 10

XPages Goes Mobile

Mobile is the technology of the age, and owning a mobile device is no longer a luxury but a necessity. This fact is becoming increasingly important in business as desktops and laptops are being superseded by tablets and smartphones. This transition has many challenges ranging from the user interface (UI) design to security. XPages and the Extension Library are in place to meet these mobile challenges. This chapter will show how to meet and overcome these obstacles.

In the Beginning...

Mobile or cellular phones are essentially two-way radios; they allow you to send and receive messages wirelessly. These kinds of devices have been around since the early 1920s. Early two-way radio communication was capable of only one station transmitting while the other was receiving because they were using the same frequency. This limitation was solved to allow simultaneous transmitting and receiving by tuning them into different frequencies, allowing people to talk and listen at the same time. Of course, it was many years before electronics, circuitry, and battery power caught up before the first truly publicly available mobile telephone was introduced. Early models required users to hold the phone with both hands because they were so big and heavy. The *brick* became smaller and cheaper, and 15 years after the first mobile phone came into being, nearly everyone in the world has one.

The mobile phone feature set evolution is interesting because it draws parallels with software: voice communication, followed by text messaging, embedded camera, the leap to smartphones, mobile apps, and finally in management of a user's social network. Communication software has had a similar progression: e-mail messaging with ccMail, Lotus Notes databases and applications, and now team collaboration and social software. Now mobile phone and communication software are merging; soon it will be hard to tell the difference and remember what it used to be like.

Trends are now moving toward businesses using smartphones, which is changing the way people communicate and collaborate. That notion presents interesting challenges to application design. For the Domino application, not only do developers have to contend with implementing a desktop and web design, but the mobile element is becoming more prevalent. Use of mobile devices in business tends to follow the features that are available. The availability of affordable mobile or cell phones has transformed the way business is conducted. Everyone from plumbers to company CEOs has been affected. There's greater flexibility and faster response times because people no longer need to be tied to one desk or location. Early smartphones included e-mail, which meant office workers could break free from their desks to engage with customers more closely. The smartphones of today are part of a technology that is expanding and advancing rapidly and may be on their way to replacing laptops and desktops. The future is mobile.

The XPages Mobile Controls in the Extension Library

The mobile space is one of the most rapidly developing areas of computing. The XPages Extension Library (ExtLib) provides several new controls and themes to make creating a mobile web experience for your Domino application as quick and easy as possible. These controls leverage the power of the Dojo Mobile framework to provide the interface metaphors and transitions familiar to users of native applications in a web setting.

Because these applications are provided over the web, an enterprise can quickly and securely roll out changes and updates to the mobile workforce while keeping tight control on sensitive data.

With Lotus Notes Domino 8.5.3 and the ExtLib, a whole avenue of application development opens. You can easily build these ancillary features onto existing XPages applications.

The Basics of the XPages Mobile Controls

An XPages mobile application is built in a way similar to any other XPages application in that both are web applications. One difference in the way an XPages mobile app is structured may be unfamiliar, however. To allow for the transition animations between the different pages, mobile apps are usually structured using a single XPage containing all the required mobile pages and controls. These may be loaded lazily on an as-needed basis to reduce bandwidth usage or loaded up front to improve performance.

Figure 10.1 shows what the XPages mobile application is composed of. It is made up of a Single Page Application control (`xe:singlePageApp`) containing one or more Mobile Pages controls (`xe:appPage`). The mobile page typically has a Page Heading control (`xe:djxmHeading`).

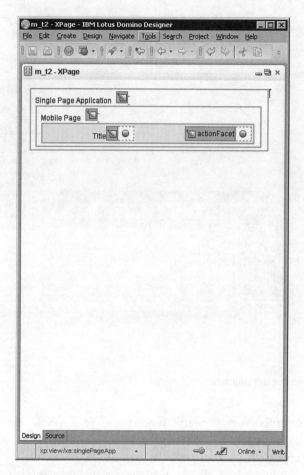

Figure 10.1 The mobile app in Designer.

You can add the other controls required for the functionality of the page to the mobile page. These may be other XPages mobile controls or even a limited number of existing XPages controls that can become valid mobile controls. All this is possible with a little bit of styling magic provided by the XPages mobile theme.

Once the new 8.5.3 ExtLib has been installed in Designer, XPages developers are presented with the mobile controls placed in their own palette, as shown in Figure 10.2. These controls are used to develop XPage mobile applications.

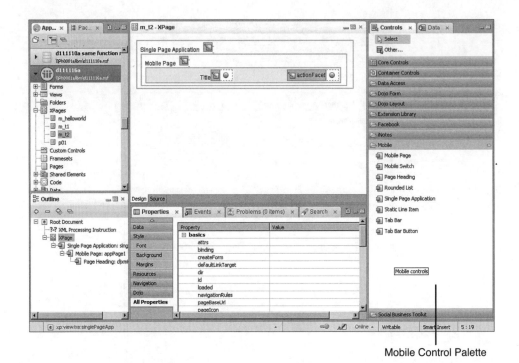

Mobile Control Palette

Figure 10.2   Mobile control palette.

The mobile controls provide specific functionality or a specific user experience that is designed to match native smartphone and tablet applications. They aren't the only controls you can use in mobile applications. Other controls can take on the mobile theme's look and feel. The controls in the Mobile palette are designed just for mobile and don't have an application elsewhere. The following sections review these controls and their use in mobilizing XPage applications.

The Single Page Application Control (`xe:singlePageApp`)

Essentially, the Single Page Application control is the container for the XPages mobile application. All components involving the mobile application, mobile pages, navigation, data reading, data input, styling, and so forth are enclosed within the Single Page Application control. In the markup, everything is contained within this control's tag, `xe:singlePageApp`, as shown in Listing 10.1.

Listing 10.1 The Single Page Application Control Contained Within the View Tag

```
<xp:view xmlns:xp="http://www.ibm.com/xsp/core"
        xmlns:xe="http://www.ibm.com/xsp/coreex">

<xe:singlePageApp
  id="singlePageApp1"
  selectedPageName="mobilePage1">
  <xe:appPage
    id="appPage1"
    pageName="mobilePage1">
    <xe:djxmHeading
      id="djxmHeading1"></xe:djxmHeading>
    <xe:djxmLineItem
      id="djxmLineItem1"
      label="Click to go to Mobile Page 2"
      moveTo="mobilePage2">
    </xe:djxmLineItem>
  </xe:appPage>
  <xe:appPage
    id="appPage2"
    pageName="mobilePage2">
    <xe:djxmHeading
      id="djxmHeading2"
      back="Back"
      moveTo="mobilePage1">
    </xe:djxmHeading>
    <xe:djxmLineItem
      id="djxmLineItem2"
      label="This is Mobile Page 2">
    </xe:djxmLineItem>
  </xe:appPage>
</xe:singlePageApp></xp:view>
```

The Single Page Application has few attributes, only one of which is needed for mobile applications. That attribute is the **selectedPageName** property, which must be set to the name of a mobile page name that exists with this container control. In the listing, the **selectedPageName** property is set to `"mobilePage1"`. Therefore, the Mobile Page (`xe:appPage`) named `"mobilePage1"` becomes the default page that the Single Page Application displays. The Single Page Application displays only one Mobile Page at a time; in Listing 10.1, this alternates between `"mobilePage1"` and `"mobilePage2"`.

The Mobile Page Control (`xe:appPage`)

Each page on a mobile application must be a mobile page. Multiple pages can be defined in two ways:

> Each page is a new XPage (including an `<xe:singlePageApp>` in each).
>
> Each page is defined inside one XPage with multiple `<xe:appPage>` tags.

Using the second method, each appPage is given an appPageId that can be used to switch pages, rather than a given URL. To move to a new `<xe:appPage>`, type the URL (the XPage filename followed by a hash [#]) and then the appPageId. An example would be **mobileHome.xsp#document**.

The Mobile Page control is the web page fragment used in a mobile application. Only one of these mobile pages is displayed at a time. Several notable properties affect the behavior of this control.

The **pageName** property is the mobile page name and the property used for navigation between the mobile pages. The singlePageApp control uses **pageName** to decide what page to show initially. You use the **resetContent** property to indicate whether the page contents should be re-created each time the page is displayed. Another property affecting performance is **preload**, which you can use to force the Mobile Page to be loaded when the whole XPage is loaded.

The Page Heading Control (`xe:djxmHeading`)

Mobile applications should have a heading. On a mobile screen, a heading is typically a bar at the top of the screen specifying the title of the page. It has various options to perform on the page, such as going backward. The **Back** button is defined in the heading tag.

```
<xe:djxmHeading id="djxmHeading1" label="Topic" back="Home"
moveTo="home"></xe:djxmHeading>
```

The **back** property is the label for the **Back** button. The **moveTo** property should contain the pageName of the Mobile Page destination.

The Heading control can also act as a container for other controls such as buttons and the mobile application's Tab Bar.

The Heading control also contains a callback or editable area for actions called **actionFacet**, which is typically a plus (+) button to create a new document. Listing 10.2 includes an example from the TeamRoom XL template. Buttons placed inside this facet take on the styling of the create buttons that are common to native buttons on that platform.

Listing 10.2   The Action Facet for a Heading Control

```
        <xp:this.facets>
           <xp:panel
             xp:key="actionFacet">
             <xp:this.rendered>
  <![CDATA[#{javascript:userBean.canCreateDocs}]]>
             </xp:this.rendered>
             <xp:button
               value="+"
               id="button1">
               <xp:eventHandler
                 event="onclick"
                 submit="true"
                 refreshMode="complete">
                 <xp:this.action>
                   <xe:moveTo
                     direction="Left to Right"
                     forceFullRefresh="true"
                     targetPage="newDiscussion"
                     transitionType="slide">
                   </xe:moveTo>
                 </xp:this.action>
               </xp:eventHandler>
             </xp:button>
           </xp:panel>
        </xp:this.facets>
```

Rounded List (`xe:djxmRoundRectList`)

As the name suggests, this is a component that displays a rectangle with rounded corners. It is mainly used as a styling container when documents are displayed and edited (see Listing 10.3 and Figure 10.3).

Listing 10.3   Rounded List Container for Data Input

```
<xe:djxmRoundRectList
    id="djxmRoundRectList1">
    <xp:label
      value="Subject: "
      id="labelSubject2"></xp:label>
```

Listing 10.3   (Continued)

```
<xp:inputText
  id="inputTextSubject2"
  value="#{document1.Subject}">
</xp:inputText>
<xp:br />
<xp:label
  value="Category: "
  id="labelCategory2"></xp:label>
<xp:inputText
  id="inputTextCategory2"
  value="#{document1.NewCats}">
</xp:inputText>
<xp:br />
<xp:inputTextarea
  id="inputTextareaBody"
  value="#{document1.Body}"
  cols="40"
  rows="10">
</xp:inputTextarea>
</xe:djxmRoundRectList>
```

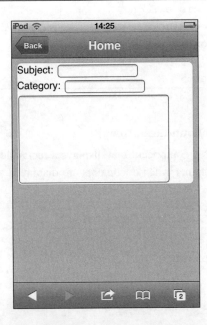

Figure 10.3   Rounded list container for a document.

Static Line Item (`xe:djxmLineItem`)

The Static Line Item control is a Dojo control mainly used to link to other mobile pages. This control can perform a number of functions. Listing 10.4 shows an example of its use as a link to a mobile page; this example would render as in Figure 10.4.

The **moveTo** property points to another mobile page contained within the same Single Page Application. For this, a hash (#) prefix may be used to enable the link to navigate to a location within the existing XPage; however, for most cases this isn't necessary because the runtime assumes that the value of the **moveTo** property is a location within the current page. You can use the **transition** property with the **moveTo** property to control how the mobile page appears to move with pages. By default, the transition is **slide**, although **fade** and **flip** are options here if desired.

Listing 10.4   Static Line Item Example

```
<xe:appPage
  id="appPage1"
  pageName="homePage">
  <xe:djxmHeading
    id="homePageHeading"
    label="Home"></xe:djxmHeading>
  <xe:djxmLineItem
    id="djxmLineItem1"
    moveTo="#viewPage"
    label="All Documents">
  </xe:djxmLineItem>
</xe:appPage>
<xe:appPage
  id="appPage2"
  pageName="viewPage"
  resetContent="false">
  <xe:djxmHeading
    id="djxmHeading1"
    label="Hello LS12"></xe:djxmHeading>
  <xe:dataView
    id="dataView1"
    pageName="documentPage"
    openDocAsReadonly="true">
    <xe:this.data>
      <xp:dominoView
        var="view1"
        viewName="xpAllDocuments"></xp:dominoView>
```

Listing 10.4   (Continued)

```
    </xe:this.data>
    <xe:this.summaryColumn>
      <xe:viewSummaryColumn
        columnName="Topic"></xe:viewSummaryColumn>
    </xe:this.summaryColumn>
  </xe:dataView>
  </xe:appPage>
```

Figure 10.4   Static Line Item control example.

You can also add images to the Static Line Item control using the **icon** property. You set the value of the property in the same way that other XPages control reference images usually reside in the same Domino application.

The **rightText** property allows an additional label to be set on this control.

Mobile Switch (`xe:djxmSwitch`)

The Mobile Switch control (`xe:djxmSwitch`) is probably best described as an on/off switch that behaves like a check box. It's not to be confused with a Switch facet control (`xe:switchFacet`), which allows the developer to dynamically change content that depends on a certain value.

The Mobile Switch control is used mainly in mobile applications for configuration, enabling an option as shown in Listing 10.5 and illustrated in Figure 10.5.

Listing 10.5   Enabling an Option with a Mobile Switch Control

```
<xe:singlePageApp
  id="singlePageApp1"
  selectedPageName="mobilePage1">
  <xe:appPage
    id="appPage1"
    pageName="mobilePage1">
  <xe:djxmHeading
    id="djxmHeading1"
    label="Mobile Switch Control">
  </xe:djxmHeading>
  <xe:djxmRoundRectList
    id="djxmRoundRectList1">
    <xp:table>
      <xp:tr>
        <xp:td>
          <xp:label
            value="Configuration Setting: "
            id="label1"></xp:label>
        </xp:td>
        <xp:td>
          <xe:djxmSwitch
            leftLabel="ON"
            rightLabel="OFF"
            id="djxmSwitch4"
            value="#{javascript:viewScope.vs01}">
            <xp:eventHandler
              event="onStateChanged"
              submit="true"
              refreshMode="complete">
              <xe:this.action><![CDATA[#{javascript:var v1 =
viewScope.vs01;
if (v1!=="off"){viewScope.put("vs01","off")
}
else{viewScope.put("vs01","on")
}}]]></xe:this.action>
            </xp:eventHandler>
          </xe:djxmSwitch>
        </xp:td>
        <xp:td>
```

Listing 10.5   (Continued)

```
                <xp:text
                    escape="true"
                    id="computedField1"
                    value="#{viewScope.vs01}">
                </xp:text>
              </xp:td>
            </xp:tr>
          </xp:table>
        </xe:djxmRoundRectList>
      </xe:appPage>
    </xe:singlePageApp>
```

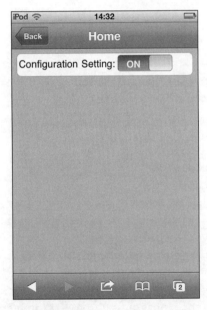

Figure 10.5   Mobile Switch control example.

There are four events attached to the Mobile Switch control; onTouchStart, onTouchEnd, onTouchMove, and onStateChanged. Each of these events is designed to be triggered conditionally. All the onTouch controls have been specifically designed to be triggered by the movement of the finger on the touch screen of a mobile device. Their behaviors are similar to the mouse events that are developed for desktop applications. In the same vein, the onStateChanged event is like an onChange event. It is triggered when the mobile switch is changed from on to off and vice versa. An example is shown in Listing 10.5.

Tab Bar (`xe:tabBar`)

The Tab Bar is mainly used as a container control for the **Tab Bar Button**. By default, the Tab Bar displays like a banner across the mobile page. In this scenario, it is usually used as an action bar at the bottom of the mobile device's screen, where black buttons will appear on a black background regardless of platform. These buttons are usually accompanied by an image on the button, as shown in Listing 10.6 and Figure 10.6.

Listing 10.6   Default Tab Bar with Buttons

```
<xe:tabBar
  id="tabBar1">
  <xe:tabBarButton
    id="tabBarButton1"
    label="Button 1"
    icon1="/act_saveandclose.gif">
  </xe:tabBarButton>
  <xe:tabBarButton
    id="tabBarButton2"
    label="Button 2"
    icon1="/authprof.gif">
  </xe:tabBarButton>
  <xe:tabBarButton
    id="tabBarButton3"
    label="Button 3"
    icon1="/intprof.gif">
  </xe:tabBarButton>
</xe:tabBar>
```

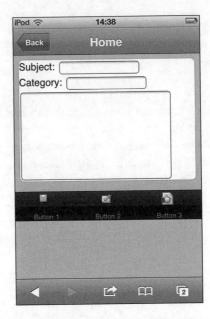

Figure 10.6   Tab Bar at the bottom of a mobile page with images.

When the **barType** property is set to `"segmentedControl"`, the Tab Bar buttons display together as one, although they're separated into their individual buttons by a vertical separator line, as shown in Listing 10.7 and Figure 10.7.

Listing 10.7   The Tab Bar as a Segmented Control

```
<xe:tabBar
    id="tabBar2"
    barType="segmentedControl">
    <xe:tabBarButton
      id="tabBarButton4"
      label="Button 1">
    </xe:tabBarButton>
    <xe:tabBarButton
      id="tabBarButton5"
      label="Button 2">
    </xe:tabBarButton>
    <xe:tabBarButton
      id="tabBarButton6"
      label="Button 3">
    </xe:tabBarButton>
  </xe:tabBar>
```

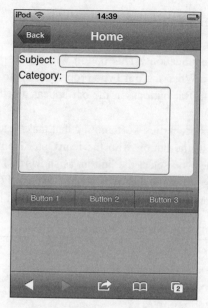

Figure 10.7 Tab Bar as a segmentedControl.

In this fashion, the segmentedControl is used for the Tab Bar in a header or on its own on the mobile page. When placed in the header, the Tab Bar's contents are merged into that of the heading, as shown in Figure 10.8.

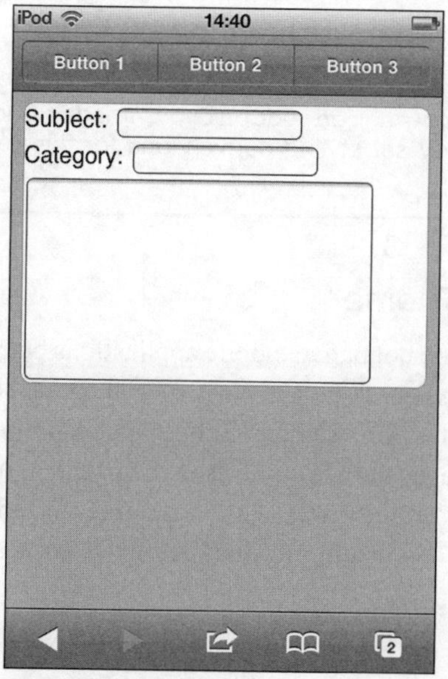

Figure 10.8 The Tab Bar in a header.

Tab Bar Button (`xe:tabBarButton`)

The Tab Bar button is similar to the conventional XPages button (`xp:button`) but with different styling for XPages Mobile applications. This button will not display as expected if it is not contained within the Tab Bar. When the **barType** property is set to `"segmentedControl"` on the Tab Bar, the multiple Tab Bar buttons on the bar appear together, as shown previously in Figure 10.7.

This control has several properties worth noting that make it applicable to mobile applications. You can add images to the button with the **icon1** and **icon2** properties. These display images depending on whether you select the button, as shown in Listing 10.8. The position of each of the images can change from the default if you use the **iconPos1** and **iconPos2** properties. This use of images is common when the Tab Bar is using its default barType setting.

Listing 10.8   Button Icon and Icon Position Properties

```
<xe:tabBarButton
  id="tabBarButton6"
  label="Button 3"
  icon1="/act_saveandclose.gif"
  icon2="/authprof.gif"
  iconPos1="top"
  iconPos2="bottom">
</xe:tabBarButton>
```

> **NOTE**
>
> When the **barType** is set to `segmentedControl`, images don't display on Apple's iOS platforms. There are already set styling conventions for this platform that excludes icon images.

The XPages Mobile Theme

XPages mobile applications are not native mobile applications but web browser applications that run on a mobile device and *appear* to be native. A special theme has been created to provide the native application look and feel for XPages mobile applications. This theme provides all the mobile styling for all the XPages mobile controls in the palette plus a few other controls like the Data View (`xe:dataView`), Outline (`xe:outline`), and Form Table (`xe:formTable`). Without this theme, XPages applications would look like regular websites on the mobile device's web browser.

This theme isn't activated or set in the same way that regular XPages themes are. It's activated per XPages that must have a prefix corresponding to a setting in the application's properties—xsp.theme.mobile.pagePrefix. So, for example, if xsp.theme.mobile.pagePrefix=mobile and the XPages are to inherit the mobile theme's look and feel, they must start with a prefix like mobileApp.xsp. When XPages is launched in the web browser, it will ignore all other themes and use the mobile theme.

Select a prefix that won't conflict with other XPages within the application. Avoid actual prefixes that are whole words or tend to form whole words in themselves. Don't use prefixes like the preceding example: mobile. Choose a pattern that makes more sense, such as "m_".

The mobile theme provides styling for many XPages controls; the Mobile controls are covered, of course, but so are the Data View (xe:dataView) and Accordion (xe:accordion). All other core, custom, and extension library controls will render in the mobile application using their existing web styling. In these cases, developers need to be selective of which controls they use and then apply their own custom styling. A case in point is using buttons (xp:button), as shown in Listing 10.9, from the TeamRoom XL template. Here the developer has created two new style classes: one for Android, "mblSaveButton_android", and another for other platforms, "mblSaveButton". These style classes are not stored in the mobile theme but in a CSS file added to the application: **.mobile.css**.

Listing 10.9   Custom Button Styling for Mobile Applications

```
<xp:button
  value="Save"
  id="button1">
  <xp:this.styleClass>
  <![CDATA[#{javascript:
   if(isAndroidCheck())
     {return "mblSaveButton_android";
}
else {
return "mblSaveButton";}
}]]>
  </xp:this.styleClass>
  <xp:this.style><![CDATA[#{javascript:
if(!isAndroidCheck())
{
return "margin-top:6px;";}
}]]></xp:this.style>
  ...
  </xp:button>
```

Listing 10.9 is an example from the TeamRoom XL template of how to style items that are outside the mobile theme. There, specific styling has been created for these elements—in this case, inline buttons. This look and feel is available as style classes stored in a custom-built CSS file from the TeamRoom application. These style classes are then applied dynamically when the application in this case is opened on an iOS platform or an Android platform. This is something the developer needs to keep in mind when styling an XPages mobile application.

Currently, the mobile theme provides styling for two main platforms: Apple's iOS and Android. The mobile theme should cover the most popular design styling cases for developers, but they may find that a control they are using doesn't have the correct or desired styling. In these cases, developers must custom-style the component and may have to do two of these styles for Apple iOS and Android. When the application runs, developers have to know which platform the application is running on and what style to apply. The XPages runtime helps with the global variable `context.getUserAgent().getUserAgent()`. It returns the name of the platform, which could be Android, iPad, or iPhone. From here, developers can decide which styling to use. XPages Mobile caches the detected browser's User-Agent string on the first request. Developers can override this by specifying a platform in the query string, such as **?platform=iphone** or `?platform=android:http://myserver/myapp.nsf/mobileApp.xsp?platform=iphone`.

Hello Mobile World Tutorial

In this tutorial, developers are shown how to build a simple XPages mobile application on an existing Domino database, which gives them the first steps to creating a mobile web experience.

This tutorial builds a mobile app from scratch, displays the contents of a view from another application, opens a document from that view, and edits and saves a document. A more detailed tutorial is available on the Lotus Notes and Domino Development wiki at http://www-10.lotus.com/ldd/ddwiki.nsf/dx/XPages_Mobile_Controls_Tutorial_.

1. Enable the App for the Extension Library and Mobile

Take any existing application and launch it in Designer. Go to the **Application Properties** and check the box for `com.ibm.xsp.extlib.library` in the **XPages Libraries** section on the **Advanced** tab. This enables the application to use the ExtLib if it hasn't been done already. Save and close the **Application Properties**.

Next, open the Application Properties, **xsp.properties**, in source mode from the Package Explorer. The Package Explorer isn't visible by default in the Domino Designer perspective. To get it to display here, select **Window → Show Eclipse Views → Package Explorer**. Once this has been launched, go to the **WebContent\WEB-INF** folder and launch the **xsp.properties** file. Then select the **Source** tab and add the prefix for the XPages to use the mobile theme. Choose any desired prefix, such as m_: in `xsp.theme.mobile.pagePrefix=m_`.

2. Create a New XPage and Mobile Application

Create a new XPage called **m_helloworld**. Note the use of the prefix here: **m_**.

On the blank XPage, add a Mobile Application control (xe:singlePageApp). Then add a Mobile Page control (xe:appPage) between the tags of the Mobile Application. Finally, add a Page Heading control (xe:djxmHeading) between the Mobile Page tags, and give the heading a label of "Hello XPages Mobile World".

Provide a name to the Mobile Page control—pageName="viewPage"—and then set the **selectedPageName** property to that page name.

This should generate the markup shown in Listing 10.10, which is enough to render a first look at the new XPages mobile application (see Figure 10.9) when launched in a mobile device's web browser.

Listing 10.10   XPages Markup of a Heading Tag Inside a Mobile Application Tag

```
<?xml version="1.0" encoding="UTF-8"?>
<xp:view
  xmlns:xp="http://www.ibm.com/xsp/core"
  xmlns:xe="http://www.ibm.com/xsp/coreex">
  <xe:singlePageApp
    id="singlePageApp1"
    selectedPageName="viewPage">
    <xe:appPage
      id="appPage1"
      pageName="viewPage">
    <xe:djxmHeading
        id="djxmHeading1"
        label="Hello XPages Mobile World">
      </xe:djxmHeading>
    </xe:appPage>
  </xe:singlePageApp>
</xp:view>
```

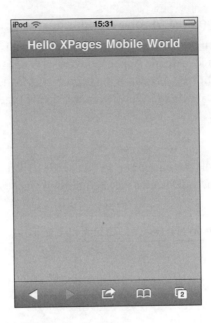

Figure 10.9   Hello XPages Mobile World example.

3. Add a View Document Collection to the Mobile Page

The next step is to create a content Mobile Application that is contained within Mobile Pages controls (`xe:appPage`).

The purpose of the mobile page viewPage is to display a list of documents, a view collection of records. The datasource for this will come from another application on the server: the ExtLib Demo App (**XPagesExt.nsf**). To display this data collection, you use a Data View (`xe:dataView`) control to connect and retrieve the data and present it in a list form.

On the source pane in Designer, drag and drop a Data View control inside the Mobile Page control. This prompts the developer to select a view datasource from the current database. However, for this simple tutorial, a view collection from another database, the **XPagesExt.nsf**, is selected. This view name is to be **AllContacts**.

Clicking **OK** on this dialog generates the markup for the XPage. From here, some minor configuration is done to the Data View to display text to represent the records per row. The **summaryColumn** property, which is also a complex property for `xe:viewSummaryColumn`, is used for this purpose. To use a Data View inside a mobile application, select a column from the original view. In this case, it will be a column named **Name**, so `columnName="Name"`.

We have selected a column named **Name**. The naming will work in this case, but in general it isn't best practice because the column title could be changed when localized, and the mobile application would likely break. It is more correct to use the programmatic name of a view column to ensure that the use case will work.

The Data View displays the view collection with the name of the contact representing the row record. At this stage, it is recommended that you restrict the number of rows to 10 so the view fits inside the small screen of the mobile device.

The markup should now look something like what is shown in Listing 10.11 and display on the mobile device like that in Figure 10.10.

An additional property is set here, too. The property `resetContent` is set to `"false"`. It will be the default page of the mobile application because we do not want the page to be re-created every time the page is displayed.

Listing 10.11   XPages Markup of a Heading Tag Inside a Mobile Application Tag

```
<xe:appPage
  id="appPage2"
  pageName="viewPage"
  resetContent="false">
  <xe:djxmHeading
    id="djxmHeading2"
    label="Hello XPages Mobile World">
  </xe:djxmHeading>
  <xe:dataView
    id="dataView1"
    rows="10">
    <xe:this.data>
      <xp:dominoView
        var="view1"
        databaseName="XPagesExt.nsf"
        viewName="AllContacts"></xp:dominoView>
    </xe:this.data>
    <xe:this.summaryColumn>
      <xe:viewSummaryColumn
        columnName="Name"></xe:viewSummaryColumn>
    </xe:this.summaryColumn>
  </xe:dataView>
</xe:appPage>
```

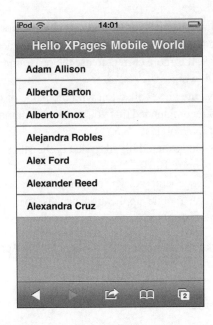

Figure 10.10   The view collection on an XPages Mobile Page.

4. Display More Rows

Typically, when a user is presented with a limited list of records from a view collection, a button is provided to allow the user to add a few more rows. This can be done in the XPages mobile applications, too; the Extension Library has a control that can provide this feature.

The Add Rows (`xe:addRows`) control is attached to any event and added through the simple Actions dialog. But first, there is an editable area on the Data View control called `"pagerBottom"` and to this add a link (`xp:link`) control. This link becomes a facet of the Data View container. A simple **Add Rows to the Data Iterator** action is added to the onClick event of the link, with the `rowCount` property set to `"5"` and the `for` property set to the ID of the Data View: `"dataView1"`, as shown in Listing 10.12.

Listing 10.12   Data View with Add Rows Simple Action

```
<xe:dataView
  id="dataView1"
  rows="7">
  <xp:this.facets>
    <xp:link
      escape="true"
      text="Load 5 more rows"
```

```
          id="link1"
          xp:key="pagerBottom">
          <xp:eventHandler
            event="onclick"
            submit="false">
            <xp:this.script>
              <xe:addRows
                for="dataView1"
                rowCount="5"></xe:addRows>
            </xp:this.script>
          </xp:eventHandler>
        </xp:link>
      </xp:this.facets>
      <xe:this.data>
        <xp:dominoView
          var="view1"
          databaseName="XPagesExt.nsf"
          viewName="AllContacts">
        </xp:dominoView>
      </xe:this.data>
      <xe:this.summaryColumn>
        <xe:viewSummaryColumn
          columnName="Name"></xe:viewSummaryColumn>
      </xe:this.summaryColumn>
    </xe:dataView
```

Figure 10.11 shows the Add Rows action: the **Load 5 More Rows** link on the mobile page. When this is selected, five rows are added to the list. Note here that the link now looks like a button. This is all part of the mobile theme, which uses buttons instead of links on mobile devices because they're easier to click.

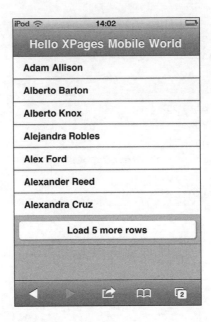

Figure 10.11   The Add Rows action.

5. Opening a Document from the Data View

The next step is to open a document from the Data View in another mobile page. For this action, another Mobile Page control is added to the Single Page Application. This is given an easily recognizable ID or pageName, **documentPage**. This ID is needed to configure the Data View **pageName** property, which should be prefixed with a hash tag, such as pageName= "#documentPage".

The hash tag is important here. If it's not used, the Data View attempts to open the document selected in that row in an XPage in the **pageName** property. With the hash tag, the navigation stays within the current XPage, as demonstrated in the following segment of a URL:

```
/m_helloworld.xsp#documentPage?documentId=D2EB6…E1DFC&action=openDocument
```

A Heading control is added to the Mobile page, which includes navigation to the view mobile page. The **back** property is the label of the **Back** button, and the **moveTo** property is set to "viewPage".

What's added next to the mobile page is a rounded rectangle list (xe:djxmRound RectList). It will be the container for the document data and provide the styling surrounding the document when it displays in the device.

After this, the mobile page is developed much like a conventional XPage. A Panel control is added to the mobile page. Then a Domino document datasource is configured to this Panel control. Labels and input controls, bound to datasources, are added to the Panel next.

Finally, the `openDocAsReadonly` property is set to `"true"` on the Data View, as shown in Listing 10.13. The document now opens in the second mobile page in read mode.

To ensure that the document selected in the data view is opened in the documentPage every time, the property `resetContent` is set to `"true"` here. Without doing that, the first document opened would remain in memory.

Listing 10.13   Opening Documents from a Data View in Another Mobile Page

```
<xe:appPage
  id="appPage2"
  pageName="documentPage"
  resetContent="true">
  <xe:djxmHeading
    id="djxmHeading2"
    label="Document Page"
    back="Back"
    moveTo="viewPage">
  </xe:djxmHeading>
  <xe:djxmRoundRectList
    id="djxmRoundRectList1">
    <xp:panel>
      <xp:this.data>
        <xp:dominoDocument
          var="document1"
          databaseName="XPagesExt.nsf"
          formName="Contact"></xp:dominoDocument>
      </xp:this.data>
      <xp:table>
        <xp:tr>
          <xp:td>
            <xp:label
              value="First name:"
              id="firstName_Label1"
              for="firstName1"></xp:label>
          </xp:td>
          <xp:td>
            <xp:inputText
              value="#{document1.FirstName}"
```

Listing 10.13   (Continued)

```
                    id="firstName1">
                </xp:inputText>
              </xp:td>
            </xp:tr>
              . . .
              . . .
          </xp:table>
        </xp:panel>
      </xe:djxmRoundRectList>
    </xe:appPage>
```

Figure 10.12 shows the changes to the viewPage, particularly the chevrons that now appear on the Data Table rows to indicate that an action applies to these rows.

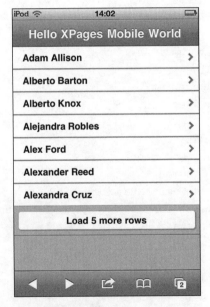

Figure 10.12   Changes to the Data View.

Figure 10.13 shows what should happen when a row is selected on the Data View. It should navigate to the documentPage and open the selected document there.

Figure 10.13 The document is opened in Read Mode.

Data View and Other View Containers in Mobile Apps

The Data View control is an enhancement of the XPages View Panel (`xp:viewPanel`) control. The way documents can be selected from rows that are opened in an XPage is built into this control. The developer doesn't need to configure further here. As demonstrated, all the developer needs to do is set the **pageName** property, and at runtime the control processes the document and opens it in the desired page. If that page has a corresponding document datasource that matches the document selected, it will be read in that page. All this is done automatically for the most part.

Extra configuration is needed if the developer chooses an alternative to the Data View, like the View Entries Tree node (`xe:dominoViewEntriesTreeNode`). In these cases, the developer needs to get the universal ID of the document in the selected row (the view datasource `var` plus `getUniversalID()`) and add a parameter on what to do with that document. Usually this involves the `openDocument` action. All this is computed inside the **href** property, as shown in Listing 10.14.

Listing 10.14 Computing the href Action to Open a Document from a View Row

```
<xe:outline
  id="outlineXPage">
  <xe:this.treeNodes>
    <xe:dominoViewEntriesTreeNode
```

Listing 10.14   (Continued)

```
          viewName="AllStates"
          labelColumn="Key"
          var="o1">
          <xe:this.href><![CDATA[#{javascript:var id =
o1.getUniversalID();
var str = "/p02.xsp?documentId="+id+"&action=openDocument";
return str}]]></xe:this.href>
          /xe:dominoViewEntriesTreeNode>
      </xe:this.treeNodes>
    </xe:outline
```

In Listing 10.14, the URL is composed to open a document in another XPage. For mobile applications, the document needs to be opened in the same XPage—another mobile page contained within the same single page application. Listing 10.15 shows how to do this—selecting a document in one mobile page and opening it in another. At first glance, there doesn't seem to be a difference. A closer look reveals one crucial difference in the page name part used to compute the URL. Instead of using a relative path to the XPage, '**/p02.xsp**' as in Listing 10.14, just the mobile page name is inserted, `"documentPage"`, and without the hash tag. This hash tag is inserted automatically during runtime so the developer doesn't have to insert it, as shown in Listing 10.15.

Listing 10.15   Opening a Document in Another Mobile Page

```
  <xe:outline
    id="outlineMobile">
    <xe:this.treeNodes>
      <xe:dominoViewEntriesTreeNode
        viewName="AllStates"
        labelColumn="Key"
        var="o1">
        <xe:this.href><![CDATA[#{javascript:var id =
o1.getUniversalID();
var str = "documentPage&documentId="+id+"&action=openDocument";
return str}]]></xe:this.href>
      </xe:dominoViewEntriesTreeNode>
    </xe:this.treeNodes>
    <xe:this.treeRenderer>
      <xe:mobileAccordionMenu></xe:mobileAccordionMenu>
    </xe:this.treeRenderer>
  </xe:outline>
```

6. Editing and Saving Document Changes

There are two actions in this section: one to edit the document and another to save the document. The Tab Bar and Tab Bar buttons are used here, but developers aren't restricted to these controls. In fact, they can use any control as long as it can perform these actions in a mobile page. All they need to worry about is the styling.

Using button or link controls in this scenario requires the developer to create custom styling. Without this, these controls display with their typical XPages web rendering. However, some container controls, like the Data View (xe:dataView) and Form Table (xe:formTable), have mobile styling. Using XPages buttons or links, these controls inherit this mobile style automatically. The developer should use these controls when developing XPages Mobile applications.

For this exercise, the Tab Bar and Tab Bar button is used because they have their own mobile styling and don't depend on other container controls. You can configure the Tab Bar Button like an existing XPages button (xp:button), although it has just one event associated with it: onClick. A conventional edit document simple action is applied for the **Edit** Tab Bar Button. And for the **Save** Tab Bar Button, a new Extension Library simple action is available: Move To Mobile Page (xe:moveTo). This action contains properties that allow it to be used for other actions and not just saving document changes. Transition after the event is catered for with the direction and **transitionType** properties. The **targetPage** property indicates to which page to transition. And with the saveDocument set to "true", document changes are submitted to the document datasource.

Listing 10.16 shows the markup of the Tab Bar and Tab Bar Buttons contained within the panel that contains the document datasource.

Listing 10.16   Edit and Save Tab Bar Buttons

```
...
</xp:table>
  <xe:tabBar
    id="tabBar1"
    barType="segmentedControl">
    <xe:tabBarButton
      id="tabBarButton1"
      label="Edit"
      rendered="#{javascript:!document1.isEditable()}">
      <xp:eventHandler
        event="onClick"
        submit="true"
        refreshMode="complete">
        <xp:this.action>
```

Listing 10.16   (Continued)

```
            <xp:changeDocumentMode
               mode="edit"
               var="document1">
            </xp:changeDocumentMode>
          </xp:this.action>
        </xp:eventHandler>
      </xe:tabBarButton>
      <xe:tabBarButton
        id="tabBarButton2"
        label="Save"
        rendered="#{javascript:document1.isEditable()}">
        <xp:eventHandler
          event="onClick"
          submit="true"
          refreshMode="complete">
          <xp:this.action>
            <xe:moveTo
               direction="Right to Left"
               forceFullRefresh="true"
               saveDocument="true"
               targetPage="viewPage"
               transitionType="slide">
            </xe:moveTo>
          </xp:this.action>
        </xp:eventHandler>
      </xe:tabBarButton>
    </xe:tabBar>
  </xp:panel>
</xe:djxmRoundRectList>
```

Figure 10.14 shows how the Tab Bar appears in the documentPage at runtime. Notice that the **Edit** button is showing and the **Save** button is not.

Figure 10.14 Mobile document in Read Mode.

Figure 10.15 shows the same mobile page when the **Edit** button is selected, which changes the mode of the document to edit mode. Here the **Save** button becomes visible.

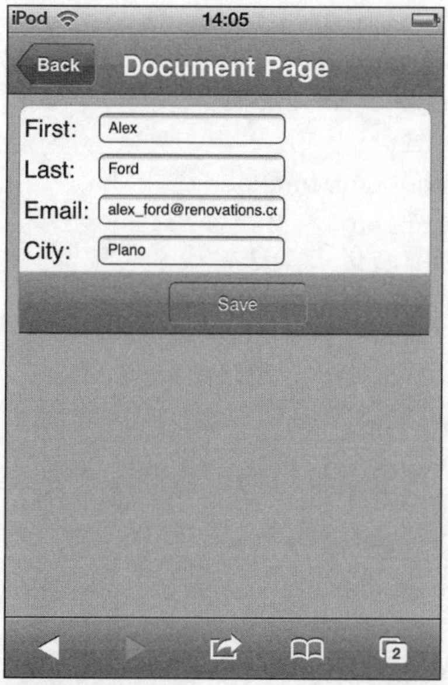

Figure 10.15 Mobile document in Edit Mode.

Using the actionFacet in the Heading for Buttons

Action buttons like these, although not the Tab Bar buttons, could also be placed in the action-Facet of the Heading control. Here they take on the mobile styling that's typical for buttons located at the top-right corner of the mobile page. Listing 10.17 shows these same Edit and Save actions but in the header.

Listing 10.17   Action Buttons in a Header

```
<xe:djxmHeading
   id="djxmHeading2"
   label="Document Page"
   back="Back"
   moveTo="viewPage">
   <xp:this.facets>
     <xp:panel
       xp:key="actionFacet">
       <xp:button
         value="Edit"
         id="buttonEdit"
         rendered="#{javascript:!document1.isEditable()}">
         <xp:eventHandler
           event="onclick"
           submit="true"
           refreshMode="complete">
           <xp:this.action>
             <xp:changeDocumentMode
               mode="edit">
             </xp:changeDocumentMode>
           </xp:this.action>
         </xp:eventHandler>
       </xp:button>
       <xp:button
         value="Save"
         id="buttonSave"
         rendered="#{javascript:document1.isEditable()}">
         <xp:eventHandler
           event="onclick"
           submit="true"
           refreshMode="complete">
           <xp:this.action>
             <xe:moveTo
```

```
                        direction="Right to Left"
                        saveDocument="true"
                        targetPage="viewPage"
                        transitionType="slide"
                        forceFullRefresh="true">
                </xe:moveTo>
            </xp:this.action>
        </xp:eventHandler>
      </xp:button>
    </xp:panel>
  </xp:this.facets>
</xe:djxmHeading>
```

For the example shown in Listing 10.17, the panel used to contain the document datasource also needs to enclose the Heading control. This is so the actions are performed on that datasource and the buttons change their rendering dynamically based on that document.

Deep Dive into the Controls in the Extension Library, with Examples of Their Use

It may surprise you as you read through this section that you may be familiar with many of the controls mentioned. These are the same Extension Library controls that are used elsewhere in this book, and they're the same controls that are used in regular XPages applications. You can exploit these same controls—with a few minor tweaks—for XPages mobile applications. That topic will be described in this section.

Outline Control

The Outline control is perfect as a menu or a way to navigate through various pages. The typical use of the outline is to display a menu of items, perhaps as a root screen or home page. A typical example of this is shown in Listing 10.18.

Listing 10.18 Outline Control with Various Navigators

```
<xe:outline
  rendererType="com.ibm.xsp.extlib.MobileOutlineNavigator"
  id="outline1">
  <xe:this.treeNodes>
    <xe:basicLeafNode
      href="#profile"
      label="My Profile: #{javascript:sessionScope.commonUserName;}">
    </xe:basicLeafNode>
```

Listing 10.18   (Continued)

```
      <xe:basicContainerNode
        label="Documents">
        <xe:this.children>
          <xe:basicLeafNode
            href="#newTopic"
            label="New Topic">
          </xe:basicLeafNode>
          <xe:basicLeafNode
            href="#allDocs"
            label="All Documents">
          </xe:basicLeafNode>
          <xe:basicLeafNode
            href="#mostRecent"
            label="By Most Recent">
          </xe:basicLeafNode>
          <xe:basicLeafNode
            href="#docsByAuthor"
            label="By Author">
          </xe:basicLeafNode>
          <xe:basicLeafNode
            href="#tags"
            label="By Tag">
          </xe:basicLeafNode>
          <xe:basicLeafNode
            href="#myDocs"
            label="My Documents">
          </xe:basicLeafNode>
        </xe:this.children>
      </xe:basicContainerNode>
    </xe:this.treeNodes>
    <xe:this.treeRenderer>
      <xe:MobileAccordionMenu></xe:MobileAccordionMenu>
    </xe:this.treeRenderer>
  </xe:outline>
```

Notice that `<xe:outline>` has its `renderType` attribute set to `"com.ibm.xsp.extlib.MobileOutlineNavigator"`. This is an example of overriding the default render-Type to provide a more appropriate styling for a mobile device. In many cases the mobile theme does this automatically, but it may be overriden if you have an alternative rendering that you'd prefer.

The Tree Nodes `<xe:this.treeNodes>` define a group of options to click on, each one of them a Basic Leaf Node `xe:basicLeafNode` in which the **href** property is the link to the mobile page. Include a hash symbol (#) before the page name to avoid any future issues with redirecting and parameter passing. You can use a Basic Container Node `xe:basicContainerNode` to create a group inside a single element in the outline when the developer might have a lot of options and want to break it into sections so the user can read it more easily. Figure 10.16 shows an example of this with the **Documents** section. Finally, the `treeRenderer` defines which way to display the sections.

Figure 10.16   The home page of the Mobile Discussion template.

The My Profile label displays the username of the person logged in; a CSS styling is applied to this `"overflow: hidden"`. This means if there is any overflow because of a long name stretching past the end of the row, it will be obscured rather than pushing text down on top of the next row.

As shown in Figure 10.16, all the functionality of the discussion template's **viewMenu** is replicated here, alongside a profile and new topic link. From this screen, the user can navigate to all the major sections of the application.

The outline has a renderer applied to it; this is not the way it appears when it's created. This renderer is used as a standard control on smartphones and is how mobile users expect to navigate through an application.

An outline with the renderer and a single leaf node is a useful way to create a link to a new page. In the document mobile page, in each reply the standard link has been replaced with this link to ensure mobile users can interact with it and understand that it opens a new page.

Hash Tags

With the mobile controls, the developer can define multiple pages inside the one XPage. The developer can set their navigation by appending a hash and then the name of the mobile page to the name of the file, such as **mobileHome.xsp#byAuthor**.

Some controls include properties that accept a mobile page as an attribute and offer other settings, such as the type of transition and the direction of movement.

Form Table Control (`xe:formTable`)

Form tables are an extremely easy way to make a detail entry or display form for a mobile device. A form table can have many form rows, each of which can have controls such as a label and text field added. See Listing 10.19.

Listing 10.19   Form Table Control

```
<xe:formTable
  id="formTable1"
  formTitle="#{profileDoc.enterWho}"
  xp:key="profile"
  style="font-size:14px; font-weight:normal;"
  formDescription="Profile document of user">
  <xe:formRow
    id="formRow1"
    labelPosition="none">
    <xp:image
      id="photo"
      alt="#{profileDoc.enterWho}"
      height="130px"
      width="130px">
      <xp:this.url><![CDATA[#{javascript:var imageName =
"profileNoPhoto-118px.png";
    var al:java.util.List =
profileDoc.getAttachmentList("thumbnailUrl");
    if(!al.isEmpty()){
    var lastItemIndex = al.size() - 1;
     if(lastItemIndex > 0){var eo:NotesEmbeddedObject =
al.get(lastItemIndex);
    imageName = eo.getHref();
    }else{
```

```
    var eo:NotesEmbeddedObject = al.get(0);
     imageName = eo.getHref();}}
     return(imageName);}]]>
       </xp:this.url>
     </xp:image>
   </xe:formRow>
   <xe:formRow
     id="formRow3"
     label="Email: "
     style="word-wrap: break-word">
     <xp:link
       text="#{profileDoc.Email}">
       <xp:this.value><![CDATA[#{javascript:"mailto:" +
profileDoc.getItemValueString('Email')}]]></xp:this.value>
     </xp:link>
   </xe:formRow>
   ...
 </xe:formTable>
```

The properties **formTitle** and **formDescription** are displayed in the top-left corner before the actual rows are displayed, as a means of giving instructions and describing the action to take. Each xe:formRow is going to be rendered as a row and in this case will contain a label and input text that is connected to a Domino document.

When you're running the sample in Listing 10.20, when the **Edit** button is selected, the document datasource behind this document is set to Edit Mode and the input text boxes are enabled; the user can change the content. The **Edit** button changes to a **Save** button.

Listing 10.20   Button with Change Dynamic Action

```
<xp:button
  id="buttonEdit"
  value="Edit">
  <xp:eventHandler
    event="onclick"
    submit="true"
    refreshMode="complete">
  <xp:this.action>
    <xp:actionGroup>
      <xp:changeDocumentMode
        mode="edit"
        var="profileDoc">
```

Listing 10.20   (Continued)

```
        </xp:changeDocumentMode>
        <xe:changeDynamicContentAction
          facetName="saveControl"
          for="dynamicContent4">
        </xe:changeDynamicContentAction>
      </xp:actionGroup>
    </xp:this.action>
  </xp:eventHandler>
</xp:button>
```

Also, the button causes a Dynamic Content control to switch the front end UI, so users can press the **Save** button when they are finished editing.

Dynamic Content Control

Previously, it was mentioned that developers can use the Dynamic Content control to change such things as groups of buttons. Dynamic content allows developers to specify multiple panels inside the container and assign them values using the xp:key property. Then when the developers define a dynamic control, they set which panel is the default. The default panel is loaded first; using an event can change which panel is loaded thereafter. In Listing 10.20, the **Edit** and **Cancel** buttons are on a panel, and **Save** and **Cancel** are on a panel that is not being rendered. When the **Edit** button is clicked, the changeDynamicContentAction action is fired, and a new panel key is specified (see Listing 10.21).

Listing 10.21   Dynamic Content Example

```
<xe:dynamicContent
  id="dynamicContent2"
  defaultFacet="viewContent">
  <xp:this.facets>
    <xp:panel
      id="panel4"
      xp:key="viewContent">

      .
</xp:panel>
    <xp:panel
      id="panel6"
      xp:key="editContent">

      ..
</xp:panel>
  </xp:this.facets>
</xe:dynamicContent
```

Dynamic controls are simple to use. The developer specifies panels inside with `xp:key=""` and a name. The default one is displayed first. Then a control in that panel or somewhere else on the page can call a `changeDynamicContent` action, where the developer can supply the name of the dynamic control and the name of the facet to change it to.

If the user created the document, an **Edit** button appears. Clicking the **Edit** button switches to an edit content section with text boxes and **Save** and **Cancel** buttons.

The dynamic control can be useful, because another screen doesn't have to be rendered. Only the section that is changing needs to be loaded, which can save resources and time. This control also provides different functionality to users.

The document view screen uses the same XPages code taken from the Discussion template to display the parent document and its replies. The only difference is that the **Read More** link was replaced with an outline with a single entry to make it more usable on a mobile device. Another issue was limiting the number of indents that are made when you reply to a response to a reresponse. The desktop version has no limit on indents, but a mobile device is limited to four indents. Any replies after that are kept at the same level as the one before it.

Data View Control

Data Views are much better than tables for displaying data on mobile devices. Tables aren't appropriate in this case because of all the formatting that takes place; the formatting is generally too wide to see most of it, or it's condensed to the point that the user can't read it. Data View takes care of this because the content is fit to the width of the device. Table 10.1 shows the column types and their uses.

Table 10.1 Column Types and Their Uses

Column Types	Use
Category Column	This is used to group items. For example, the By Most Recent View from the Discussion Template groups data by creation date.
Summary Column	This column is placed to the left of the row and is its main focus. For example, in most of the Data Views in this application, the summary row is the subject of the post.
Icon Column	This column is used to assign icons to a row.
Extra Column	There can be multiple extra columns that are placed in the order they are defined. For example, adding a second column after the first will display on the right and so on.

However, the layout of the Data View is a little bit different when a renderer is applied to it. In the All Documents page, the summary row is in the top left and the extras appear beneath it.

When developers are using a category column, such as the ones used in Most Recent or By Author from the Discussion template, they need to make sure the expand level is set correctly. (Not including it returns a default value, which is acceptable.) The expand level is a property that denotes whether replies are included; only the parent documents are displayed, but anything categorized won't display if the expand level is set not to allow replies (see Listing 10.22).

Listing 10.22   Expand Level Example

```
  <xp:this.expandLevel>
<![CDATA[#{javascript:if(sessionScope.ec==null ||
sessionScope.ec==0){return 1}{return 0}}]]>
  </xp:this.expandLevel>
```

The developer can add facets to a row. On the All Documents page on the Discussion XL template's mobile application, a panel has been added to the detail facet and text has been added to the panel. The panel is the abstract of the post content.

More Link

Every Data View page should have a **More** link at the bottom that is equivalent to the desktop's **Next** button. With a Data View, the developer specifies how many rows are displayed at the start. The developer should try not to have too many rows, because it will take longer to load the first view the user wants to see. In the example in Listing 10.23, the first 10 rows are loaded, and each time the user presses **More**, an additional 5 are added to the view. This task is done relatively easily using the addRows tag (xe:addRows). The code shows the addRows tag, but it also determines whether the **More** link needs to be displayed.

Listing 10.23   More Link Example

```
<xp:this.facets>
  <xp:link
    escape="true"
    text="More..."
    id="link6"
    xp:key="pagerBottom">
    <xp:this.rendered>
    <![CDATA[#{javascript:
     var num = parseInt(dominoView2.getTopLevelEntryCount());
     if(num > 10)
     return true;
     else
       return false;}]]>
```

```
      </xp:this.rendered>
      <xp:eventHandler
        event="onclick"
        submit="false">
        <xp:this.script>
          <xe:addRows
            rowCount="5"
            for="dataView2"
            disableId="link6">
          </xe:addRows>
        </xp:this.script>
      </xp:eventHandler>
    </xp:link>
  </xp:this.facets>
```

This code adds a label as the bottom-left facet of the Data View. Some of these Domino views are categorized; the categorized rows count as rows when Add Rows is used.

> **NOTE**
>
> The Data View never adds blank rows. If you have an addRows tag that says to add five rows and only three are left, only three rows are added.

Filter Data

In a similar way to the desktop version, the developer can specify a filter for the data that is applied to the Category column: categoryFilter. So, for example, in Listing 10.24, the My Documents page is similar to the By Author page with the exception of adding a category filter of the username of the logged-in user. The result is one category being returned instead of many.

Listing 10.24   Category Filtering Example

```
<xe:this.data>
  <xp:dominoView
    var="dominoView"
    viewName="xpAuthorPosts"
    dataCache="full"
    categoryFilter="#{javascript:sessionScope.authorName}:Main">
  </xp:dominoView>
</xe:this.data>
```

Multiple Controls

The last thing you need to know about Data Views is how to combine them with other controls. A Data View is like any other control; it doesn't need to be the size of the page. Listing 10.25 is an example of a form table and two Data Views. The user can click on a username onscreen to view the details of that user.

The first part of the listing is the same as the Profile View except that it searches for the username that was clicked on. Two Data Views must exist, because the Data View returns just one of the sections at a time when it's filtering the categories. Viewing both sections side by side requires the developer to have two views.

Listing 10.25   Multiple Controls

```
<![CDATA[#{javascript:
var nNotesName:NotesName = session.createName(sessionScope.authorName);
var sCanonicalName:String = nNotesName.getCanonical();
var nameAbbreviated = nNotesName.getAbbreviated();


var text =  res.getString("authorProfile.description") + ": " +
nameAbbreviated;


//Details
var db:NotesDatabase = database;
var view:NotesView = db.getView(VIEW_PROFILES);
view.setAutoUpdate(false);
var entry:NotesViewEntry =
view.getEntryByKey(nNotesName.getCanonical(), true);
if (entry != null)
{
var cols = entry.getColumnValues();
//viewScope.mAlocation = cols[location];
viewScope.mAemail = cols[COLUMN_EMAIL];
viewScope.mAphone = cols[COLUMN_PHONE];
viewScope.mArole = cols[COLUMN_ROLE];
viewScope.mAgoal = cols[COLUMN_GOAL];
viewScope.mAprofileFound = true;
}
else
{
viewScope.profileFound = false;
}
return text;}]]>
```

Move to Mobile Page Action

Similar to a redirect with the understanding of how the hash tags work, the Move To (xe:moveTo) mobile page action allows the developer to specify properties such as the type of transition the developer would like to see and the direction it moves. The target page is the mobile page (for example, **document** would be the target, not **mobileHome.xsp#document**). See Listing 10.26.

Listing 10.26   Move To Example

```
<xp:this.action>
  <xe:moveTo
    transitionType="slide"
    direction="Left to Right"
    forceFullRefresh="true"
    targetPage="replyThread?action=openDocument
&amp;documentId=#{javascript:dominoDoc.getNoteID()}
&amp;parentNoteID=#{javascript:dominoDoc.getNoteID()}">
  </xe:moveTo>
</xp:this.action>
```

One important property is **forceFullRefresh**. Sometimes when you're moving between pages, you want nothing to be saved. Without **forceFullRefresh**, after entering a new topic and returning to the screen, the previous elements you entered will still be there, which could affect security because of passwords and usernames.

The Move To action also allows the user to save the document. In other words, this action can leave the current screen and update a document.

Heading (`xe:djxmheading`)

The heading is just a normal control that displays the title of the mobile page and can have a **Back** button declared to return to a previous page. The Heading also has events. Developers can't apply an event handler to this type of control, so they have to add content to the events the same way as a property. These events can be useful for running code similar to what was loaded before/after page load that is missing from defining all pages in the same file (see Listing 10.27).

Listing 10.27   A Mobile Page Heading

```
<xe:djxmHeading
  id="djxmHeading1"
  label="Home"
  back="Home"
  moveTo="home">
```

Listing 10.27   (Continued)

```
    <xp:this.onShow>
<![CDATA[#{javascript:
sessionScope.from = "allDocs";
sessionScope.fromName = "All Docs";
}]]>
    </xp:this.onShow>
  </xe:djxmHeading>
```

This example shows a heading defined with a **Back** button to the home page. The onShow event updates a session variable that the page currently on is the all documents page. Using this session variable is not required; it is an example of using dynamic breadcrumbs on the application. That is, instead of hard-coding back buttons, the developer could query this session variable.

Large Content

One problem with making a mobile version that connects to the same datasource as a desktop is that the desktop version can have a rich text box, meaning large tables can be in the data. That, in turn, can cause a mobile page that displays it to stretch out. A dijit, xsp.largeContent, has been created to handle this problem; Listing 10.28 is an example of how to call it.

Listing 10.28   Outline Control with Various Navigators

```
<div
    id="largeContentDiv"
    dojoType="xsp.largeContent"
    content="#{dominoDoc.Body}"
    url="largeContent#{sessionScope.backURL}"
    from="document">
</div>
```

The example in Listing 10.28 contains all three available properties: **content** is used to specify the content to be displayed; **url** is used to specify the URL to the page that will display this content; and the **From** property is used to tell which mobile page that the transition will be called on (that is, the mPage ID).

The control takes the content that has been given to it and renders it in a div. Then it looks at this div to determine its scroll width. If the width is greater than a threshold, a button is rendered. (The div is set to hide overflow, so it won't stretch the screen if it's wide.) The button is linked to the page defined by the URL that's passed in. This way if the content is large, it gets cut off, and the user sees a button to view the content on a separate page that has no mobile controls. Nothing will be affected by the size of the content.

The `xsp.largeContent` dijit is found only in the Discussion XL and TeamRoom XL templates. It is not distributed as part of the ExtLib plugins. To use the `xsp.largeContent` dijit, developers must implement this feature in their own NSF.

Using Dojo to Modify Controls

Dojo is a powerful tool to have alongside XPages. Using dojo.query, you can easily access elements using a simple query syntax that's based on CSS selectors. This allows you to quickly perform operations on one or more elements.

For example, if you wanted to add `'[XPages]'` to every link on the page, you could use the following:

```
dojo.query('a').addContent('[XPages]');
```

Selecting with the ID selector is not recommended. Because of the way XPages renders the underlying HTML, it can be difficult to predict the value of an ID unless you calculate it on the server. That's why it's often easier to use a unique styleClass instead.

What follows is an example of a unique styleClass, where we hide a particular label row:

```
dojo.query('.labelRows1').style('display', 'none');
```

XPages Mobile Phone Application Gotchas

Developers need to remember numerous things when developing Mobile XPages application as opposed to regular XPages applications. For the most part, they can continue as they are, developing XPages, and they will work on a mobile device, with a couple of mobile rendering stylings, of course. However, there are a few things to look out for when developing XPages for mobile.

The Differences Between Web App and Mobile App Layout

There are a number of differences between XPages web applications and XPages mobile applications that don't always translate between the two.

Tables

Tables don't lend themselves well to mobile applications. A lot of formatting is applied to views like All Documents and Most Recent, leaving superfluous blank space. Mobile applications just don't have room for that blank space because of their limited screen size. Trying to make the content fit would mean that little of the data would be displayed.

The Data View component in the Extension Library is the mobile phone's equivalent of displaying data in a table. This allows developers to render the same data but in a way that fits the screen. More importantly, it is the standard means of displaying data that mobile users will be familiar with.

Menus

In desktop applications, menus generally go along the left or the top. (The Discussion template defines a component called a menuView that is in the top-left corner.) This layout doesn't suit mobile applications, however, because the controls would be quite small. The mobile equivalent involves using an outline and giving it a rendererType to display it as a standard mobile control.

Tag Clouds

The Discussion template uses tag clouds along the left to filter authors who have left posts and tags that people have assigned to their post. This template renders in a mobile application, but if it's not the width of the screen, it can be quite hard to use. When the template is that size, it is visually poor as a design element for mobile.

Link Tags

Link tags don't lend themselves well to mobile applications. That can become a problem when there are many close to each other, because they can be hard to click with a finger on a touch screen. Mobile users are used to seeing either a button or an outline with a single basic leaf node. Applications should be tailored to the market that will be using them.

Custom Controls

With mobile applications, defining each mobile page as a Custom Control can be useful. Defining them in a single file can make it hard to navigate the code searching for a problem. Simply delete everything that would have gone between the Mobile Page control tags (`<xe:appPage>`) and place it in a Custom Control. Then add back the Custom Control reference between the same mobile page. No further changes are needed.

The Discussion and TeamRoom template applications use this technique, which is shown in Listing 10.29.

Listing 10.29   Mobile Pages Containing Custom Controls

```
<xe:singlePageApp
   id="DiscussionApp"
   selectedPageName="mostRecent">
   <xe:appPage
     resetContent="true"
     id="home"
     pageName="home">
     <xc:mobile_home></xc:mobile_home>
   </xe:appPage>
   <xe:appPage
     resetContent="true"
```

```
      preload="true"
      id="profile"
      pageName="profile">
      <xc:authorProfileForm></xc:authorProfileForm>
   </xe:appPage>
   <xe:appPage
      resetContent="true"
      preload="true"
      id="newTopic"
      pageName="newTopic">
      <xc:mobile_newTopic></xc:mobile_newTopic>
   </xe:appPage>
   ...
</xe:singlePageApp>
```

Setting a Right Navigation Button

On the iPhone, the developer can define a right navigation button, which is the same as the **Back** button, to a **Save** or **Edit** button. The Heading control contains a callback or editable area called actionFacet to allow the developer to locate actions on the top right of a mobile page, as shown in Listing 10.30.

Listing 10.30 Right Navigation Button Example

```
<xp:this.facets>
   <xp:button
      value="Save"
      id="button2"
      xp:key="actionFacet">
      <xp:eventHandler
         event="onclick"
         submit="true"
         refreshMode="complete">
         <xp:this.action>
            <xe:moveTo
               saveDocument="true"
               targetPage="#{javascript:sessionScope.from}"
               direction="Left to Right"
               transitionType="slide"
               forceFullRefresh="true">
            </xe:moveTo>
```

Listing 10.30   (Continued)

```
        </xp:this.action>
      </xp:eventHandler>
    </xp:button>
  </xp:this.facets>
```

What Stays the Same?

There are a number of techniques the XPages developer will not have to rethink when developing XPages mobile applications.

Repeat List/Table Used to Display Replies

It was previously mentioned that you shouldn't really use tables; however, there is one exception. One section of the Discussion application displays replies. A table can be used to lay out the controls placed on that page. Using a repeat to display multiple replies works well on a mobile device. What's more, that entire section of code can nearly be copied and placed in another.

JavaScript

With a few exceptions, any JavaScript—whether in a script file or used in CDATA sections, for example—will not need to be changed. The same code will work in both web applications, be it on a desktop or mobile device.

Events

For the most part, events used in buttons and links will work if the developer can change the URL, because it won't have hash tags for XPage mobile pages. Sometimes it's necessary to change the event to a Move To mobile page action.

Domino Documents

Domino document datasources port quite well from a regular XPages app to an XPages Mobile app. Developers shouldn't run into as many problems as with JavaScript, because they can define a Domino document inside a mobile page. A document is applied to the container it is in. So, for example, creating one datasource inside a panel means only objects in that panel can access it.

What Has Changed?

However, there are a few areas the developer needs to be mindful of when hoping to bring existing XPages functionality to the mobile application.

Rich Text

Traditional and XPages Rich Text content is not rendered inside an XPage mobile application because it becomes incomprehensible when it's scaled down to a small screen even though the rich text will display in read mode. Generally, the solution is to replace the rich text control with a multiline editbox (`xp:inputTextarea`), but that solution means that the user won't have features associated with a rich text format.

> **NOTE**
>
> If developers intend to use some kind of text box in place of a rich text editor, they need to set the **escape** property to false if both applications are connecting to the same data-source. Otherwise, if the desktop version has a rich text box allowing for table creation, the user will see the tags used to create it rather than the table itself.
>
> Escaping is the default behavior, and removing that option is likely to cause security concerns. That's why it's recommended that this text be run through the Active Content Filter if escaping is turned off. The Active Content Filter is configured through the **htmlFilter** and **htmlFilterIn** properties of the input control in XPages.

Tablet devices in general have a bigger screen, so rich text can be displayed more easily without having to resort to using the "large content technique" as mentioned previously in this chapter. Here rich content should display in Read Mode and Edit Mode although this does depend on the operating system of the tablet.

> **NOTE**
>
> At the time of writing, support for rich text editing in mobile browsers is still very limited; only the very latest devices have the capabilities to do so. In addition, an issue in Notes Domino 8.5.3 with the XPages runtime's wrapping of the CKEditor editor, the default rich text editor in XPages, is that it isn't possible to edit rich text in a mobile device. The suggested workaround for this issue is to use the Dojo rich text editor in place of the CKEditor. IBM aims to address this issue in future releases.

Renderers

Certain components can have a renderer attached to them to make them display differently. For example, if you add an outline and give it leaf nodes, it displays something like a bulleted list. However, adding `com.ibm.xsp.extlib.MobileOutlineNavigator` to the **rendererType** property makes it display as a standard mobile tableView object, which is normally used on mobile devices to navigate pages or as a main menu.

File Upload

File upload doesn't work because mobile directories aren't the same as desktop directories, and for the most part, the file system on mobile devices isn't accessible through the browser or web view.

Breadcrumbs

For mobile applications, developers must provide a means of moving back to previous screens. The mobile header tags allow developers to specify a **Back** button and a link to the given page. There are two ways to accomplish this:

- Hard-code **Back** buttons to force a certain flow if the layout of the app means that a given page is the only possible one to return to.
- Use JavaScript and session scope to keep track of the previous page, and dynamically generate the **Back** button on the page's creation.

Setting Back Button

Setting the Heading property **moveTo** to `"document"` is an example of hard-coding the **Back** button. It is recommended that this should be calculated dynamically as shown in Listing 10.31. Here the property is given a session scoped variable `"from"` to allow this button's destination to be determined dynamically.

Listing 10.31   Setting the Back Page with JavaScript

```
<xp:this.moveTo>
    <![CDATA[#{javascript:var from = sessionScope.get("from"); return
from;
    }]]>
</xp:this.moveTo>
```

Setting Back Title

Similarly, **backButtonTitle** and **back** are the properties for setting the titles in the given controls. The developer can use the same session variable for the title, but it might not make a good design because of the names assigned.

Setting Current Page

The idea behind the breadcrumb is that every time the user navigates to a new page using some sort of `onLoad` method (maybe of a component), the user accesses the session scope variable and modifies it to the current page. Therefore, when the following page loads, it reads the last screen.

```
#{javascript:sessionScope.from = "docsByAuthor"; sessionScope.fromName
= "By Author";
```

Sometimes it can be an issue to refresh the current page. Going back to a page may not allow it to run again because it is not being reloaded. An example of a place to use this is using an execute script action inside a control during an event such as a click.

Conclusion

The new mobile XPages controls in the ExtLib have broken new ground for Domino application development. They pull this technology into the present day and beyond, while still keeping to the core Domino philosophy of building powerful applications rapidly. There are many challenges ahead while mobile standards converge. The XPages mobile controls have met these challenges, and future developments may even see these features lead the way.

CHAPTER 11

REST Services

REpresentational State Transfer (REST) is a set of principles, introduced in 2000 by Roy Fielding (http://www.ics.uci.edu/~fielding/pubs/dissertation/rest_arch_style.htm), that define a communication protocol used when constructing a web application. REST exploits the power and openness of HTTP using simple and clean calling conventions. It is easy to look at a REST statement and discover the method for data access. Its simplicity also makes it easy to use in basic scripting. Typically, REST references today describe a web service that uses the HTTP protocol in conjunction with a custom application programming interface (API) and XML or JSON (JavaScript Object Notation) to alter or query the state of a remote resource.

Beginning with IBM Lotus Notes Domino 8.5.3, a REST service provides a way of having a non-Domino server accessing Domino data without installed software and without using Corba. The Domino REST services conform to JsonRestStore's expectations for data structure and let the developer quickly wire an application to data components such as a Dojo Data Grid, iNotes List, iNotes Calendar, or a conventional XPages view container like a view panel, which render these REST services directly in an XPage.

The REST services are customizable by use of properties and parameters. These parameters allow the user fine-grained control over the data and the output. If the existing services cannot satisfy a specific use case, a developer can modify the source code available on OpenNTF to generate the desired implementation and output. The XPages Extension Library also includes Apache Wink for REST services. This allows the developer a way to produce custom REST service without exposing the underlying physical document model.

REST is important to the new Web 2.0 programming model. New technologies like OpenSocial and Android are embracing REST services to allow remote clients access to server-side data. The XPages Extension Library has RESTful services in place, opening a whole range of exciting data-handling options for the XPages developer.

REST Services in the XPages Extension Library

The basic REST service design establishes a mapping between Create, Read, Update, and Delete (CRUD) operations to a protocol. Although HTTP is not required, most REST services are, in fact, implemented using the HTTP methods POST, GET, PUT, and DELETE, as in Table 11.1.

Table 11.1   HTTP Methods Mapped to CRUD Operations

HTTP Methods	CRUD Operations
POST	To create a resource on the server
GET	To read a resource on the server
PUT	To update a resource on the server
DELETE	To delete a resource on the server

The XPages Extension Library now includes a new set of RESTful, which follow the first principles of REST, services collectively called Domino REST services. These REST services allow developers access to the following Domino objects in JSON format (see Table 11.2).

Table 11.2   List of Domino REST Services and the Supported CRUD Operations

Domino REST Services	Supported CRUD Operations
Database Collection Service	Read the list of databases on the server
View Collection	Read the list of views and folders in a database
View Service	Create, read, update, and delete the entries in a view or folder
View Design Service	Read the design of a view or folder
Document Collection Service	Read the list of documents based on a query
Documents Service	Create, read, update, and delete documents

There are two ways to consume Domino REST services: access them from an XPages REST Service control, or access them as a built-in service. When you access them as a built-in service, they are called the Domino Data Service. Because the same service is being accessed, the user can expect consistent output regardless of how the service is accessed. The services provided by the REST Service control are known as extensions to the REST service. The REST Service control also provides the ability to use additional services that are not included with the Domino Data Service.

Each of these REST services has a unique set of properties or parameters you can set to customize the service's behavior. It is important to note that the same parameters are exposed as properties of the REST Service control that can be set in the Designer user interface (UI), as shown in Figure 11.1. The properties of the REST Service control change depending on the service or resource selected. For example, a developer can search a view using the search parameter or set the search property exposed through the REST Service control. The parameters and output available for each service listed in Table 11.2 are described in detail near the end of this chapter in the section called "Accessing Data Services from Domino as a Built-In Service."

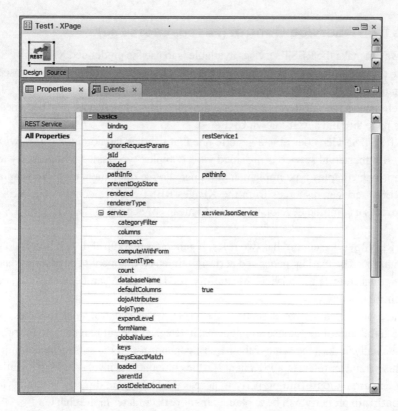

Figure 11.1   The properties for View Service displayed in the Domino Designer UI of the REST Service control.

In most cases, a developer would want to use a REST Service control in an XPage application and use the built-in standalone service in an application that does not use XPages. A Dojo application is not an XPage application, but it may use the standalone service to access Domino data.

In addition to the services described, there is a way for Java developers to create custom REST services. This may be required if the REST services provided with the XPage Extension Library do not meet the particular needs of a developer. The developer can create a custom REST service using the REST Service control or by creating a custom servlet or by using the DAS. More details on developing a custom REST service will be described later in this chapter.

Many of the examples in this chapter are referencing content from the XPages Extension Library Demo database (**XPagesExt.nsf**) that is part of the download from OpenNTF. It includes a REST tab that has several samples that demonstrate the REST Data Service in action. These samples are highlighted further along in this chapter.

XPages REST Service Control (`xe:restService`)

One easy way to make the REST services available is to use the predefined XPages REST Service control (`xe:restService`). The data from the REST services extensions is exposed to other controls on the page that directly reference the REST Service control. For example, a Dojo Data Grid can reference a REST Service control on the same page. The service also becomes available outside the page through a well-known URL.

The REST Service control is a generic one that handles the communication with the runtime layer. But the actual service is provided via a complex type added as a property to the control. There is one complex type implementation per service implementation. You can access the Domino REST services resources from the XPages REST Service control. The REST Service control provides a common development UI and means of accessing the selected REST services extensions.

The REST Service control has two roles. It generates markup at design time, and it acts as a server at runtime. The markup generated at design time is a fragment of JavaScript that creates a Dojo store connecting to the service. At runtime, the Dojo store can be accessed via the REST Service control in a few ways.

In the context of an XPage, at runtime, the REST Service control looks for other components bound to it. If the control finds those components, it delegates the entire request to the other components. Incidentally, it does the same if the request contains a `$$axtarget` parameter in the query string. If this parameter refers to a JSF client ID, the component is invoked within its full context.

You can use the **pathInfo** property to access the Dojo store directly without XPages context. The **pathInfo** property will be explained in more detail later in the chapter.

Standard Attributes for REST Service Control

Service

From the REST Service control, the developer can select one of the many REST services extension types listed in Table 11.3. These services are described in detail in later sections of this chapter.

Table 11.3   REST Services Extension Types

REST Service Control	Extension Type
Database Collection Service	xe:databaseCollectionJsonService*
View Collection	xe:viewCollectionJsonService*
View Service	xe:viewJsonService* xe:viewItemFileService xe:viewJsonLegacyService xe:viewXmlLegacyService xe:calendarJsonLegacyService
View Design Service	xe:viewJsonService*
Document Collection Service	xe:documentJsonService*
Documents Service	xe:documentJsonService*

(*Denotes that the service is also available as a built-in service)

id

The data is exposed to other controls using the **id** property of the REST Service control.

pathInfo

The REST service data is exposed to an HTTP request using the **pathInfo** property of the REST Service control. When a **pathInfo** is used, the REST service is not executed in any particular context. It is more efficient to access the REST data without a context if the context is not relevant to the application. The following is an example of using the **pathInfo** in an HTTP request URL:

```
http://{host}/{database}/{xpage}/{pathInfo}?{optional parameters}
```

When the REST control is accessed in the context of an XPage, there is additional overhead base on its relationship with the other controls on the page. For example, if the REST control is used as the datasource of the Repeat control, then the repeat will be handled. Although it is unlikely, a developer can access the REST control in the context of the page by using the $$axtarget parameter in the query string. In most instances, a developer will use the **pathInfo** to access the REST control data without the overhead of the XPage.

NOTE

Using pathInfo is faster than $$axtarget from a runtime perspective, because it doesn't require a particular context. It is also the only reliable way to expose the service to other pages. Use the **pathInfo** property when accessing data outside the context of an XPage.

---

ignoreRequestParams

The REST Service control exposes a subset of the properties in Designer that can be set from HTTP as parameters. You can ignore the HTTP parameters by setting the REST Service control property **ignoreRequestParams** to `true`.

preventDojoStore

You can use the REST Service control property **preventDojoStore** to prevent the Dojo store from being generated as part of the page markup.

> **NOTE**
>
> The Dojo store class depends on the service that is being selected.

Standard Attributes for Each Service Type

Depending on the REST Service control selected, the developer receives additional properties that map to the parameter that service supports. For example, the view service supports setting the form field on new documents. It can be set as a URL parameter form or as a REST Service control property **formName**. In most cases, the name of the service property matches the parameter.

Hello REST World 1: Using the pathInfo Property

Example of an XPage that Uses the REST Service Control

This section walks through the steps of how to build and reference an XPage that uses the REST Service control to access a Domino REST service. You will access the View Service (`xe:viewJsonService`) using the **pathInfo** property of the REST Service control. You can use the same steps to access any of the other REST data services.

From Domino Designer, add the REST Service control to a new XPage called **MyXPage**. Then enter **myPathInfo** for the **pathInfo** property of the REST Service control. The **pathInfo** is used in the URL to access the REST service from an HTTP request. Next, select the REST service by selecting `xe:viewJsonService` for the service property of the REST Service control. When the service is selected, the properties available for the REST service change based on the service selected. Enter **AllContacts** for the **ViewName** property. Now set the property **default-Columns** to `true`; the default is `false`. Only the system columns are included in the output. Setting this property to `true` outputs all the columns. You can view the generated XPage markup in the **Source** tab; see Listing 11.1.

Listing 11.1   XPage Markup of an XPage That Uses the REST Service Control

```
<xe:restService
  id="restService1"
  pathInfo="myPathInfo">
  <xe:this.service>
    <xe:viewJsonService
      viewName="AllContacts"
      defaultColumns="true">
    </xe:viewJsonService>
  </xe:this.service>
</xe:restService>
```

To initiate an HTTP GET request using the **pathInfo** property, enter the following URL from a browser:

```
http://myDominoServer/XPagesExt.nsf/MyXPage.xsp/myPathInfo
```

You use the **pathInfo** property (**myPathInfo**) to access the REST service from an HTTP request; otherwise, the XPage is displayed. The response in JSON is a list of entries in the **All-Contacts** view in JSON format. The content looks similar to the response described in the "View JSON Service" section later in this chapter.

Hello REST World 2: Computed Column to Join Data

Example of a REST Service Control with a Computed Column

You can use the XPages REST Service control to create computed columns. Computed columns allow you to use JavaScript to do two things: create an additional column that does not exist in the view, and access data and formula values. The XPages Extension Library sample **REST_Dojo-GridJsonRest.xsp** contains a computed column called **ShortName**. Here a short name is computed by getting the text left of the @ from an existing column value **Email**.

Now you'll learn how to build the computed column that looks up the state name in a different table from the state abbreviation. Start by setting the **var** property of the service (xe:viewJsonService) to **entry**, which represents the view entry. Then add a column (xe:restViewColumn) to the **columns** (xe:this.columns) property of the REST Service control. Set the name property to **StateName**, and set the **value** property to a computed value using the script editor. This sample exploits the function @DbLookup, which looks in the specified view (or folder) and finds all documents containing the key value in the first sorted column within the view. Specifically, you need to sort the first column (**Key**) in the **AllState** view in the XPage Extension Library sample database so the lookup will work. You can view the generated XPage markup in the **Source** tab (see Listing 11.2).

Listing 11.2   XPage Markup of a REST Service Control with a Computed Column

```
<xe:restService
    id="restService1">
    <xe:this.service>
      <xe:viewJsonService
        viewName="AllContacts"
        defaultColumns="true"
        var="entry">
        <xe:this.columns>
          <xe:restViewColumn
            name="StateName">
            <xe:this.value><![CDATA[#{javascript:
  var state = entry.getColumnValue("State")
  if(state) {
  return  @DbLookup("", "AllStates", state, "Name")
  }
  return ""
}]]></xe:this.value>
          </xe:restViewColumn>
        </xe:this.columns>
      </xe:viewJsonService>
    </xe:this.service>
  </xe:restService>
```

Hello REST World 3: REST Service in a Data Grid

Example of Binding a Grid to a REST Service Control

This section explains how to bind a Dojo Data Grid (xe:djxDataGrid) control to the REST Service control. Place the Dojo Data Grid on the XPage and set the storeComponentId to **rest-Service1**. Next, add Dojo Data Grid Column (xe:djxDataGridColumn), and set the field property for each column displayed in the grid. For example, to display the **Email** column, set the field property of the column to **Email**. You can also display the computed column created previously. Simply adding another column and setting the field property of the column to **StateName** displays the computed column. The **pathInfo** property of the REST Service control is not relevant when binding to a control like a grid. You can view the generated XPage markup in the **Source** tab (see Listing 11.3).

Listing 11.3   XPage Markup of Dojo Data Grid Bound to the REST Service Control

```
<xe:djxDataGrid
  id="djxDataGrid1"
  storeComponentId="restService1">
  <xe:djxDataGridColumn
    id="djxDataGridColumn1"
    field="EMail">
  </xe:djxDataGridColumn>
  <xe:djxDataGridColumn
    id="djxDataGridColumn2"
    field=" StateName">
  </xe:djxDataGridColumn>
</xe:djxDataGrid>
```

Domino REST Service from XPages Samples

As mentioned previously, a good resource for using Domino REST services from XPages is the sample database **XPagesExt.nsf**, which is included with the XPages Extension Library download. This sample application includes a **REST** tab that has several samples demonstrating the REST Data Service, as shown in Figure 11.2. You can open the samples in a browser and in Designer. They will inspire you to use them your own applications.

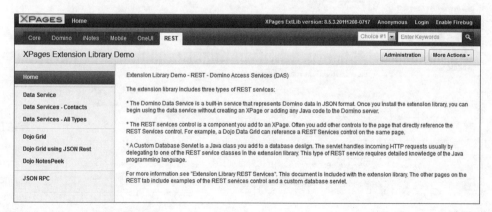

Figure 11.2   REST samples.

Data Service

The **Data Service** page contains an example that demonstrates each of the services included with the Domino Data REST service. A button launches a URL that references each service from a REST Service control, as shown in Figure 11.3. To execute the sample, click its button, and the JSON output of the associated service is displayed. You can use the sample output to aid developers who intend to parse the JSON to create RESTful applications.

When you click the **Database Collection** button, it emits the JSON output from the **Database Collection JSON Service**. Specifically, this is a JSON representation of the databases on the server. Clicking the **View Collection** button results in JSON output for views and folders in the sample database. To get the content of a view (from **View Collection JSON Service**) or the design of a view, select the view in the drop-down and click **View Entries Collection** or **View Design Collection**, respectively. Similarly, you can get content of a document in JSON by selecting a document UNID from the drop-down and clicking the **Document** button. You can use the Document Collection JSON Service to execute a full text search of the database by entering a query string in the text field and clicking the **Document Collection** button.

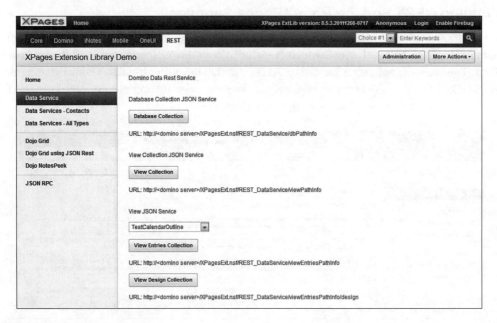

Figure 11.3   Data Service.

Data Services—Contacts and All Types

The Data Services—Contacts and **All Types** pages contain examples of custom and legacy services. Like the Data Service example, a button launches a URL that references the service described. Click the button for the sample, and the JSON or XML output of the associated service is displayed. These examples are targeted to both legacy application developers and custom application developers.

XML output for views has been a feature of Domino for more than a decade. Several years ago, the feature was enhanced to support JSON output. The buttons for **Legacy ReadView-Entries** demonstrate how to call the existing ReadViewEntries with XML and JSON format. In addition, new implementations for these legacy services, called viewXmlLegacyService and viewJsonLegacyService, are provided in Java. They emulate ReadViewEntries as XML and JSON, respectively. Applications that depend on ReadViewEntries continue to work, and now even more options are available. In fact, if the Java implementation of ReadViewEntries does not suit a developer's needs, the Java code can be modified.

In rare instances, some of the Data Services provided may not suit a developer's needs. In this case, a developer with Java experience can choose to create a Custom Database Servlet or a Custom Wink Servlet. A Custom Database Servlet is a Java class that can be added to a database design. The servlet typically handles incoming HTTP requests by delegating to one of the REST service classes in the extension library. A Custom Wink Servlet is the most advanced type of REST service. The open source Apache Wink project defines a service. The servlet is contained in a plug in that is deployed directly to Domino's OSGi framework.

Dojo Grid Using JSON Rest Data Services

The **Dojo Grid Using JSON Rest** page contains an example that demonstrates a Dojo Data Grid referencing a REST Service control on the same page (see Figure 11.4). The REST Service control uses `xe:viewJsonService` to access the **AllContacts** view. The data from the REST services is exposed to grid control using the **id** property of the REST Service control. Specifically, the **storeComponentId** of the `xe:djxDataGrid` is set to the **id** (restService1) of the REST Service control. The contents of the **AllContacts** view are then displayed in the grid.

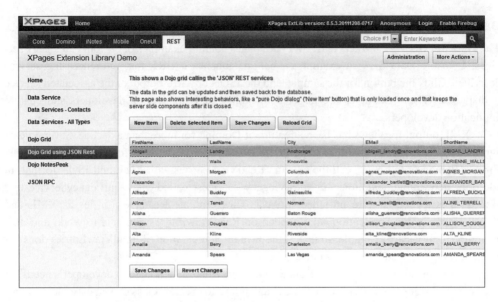

Figure 11.4   Dojo Grid calling JSON REST services.

You can update the data in the grid and then save it to the database. Because you are accessing a view, you can update only the columns that reference items. This page also shows a pure Dojo dialog (from the **New Item** button) that is only loaded once and keeps the Server-Side components after it is closed. You can use JavaScript to create a new item in the database using Dojo REST Store. The View JSON Service is shown in Listing 11.4.

Listing 11.4   View JSON Service Example

```
var firstName = dijit.byId('#{id:dlgFirstName}').getValue();
var lastName = dijit.byId('#{id:dlgLastName}').getValue();
var email = dijit.byId('#{id:dlgEMail}').getValue();
var city = dijit.byId('#{id:dlgCity}').getValue();

var newItem = {
"FirstName":firstName,
"LastName":lastName,
"Email":email,
"City":city
};
var grid = dijit.byId('#{id:djxDataGrid1}');
var store = grid.store;
store.newItem(newItem);
```

```
store.save();
store.close();
grid._refresh();
```

Dojo NotesPeek

The **Dojo NotesPeek** page contains an example that demonstrates using the built-in Domino Data REST services as a Dojo Application. A button launches a URL that references the DojoNotesPeek application, as shown in Figure 11.5. The built-in service requires the data service to be enabled for each server, database, and view. Therefore, DojoNotesPeek can access only data service–enabled applications. Accessing a database or view that has not been enabled results in the error `Sorry, an error occurred`. The steps to enable this service per element are described in the later section "Accessing Data Services from Domino as a Built-In Service."

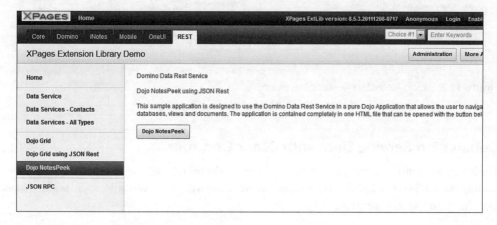

Figure 11.5 Dojo NotesPeek—launch page.

The application consists of three Dojo grids (`dojox.grid.DataGrid`) connected to three Dojo stores (`dojox.data.JsonRestStore`). The stores reference the Database Collection JSON Service, View Collection JSON Service, and View JSON Service. The three grids render a list of databases, a list of views corresponding to the selected database, and the contents of the view (see Figure 11.6). Selecting and clicking on a row from the view opens a new window that renders HTML of the JSON document.

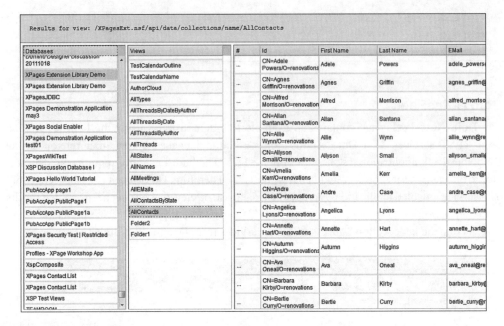

Figure 11.6   Dojo NotesPeek—running example.

Consuming Service Data with Other Controls

The XPages Extension Library Demo app includes an **iNotes** tab that has several samples demonstrating the REST Data Service consuming service data with other controls, such as the iNotes List View and iNotes Calendar.

iNotes List View

The iNotes List View (`xe:listView`) is a powerful control that renders the output of `xe:viewJsonService` as it would be displayed in the Notes Client. The JSON output from a categorized view appears categorized with collapsible sections, as shown in Figure 11.7. Columns defined as icons appear as icons instead of the number that defines them.

The iNotes List View control works like the Dojo grid—`xe:djxDataGrid`—in the way it uses `xe:viewJsonService` to access the JSON output of a view. The data from the REST services is exposed to iNotes List View control by setting the **storeComponentId** of the `xe:listView` to the ID (**restService1**) of the REST Service control. The result is the content of the view displayed in the list.

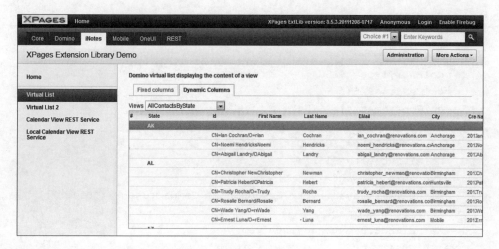

Figure 11.7 iNotes List View—running example.

iNotes Calendar

The iNotes Calendar—`xe:calendarView`—is another powerful control that behaves like the calendar in the Notes Client, as shown in Figure 11.8. It can show the calendar layout as one day, two days, five days, one week, two weeks, a month, or a year by setting the type. The data from the REST services is exposed to the iNotes List Calendar control by setting the **store-ComponentId** of the `xe:calendarView` to the ID (**restService2**) of the REST Service control. You can view the generated XPage markup in the Source tab (see Listing 11.5).

Listing 11.5 XPage Markup of iNotes List Calendar Bound to a REST Service Control

```
<xe:restService
  id="restService2"
  pathInfo="/inoteslegacyjson"
  preventDojoStore="false">
  <xe:this.service>
    <xe:calendarJsonLegacyService
      viewName="TestCalendar"
      var="entry"
      contentType="text/plain"
      colCalendarDate="$134"
      colEntryIcon="$149"
      colStartTime="$144"
```

Listing 11.5   (Continued)

```
        colEndTime="$146"
        colSubject="$147"
        colEntryType="$152"
        colChair="$153"
        colConfidential="$154"
        colStatus="$160"
        colCustomData="$UserData"
        colAltSubject="$151">
        <xe:this.compact>
        <![CDATA[#{javascript:sessionScope.CompactJson2=="true"}]]>
        </xe:this.compact>
      </xe:calendarJsonLegacyService>
    </xe:this.service>
  </xe:restService>

  <xe:calendarView
    id="calendarView1"
    jsId="cview1"
    summarize="false"
    type="#{javascript: null == viewScope.calendarType? 'M' :
viewScope.calendarType }
"
    storeComponentId="restService2">
  </xe:calendarView>
```

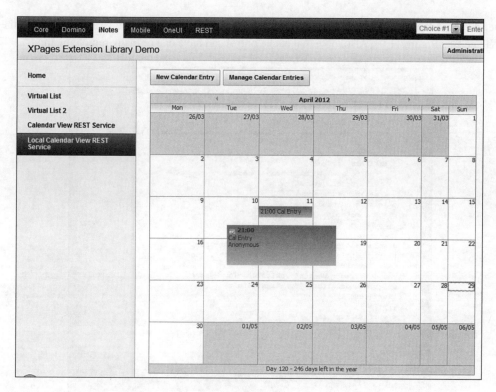

Figure 11.8   iNotes Calendar—running example.

Calling a Remote Service from Domino

The XPages Extension Library Demo includes a sample that demonstrates how to make a JSON-RPC to the Domino server. JSON-RPC is a stateless, lightweight remote procedure call (RPC) protocol. It is an important part of the REST service because OpenSocial defines REST and RPC protocols to give remote clients access to Server-Side data. Clients in Android applications also take advantage of JSON-RPC in applications.

Shindig and JSON-RPC allow multiple methods to be called at once, thus minimizing the number of requests to the server. This can be a huge saving in connections and resources, which can increase performance and scalability. This feature is not currently supported at the time of this writing, but it is being investigated for a future release of the Extension Library.

JSON-RPC Service

Remote Services—`xe:jsonRpcService`—is a versatile control that allows RPCs to the Domino server using JSON-RPC. JSON-RPC is a protocol that enables a procedure to execute in another process or on another computer (in this case, a Domino server). The value of JavaScript is set on the server, and the client uses **dojo.rpc**. The markup to support this is generated in the XPage (see Figure 11.9). Also, note that each control can have one or many remote methods.

Figure 11.9   Markup generated from JSON-RPC control.

Listing 11.6 demonstrates that JSON-RPC can be used to call @Functions on the Domino server. The function @DbLookup looks up a user's email from the **AllNames** view. This listing also shows how an argument (xe:remoteMethodArg) known as **userName** defined in the method (xe:remoteMethod) can be passed to @DbLookup.

Listing 11.6   JSON-RPC Example

```
<xe:jsonRpcService
    id="jsonRpcService1"
    serviceName="userinfo">
    <xe:this.methods>
        <xe:remoteMethod
            name="dblookup">
```

```
   <xe:this.script><![CDATA[
return (@DbLookup("", "AllNames", userName, "Email"));
]]>
   </xe:this.script>
   <xe:this.arguments>
     <xe:remoteMethodArg
       name="userName">
     </xe:remoteMethodArg>
   </xe:this.arguments>
   </xe:remoteMethod>
  </xe:this.methods>
 </xe:jsonRpcService>
```

You can place the script to call in a button. In a real application, the argument is from a drop-down or edit control, but here we just pass a hard-coded value (`"Linda Lane"`) to the `dblookup` method, as shown in Listing 11.7.

Listing 11.7 JSON-RPC Example

```
<xp:button
  value="Lookup User Email"
  id="button1">
  <xp:eventHandler
    event="onclick"
    submit="false">
    <xp:this.script><![CDATA[
var deferred = userinfo.dblookup("Linda Lane")
deferred.addCallback(function(result) {
alert(result)
});]]>
    </xp:this.script>
  </xp:eventHandler>
</xp:button>
```

Consuming Service Data from External Applications

OpenSocial Gadgets

According to Google, OpenSocial is a set of common APIs for building social applications across many websites. It consists of both JavaScript APIs and REST/RPC protocols for server-to-server interactions. In general, OpenSocial gadgets are XML files similar to the Dojo NotesPeek application that reference the OpenSocial API. Based on this definition, using the Domino REST services to build OpenSocial gadgets seems like a perfect fit. Google provides a plethora of information on OpenSocial. The XML markup to create a simple gadget using Domino REST service is shown in Listing 11.8. Figure 11.10 shows this simple OpenSocial gadget accessing the View JSON Service.

Listing 11.8   OpenSocial Gadget Example

```xml
<?xml version="1.0" encoding="UTF-8" ?>
  <Module>
    <ModulePrefs
      title="Simple Data Service Gadget"
      height="500">
      <Require
        feature="osapi" />
      <Require
        feature="minimessage" />
      <Optional
        feature="dynamic-height" />
    </ModulePrefs>
    <Content
      type="html">
<![CDATA[
<div id="content_div"></div>
<script type="text/javascript">

var g_msg = new gadgets.MiniMessage(__MODULE_ID__);

function getAllDocuments(context) {
 var url =
"http://xyz.comexample.com/XPagesExt.nsf/api/data/collections/name/AllT
ypes?ps=100";
 osapi.http.get({ "href": url, "format": "json",
  "refreshInterval": 0,
  "headers":
  {"Authorization": ["Basic YWRtaW46YXRsYW50aWM="]}
 }).execute(getAllDocumentsResponse);
}
```

```
function getAllDocumentsResponse(data) {
 var documents = null;
 var html = "<font color=grey size=2>";
 if ( data != null && data.content != null ) {
  documents = data.content;
  for (var i = 0; documents != undefined && i < documents.length; i++)
{
   html += "UNID: " + documents[i]['@unid'] + "<br>";
   html += "Form: " + documents[i]['@form'] + "<br>";
   html += "NoteID: " + documents[i]['@noteid'] + "<br>";
   html += "<right>";
   var jsonLink = "<a href=\"" + documents[i]['@link'].href + "\">" +
"JSON" + "</a>";
   html += jsonLink + "<br>";
   html += "</right>";
   html += "<hr/>";
  }
 }
 else {
  html = "No documents.";
 }
 html += "</font>";
 document.getElementById('content_div').innerHTML = html;
 gadgets.window.adjustHeight();
}


 gadgets.util.registerOnLoadHandler(getAllDocuments);
</script>
]]>
     </Content>
   </Module>
```

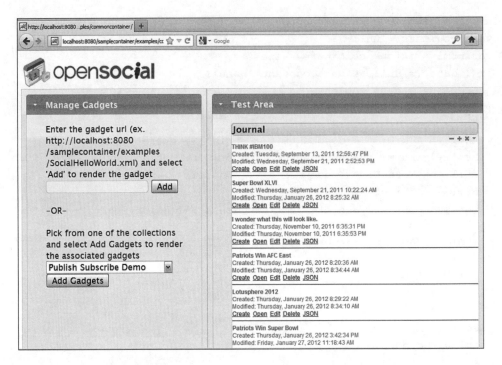

Figure 11.10   OpenSocial gadget.

Accessing Data Services from Domino as a Built-In Service

You can access a subset of the Domino REST services as a built-in service. These services are collectively called the Domino Data Service when they're accessed as a built-in service, and individual components are called resources. An administrator typically doesn't want the data service to handle requests on every Domino server because it could expose details of applications not easily visible in the UI.

The data service is disabled by default. Domino Data Service uses a three-tiered approach for limiting access. The administrator needs to specifically enable the data service for each server, database, and view. The following sections describe how to enable the data service. For more information, please see the *Domino Data Service User Guide* (**Extension Library REST Services.pdf**) and *Domino Data Service Reference* (**DominoDataServiceDoc.zip**), which is included with the XPage Extension Library download from OpenNTF.

Once enabled, the data service starts along with the HTTP task. Because the data service is a built-in service, the developer can use it without creating an XPage or adding Java code to the Domino server. The built-in data service requires Domino 8.5.3 (or greater).

Enabling the Service on the Domino Server

The data service is loaded whenever the Domino HTTP task is started. However, an administrator typically doesn't want the data service to handle requests on every Domino server. The administrator needs to deliberately enable the data service in the appropriate Internet Site document on each server. To enable the data services, add the **Data** keyword to the **Enabled Services** field on the Internet Site document for the server (see Figure 11.11). A restart of the server is required for the changes to take place.

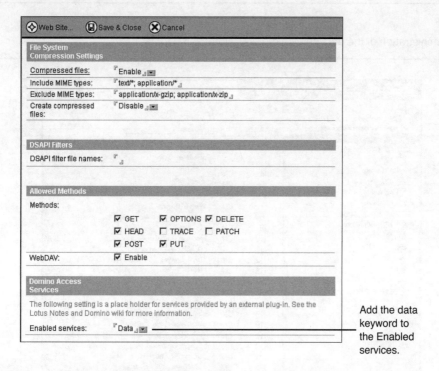

Add the data keyword to the Enabled services.

Figure 11.11   Add the data keyword to the **Enabled services** field on the Internet Site document.

NOTE

The preceding instructions assume the server is configured using Internet Site documents. If the server is not configured this way, enable the data service in the server document. See the *Domino Data Service User Guide* available in the XPage Extension Library download on OpenNTF for more information:

http://www.openntf.org/internal/home.nsf/releases.xsp?action=openDocument&name=XPages%20Extension%20Library

Enabling the Service for a Database

By default, the data service does not have access to each database. Just as the administrator needed to enable the data service for a server, the data service for a database needs to be deliberately enabled. To enable the data services for a database, use the Notes Client to open the Application properties for the database. Then change the field labeled **Allow Domino Data Service** on the bottom of the **Advanced** tab to **Views and Documents**, as in Figure 11.12.

> **TIP**
> Administration of the data service requires Notes 8.5.3 (or later).

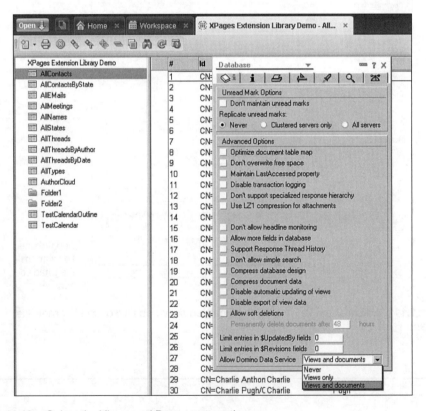

Figure 11.12   Select the Views and Documents option.

You can also set this property from Domino Designer, as shown in Figure 11.13. Close the database or close the project for the change to take effect.

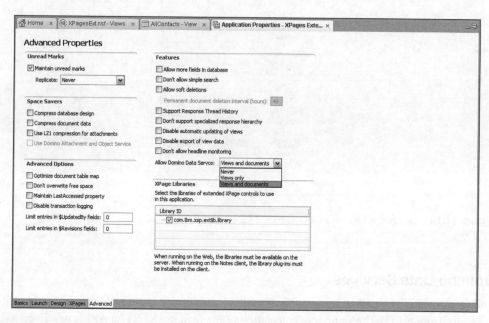

Figure 11.13   Select the Views and Documents option in the Application Properties.

Enabling the Service for View and Documents

By default, the data service does not have access to each view in a database. The data service for a view or folder needs to be deliberately enabled. To enable the data service for a view or folder, use the Domino Designer to open the **View Properties** for the view or folder. Then select the check box labeled **Allow Domino Data Service Operations** on the **Advanced** tab of the View properties box (see Figure 11.14).

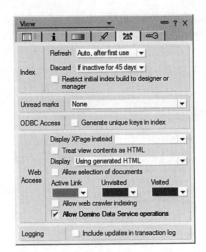

Figure 11.14   Set Allow Domino Data Service Operations.

Domino Data Services

This section describes each resource of the Domino Data Service and how to call each as a built-in service from HTTP. The same implementation of the Domino RESTful API is described as a resource when it's called as a built-in service and described as a service when it's used in the context of the REST Service control. Because this book is primarily about XPages, the term service is used. However, the same implementation can be referred to as a resource in other documentation that is focused on the built-in service and in the context of the Domino Data Service.

The REST Service control can also access each resource of the Domino Data Services. To change the resource, simply select a different service type in the design properties. To reference the service from HTTP, use a URL with the database, XPage, and **pathInfo** property, as described in the previous section "Standard Attributes for REST Service Control." Where possible, the JSON format output by the REST service is consumable by the Dojo data store JsonRestStore.

Database JSON Collection Service

The Database JSON Collection Service supports the HTTP method GET.

GET

To get the list of databases on a server, send an HTTP GET request to the database collection resource uniform resource identifier (URI):

```
http://{host}/api/data
```

The data service returns a response in JSON format, like what's shown in Listing 11.9.

Listing 11.9   Data Service Response

```
[
  {
      "@title":"Administration Requests",
      "@filepath":"admin4.nsf",
      "@replicaid":"852555510361A2F4",
      "@template":"StdR4AdminRequests",

"@href":"http:\/\/example.com\/admin4.nsf\/api\/data\/collections"
  },

  ...

  {
      "@title":"XPages Extension Library Demo",
      "@filepath":"XPagesExt.nsf",
      "@replicaid":"8525786555581FD3",
      "@template":"",

"@href":"http:\/\/example.com\/XPagesExt.nsf\/api\/data\/collections"
  }
]
```

View JSON Collection Service

The View JSON Collection Service supports the HTTP method GET.

GET

To get the list of views and folders in a database, send an HTTP GET request to the view collection resource URI:

```
http://{host}/{database}/api/data/collections
```

The data service returns a response in JSON format, like what is shown in Listing 11.10.

Listing 11.10   Data Service Response

```
[
  {
      "@title":"TestCalendarOutline",
      "@folder":false,
```

Listing 11.10   (Continued)

```
    "@private":false,
    "@modified":"2011-04-29T13:02:20Z",
    "@unid":"F598C2D31E4E12F68525786500660B7E",

"@href":"http:\/\/example.com\/XPagesExt.nsf\/api\/data\/collections\
/unid\/F598C2D31E4E12F68525786500660B7E"
  },

  ...

  {
    "@title":"AllContacts",
    "@folder":false,
    "@private":false,
    "@modified":"2011-04-29T13:02:20Z",
    "@unid":"CD40A953ABDE036A8525786500660C27",

"@href":"http:\/\/example.com\/XPagesExt.nsf\/api\/data\/collections\
/unid\/CD40A953ABDE036A8525786500660C27"
  },

  ...
]
```

View JSON Service

The View JSON Service supports the HTTP methods GET, PUT, PATCH, POST, and DELETE.

GET

To get a list of entries in a view or folder, send an HTTP GET request to the view entry collection resource URI:

```
http://{host}/{database}/api/data/collections/unid/{unid}?{parameters}
```

```
http://{host}/{database}/api/data/collections/name/{name or alias}?
{parameters}
```

Table 11.4 lists parameters that are available to use in a GET request.

Table 11.4 Parameters Are Available to Use for a GET Request

Parameter	Description
start	Where to start getting items.
count	Number of entries to get.
si	Used with ps and page to set the start index.
ps	Used with si and page to set the page size.
page	Used with si and ps to set the page.
Search	Full text search of view.
searchmaxdocs	Limits the output of the search parameter.
sortcolumn	Sort item based on column.
sortorder	Sort order of ascending or descending based on design.
startkeys	Start at key based on sorted column.
keys	Select only items that match criteria.
ceysexactmatch	Used with keys to limit to exact match.
expandLevel	Get only the entries at the level and higher used to limit results within a category.
category	Only display the entries for this category.
parentid	Get response children for this parent.
entrycount	Used to emit the Content-Range header with the count. Set to false to disable the output of the Content-Range header. You can use this as a performance optimization because it avoids getting the count, which can be costly.

For example, the following URI corresponds to the **AllContacts** view in the XPage Extension Library sample database:

```
http://example.com/XPagesExt.nsf/api/data/collections/name/AllContacts
```

The data service returns a response in JSON format, like what is shown in Listing 11.11.

Listing 11.11   Data Service Response

```
[


"@href":"http:\/\/example.com\/XPagesExt.nsf\/api\/data\/collections\
/name\/AllContacts\/unid\/AAE5C9A07AF9C1A7852578760048C0D6",
      "@link":
      {
          "rel":"document",

"href":"http:\/\/example.com\/XPagesExt.nsf\/api\/data\/documents\/unid
\/AAE5C9A07AF9C1A7852578760048C0D6"
      },
      "@entryid":"1-AAE5C9A07AF9C1A7852578760048C0D6",
      "@unid":"AAE5C9A07AF9C1A7852578760048C0D6",
      "@noteid":"9AA",
      "@position":"1",
      "@read":true,
      "@siblings":200,
      "@form":"Contact",
      "Id":"CN=Adela Rojas\/O=renovations",
      "FirstName":"Adela",
      "LastName":"Rojas",
      "EMail":"adela_rojas@renovations.com",
      "City":"Paterson",
      "State":"NJ",
      "created":"2011-04-18T13:14:39Z",
      "$10":"Adela Rojas"
  },
  ...


]
```

When view entries are retrieved, the response also includes a Content-Range header indicating how many entries are included. For example:

```
Content-Range: items 0-9/201
```

This header indicates that the data service returned entries 0 through 9 from a total of 201 entries. To get the next 10 entries, you must send a GET request with additional URL parameters:

```
http://example.com/xpagesext.nsf/api/data/collections/name/AllContacts?
ps=10&page=1
```

In this example, the `ps` parameter specifies the page size, and the `page` parameter specifies which page to get. In this case, get the second page. (Page numbers are zero-based.) The data service returns the second page of data and a new `Content-Range` header like this:

```
Content-Range: items 10-19/201
```

PUT

This replaces (completely updates) a document in a view or folder. You can only update columns that map directly to fields. The supported parameters are listed in Table 11.5. The `parentid`, `form`, and `computewithform` parameters are described in more detail later in this chapter in the section "Document JSON Service" under HTTP method PUT.

```
http://{host}/{database}/api/data/collections/unid/{unid}/unid/{unid}?
{parameters}
```

```
http://{host}/{database}/api/data/collections/name/{name}/unid/{unid}?
{parameters}
```

Table 11.5 Parameters for PUT Request

Parameter	Description
`parentid`	Creates a response child for this parent
`form`	Creates a document with this form
`computewithform`	Run a validation formula based on the form

NOTE

Parameters are the same for PUT, PATCH, and POST, and are listed in Table 11.5.

PATCH

This is used to partially update a document in a view or folder. Only columns that map directly to fields can be updated. The supported parameters are listed in Table 11.5.

```
http://{host}/{database}/api/data/collections/unid/{unid}/unid/{unid}?
{parameters}
```

```
http://{host}/{database}/api/data/collections/name/{name}/unid/{unid}?
{parameters}
```

POST

This creates a document in a view or folder. Only columns that map directly to fields can be created. The supported parameters are listed in Table 11.5.

```
http://{host}/{database}/api/data/collections/unid/{unid}?{parameters}
```

```
http://{host}/{database}/api/data/collections/name/{name}?{parameters}
```

DELETE

To delete a document, an HTTP DELETE request is sent to the URI. If the data service deletes the document without errors, it returns an HTTP status code of 200.

```
http://{host}/{database}/api/data/collections/unid/{unid}/unid/{unid}
```

```
http://{host}/{database}/api/data/collections/name/{name}/unid/{unid}
```

View Design JSON Service

The View Design JSON Service supports the HTTP method GET.

GET

To read the design of a view or folder, send an HTTP GET request to the view design resource URI:

```
http://{host}/{database}/api/data/collections/unid/{unid}/design
```

```
http://{host}/{database}/api/data/collections/name/{name or
alias}/design
```

For example, the following URI corresponds to the **AllContacts** view in the XPages Extension Library sample database:

```
http://example.com/XPagesExt.nsf/api/data/collections/name/AllContacts/
design
```

The data service returns a response in JSON format, like what's shown in Listing 11.12.

Listing 11.12   Data Service Response

```
[
    ...    {
        "@columnNumber":3,
        "@name":"FirstName",
        "@title":"First Name",
        "@width":10,
        "@alignment":0,
        "@hidden":false,
        "@response":false,
        "@twistie":false,
        "@field":true,
        "@category":false
    },
    {
        "@columnNumber":4,
        "@name":"LastName",
        "@title":"Last Name",
        "@width":12,
        "@alignment":0,
        "@hidden":false,
        "@response":false,
        "@twistie":false,
        "@field":true,
        "@category":false
    },
    ...
]
```

Document Collection JSON Service

The Document Collection JSON Service supports the HTTP method GET.

GET

You can use the HTTP GET request to list all the documents in the database. You can use the `since` and `search` parameters to filter the list as described further in Table 11.6.

```
http://{host}/{database}/api/data/documents?{parameters}
```

Table 11.6   Parameters for the Document Collection JSON Service

Parameter	Description
since	Used to get all the documents since some date time.
search	Used to search for documents based on a query

For example, you can use the following URI to search for all documents that contain `Tempe` in the XPage Extension Library sample database:

```
http://example.com/XPagesExt.nsf/api/data/documents?search=Tempe
```

The data service returns a response in JSON format, like what is shown in Listing 11.13.

Listing 11.13   Data Service Response

```
[
  {
      "@modified":"2011-04-18T13:14:41Z",
      "@unid":"08F7227475F21A2C852578760048C131",

"@href":"http:\/\/example.com\/XPagesExt.nsf\/api\/data\/documents\
/unid\/08F7227475F21A2C852578760048C131"
  }
]
```

Document JSON Service

The Document JSON Service supports the HTTP methods GET, PUT, PATCH, POST, and DELETE.

GET

You can use the HTTP GET request to obtain a document in the database. The supported parameters are listed in Table 11.7.

```
http://{host}/{database}/api/data/documents/unid/{unid}?{parameters}
```

Table 11.7 Parameters for the Document JSON Service

Parameter	Description
strongtype	Provide type information with output
markread	Disable the read mark on get
hidden	Emit supported Notes $ fields

Attachments are supported as a URI reference to the resource. For example, you can use the following URI to obtain a document from the XPage Extension Library sample database:

```
http://example.com/XPagesExt.nsf/api/data/documents/unid/B08E87F21FE84F
AB49257826004FEB5E
```

The data service returns a response in JSON format, like what is shown in Listing 11.14.

Listing 11.14 Data Service Response for a Document with an Attachment

```
{

"@href":"http:\/\/example.com\/XPagesExt.nsf\/api\/data\/documents\
/unid\/B08E87F21FE84FAB49257826004FEB5E",
    "@unid":"B08E87F21FE84FAB49257826004FEB5E",
    "@noteid":"38CA",
    "@created":"2011-01-28T14:32:55Z",
    "@modified":"2011-03-24T19:34:07Z",
    "@authors":"CN=Admin\/O=Peaks",
    "@form":"AllTypes",
    "$UpdatedBy":"CN=Admin\/O=Peaks",
    "$Revisions":"01\/28\/2011 09:32:56 AM;02\/08\/2011 03:31:22 PM ",
    "fldText":"One",
    "fldNumber":1,
    "fldDate":"2010-01-01",
    "fldTime":"01:00:00",
    "fldDateTime":"2010-01-01T06:00:00Z",
    "fldDialogList":"c1",
    "fldText2":
    ["One","Two","Three"
    ],
    "fldNumber2":
    [1,2,3
    ],
    "fldDate2":
```

Listing 11.14   (Continued)

```
    ["2010-01-01","2010-01-02","2010-01-03"
    ],
    "fldTime2":
    ["01:00:00","02:00:00","03:00:00"
    ],
    "fldDateTime2":
    ["2010-01-01T06:00:00Z","2010-01-02T07:00:00Z","2010-01-
03T08:00:00Z"
    ],
    "fldDialogList2":
    ["c1","c2","c3"
    ],
    "fldRichText":
    {
        "contentType":"text\/html",
        "data":"<br \/>\r\n<font color=\"#FF0000\">This is
red.<\/font><br \/>\r\n<font color=\"#008000\">This is
green.<\/font><br \/>\r\n<font color=\"#0000FF\">This is
blue.<\/font><br \/>\r\n<br \/>\r\n<a class=\"domino-attachment-link\"
style=\"display: inline-block; text-align: center\"
href=\"http:\/\/example.com\/XPagesExt.nsf\/0\/b08e87f21fe84fab49257826
004feb5e\/$FILE\/Picture.JPG\" title=\"Picture.JPG\"><img
src=\"http:\/\/example.com\/XPagesExt.nsf\/0\/b08e87f21fe84fab492578260
04feb5e\/fldRichText\/0.158?OpenElement&FieldElemFormat=gif\"
width=\"72\" height=\"34\" alt=\"Picture.JPG\" border=\"0\" \/><span
class=\"domino-caption\" style=\"display:
block\">Picture.JPG<\/span><\/a>",
        "attachments":
        [
            {
"@href":"http:\/\/example.com\/XPagesExt.nsf\/0\/b08e87f21fe84fab492578
26004feb5e\/$FILE\/Picture.JPG"
            },
            {

"@href":"http:\/\/example.com\/XPagesExt.nsf\/0\/b08e87f21fe84fab492578
26004feb5e\/fldRichText\/0.158?OpenElement&FieldElemFormat=gif"
            }
        ],
        "type":"richtext"
    }
}
```

PUT

To replace (completely update) a document, send a PUT request to document resource URI. The supported parameters are listed in Table 11.5.

```
http://{host}/{database}/api/data/documents/unid/{unid}?{parameters}
```

When sending a PUT request, include a Content-Type header, as shown in Listing 11.15.

Listing 11.15   The PUT Request to Change the Content-Type Header

```
Content-Type: application/json

{
    "Id":"CN=Adela Rojas\/O=renovations",
    "FirstName":"Adela",
    "LastName":"Rojas",
    "City":"Newark",
    "State":"NJ",
    "EMail":"adela_rojas@renovations.com"
}
```

The preceding request changes Adela Rojas's city from Paterson to Newark. If the data service completes the request without errors, it returns an HTTP status code of 200 without a response body.

> **TIP**
>
> When sending a PUT request, don't include any @ properties like @unid and @href. These properties are considered metadata. The data service ignores any attempt to update metadata.

Usually when a document is to be updated, the business logic contained in a specific form must be executed. To do this, send a PUT request with additional URL parameters:

```
http://example.com/xpagesext.nsf/api/data/documents/unid/AAE5C9A07AF9C1
A7852578760048C0D6?form=Contact&computewithform=true
```

In this example, the form parameter specifies the Contact form. The computewithform parameter is true, instructing the data service to execute the Contact form's business logic.

PATCH

To partially update a document, send a PATCH request to document resource URI with the available parameters shown in Table 11.5.

```
http://{host}/{database}/api/data/documents/unid/{unid}?{parameters}
```

POST

To create a document, send an HTTP POST. The available parameters are shown in Table 11.5.

```
http://{host}/{database}/api/data/documents?{parameters}
```

When sending a POST request, you must send a Content-Type header, as shown in Listing 11.16.

Listing 11.16   Create a New Document Example Using JSON in a POST Request

```
Content-Type: application/json

{
    "FirstName":"Stephen",
    "LastName":"Auriemma",
    "City":"Littleton",
    "State":"MA",
    "EMail":"sauriemma@renovations.com"
}
```

If the data service is able to create the document without errors, it returns an HTTP status code of 201. The response also includes a Location header identifying the URI of the new document resource:

```
Location:
http://example.com/.../api/data/documents/unid/3249435909DCD22F852578A7
0063E8E5
```

Usually when a new document is created, the business logic contained in a specific form needs to be run. To do so, send a POST request with additional URL parameters. For example:

```
http://example.com/xpagesext.nsf/api/data/documents?form=Contact&
computewithform
```

The form and computewithform parameters are described in the preceding section "Document JSON Service" under the HTTP method PUT.

A user may want to create a document that is a response to another document. Doing this involves sending a POST request with a `parentid` parameter. For example:

```
http://example.com/xpagesext.nsf/api/data/documents?form=Discussion&
computewithform =true&parentid=440FA99B2F0F839E852578760048C1AD
```

If the POST request succeeds, the data service creates a response to the document with a UNID of `440FA99B2F0F839E852578760048C1AD` the parent.

DELETE

To delete a document, send an HTTP DELETE request to the document resource URI. If the data service deletes the document without errors, it returns an HTTP status code of 200.

```
http://{host}/{database}/api/data/documents/unid/{unid}
```

Computed Items

You can use the XPages REST control to create computed items. This feature is similar to computed columns mentioned previously. It's a powerful feature that allows the developer to create additional items that do not exist in the document using JavaScript and access data and formula values. In the following example, a short name is computed by getting the text left of the @ from an existing item value **Email**.

Here's how to create a computed item in an XPage:

1. Add a REST Service control to the page and set the service property to `xe:document JsonService`.

2. Start by setting the **var** property of the service (`xe:documentJsonService`) to **document**, which represents the Notes document.

3. Add an item (`xe:restDocumentItem`) to the items (`xe:this.item`) property of the REST Service control.

4. Set the name property to **ShortName**.

5. Set the value property to a computed value using the script editor.

6. Type the following script into the script editor, as in Listing 11.17.

Listing 11.17   JavaScript for a Computed Item Value

```
var e = document.getItemValue("EMail")
if(e) {
       var p = @UpperCase(@Left(e,"@"))
       return p
}
return ""
```

To see the results, access the service from a browser by entering the following URL, but replace the UNID B53EE32CCC6B79218525790300512A36 with the UNID of an actual existing document:

```
http://myDominoServer/XPagesExt.nsf/MyXPage.xsp/myPathInfo/B53EE32CCC6B
79218525790300512A36
```

The data service returns a response in JSON format, like what is shown in Listing 11.18.

Listing 11.18   Data Service Response for the Request with a Computed Item Called Shortname

```
{
    "@unid":"B53EE32CCC6B79218525790300512A36",
    "@noteid":"1A22",
    "@created":"2011-09-06T14:46:32Z",
    "@modified":"2011-09-06T14:46:32Z",
    "@authors":"Anonymous",
    "@form":"Contact",
    "$UpdatedBy":"Anonymous",
    "State":"MA",
    "LastName":"Auriemma",
    "City":"Littleton",
    "FirstName":"Stephen",
    "EMail":"sauriemma@renovations.com",
    "shortname":"SAURIEMMA"
}
```

Developing Custom REST Services

For the most part, this chapter has discussed consuming existing services provided by the XPage Extension Library. In addition to consuming REST services, the XPages Extension Library includes a framework to develop a custom a REST service that meets a particular need. This section introduces another way to develop a custom a REST service and compares their capabilities. Knowledge of Java and REST services is required.

Developing Custom REST Services:

The **Custom XPages REST Service Control Extension** is a service that you can select from a REST Service control. You can modify the code provided on OpenNTF for the XPages Extension Library and customize one of the existing services of the implementation to generate the desired implementation and output.

A **Custom Database Servlet** is a Java class that you can add to a database design. The servlet typically handles incoming HTTP requests to one of the REST service classes in the extension library. This type of REST service requires detailed knowledge of the Java programming language, but you have complete control over the definition of the service.

A **Custom Wink Servlet** is the most advanced type of REST service. The Java developer can use the open source Apache Wink project to define the service. The developer's servlet needs to be contained in a plugin deployed directly to Domino's OSGi framework. The service is not tied to a single database; it can access any data chosen and represent it in any format.

Conclusion

The XPages Extension Library has a variety of RESTful services and controls for accessing Domino data. At the heart is the REST Service control that provides one interface for developing applications that consume REST services. There are several XPage UI controls, including the iNotes List and iNotes Calendar, that can consume and render these REST services directly in an XPage. An XPage application is not required to consume REST services using the XPage Extension Library. For example, a Dojo application can consume as a standalone REST service without any reference to an XPage. In addition to consuming REST services, the XPages Extension Library includes a framework for producing a custom REST service.

CHAPTER 12

XPages Gets Relational

Until recently, native access to data in XPages has been restricted to data stored within the Notes Storage Facility (NSF). Access to Relation Database Management Systems (RDBMS) data was only available by direct access to the core Java Database Connectivity (JDBC) application programming interfaces (APIs), and even then surfacing that data to standard XPages controls required a strong understanding of the XPages runtime. Now, in the Experimental package of the Extension Library (ExtLib) but not included in Upgrade Pack 1 (UP1), read-only and full read/write access to relational databases becomes a reality. This release opens the door to utilize XPages as the integration point between disparate systems.

Through the use of these components, relational data can be utilized in the same manner that data from the NSF is used to populate components such as view panels and edit controls. This allows you to directly integrate and extend non-Notes-based data from enterprise applications without having to synchronize it to an NSF.

This chapter reviews concepts behind integrating relational data and the new relational database components that the ExtLib provides, including JDBC, the Connection Pool and Connection Manager, the datasources, and the Java and Server-Side JavaScript (SSJS) APIs included to help integrate relational data into an XPages application.

Accessing Relational Data Through JDBC

Because XPages is an implementation of Java Server Faces (JSF), it would make sense that access to relational data would be made through the standard APIs that provide Java programmers with connectivity to those datasources. These APIs, known as Java Database Connectivity, or JDBC for short, define how Java applications, serving as the client, may access a database. The ExtLib utilizes JDBC to provide connections to other data stores, so a little background information on how JDBC operates will make implementing relational datasources in XPages easier.

JDBC uses a driver manager to load a vendor-specific implementation of a Java class that is responsible for the low-level communication between the application and the database. Depending on the type of database and the connection used, this driver may implement any one of a number of driver types of connectivity models. For example, a JDBC driver may be what is called a type 1 driver, or a JDBC-Open Database Connectivity (ODBC) bridge, where the calls to the JDBC driver are converted into ODBC calls and then executed against the datasource using ODBC. Alternatively, the JDBC driver may have direct native access to the database and may be able to manipulate and update the database directly. This driver model is known as a type 4 driver. The XPages ExtLib ships with prebuilt connectivity to a type 4 driver for Apache Derby, which is a lightweight open source relational database implemented entirely in Java. Other types of drivers integrate platform-specific libraries (type 2 drivers) or connectivity to a middleware application server (type 3 driver) that acts as an intermediary to access the data. The type of driver available to provide connectivity to a given database may depend on factors such as the database platform and the Client-Side operating system. Any available JDBC driver compatible with the JDBC version in use in the Java Virtual Machine (JVM) can provide connectivity for an XPages datasource. Figure 12.1 illustrates how these JDBC drivers and the JDBC API interacts with the datasources to provide SQL access to an XPages application.

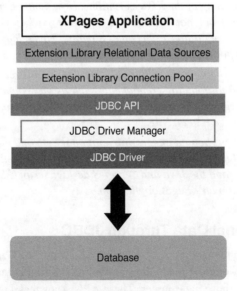

Figure 12.1   XPages JDBC connectivity model.

Installing a JDBC Driver

The only built-in database connectivity provided out of the box with the ExtLib is to an Apache Derby database, which is included only as a demonstration datasource since it is not intended for production use. As a result, one of the first steps to implementing relational data in an XPages application is acquiring and installing the appropriate JDBC driver for the RDBMS that will be accessed. The examples in this chapter will be connecting to an instance of IBM DB2® Express-C, which is the free community edition of IBM's powerful and popular relational and XML data server available at http://www-01.ibm.com/software/data/db2/express/download.html. As seen in Figure 12.2, from this page, you can download the full DB2 Express-C package in installable or virtual machine form, or you can just download the database drivers. Other RDBMS drivers will be available from the vendor of the RDBMS and may be included on the distribution media or downloadable from their site.

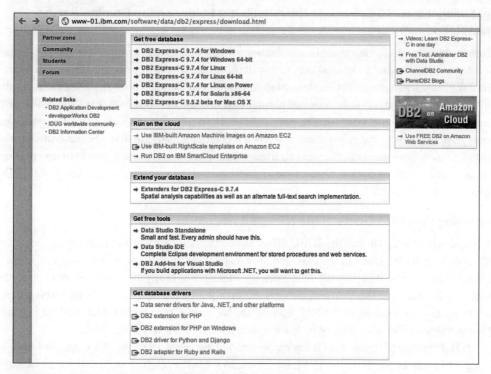

Figure 12.2   Downloading the DB2 JDBC Driver from IBM.com.

Included in the DB2 Express-C installation is a type 4 JDBC driver composed of two files, **db2jcc4.jar** and **db2jcc_license_cu.jar**, as seen in Figure 12.3. These files must be available to the Domino JVM. This chapter covers all three ways to install the JDBC driver, but only one is recommended because the other methods have drawbacks.

> **NOTE**
>
> The **db2jcc_license_cu.jar** filename may vary because of the licensed options of the DB2 server. The community edition includes the **db2jcc_license_cu.jar** license file.

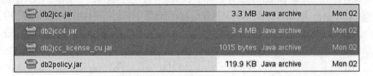

🗄 db2jcc.jar	3.3 MB Java archive	Mon 02
🗄 db2jcc4.jar	3.4 MB Java archive	Mon 02
🗄 db2jcc_license_cu.jar	1015 bytes Java archive	Mon 02
🗄 db2policy.jar	119.9 KB Java archive	Mon 02

Figure 12.3 The DB2 Express-C drivers located in the DB2 installation folder on Linux.

Installing the JDBC Driver into the jvm/lib/ext Folder on the Domino Server (Not Recommended)

Copying the two JAR files and placing them into the **jvm/lib/ext** folder of the Lotus Domino server's installation is the simplest way to install the driver. The driver needs to call methods that the Java Security Manager (as implemented in Domino by default) does not allow. Placing the driver in this folder grants it the required permissions because the code base is in this trusted location. However, if you do not use the optional Database Connection Pool, discussed later, you must load and register the driver manually when it is required. Additionally, because this type of installation requires access to the server's file system, it may not be an acceptable option in some Lotus Domino environments. Due to these drawbacks, this approach of installing the JDBC driver into the **jvm/lib/ext** folder is not recommended.

Installing the JDBC Driver in the NSF (Not Recommended)

Alternatively, you can install the JDBC driver inside the NSF. Similar to installing on the server file system, a JDBC driver in the NSF requires manual registration. However, the NSF is not a trusted location, and it causes the Java Security Manager to block the execution of code in the JAR file. To overcome this problem, modify the **java.policy** file in the server's **jvm/lib/security** folder, adding the location of the NSF as a trusted location. Doing so instructs the Java Security Manager to allow the execution of code located in the JAR from within the NSF.

This method of installation is not recommended, however, since the JDBC Driver Manager is a global instance for the entire JVM. Because a JAR file in each NSF is on a different path, the Driver Manager loads each JAR instance separately. If two NSFs contain the same driver, each instructs the Driver Manager to load its own JAR, essentially causing multiple versions of the same driver to be loaded, the Driver Manager becomes confused, and instability results. Moreover, an NSF can be discarded from memory after a period of inactivity, leaving the JDBC registry in a bad state, and even introducing memory leaks.

Installing the JDBC Driver via an OSGi Plugin (Recommended Approach)

The recommended approach is to deploy the driver via an OSGi plugin. This allows the code to be executed from a trusted location and the driver to be dynamically loaded, only once and as needed, automatically by the JDBC Driver Manager. You can package the plugin into an update site and deploy it automatically in the same manner that you deploy ExtLib to servers through the use of the update site database as described in Chapter 2, "Installation and Deployment of the XPages Extension Library." Doing so removes the need to directly deploy the drivers to the server's file system and simplifies distributing and managing the drivers across multiple servers.

Although it's not difficult, the development of an OSGi plugin may be new to many Lotus Notes and Domino developers. Lack of knowledge on how to accomplish the task may make it seem more difficult that it needs to be. The ExtLib comes with a sample OSGi plugin for the Apache Derby driver that can serve as a template for other drivers.

You can develop the plugin using either Domino Designer in the Plug-In Development Perspective or the Eclipse Integrated Development Environment (IDE) (which you can download from http://www.eclipse.org/downloads). As seen in Figure 12.4, the user interface for the Eclipse IDE should be familiar to most Domino developers because Domino Designer 8.5 and later is based on the Eclipse IDE. Regardless of the environment chosen to create the plugin, the steps are the same.

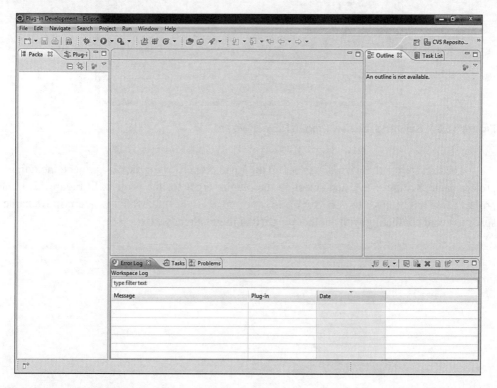

Figure 12.4 The Eclipse 3.5 Galileo IDE.

You begin creation of an OSGi plugin by switching Domino Designer to the Plug-In Development Perspective by selecting **Window** → **Open Perspective** → **Other**, locating and selecting **Plug-In Development**, and then clicking **OK**. Once you're inside the Plug-In Development perspective, you can start the project by creating a new **Plug-In Project**, found in the New Project Wizard by selecting **File** → **New** → **Project** in the IDE. Then expand the **Plug-In Development** category and click **Next**, as seen in Figure 12.5.

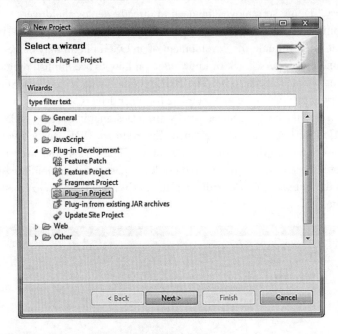

Figure 12.5   Selecting the new Plug-In Project Wizard.

The first step in the wizard is to set up the basic properties for the new project, including a project name, setting paths, and selecting the plugin target for the project. In Figure 12.6, the project name has been set to `com.ZetaOne.JDBC.drivers.DB2`, which is a descriptive namespace to avoid conflicting with another plugin that might already exist.

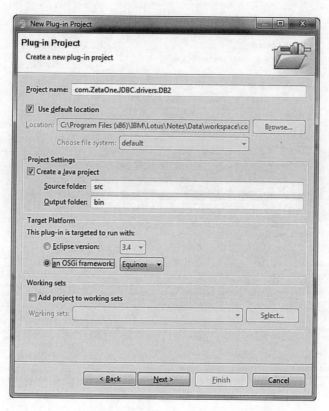

Figure 12.6   Setting the project's name and settings.

After setting the project properties, you set the properties for the plugin, including the ID, version, and provider. Then set the Execution Environment to **No Execution Environment** and deselect **Generate an Activator, a Java Class That Controls the Plug-In's Life Cycle** (see Figure 12.7).

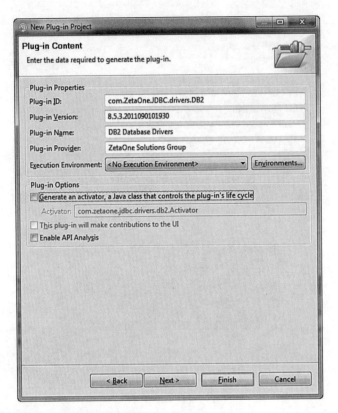

Figure 12.7   Setting the plugin's name and settings.

Finally, in the last window of the wizard, deselect the **Create a Plug-In Using One of the Templates**, as shown in Figure 12.8. Click the **Finish** button to generate the project stub.

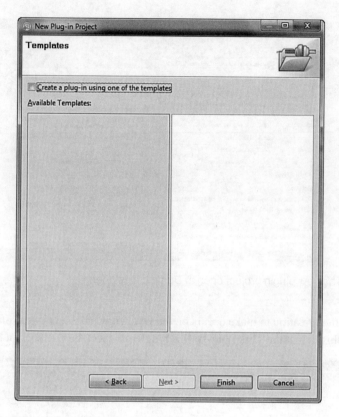

Figure 12.8   Finishing the New Plug-In Project Wizard.

As seen in Figure 12.9, after the project is created, Domino Designer opens it. The project folder appears in the Package Explorer; furthermore, the project **Overview**, where the settings for the project are maintained, is displayed. To complete the project, the JDBC driver JARs need to be imported into the project, several settings within the project need to be modified, and an extension must be built to provide the driver to the XPages runtime environment.

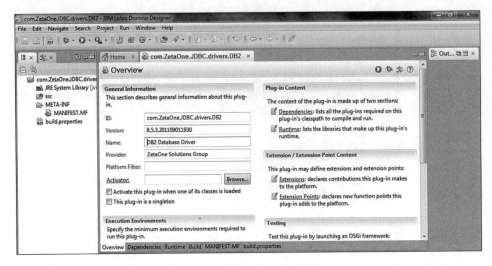

Figure 12.9 The new plugin project open in Domino Designer.

The first modification to make occurs on the **Overview** tab. Identify the plugin as a singleton. To enable this, select the **This Plug-In Is a Singleton** check box, as seen in Figure 12.10.

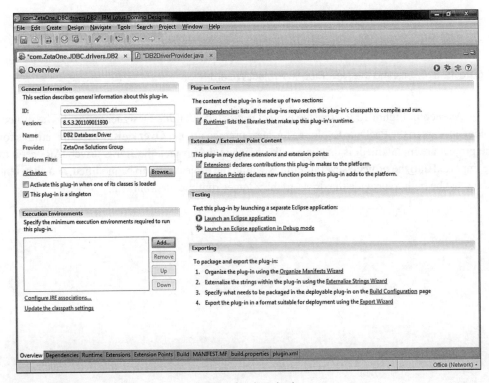

Figure 12.10 Enabling the singleton setting for the plugin.

To deploy the JDBC driver, import the driver JAR files from Figure 12.3 into the **lib** folder of the plugin project. To import them, right-click the project in the Package Explorer and select the **Import** option, as seen in Figure 12.11.

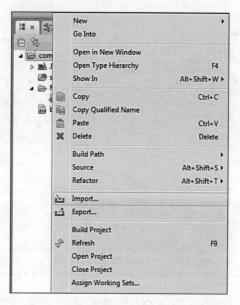

Figure 12.11   Importing the JDBC driver JARs into the project.

Clicking the **Import** menu item opens the Import Select dialog that allows you to select the type of import to be performed (see Figure 12.12). For this example, the JDBC driver JAR files are on the file system, so select **File System** and click **Next**.

Figure 12.12   Selecting the Import type for the import of the JDBC driver JAR files.

Then in the File System Import dialog, you locate the folder containing the driver JARs by clicking the **Browse** button. Select the individual files for import. For DB2, you need to import both the driver (**db2jcc4.jar**) and the license (**db2jcc_license_cu.jar**). In the field for **Into folder**, **/lib** is added to the end of the project file, so the JARs are added to a **lib** folder within the project, as seen in Figure 12.13, and the **Finish** button is clicked.

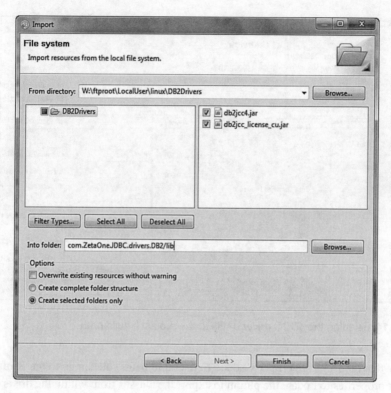

Figure 12.13 Importing the DB2 JDBC driver JARs into the lib folder of the project.

Once the import has completed, the new **lib** folder appears under the project in the Package Explorer. To make the JARs available to the project, you must add them to the project's Build Path by expanding the **lib** folder, selecting the JAR files, right-clicking them, and selecting **Build Path → Add to Build Path** from the pop-up menu (see Figure 12.14). Once you have added the JARs to the build path, a new folder named **Referenced Libraries** appears with the JAR files underneath.

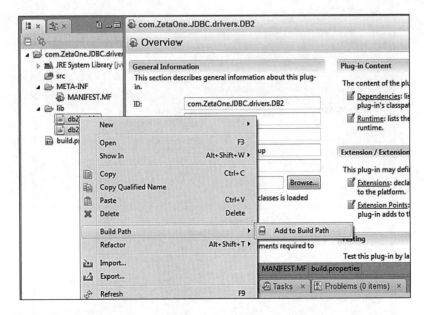

Figure 12.14   Adding the JDBC driver JARs to the project's build path.

Now that the JARs are properly added to the build path, you can go to the **Runtime** tab of the project properties to update the plugin to export the classes from within the driver JARs. The classes are exported by clicking the **Add** button under **Exported Packages** and selecting all the packages that appear in the dialog (see Figure 12.15).

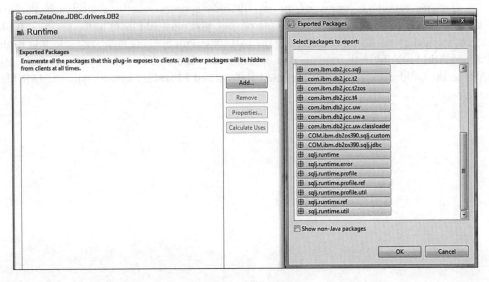

Figure 12.15   Selecting the classes the plugin will export.

Additionally, you need to add the JARs in the project to the classpath, which is set on the **Runtime** tab. Adding the JARs to the classpath is done under **Classpath** by clicking the **Add** button and expanding and selecting the JARs in the **lib** folder, as seen in the JAR selection dialog displayed in Figure 12.16.

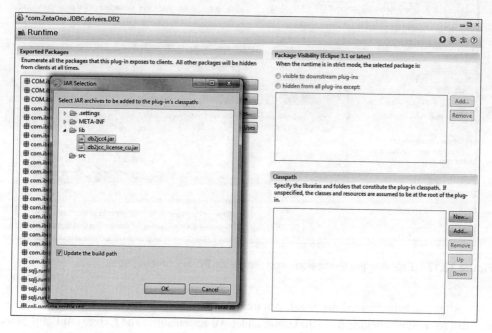

Figure 12.16 Adding the JDBC driver JARs to the classpath.

The next step in prepping the OSGi plugin is to create a driver provider and plug it into the proper extension point. To identify the extension point, the **Extension** and **Extension Point** pages must be enabled for the project. To do this, on the **Overview** tab, click the **Extensions** link under **Extensions / Extension Point Content**. Domino Designer confirms that the pages should be displayed, as seen in Figure 12.17.

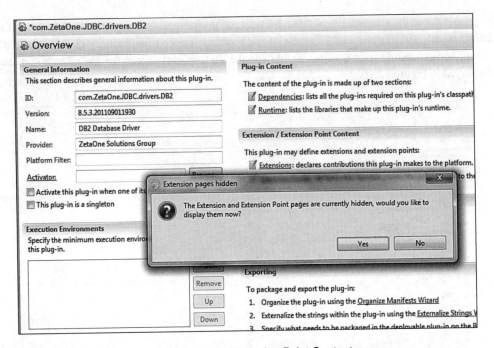

Figure 12.17   Enabling the Extensions and Extension Point Content pages.

After you have enabled the pages, you use the **Extensions** page to add the extension point that will be used by clicking the **Add** button under **All Extensions**. The **Extension Point Selection** dialog appears. You select the extension point by typing the beginning of its name in the **Extension Point Filter** edit box (see Figure 12.18). The extension point to be selected is `com.ibm.commons.Extension`.

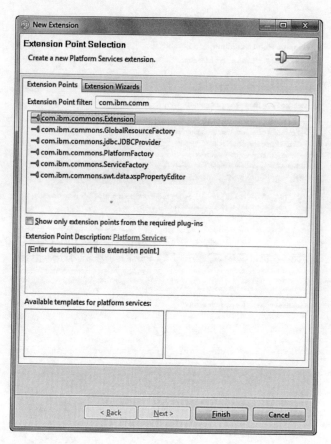

Figure 12.18 Selecting the extension point in the Extension Point Selection dialog.

Once you have located the extension point, select it from the list, and click the **Finish** button. Domino Designer confirms that the plugin com.ibm.commons should be added to the list of dependencies, as seen in Figure 12.19.

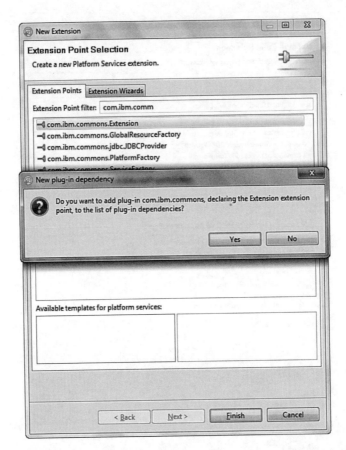

Figure 12.19   Confirming the addition of the `com.ibm.commons` plugin to the dependencies.

After you have added the extension point, under the **All Extensions** header, expand the extension and select the **(service)** item. On the right side of the window, enter a type and Java class to provide the extension. Populate the type field with `com.ibm.common.jdbcprovider`. The class is the fully qualified name of a Java class that you need to create in this project. In this example, the class name is derived from the namespace for the project and the class name `DB2DriverProvider`, as seen in Figure 12.20.

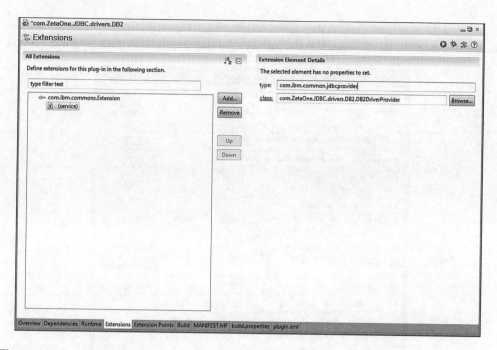

Figure 12.20 Populating the `com.ibm.common.jdbcprovider` extension point with the `DB2DataProvider` class.

Once you have populated the extension point, you must create the `DB2DriverProvider` class. You do this by right-clicking the **src** folder in the project and selecting **New → Class**, as seen in Figure 12.21.

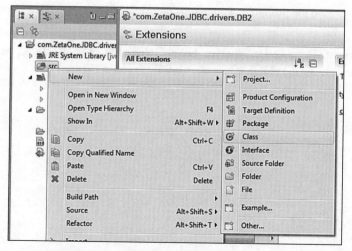

Figure 12.21 Launching the New Java Class Wizard.

Once the New Java Class dialog opens, as pictured in Figure 12.22, you can enter some of the basic settings for the class, such as the package and class name. Then click the **Finish** button.

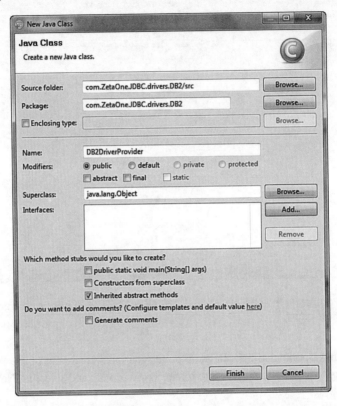

Figure 12.22   Setting the properties for the new DB2DriverProvider Java class.

At this point, Domino Designer or Eclipse reads the project settings and creates the required source code for the plugin's Java class, as displayed in Figure 12.23.

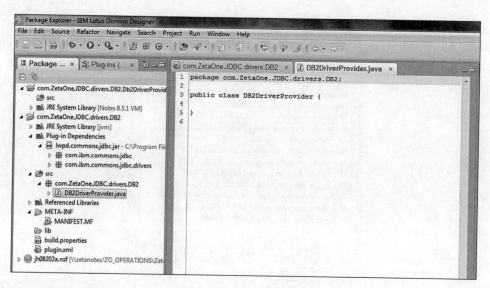

Figure 12.23 The `DB2DriverProvider` Java class stub.

The `DB2DriverProvider` class depends on two classes that must be included in the dependencies of the plugin. You can resolve these dependencies by adding the `com.ibm.commons.jdbc` plugin to the dependencies list, found on the **Dependencies** tab of the Manifest. Click the **Add** button, and the Plug-In Selection dialog is displayed. Within the dialog, the edit box serves as a filter selection to list plugins that are below. In the filter box, when you enter `com.ibm.commons`, the list of matching plugins is displayed (see Figure 12.24). Once you find the `com.ibm.commons.jdbc` plugin, select it and click **OK**.

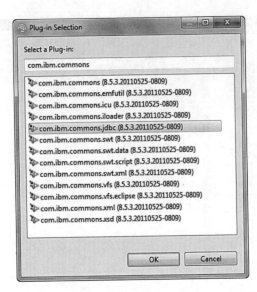

Figure 12.24   Adding the `com.ibm.commons.jdbc` plugin to the plugin dependencies.

After you resolve the dependency, you can finish the driver provider class. The class must implement the `com.ibm.commons.jdbc.drivers.JDBCProvider` interface and contain two methods: `loadDriver(String   className)` and `getDriverAliases()`. The `load-Driver()` method should check the name of the requested driver passed in `className`. If it matches the driver's class, a new instance of the driver should be returned; otherwise, null should be returned. You can use the `getDriverAliases()` method to retrieve any driver aliases. Generally, it returns null. Figure 12.25 shows a sample implementation of the class for the DB2 driver.

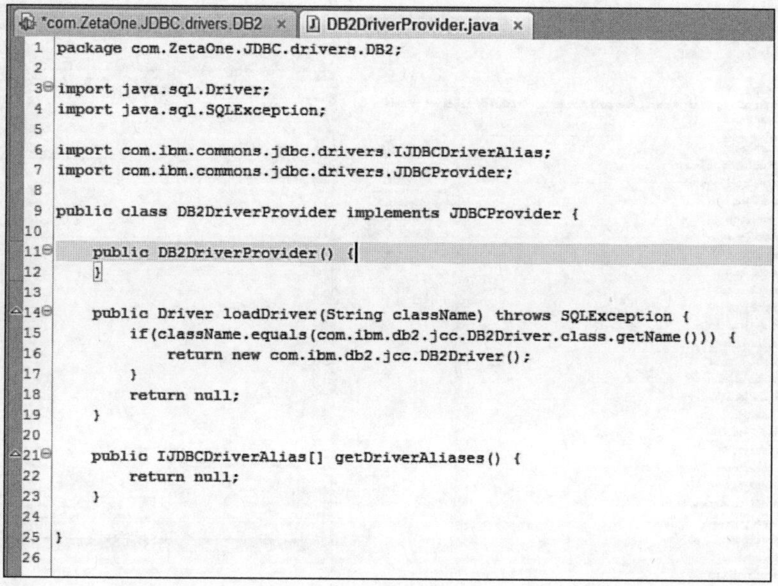

```
com.ZetaOne.JDBC.drivers.DB2  ×   DB2DriverProvider.java  ×
  1  package com.ZetaOne.JDBC.drivers.DB2;
  2
  3⊖ import java.sql.Driver;
  4  import java.sql.SQLException;
  5
  6  import com.ibm.commons.jdbc.drivers.IJDBCDriverAlias;
  7  import com.ibm.commons.jdbc.drivers.JDBCProvider;
  8
  9  public class DB2DriverProvider implements JDBCProvider {
 10
 11⊖     public DB2DriverProvider() {
 12      }
 13
 14⊖     public Driver loadDriver(String className) throws SQLException {
 15          if(className.equals(com.ibm.db2.jcc.DB2Driver.class.getName())) {
 16              return new com.ibm.db2.jcc.DB2Driver();
 17          }
 18          return null;
 19      }
 20
 21⊖     public IJDBCDriverAlias[] getDriverAliases() {
 22          return null;
 23      }
 24
 25  }
 26
```

Figure 12.25   The full DB2 driver provider class.

Once you have created the driver provider class, select the class for export. You do this in the Manifest by clicking **Add** under **Exported Packages** on the **Runtime** tab. The driver provider package should appear for selection, as shown in Figure 12.26.

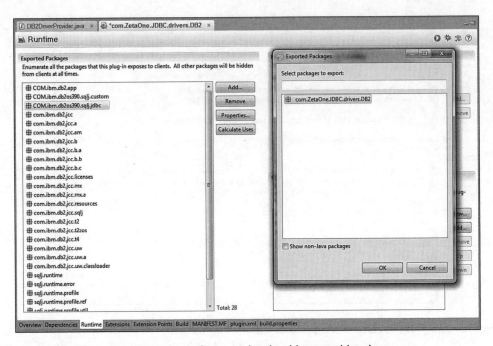

Figure 12.26   Exporting the package that contains the driver provider class.

At this point, you can save the plugin project. It is ready to export and deploy to the server. As discussed earlier, there are two ways to deploy the OSGi plugin: by either exporting the plugin and then placing the OSGi driver package directly on the server's file system, or deploying the plugin via an update site in an NSF-based update site. The export process to place the plugin on the server's file system is quick and can be accessed by right-clicking the project in **Package Explorer** and selecting **Export** from the pop-up menu. In the Export Select dialog that appears (see Figure 12.27), under **Plug-In Development**, select the **Deployable Plug-Ins and Fragments** option, and click the **Next** button to perform the export.

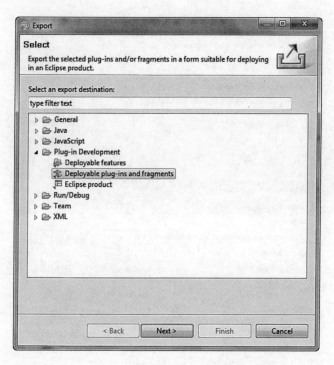

Figure 12.27   Selecting the Deployable Plug-Ins and Fragments export.

In the Export dialog, select the plugin project for export. Then set the export path in the **Directory** field on the **Destination** tab, shown in Figure 12.28, and click the **Finish** button.

Figure 12.28   Exporting the plugin using the Deployable Plug-Ins and Fragments Wizard.

The export processes the plugin, as seen in Figure 12.29; the result of the export is a JAR in the location selected during the export.

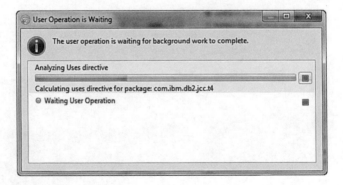

Figure 12.29   The plugin export in progress.

You can deploy this JAR file, as seen in Figure 12.30, to the **<data>\domino\workspace\ applications\eclipse\plugins** directory of the Domino server. Placing the JAR in this directory should make the drivers available to the XPages runtime.

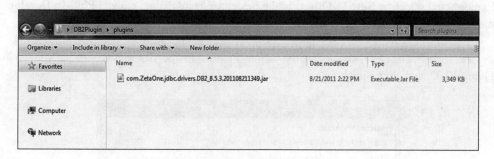

Figure 12.30   The result of the project is a plugin JAR file.

To verify that the drivers are available, you can query the OSGi console in Domino with the command `tell http osgi ss com.ZetaOne`, where `com.ZetaOne` is a filter that restricts the list of results. The filter should be the beginning of the name of the class, long enough to uniquely identify it and display it in the results (see Figure 12.31).

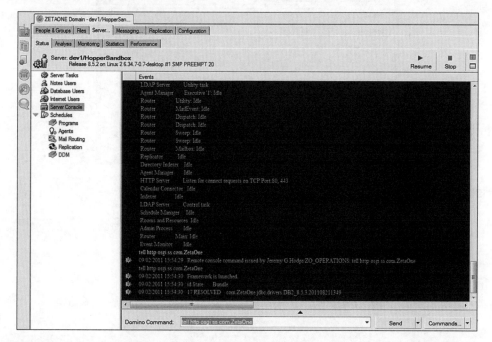

Figure 12.31   Querying OSGi on the console to determine whether the plugin is resolved.

For 8.5.3 and above, the preferred method for distributing the plugin is through an Eclipse update site using the Domino update site database that was described in Chapter 2. You create the update site in two steps. First create a Feature project by right-clicking inside the Package Explorer and selecting **New** → **Other**. In the Select a Wizard dialog, expand **Plug-In Development**, select **Feature Project**, and click **Next**.

In the **Feature Properties** page, add a project name, such as com.ZetaOne.JDBC. drivers.DB2.feature, and update the various **Feature Properties**, similar to what you see in Figure 12.32, and click **Finish**.

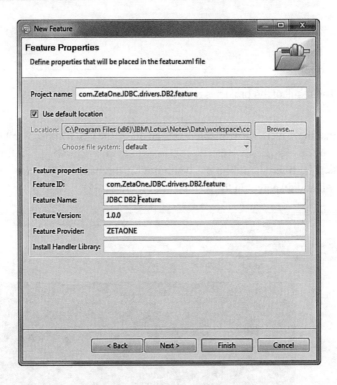

Figure 12.32   Creating a new Feature Project for the DB2 drivers.

When the new feature project opens, switch to the **Plug-Ins** tab, and click the **Add** button under **Plug-Ins and Fragments**. In the Select a Plug-In dialog, type com.ZetaOne in the Edit box to filter the list of plugins, and select the DB2 driver plugin shown in Figure 12.33. Then save the project.

Figure 12.33   Adding the DB2 JDBC Plug-in to the frature project.

The final steps in creating the update site are to create the actual update site project by right-clicking in the **Package Explorer**, again selecting **New → Other**, expanding Plug-In Development, selecting **Update Site Project**, and clicking **Next**. In the Update Site Project Wizard, enter a project name such as com.ZetaOne.JDBC.drivers.DB2.updateSite and click **Finish**. Once the update site project opens, click the **New Category** button. Give the category a unique **Name** and **Label**. Then click the **Add Feature** button. In the Select a Feature dialog, type com.ZetaOne in the Filter box and select the DB2 driver feature. The final update site project should look similar to Figure 12.34.

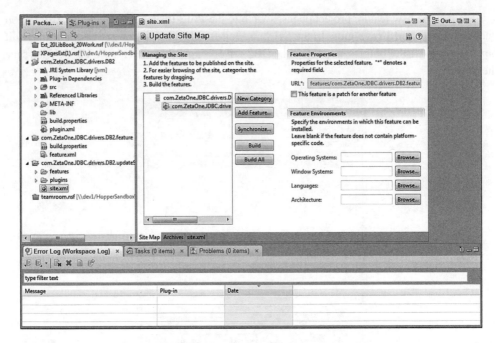

Figure 12.34   The final Update Site project for the DB2 drivers.

To import the plugin into the update site, click the **Synchronize** button. In the Features Properties Synchronization dialog, select the **Synchronize All Features on This Site** option and click **Finish**. Finally, to create the actual update site, click the **Build All** button. After the build process has completed, the update site has been created and is ready for import into the update site application from the project's folder in your workspace (for example **C:\Program Files\IBM\Lotus\Notes\Data\workspace\com.ZetaOne.JDBC.drivers.DB2.updateSite**). Import the update site into the NSF update site database in the same manner that you imported the ExtLib in Chapter 2. The driver will be available on any server where the NSF-based update site is installed.

Creating a Connection to the RDBMS

Now that the JVM has access to the JDBC drivers, the next step is setting up the connection between the driver and the RDBMS. You can establish connections to an RDBMS by creating connections in the NSF.

Creating Connection Files

The connection file is a simple XML file that contains the driver, a uniform resource locator (URL) pointing to the server, and other connection-related information. The connection file is named ***connectionName*.jdbc**, where *connectionName* is the unique name that will be given to the connection and the name used when access to the datasource is required. The format for the ***connectionName*.jdbc** file is shown in Listing 12.1.

Listing 12.1   Definition of a JDBC Connection File

```
<jdbc type="connection-pool-type">
    <driver>driver-class</driver>
    <url>url-to-database</url>
    <user>user-name</user>
    <password>password</password>
</jdbc>
```

Table 12.1 describes each of the field definitions used within the JDBC connection file.

Table 12.1   JDBC Connection File Field Definitions

Field Value Name	Field Value Description
connection-pool-type	Defines the implementation type of the connection pool that this connection will use. The default is `simple`. `Simple` is the only current connection pool implemented, but future releases of the ExtLib may include an implementation of Apache DBCP. Additional parameters to the connection pool can be provided through an additional section within the JDBC connection file detailed in Listing 12.2.
driver-class	The fully qualified Java class name of the driver that makes the connection. The driver vendor should have the driver class documented for your reference.
url-to-database	The JDBC URL to the database this connection will connect to. (See the later section, "Specifying the Database URL.")
user-name	The username used for the connection.
password	The password for `user-name`'s access to the database.

As mentioned in the `connection-pool-type` definition in Table 12.1, there are additional parameters you can set in the JDBC connection file to control the settings for the connection pool for this connection. To set these, you use an additional section that's included at the end of the connection file. The section is enclosed by a tag set using the name of the selected `connection-pool-type`. For example, if the `connection-pool-type` is set to `simple`, the tag set would be `<simple>...</simple>`. Enclosed within the tag set are the `connection-pool-type` specific settings for that connection. Listing 12.2 defines the parameters and default values for the `simple` `connection-pool-type`, and Table 12.2 defines each of the parameter's usage.

Listing 12.2   Simple Connection Pool Optional Parameters and Default Values

```
<simple>
  <minPoolSize>10</minPoolSize>
  <maxPoolSize>20</maxPoolSize>
  <maxConnectionSize>200</maxConnectionSize>
  <useTimeout>0</useTimeout>
  <idleTimeout>0</idleTimeout>
  <maxLiveTime>0</maxLiveTime>
  <acquireTimeout>10000</acquireTimeout>
</simple>
```

Table 12.2   Connection File Connection Pool Parameter Definitions for the `Simple` Pool Type

Field Value Name	Field Value Description
minPoolSize	Defines the minimum number of JDBC connections that will be maintained in the connection pool. The default value is 10. This means that at all times, 10 opened JDBC connections will be available in the connection pool.
maxPoolSize	Defines the maximum number of connections the connection pool will hold open. The connection pool will open a connection for any connection request up to maxConnectionSize, but open connections above maxPoolSize will be closed when they are returned to the pool.
maxConnectionSize	The maximum number of JDBC connections allowed at any one time. The default value is 200. Once maxConnectionSize connections are opened, any new connection requests are placed into a queue for acquireTimeout seconds. If the number of connections drops below maxConnectionSize, the connection is established; otherwise, an exception is thrown.
useTimeout	When set to a value of 1 (one), connections held longer than idleTimeout are automatically returned to the connection pool, ensuring all connection requests are returned to the pool.
idleTimeout	If a connection (before returning it to the pool) has been idle for this amount (in seconds), it is automatically closed and returned to the pool. This ensures that all connections requested by applications are returned to the document pool.
maxLiveTime	Defines the maximum lifetime for a JDBC connection. Connections idle for longer than maxLiveTime are closed, allowing the connection pool to optimize the number of open connections held in the pool during low usage periods.
acquireTimeout	The maximum number of seconds a connection waits in the queue while connections exceed maxConnectionSize. If the timeout is exceeded, the request is dropped and an exception is thrown.

Figure 12.35 shows a fully formed implementation of a JDBC connection file in Domino Designer with both the JDBC connection and the connection pool values set and customized. At the time of this writing, it is planned to include a way to create a global connection for all applications on the server. Discussions are ongoing as to how this global connection and connection pool would be created and managed (for example, whether it would be in the server's **names.nsf** or a separate database). Review the release notes in future releases of the ExtLib for more information on this option.

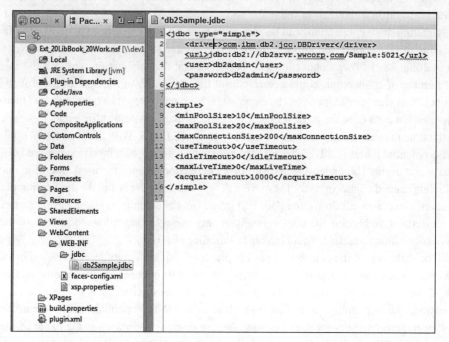

Figure 12.35 A sample NSF-specific DB2 connection in the WebContent\WEB-INF\jdbc folder.

Specifying the Database URL

The syntax of the URL is defined by the driver you are trying to access, but it is generally defined as `jdbc:DRIVER:server:port:additional-parameters`. For example, a DB2 connection, connecting to the database northwood on server db2.wwcorp.com on port 5021 would be `jdbc:db2://db2.wwwcorp.com:5021/northwood`. For a local Apache Derby database however, the connection URL `jdbc:derby:${rcp.data}\derby\XPagesJDBC; create= true` would connect to a derby database file **derby/XPagesJDBC** located in the local data directory. Notice in the previous example the use of the configuration property **rcp.data** in the computed expression `${rcp.data}`. The connection files can take advantage of computed properties in their definitions.

Creating Connections and the Connection Pool

The XPages runtime environment implements a simple connection pool to improve performance, concurrency, and scalability. A connection pool is a global object within the XPages runtime that manages the open connections to JDBC datasources. When an XPage object needs to interact with a JDBC datasource, it can request a connection from the connection pool. This pool is likely to have already established connections to the datasource because other XPages and processes have requested access previously. If the specific connection requested is not in the pool, the connection is established and then stored in the pool.

Creating these connections can be expensive because of the overhead in network traffic and processing time in connection initialization. If every XPage session on the Domino server had to open and manage its own connection to a database, and the application was heavily used, the sheer number of connections could severely limit the scalability of the application. Likewise, if the connection was instead managed by every page, each page would have to open and then close the connection each time the page was accessed. Performance would suffer greatly as each page took the time to open and process the connection to the RDBMS. With the connection pool, each of these potential issues is solved because the pool can share these connections between different sessions and users. The expensive start-up of a connection is only incurred when the pool has insufficient cached connections for the current demand that the users and the application place on the server. Once demand drops, the pool will prune out stale connections, releasing and closing the connections, and tuning the pool to maintain only enough connections to service all the concurrent connection requests without having to initialize new ones.

The existence of the connection pool is practically unknown to developers and creates no extra effort. The connection pool and the management of its connections are automatic. Once the JDBC driver is provided to the runtime environment and the connection is defined via the JDBC connection, Java Naming and Directory Interface (JNDI) publishes the connection at `java:comp/env/jdbc/`*connectionName*, where *connectionName* is the name of the connection used in XPages RDBMS component's **connectionName**. (*connectionName* is also the filename of the connection file in the **WebContent/WEB-INF/jdbc** folder of the NSF. If you exclude the jdbc/ prefix from the connection name, the runtime automatically adds it.) When the XPage request ends, the JNDI implementation ensures the connection is properly returned to the pool, without having to explicitly close it. However, it is best practice when acquiring a connection programmatically from the pool to close it as soon as it is no longer required. This keeps the connection pool from establishing too many connections and overusing system resources.

Using Relational Datasources on an XPage

The ExtLib's RDBMS support adds two new datasource types for use with data-aware components. Both `xe:jdbcQuery` and `xe:jdbcRowSet` components provide access to RDBMS data to controls in an XPage, but they have different uses and performance implications. The `xe:jdbcQuery` component returns a data set based on a query statement and stores its data using a JDBC result set. The returned record set is read-only and caches data up to `maxBlockCount` pages of data at one time. It is optimal for large read-only data sets, where the result set would be displayed in a view-like interface such as a data table. Conversely, the `xe:jdbcRowSet` is based on a JDBC `CachedRowSet` object, and the results (up to a maximum number of rows) of the query are loaded and cached in memory. The larger the returned record set, the more memory the results consume. The `xe:jdbcRowSet`, however, is a read-write data set. The cached records capture all changes to the record set and hold the changes in cache until the data is committed back to the RDBMS.

Adding a JDBC Datasource to an XPage

> **NOTE**
>
> To enable these new datasources, you must first enable the ExtLib in the application. The ExtLib is enabled the first time you use an ExtLib component from the component palette, or you can manually enable it in the Application Properties' Advanced panel. Until the ExtLib is enabled, the relational datasources do not appear in the list of datasource types on data-aware components.

The JDBC datasources are available anywhere that an `xp:dominoDocument` or `xp:dominoView` datasource would be. In the **Data** tab of a data-aware component (that is, the XPage itself, or in a View Panel), you can click the **Add** button to select the available datasources. Once added, the property list appears in any control where a datasource can be added, as shown in Figure 12.36.

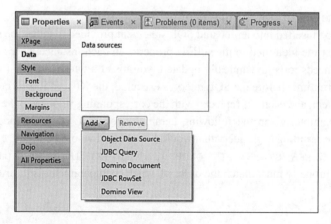

Figure 12.36 Adding a JDBC datasource to an XPage.

Creating a connection to a datasource requires at least two properties to be populated. These properties are either **connectionName** or **connectionURL** and either **sqlFile**, **sqlQuery**, or **sqlTable**. As previously discussed, the **connectionName** is the JNDI name of a connection defined by a JDBC connection file. The **connectionUrl** property takes precedence over the **connectionName** property and provides a direct JDBC URL to the database, such as `jdbc:db2://db2srvr.wwcorp.com:5021/database:user=db2adm;password=db2adm;`. Utilization of the **connectionUrl** bypasses the JDBC Connection Pool and should be used for testing only. The **sqlFile**, **sqlQuery**, and **sqlTable** properties establish the SQL statement to retrieve the data. Only one of the three properties defines the SQL statement. The precedential order for properties is **sqlTable**, **sqlQuery**, and **sqlFile**. **sqlFile** is used only if both **sqlQuery** and **sqlTable** are empty, and **sqlQuery** is used only if **sqlTable** is empty.

Specifying the SQL Statement

Use of the **sqlTable** property instructs the JDBC datasource to return a SQL table, view, or stored procedure. The value of the **sqlTable** property should be the name of the table, view, or stored procedure from which the datasource should retrieve its result set. The SQL query executed when using the **sqlTable** property is `SELECT * FROM sqlTable`. You can use a custom SQL query statement by populating either the **sqlQuery** or the **sqlFile** property. The **sqlQuery** property directly specifies the query. The **sqlFile** property specifies the filename of a text file (with the file extension **.sql**) containing the SQL query stored in the **WebContent/WEB-INF/jdbc** folder of the NSF. The SQL statement in both **sqlQuery** and **sqlFile** can be parameterized by using the **sqlParameters** property.

Adding Parameters to a SQL Statement

Parameters can be inserted into a prepared SQL statement provided in either the **sqlQuery** property or in the text file identified in the **sqlFile** property. In each instance where a portion of the SQL statement needs to be dynamically updated, you insert a question mark (?) character as a placeholder. At runtime, before the SQL query is executed, the XPages RDBC components evaluate SQL statement, and each ? is replaced with the corresponding value from the **sqlParameters** property. For example, given the following parameterized SQL statement and parameters in Figure 12.37, the resulting SQL query that would be executed would be `SELECT TOP 10 FROM ORDERCOUNTS WHERE STATE='MI' ORDERBY QUANTITY`. The order of parameters in the **sqlParameters** property must match the order in which each parameter is inserted into the SQL statement.

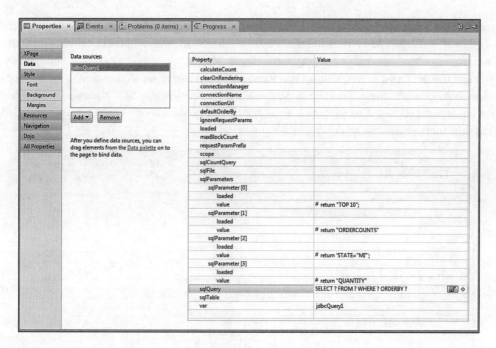

Figure 12.37 Parameterizing a SQL statement.

It is highly recommended that prepared SQL statements with parameters be used rather than calculating dynamic queries. Doing so increases performance because the query can be cached rather than having to be recomputed on each request. In addition, the use of the prepared SQL statement with parameters increases security, preventing SQL injection attacks.

Working with the `xe:jdbcQuery` Datasource

As previously mentioned, the `xe:jdbcQuery` datasource is a read-only datasource that's ideal for displaying large amounts of data because of the way data is cached for the datasource. Unlike the `xe:jdbcRowSet`, which caches the entire result set by default, the `xe:jdbcQuery` caches blocks of data.

A block of data is the result set returned to fulfil a "page" of data. For example, using the View Panel that displays 30 rows of records, those 30 lines are one page. The **maxBlockCount** property of the `xe:jdbcRowSet` controls the number of blocks that can be cached. If a database connection is slow, increasing the number of cache blocks can increase performance, but it comes at the expense of server memory. By default, the `xe:jdbcRowSet` does not perform caching. (**maxBlockCount** is set to 0.)

The `xe:jdbcQuery` datasource, displayed in Figure 12.38, supports page and record counts for the implementation of a pager. When it's set to true, the **calculateCount** property manipulates the SQL statement for the query to add a `COUNT(*)` function to the statement to return the number of rows available to the data set. For example, if the generated SQL statement is `SELECT * FROM tableName WHERE COUNTY="BRANCH"`, the component converts the statement to `SELECT * COUNT(*) FROM tableName WHERE COUNTY="BRANCH"`. Additionally, you can use the properties **sqlCountQuery** and **sqlCountFile** to set a custom SQL query statement to generate the count. This allows the use of a higher-performing SQL statement to generate the count that excludes directives such as `ORDERBY` that would increase computational overhead and time for the execution of the `count` statement.

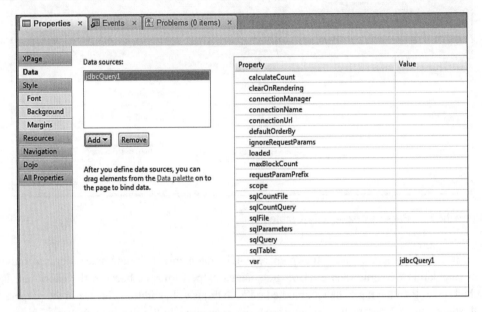

Figure 12.38   The `xe:jdbcQuery` datasource added to an XPage.

The `xe:jdbcQuery` component supports setting a default sort order through the use of the **defaultOrderBy** property. Setting the value of the property to a list of comma-separated column names establishes the default sort order. The datasource also supports user-sorted columns, which override the **defaultOrderBy** property.

Working with the `xe:jdbcRowSet` Datasource

The `xe:jdbcRowSet` datasource, pictured in Figure 12.39, is optimal for smaller data sets. This datasource reads and caches all records in the dataset by default. The more records the SQL statement returns, the more memory the component consumes. You can limit the total number of cached records by setting the **maxRows** property. It is a read-write datasource; changes made to the records are held in the cache until the entire record set is committed to the RDBMS. Unlike the `xe:jdbcQuery`, `xe:jdbcRowSet` does not support a full record count for paging. The record count available from the datasource is the current number of records currently cached in the datasource.

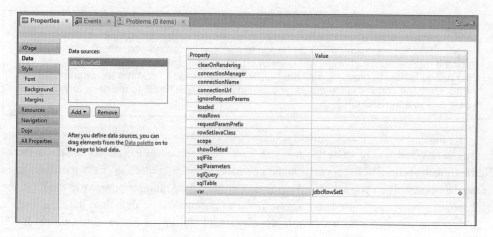

Figure 12.39 The xe:jdbcRowSet datasource added to an XPage.

Properties Common to Both the xe:jdbcQuery and xe:jdbcRowSet Datasources

In addition to the standard component properties that all datasources have, such as **ignoreRequestParams**, **scope**, **var**, and **loaded**, both data JDBC sources contain the property **clearOnRendering**. This property, when set to true, instructs the data set to clear all caches before the XPage has rendered, forcing the XPage to acquire the latest data from the RDBMS.

JDBC Datasources and Concurrency

In the typical XPages application based on NSF data, the application architecture exists prebuilt into the platform to deal with concurrent data access. If you're building applications on the platform, you don't need to worry about issues resulting from concurrent data editing related to the semi-automated nature of resolving the issue. With an RDBMS, concurrent data editing is a real concern; transactions can read and write records without an indication that a conflict has occurred. Because an XPages application is multi-threaded and can serve many requests concurrently, multiple users modifying the same data set can raise concerns about data integrity.

Additionally, when a single XPage contains more than one JDBC connection to the same connection, a performance hit can be incurred because each JDBC datasource executes its transaction independently. At the end of each transaction, a commit is made to update the transaction to the RDBMS. Each one of these commits adds overhead to the process, but a commit is not needed after every transaction if multiple transactions are going to be made to the same datasource.

NOTE

A commit is the process by which a change to a record becomes permanent in an RDBMS. During a transaction, a change, or series of changes, is performed against a database, but the change is held in memory until the RDBMS is instructed to commit the change permanently. Until the commit is executed, you can instruct the RDBMS to roll back any changes made during a transaction.

By placing an `xe:jdbcConnectionManager` component on the XPage, you can alleviate both issues. When you're using the `xe:jdbcConnectionManager`, you set the **connection-Name** (or **connectionURL**) property on the `xe:jdbcConnectionManager` component instead of the datasource. Then you set each datasource's **connectionManager** property to the ID of the appropriate `xe:jdbcConnectionManager` component. By default, the `xe:jdbc-ConnectionMananger`'s **autoCommit** property is set to false; you can execute multiple JDBC calls within a single transaction with a single commit after the grouped transaction, negating the performance hit.

The Connection Manager can also set a transactional isolation level using the **transaction-Isolation** property to help alleviate concurrency issues and maintain data integrity. Three different concurrency issues exist. Each of the five levels of transaction isolation is meant to alleviate different issues of concurrency, with varying impacts on performance.

A concurrency conflict occurs when two separate connections start a transaction simultaneously and want to interact with the same record. The three types of concurrency conflicts are Dirty Read, Unrepeatable Read, and Phantom Read. Each concurrency conflict can cause data integrity issues for different reasons.

A Dirty Read occurs when the first transaction changes the value of **fieldA** from A to a value of B. The second transaction then reads the same record and is given the new value of B. The second transaction then commits a change back to the RDBMS, with **fieldA** now equalling B. Finally, the first transaction encounters some state that would cause the transaction to roll back, but the record has already been committed with the value of **fieldA** being equal to B by the second transaction, causing invalid data to be stored in the record.

An Unrepeatable Read occurs when the first transaction reads the record and retrieves the value A from **fieldA**. The second transaction then initiates a change to **fieldA**, setting the value to B, and then commits the change. Transaction 1 then rereads the record and retrieves the new **fieldA** value of B, while continuing to process and eventually committing the record.

A Phantom Read occurs when a transaction reads a record set with a SELECT statement that causes a set number of records to be returned (for example, five records). The second transaction then inserts and commits a new record that matches the SELECT criteria. The first transaction re-executes the SELECT and returns six records.

Table 12.3 identifies each of the five levels of transaction isolation, the concurrency conflicts they address, and their impact to performance.

Table 12.3 Transaction Isolation Levels and Performance Impact

	Dirty Read	Unrepeatable Read	Phantom Read	Performance
TRANSACTION_NONE	n/a	n/a	n/a	Fastest
TRANSACTION_READ_UNCOMMITED	No Protection	No Protection	No Protection	Fastest
TRANSACTION_READ_COMMITED	Protected	No Protection	No Protection	Fast
TRANSACTION_REPEATABLE_READ	Protected	Protected	No Protection	Medium
TRANSACTION_SERIALIZABLE	Protected	Protected	Protected	Slow

The `xe:jdbcConnectionManager` also provides a method binding called `initConnection` that allows you to hook into the connection initialization routine to perform tasks. The connection object is available using the variable `connection` from within the method.

Note that the available isolation methods depend on what the RDBMS implements. Be sure to consult the database vendor's documentation to confirm what levels of isolation are implemented.

Server-Side JavaScript JDBC API for XPages and Debugging

Several @Functions have been added to Server-Side JavaScript to enable programmatic interaction with JDBC datasources. Each @Function performs a transaction of a specific type and makes programmatic access to JDBC data as easy as access to NSF data. Those methods that operate on a record set do not commit after they are called. It is up to you to ensure that either `autoCommit` is turned on (it is by default) or a call to commit is made at the appropriate time. Each of the @Functions is discussed next.

@JdbcGetConnection(data:string)

The `@JdbcGetConnection` function, an example of which appears in Listing 12.3, returns a JDBC connection for use within the other @Functions and is a shortcut to the JNDI call. The `data` parameter is the name of the connection to return. The connection follows the same rules as the `connectionName` parameter used in the JDBC datasources. The connection is released back to the connection pool when the request is completed.

When you're using `@JdbcGetConnection`, you should wrap the code block in a `try...finally` block. Inside the `finally` block, the connection should be closed. This ensures that the connection is properly closed and returned to the connection pool, even if an exception is raised.

Listing 12.3   @JdbcGetConnection(data string)

```
var con:java.sql.Connection;
try {
  con = @JdbcGetConnection("HR");
  // Execute additional operations here…
} finally {
  con.close();
}
```

@JdbcDbColumn(connection:any, table:string, column:string) : Array
@JdbcDbColumn(connection:any, table:string, column:string,
where:string) : Array
@JdbcDbColumn(connection:any, table:string, column:string,
where:string, orderBy:string) : Array
This method returns an array of all the values from the specified column in the selected table. You can use the results of this call, for example, to populate the selection values in a comboBox. You can filter the values by providing a SQL where clause in the where parameter. You can provide a comma-separated list of column names by which to sort the results in the orderBy parameter.

Listing 12.4 illustrates the simplest form of use for the method, taking the connection upon which to act, the table from which to retrieve the column, and the column's name as parameters.

Listing 12.4   @JdbcDbColumn(connection:any, table:string, column:string):
Array

```
var con:java.sql.Connection;
try {
  con = @JdbcGetConnection("HR");
  var results:Array =
        @JdbcDbColumn(con, "employees", "employeeNumber");
} finally {
  con.close();
}
```

Listing 12.5 builds upon the example from the previous listing and adds the additional where parameter. The where parameter filters the results of the function by appending a SQL where clause, which is passed as the where parameter, to the SQL statement. In this example, the results returned from Listing 12.5 are filtered down to records where the value of the field Active is set to Y.

Listing 12.5 @JdbcDbColumn(connection:any, table:string, column:string, where: string): Array

```
var con:java.sql.Connection;
try {
  con = @JdbcGetConnection("HR");
  var results:Array =
      @JdbcDbColumn(con, "employees", "employeeNumber",
            "Active='Y'");
} finally {
  con.close();
}
```

The orderBy parameter sorts the results of the function by appending a SQL order by clause, which is passed as the orderBy parameter, to the SQL statement. Listing 12.6 adds this additional orderBy parameter to the results of Listing 12.5 and sorts the results by last name and then first name.

Listing 12.6 @JdbcDbColumn(connection:any, table:string, column:string, where: string, orderBy: String): Array

```
var con:java.sql.Connection;
try {
  con = @JdbcGetConnection("HR");
  var results:Array =
      @JdbcDbColumn(con, "employees", "employeeNumber",
            "Active='Y'", "employeeLast, employeeFirst");
} finally {
  con.close();
}
```

@JdbcDelete(connection:any, table:string, where:string) : int
@JdbcDelete(connection:any, table:string, where:string, params:Array) : int
This method deletes a set of records from the specified table in the specified connection that meet the criteria specified in the where parameter. The return value of the @Function is the number of rows affected by the delete statement. In the JDBC @Functions, connection can be either a java.sql.Connection object returned from @JdbcGetConnection or a string specifying the name of the connection to be used. Listing 12.7 demonstrates the simplest form of @JdbcDelete, performing a simple unparameterized query to the employees table of the HR connection to delete a record, where the employeeNumber field matches the value 1234.

Listing 12.7   `@JdbcDelete(connection:any, table:string, where: string): int`

```
var cnt:int = @JdbcDelete("HR", "employees", "employeeNumber='1234'");
```

Additionally, through the use of the optional `params` parameter, you can send an array of values to parameterize the SQL table or `where` parameters. In each instance where a portion of the SQL statement needs to be dynamically updated, as Listing 12.8 demonstrates, you can insert a question mark (?) character as a placeholder. Before executing the SQL query, the SQL statement is evaluated, and each ? is replaced with the corresponding value from the params parameter. The return value from the function is the number of records deleted from the selected table. Notice in Listing 12.8 that after the call to @ JdbcDelete the code checks to ensure the connection's auto commit is set to true. If it isn't, the code permanently commits the change to the dataset.

Listing 12.8   `@JdbcDelete(connection:any, table:string, where: string): int`

```
var con:java.sql.Connection;
try {
  con = @JdbcGetConnection("HR");
  var parms = ['employees','1234'];
  var cnt:int =
      @JdbcDelete(con, "?", "employeeNumber='?'",parms);
  If (!con.getAutoCommit()) {
    con.commit();
  }
} finally {
  con.close();
}
```

@JdbcExecuteQuery(connection:any, sql:string) : java.sql.ResultSet
@JdbcExecuteQuery(connection:any, sql:string, params:Array) :
java.sql.ResultSet
This method executes a custom SQL statement and returns the results of the query as a `java.sql.ResultSet` object. Listing 12.9 demonstrates executing a simple query that returns all the records found in the employees table from the HR connection where the ACTIVE field is set to Y.

Listing 12.9   `@JdbcExecuteQuery(connection:any, sql: string):` `java.sql.ResultSet`

```
var con:java.sql.Connection;
try {
  con = @JdbcGetConnection("HR");
```

```
var results:java.sql.ResultSet =
      @JdbcExecuteQuery(con,
        "SELECT * FROM employees WHERE ACTIVE='Y'");
} finally {
  con.close();
}
```

You can also pass the optional `params` parameter to `@JdbcExecuteQuery` to construct the query from a parameterized query. The value of the params parameter is an array of values you can use to parameterize the SQL table or `where` parameters. In each instance where a portion of the SQL statement needs to be dynamically updated, you can insert a question mark (?) character as a placeholder. Before you execute the SQL query, the SQL statement is evaluated, and each ? is replaced with the corresponding value from the `params` parameter.

Listing 12.10 `@JdbcExecuteQuery(connection:any, sql: string, params: string): java.sql.ResultSet`

```
var con:java.sql.Connection;
try {
  con = @JdbcGetConnection("HR");
  var params = ['employees','1234'];
  var results:java.sql.ResultSet =
        @JdbcExecuteQuery(con,
          "SELECT * FROM ? WHERE ACTIVE='?'", params);
} finally {
  con.close();
}
```

`@JdbcInsert(connection:any, table:string, values:any) : int`
The `@JdbcInsert` function inserts a new record with values specified in the `values` parameter. The `values` parameter can be either a Java map or an array. For a Java map, the field names are specified as the map keys. For an array, the values can specify either `columnName=value` or just the field values. When the array specifies just field values, they must correspond to the column order of the specified table. The return value is the number of records inserted. Listing 12.11 demonstrates using the `@JdbcInsert` function with a simple JavaScript array to provide the values for each column of the new row in the specified table.

Listing 12.11   @JdbcInsert(connection:any, table: string, values: any): int

```
var con:java.sql.Connection;
try {
  con = @JdbcGetConnection("HR");
  // Specifying the values as an array of values
  var vals = [ "1234", "Y", "Smith", "Joe" ];
  var results:int = @JdbcInsert(con, 'employees', vals);
  if (!con.getAutoCommit()) {
    con.commit();
  }
} finally {
  con.close();
}
```

Listing 12.12 demonstrates using the @JdbcInsert function with a simple JavaScript array, where each entry in the array is a name/value pair that specifies which value goes into which column within the table.

Listing 12.12   @JdbcInsert(connection:any, table: string, values: any): int

```
var con:java.sql.Connection;
try {
  con = @JdbcGetConnection("HR");
  // Specifying the values as an array of name=value pairs
  var vals = [ "employeeNumber='1234'", "Active='Y'",
"lastName='Smith'", "firstName='Joe'" ];
  var results:int = @JdbcInsert(con, 'employees', vals);
  if (!con.getAutoCommit()) {
    con.commit();
  }
} finally {
  con.close();
}
```

Listing 12.13 demonstrates using the @JdbcInsert function with a java.util.HashMap, where each entry in the map is a name and value pair that correlates to the column name and value that will be inserted into the new row.

Listing 12.13   @JdbcInsert(connection:any, table: string, values: any): int

```
var con:java.sql.Connection;
try {
  con = @JdbcGetConnection("HR");
  // Specifying the values using a Java HashMap
  var vals:java.util.HashMap = new java.util.HashMap();
  vals.put("employeeNumber","1234");
  vals.put("Active","Y");
  vals.put("lastName","Smith");
  vals.put("firstName","Joe");
  var results:int = @JdbcInsert(con, 'employees', vals);
  if (!con.getAutoCommit()) {
    con.commit();
  }
} finally {
  con.close();
}
```

Listing 12.14 demonstrates yet another way to use the @JdbcInsert function, this time with the JSON object, where the variable name of each member of the object represents the column name, and the value assigned is the value that will be inserted into that column.

Listing 12.14   @JdbcInsert(connection:any, table: string, values: any): int

```
var con:java.sql.Connection;
try {
  con = @JdbcGetConnection("HR");
  // Specifying the values as a simple JavaScript object
  var vals = {
    employeeNumber: "1234",
    Active: "Y",
    lastName: "Smith",
    firstName: "Joe"
  };
  var results:int = @JdbcInsert(con, 'employees', vals);
  if (!con.getAutoCommit()) {
    con.commit();
  }
} finally {
  con.close();
}
```

@JdbcUpdate(connection:any, table:string, values:any) : int

@JdbcUpdate(connection:any, table:string, values:any, where:string) : int

@JdbcUpdate(connection:any, table:string, values:any, where:string,
params:Array) : int

This method updates one or more records that match the `where` clause with values specified in the `values` parameter. Like `@JdbcInsert`, the `values` parameter can be a JavaScript array, a JavaScript object, or a Java map.

The optional `where` parameter appends a `where` clause to the generated SQL statement that filters the list of records that will receive the update. Pass the entire contents of the where conditional (without the `WHERE` keyword) as the value of the `where` parameter.

The optional `params` parameter is an array of values you can use to parameterize the SQL table or `where` parameters. In each instance where a portion of the SQL statement needs to be dynamically updated, you can insert a question mark (?) character as a placeholder. Before executing the SQL query, the SQL statement is evaluated, and each ? is replaced with the corresponding value from the `params` parameter.

The return value is the number of records updated. For this method, connection can be either a `java.sql.Connection` object returned from `@JdbcGetConnection` or a string specifying the name of the connection to be used.

Listing 12.15 is an example of a parameterized `@JdbcUpdateFunction` using the `where` clause.

Listing 12.15   `@JdbcUpdate(connection:any, table: string, values: any,`
`where: string, params: string): int`

```
var con:java.sql.Connection;
try {
  con = @JdbcGetConnection("HR");
  // Specifying the values as a Java Hash Map
  var vals:java.util.HashMap = new java.util.HashMap();
  vals.put("Active","?");
  var parms = [ "N" ];
  var results:int =
    @JdbcInsert(con, 'employees', vals,
        "employeeNumber='1234'", parms);
  if (!con.getAutoCommit()) {
    con.commit();
  }
} finally {
  con.close();
}
```

Debugging with the `xe:dumpObject` Component

For debugging purposes, the ExtLib's dump object `xe:dumpObject`, which is available under the **Create → Other** menu by expanding the **Extension Library** category and selecting **Dump Object**, is able to dump the database metadata and the contents of a JDBC datasource to an HTML table. The dump is executed by adding the `xe:dumpObject` component to the XPage and selecting the JDBC datasource to be dumped. Listing 12.16 illustrates how to use the dump object with an `xe:jdbcQuery` datasource.

Listing 12.16   Using the `xe:dumpObject` with a JDBC Datasource

```xml
<?xml version="1.0" encoding="UTF-8"?>
<xp:view
  xmlns:xp="http://www.ibm.com/xsp/core"
  xmlns:xe="http://www.ibm.com/xsp/coreex"
  dojoParseOnLoad="true"
  dojoTheme="true">

  <xp:this.data>
    <xe:jdbcQuery
      var="jdbcQuery1"
      connectionName="HR"
      sqlFile="activeEmployees.sql">
    </xe:jdbcQuery>
  </xp:this.data>

  <xe:dumpObject
    id="dumpObject1"
    objectNames="jdbcQuery1">
  </xe:dumpObject>
</xp:view>
```

Java JDBC API for XPages

Two Java classes are included with the RDBMS support in the ExtLib that give you additional tools to work with RDBMS datasources in your XPages application. The class `com.ibm.extlib.util.JdbcUtil` provides several methods to acquire connections, check for tables, and load SQL statement design resource files from the NSF. The `com.ibm.xsp.extlib.jdbc.dbhelper.DatabaseHelper` class has functions to aid in the generation and issuance of SQL statements to a given connection.

The `com.ibm.xsp.extlib.jdbc.DatabaseHelper` class is designed mainly to assist in the generation and issuance of SQL commands to an RDBMS. Several methods, named `appendSQL`*`Type`*`()`, take a `StringBuilder` object as the first parameter and the appropriately typed value as the second and append the value to the `StringBuilder` object. The available `StringBuilder`-related methods are listed in Listing 12.17.

Listing 12.17   `appendSQLType()` Methods to Build a SQL Statement Using a `StringBuilder`

```
appendSQLBoolean(StringBuilder, boolean)
appendSQLDate(StringBuilder, Date)
appendSQLDouble(StringBuilder, double)
appendSQLFloat(StringBuilder, float)
appendSQLInteger(StringBuilder, int)
appendSQLLong(StringBuilder, long)
appendSQLNull(StringBuilder)
appendSQLShort(StringBuilder, short)
appendSQLString(StringBuilder, String)
appendSQLTime(StringBuilder, Time)
appendSQLTimestamp(StringBuilder, Timestamp, Calendar)
appendUnicodeSQLString(StringBuilder, String)
```

Additionally, several methods that return just the SQL statement-compatible string version of a value are available as `getSQLType()`. Listing 12.18 lists these methods.

Listing 12.18   getSQL

```
getSQLBoolean(boolean)
getSQLDate(Date)
getSQLDouble(double)
getSQLFloat(float)
getSQLInteger(int)
getSQLLong(long)
getSQLNull()
getSQLShort(short)
getSQLString(String)
getSQLTime(Time)
getSQLTimeStamp(Timestamp, Calendar)
getUnicodeSQLString(String)
```

In addition to the methods to help build SQL queries using a string builder, Table 12.4 lists several additional helper methods that can be used for various JDBC actions.

Table12.4 Additional Methods to Perform Other JDBC-Related Actions

Method Name	Method Description
`escapeString(String)`	Escapes string values to be included in a SQL statement.
`findHelper(Connection)`	Static method for locating the proper `Database-Helper` class for a given connection's database driver type. Only valid types currently are Derby and Generic.
`getType()`	Returns the type (enum of `com.ibm.xsp.extlib.jdbc.dbhelp.DatabaseHelper.type`) of the `Database-Helper` class. Currently either Generic or Derby.
`sendBatch(Connection, List<String>)` `sendBatch(Connection, List<String>, boolean)`	Executes a series of SQL statements on the given connection. SQL statements are sent in the `List<String>` parameter. When true, the optional `boolean` parameter issues the statements as a transaction, committing the changes after issuing the statements, and rolling back the transaction if any SQL statement fails.
`supportsBoolean()`	Returns `true` or `false` indicating whether the database type supports Boolean types.

In addition to the `DatabaseHelper` class, the `com.ibm.xsp.extlib.util.JdbcUtil` class, detailed in Table 12.5, includes several methods that are useful for Java development in XPages. The class mainly focuses on getting and creating connections, reading SQL design elements, and listing and checking for the existence of tables.

Table 12.5   Method Summary for `com.ibm.xsp.etlib.util.JdbcUtil` Class

Method Name	Method Description
`readSqlFile(String)`	Loads and reads a SQL statement design element from the **WebContent/WEB-INF/jdbc** folder of the NSF and returns the SQL statement contained within.
`listTables(Connection, String schemaPattern, String tableNamePattern)`	Returns a list of tables that match the table name and schema pattern specified.
`tableExists(Connection, String tableName)`	Returns `true` if the specified `tableName` exists.
`tableExists(Connection, String schema,String tableName)`	Returns `true` if the specified `tableName` exists with the specified schema.
`createConnectionFromUrl (FacesContext,String connectionUrl)`	Returns a `java.sql.connection` for the given `connectionUrl`.
`createManagedConnection (FacesContext, UIComponent component, String connectionName)`	Returns a `java.sql.connection` managed by an `xe:connectionManager` owned by a component for the given `connectionName`. Pass in `null` as the component to use for the current view root.
`createNamedConnection (FacesContext, String connectionName)`	Creates and returns a new connection for the specified `connectionName`.
`findConnectionManager (FacesContext,UIComponent component, String connectionName)`	Returns the connection manager for a given component and `connectionName`.
`getConnection(FacesContext, String connectionName)`	Returns a connection to the specified `connectionName` by calling `createNamedConnection`.
`getCountQuery(String)`	Coverts a `SELECT` SQL statement to a `COUNT` SQL statement.

Conclusion

With the addition of relational database access to XPages, the ability for the platform to truly become an integration point between disparate systems in the enterprise becomes a reality. Although support of RDBMS is new to XPages and the tools to integrate it into the Domino Designer UI are still forthcoming, RDBMS in XPages is already a powerful new tool in the XPage developer's arsenal. With a little work and a good understanding of RDBMS systems design, application developers will find it easy to create and deploy high-performing and highly scalable applications that cross both Lotus Domino and RDBMS stacks.

CHAPTER 13

Get Social

There is a lot of talk about "social" these days—social applications, social business, social media, social services, and so forth. The theme of Lotusphere 2012 was "Business. Made Social." Social has certainly become something of a buzzword.

Social has a lot of definitions. Some of these definitions are high-level marketing statements, others are limited to public social websites, and still more are limited to cloud computing. This chapter uses a definition of social applications in the context of XPages, custom application development, and IBM Lotus Domino/IBM XWork Server. It describes the new requirements, maps them to technologies, and shows how the Extension Library (ExtLib) helps implement these new requirements.

IBM Lotus Domino has always been a collaborative platform. For good reasons, many customers, partners, and users consider Domino a social platform for helping businesses work together more effectively. In addition to all the social functionality that Domino has always offered, the XPages ExtLib now adds functionality to support the new IT landscape and requirements.

Going Social

Today, people are connected more than ever, blurring the lines between their business and private life. Employees have Twitter accounts that they use to tweet both private and business messages. Also, many employees use their private smartphones to access business applications and data. Furthermore, information is scattered, within enterprises and in public social networks, on site systems, and on the cloud. The inbox is no longer only the mail inbox; new notifications also come in via Connections, Facebook, Google+, Twitter, and LinkedIn.

Consequently, there are new requirements for technologies to integrate and interoperate between heterogeneous systems. Technically, this often means REST application programming interfaces (APIs), which are the new lightweight and easy-to-consume web services that most services now support. HTTP requests are invoked to read and write data that is serialized as JSON or XML/Atom. Most services support OAuth (which is described later in the chapter) to delegate authorization so that custom applications can access information about these services. The XPages ExtLib provides utilities that make the usage of REST APIs really easy, including a new storage facility for OAuth application and user tokens.

Social applications always involve people, so they have to deal with users' profile information. The ExtLib comes with concepts to access the profile information of users not only from Lotus Domino, but also from these other services. And for some typical scenarios, the XPages ExtLib comes with reusable user interface controls, Sametime® live name, Connections business card, files control for Connections, and more.

Given the way collaboration software has evolved over the past 20 years, these new social tools are set to enable you to exploit this social business landscape.

Get Started

To enable building of social applications, various functionality and samples are available as part of the XPages ExtLib (http://extlib.openntf.org). At the time of writing, these tools are available only from the main download from OpenNTF.

Plugin

The ExtLib comes with a plugin called **com.ibm.xsp.extlibx.sbt**. This plugin contains the core APIs to invoke REST service calls and handle OAuth. Typically, this plugin is only consumed as-is rather than being extended or changed.

OAuth Token Store Template

The Domino template OAuth Token Store (**WebSecurityStore.ntf**) in the XPages ExtLib Open-NTF project stores both the application keys and the user tokens to invoke REST services via OAuth.

The Social Enabler Sample Database

The database **XPagesSBT.nsf** in the XPages ExtLib project contains various samples for how to do REST calls, how to do OAuth, and how to consume other services' datasources. It also contains controls showing how to access files from IBM Connections, LotusLive, and Dropbox from XPages.

Setup

You need to extract the **XPagesSBT.nsf** and the **WebSecurityStore.ntf** from the downloaded zip from the OpenNTF ExtLib project. Put this database and template in the Domino data directory and then sign it with an ID that can run unrestricted methods and operations on the server. The new application called **websecuritystore.nsf** should be created from the OAuth Token Store template.

After this, you can open the home page (http://myServer/XPagesSBT.nsf/Home.xsp), from which you can navigate to the different samples.

NOTE

You can't run all samples out of the box; several of them require configuration. For example, you need to add your own application tokens when accessing OAuth services such as Dropbox.

OAuth

OAuth is an open protocol that allows secure API authorization in a simple and standard method from desktop and web applications. Many popular services today use it, including Facebook, Twitter, and Dropbox. More and more IBM products are adding support for this protocol, with some offerings, such as LotusLive, supporting it already.

The web page http://oauth.net/ describes OAuth in more detail. You can also access various libraries to access OAuth services, one of which is http://oauth.net/code/.

The XPages ExtLib makes it easy to access OAuth services, encapsulating all the complexity such as **OAuth dance** (exchange of keys). Furthermore, the ExtLib comes with a web security store in which both application and user token can be securely stored and managed.

The following sections describe how to configure and use OAuth with XPages.

OAuth Dance

Here is a sample of how OAuth works for the **DropboxOAuth.xsp** accessing Dropbox, as shown in Figure 13.1. The Social Enabler database contains simple samples for the various services, which also print out debug information—including the tokens. You can find the samples in the XXXOAuth XPages (for example, **DropboxOAuth.xsp**).

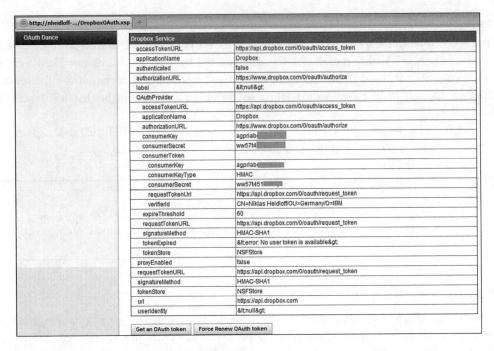

Figure 13.1   OAuth Dance Dropbox example.

When users click the **Get an OAuth Token** button, they are redirected to a Dropbox page prompting them for authentication, as shown in Figure 13.2.

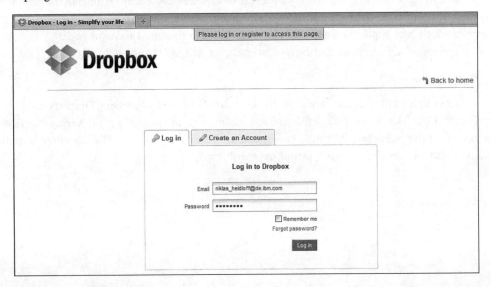

Figure 13.2   Authentication prompt.

After users have logged in, they need to give the XPages application permission to access their information and act on their behalf (see Figure 13.3).

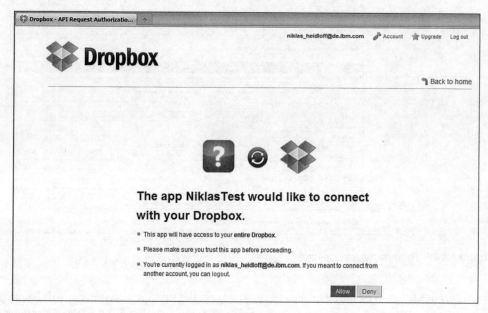

Figure 13.3   Access permission to third-party service.

After this, users are redirected to the XPages application, which now has access, in this case, to Dropbox. To test whether you can invoke REST calls, click the button **Call the Dropbox Service - Authenticated**, as shown in Figure 13.4.

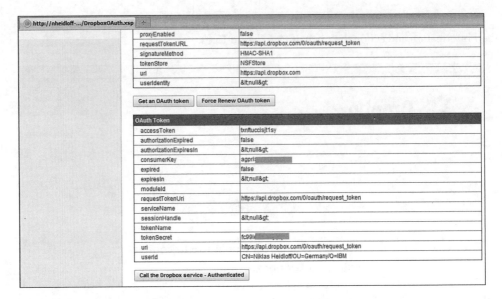

Figure 13.4   Third-party service test.

This dance has to be only executed once. After this, the keys are stored in the Web Security Store database. When tokens expire, they are renewed automatically until the specific service's expiration date. Some services allow you to define the period of token validity, such as one month. In this case, users get prompted again to grant the application access again.

OAuth Token Store Template

You can use any database created from the OAuth Token Store template (**WebSecurityStore.ntf**) to store both the application keys and the user tokens to invoke REST services via OAuth. It is envisaged that only one token store database will be on a server. Although it's not a restriction, you can use multiple OAuth Token Store databases to take advantage of various use cases for social applications. You may not want to use the same OAuth application information for all applications connecting to a particular service. For example, you may need a way for a said XPages application to use certain Twitter OAuth app information; and in this case, you need a different token.

To access services via REST and OAuth, you first need to get your own application keys and secrets. Each service is different, so it is recommended that for whatever service you want to obtain for the application, you consult the service's website, or documentation, which describes how and where this can be done. For example, for Dropbox, this can be done on http://www.dropbox.com/developers, as shown in Figure 13.5, which shows the details of a particular application.

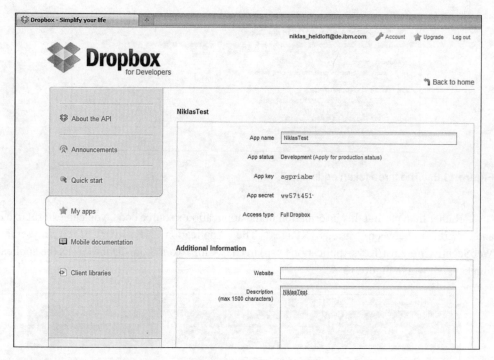

Figure 13.5   Service information.

As said, each service is different. And each service provider is likely to change the require-ments from time to time. You need to be mindful of these events, because applications that use these services are likely to suffer, so they need maintenance. It is recommended that application owners put strategies and procedures in place to cover such eventualities.

NOTE

To register applications for LotusLive and the IBM Social Business Toolkit (SBT), go here:
LotusLive: http://www-10.lotus.com/ldd/bhwiki.nsf/dx/How_to_get_a_new_oauth_key (For LotusLive please contact your LotusLive administrator to ask for a key)
SBT: http://www-10.lotus.com/ldd/appdevwiki.nsf/dx/Using_OAuth_to_integrate_with_the _IBM_Social_Business_Toolkit_sbt

---

Each service, besides having its own keys and secrets, has its own REST endpoints, usually three. Figure 13.6 shows these endpoints for Dropbox: **Request Token**, **Authorize the Request Token**, and **Upgrade to an Access Token**.

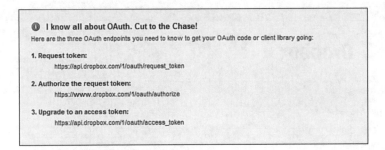

Figure 13.6   The three token endpoints.

Rather than putting this information in the application's source code, you can externalize it and share it between various XPages. The Application Keys view (http://myserver/ WebSecurityStore.nsf/KeysApplications.xsp) in an OAuth Token Store database lists the application keys, shown in Figure 13.7.

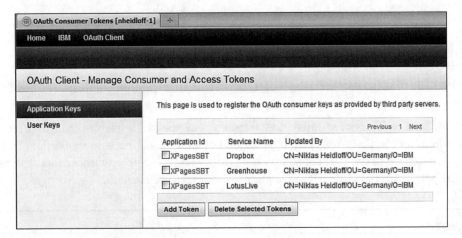

Figure 13.7   Applications Keys view.

From this view, you can add your own application's keys, as shown in Figure 13.8.

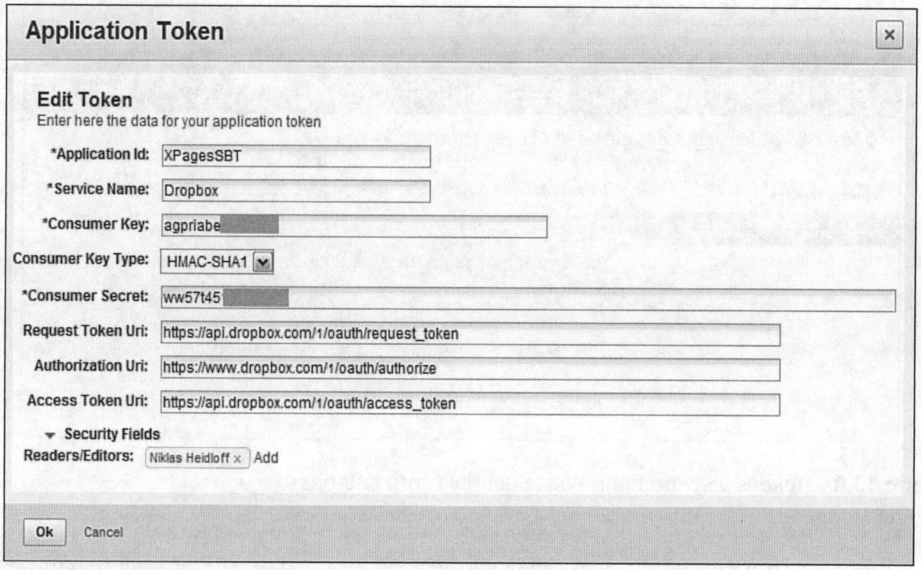

Figure 13.8   Adding a key.

Application ID and **Service Name** together are the unique key. They need to map to the configuration in **faces-config.xml**, as shown in Listing 13.1.

Listing 13.1   The Application's faces-config.xml

```
<managed-property>
  <property-name>serviceName</property-name>
  <value>Dropbox</value>
</managed-property>
<managed-property>
  <property-name>appId</property-name>
  <value>XPagesSBT</value>
</managed-property>
```

Under **Consumer Secret** and **Consumer Key**, you need to enter the credentials resulting from the application registrations. Furthermore, you need to enter the three OAuth endpoints here.

Under the **Security Fields** section in the field **Readers**, you can add more people with read access. By default, it's only the user who created the document and the database managers who have access. You need to add other users here to give them access.

The **User Keys** view (http://myserver/WebSecurityStore.nsf/KeysUsers.xsp) contains a list of user tokens, as shown in Figure 13.9. These tokens are added after users have given the application access to the various social services.

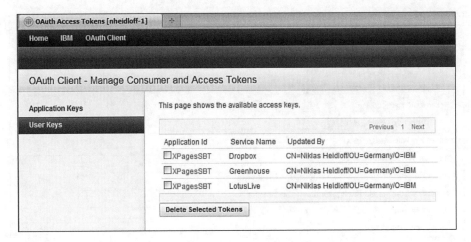

Figure 13.9   Tokens view from the Web Security Store database.

From the **User Keys** view, you can delete specific user tokens. If you want to request new keys for debugging purposes, you need to delete the tokens here and restart the HTTP server (restart task http) because the tokens are cached in memory. Theoretically, you could add and edit the tokens here, but the infrastructure usually does this automatically. By default, only the user who owns the token and the database managers have access to a user's tokens

Figure 13.10 shows a user key token as stored in the OAuth Token Store.

Figure 13.10   Token access details.

Configure Applications to Use OAuth

Now that the application keys are stored in an OAuth Token Store database, you can almost call REST services. But first, further configuration is needed in the custom application to point to the Token Store database.

If you have put this database in an alternate directory other than the root, then in the Java perspective (or Project Explorer view in the Designer perspective), you can open the file **WebContent/WEB-INF/faces-config.xml** to link the OAuth Security Store database to the application, as shown in Listing 13.2.

Listing 13.2 The OAuth Token Store's faces-config.xml

```xml
<managed-bean>
  <managed-bean-name>NSFStore</managed-bean-name>
  <managed-bean-class>
com.ibm.xsp.extlib.sbt.security.oauth_10a.store.OAuthNSFTokenStore
  </managed-bean-class>
  <managed-bean-scope>application</managed-bean-scope>
  <managed-property>
    <property-name>database</property-name>
    <value>WebSecurityStore.nsf</value>
  </managed-property>
</managed-bean
```

REST API Calls and Endpoints

XPages applications need uniform resource locators (URLs) and credentials to call REST services. To make this as easy as possible, the XPages ExtLib provides mechanisms to encapsulate and manage this complexity.

In the XPages ExtLib, the URL and the credentials are encapsulated in an object called an endpoint. An endpoint is defined via a managed bean, with some managed properties as parameters. Multiple endpoint implementations are provided, each of them proposing a different authentication/authorization mechanism.

Here are the available implementations:

- **com.ibm.xsp.extlib.sbt.services.client.endpoints.OAuthEndpointBean**—
  Connects to the service using OAuth tokens. OAuth should be the preferred method when calling REST services.

- **com.ibm.xsp.extlib.sbt.services.client.endpoints.AnonymousEndpointBean**—
  Connects to the service as anonymous, without credentials.

- **com.ibm.xsp.extlib.sbt.services.client.endpoints.FacebookEndpoint**—Connects to Facebook using the Facebook application key.

- **com.ibm.xsp.extlib.sbt.services.client.endpoints.BasicEndpointBean**—Connects to the service using basic authentication, with a username and a password. This is generally not advised, particularly if HTTPS is not being used. But it is simple and convenient for demo purposes. Furthermore, this is the only method some servers provide.

More implementations, such as a SAML or a LTPA item, may be added later.

Endpoint Configuration

This section describes the different endpoint configurations. All of them are done in the file **WebContent/WEB-INF/faces-config.xml** again.

OAuthEndpointBean

Listing 13.3 shows how this is done for the **OAuthEndpointBean**.

Listing 13.3   OAuthEndpointBean in the faces-config.xml File

```
<managed-bean>
    <managed-bean-name>dropbox</managed-bean-name>
    <managed-bean-
class>com.ibm.xsp.extlib.sbt.services.client.endpoints.OAuthEndpoint
Bean</managed-bean-class>
    <managed-bean-scope>application</managed-bean-scope>
    <!-- Endpoint URL -->
    <managed-property>
      <property-name>url</property-name>
      <value>https://api.dropbox.com</value>
    </managed-property>
    <managed-property>
      <property-name>serviceName</property-name>
      <value>Dropbox</value>
    </managed-property>
    <managed-property>
      <property-name>appId</property-name>
      <value>XPagesSBT</value>
    </managed-property>
    <!-- OAuth parameters -->
    <managed-property>
      <property-name>tokenStore</property-name>
      <value>NSFStore</value>
    </managed-property>
  </managed-bean>
```

The bean name is the variable that you can use later in an XPage. It needs to have the class `com.ibm.xsp.extlib.sbt.services.client.endpoints.OAuthEndpointBean`. The **appId** and the **serviceName** need to map to the names defined in the token store. The `url` is the base URL of the REST service. The **tokenStore** value needs to point to the token store bean that you have defined.

AnonymousEndpointBean

An example of how to configure the **AnonymousEndpointBean** is shown in Listing 13.4.

Listing 13.4   faces-config.xml Example for the AnonymousEndpointBean

```
<managed-bean>
  <managed-bean-name>lotusliveAnonymous
  </managed-bean-name>
  <managed-bean-class>

com.ibm.xsp.extlib.sbt.services.client.endpoints.AnonymousEndpointBean
  </managed-bean-class>
  <managed-bean-scope>application</managed-bean-scope>
  <managed-property>
    <property-name>url</property-name>
    <value>https://apps.test.lotuslive.com
    </value>
  </managed-property>
</managed-bean>
```

In this case, the class name is `com.ibm.xsp.extlib.sbt.services.client.end-points.AnonymousEndpointBean,` and the **url** needs to be defined.

FacebookEndpoint

This endpoint type, **FacebookEndpoint**, is used to connect to Facebook. To connect to Facebook and to use its JavaScript SDK, a Facebook API key is needed so that you can be connected, as shown in Listing 13.5. Follow the dedicated site for this purpose (https://developers.facebook.com/apps).

Listing 13.5   The faces-config.xml Configuration for the FacebookEndpoint

```
<managed-bean>
  <managed-bean-name>facebook</managed-bean-name>
  <managed-bean-class>
    com.ibm.xsp.extlib.sbt.services.client.endpoints.FacebookEndpoint
  </managed-bean-class>
  <managed-bean-scope>application</managed-bean-scope>
```

Listing 13.5   (Continued)

```
<managed-property>
  <property-name>url</property-name>
  <value>http://www.facebook.com/</value>
</managed-property>
<managed-property>
  <property-name>serviceName</property-name>
  <value>Facebook</value>
</managed-property>
<managed-property>
  <property-name>appId</property-name>
  <value>XPagesSBT</value>
</managed-property>
<!-- OAuth parameters -->
<managed-property>
  <property-name>tokenStore</property-name>
  <value>NSFStore</value>
</managed-property>
</managed-bean>
```

BasicEndpointBean

Listing 13.6 shows the **BasicEndpointBean** configuration.

Listing 13.6   faces-config.xml Example for BasicEndpointBean

```
<managed-bean>
  <managed-bean-name>greenhouseConnections
  </managed-bean-name>
  <managed-bean-class>
com.ibm.xsp.extlib.sbt.services.client.endpoints.BasicEndpointBean
  </managed-bean-class>
  <managed-bean-scope>session</managed-bean-scope>
  <managed-property>
    <property-name>url</property-name>
    <value>https://greenhouse.lotus.com
    </value>
  </managed-property>
  <managed-property>
    <property-name>proxyEnabled</property-name>
```

```
        <value>true</value>
    </managed-property>
    <managed-property>
        <property-name>passwordStore</property-name>
        <value>PwdStore</value>
    </managed-property>
    <managed-property>
        <property-name>authenticationPage
        </property-name>
        <value>_BasicLogin?endpoint=greenhouseConnections
        </value>
    </managed-property>
</managed-bean>
```

Set the managed bean class to `com.ibm.xsp.extlib.sbt.services.client.endpoints.BasicEndpointBean` and provide the **url**.

The **passwordStore** points to the managed bean that defines where to store user credentials when users choose the option **Save My Credentials and Keep Me Signed In Across Sessions** on the login page. In this case, the credentials used for basic authentication are stored encrypted and are accessible for the user in the database defined in the managed bean **PwdStore**, which happens to be the same token store database shown in Listing 13.7.

Listing 13.7   PwdStore Sample faces-config.xml

```
<managed-bean>
    <managed-bean-name>PwdStore</managed-bean-name>
    <managed-bean-class>
        com.ibm.xsp.extlib.sbt.security.password.store.BANSFPasswordStore
    </managed-bean-class>
    <managed-bean-scope>application</managed-bean-scope>
    <managed-property>
        <property-name>database</property-name>
        <value>WebSecurityStore.nsf</value>
    </managed-property>
</managed-bean>
```

In addition, you need to define an XPage to perform the authentication. In the authentication page, you need to call the login method of the endpoint with the username, the password, and whether to keep the credentials in the memory store, as shown in Listing 13.8. With the `redirect` method to the previous page, this page is displayed again.

Listing 13.8   BasicLogin XPage Markup

```
<xp:panel
  tagName="p"
  styleClass="lotusFormField">
  <xp:label
    value="User Name:"
    id="label1"
    for="userInput"></xp:label>
  <xp:inputText
    id="userInput"
    size="30"
    style="margin-left:4.0px"></xp:inputText>
</xp:panel>
<xp:panel
  tagName="p"
  styleClass="lotusFormField">
  <xp:label
    value="Password:"
    id="label2"
    for="passwordInput">
  </xp:label>
  <xp:inputText
    id="passwordInput"
    password="true"
    size="30"
    style="margin-left:12.0px">
  </xp:inputText>
</xp:panel>
<br></br>
<xp:panel
  tagName="p"
  styleClass="lotusFormField">
  <xp:checkBox
    text="Save my credentials and keep me signed in across sessions"
    id="ckKeep"
    style="font-weight:normal">
  </xp:checkBox>
</xp:panel>
<br></br>
<xp:div
```

```
    rendered="#{javascript:compositeData.loginButton}"
    styleClass="lotusBtnContainer">
    <xp:button
      value="Login"
      id="button1"
      styleClass="lotusFormButton">
      <xp:eventHandler
        event="onclick"
        submit="true"
        refreshMode="complete">
        <xp:this.action><![CDATA[#{javascript:var ep =
@Endpoint(compositeData.endpoint)
var u = getComponent("userInput").getValue();
if(u) {
 var p = getComponent("passwordInput").getValue();
 var k = getComponent("ckKeep").isChecked();
 if(ep.login(u,p,k)) {
  ep.redirect()
 }
}
}]]></xp:this.action>
      </xp:eventHandler>
    </xp:button>
    <br></br>
    <br></br>
  </xp:div>
```

Figure 13.11 shows the authentication page.

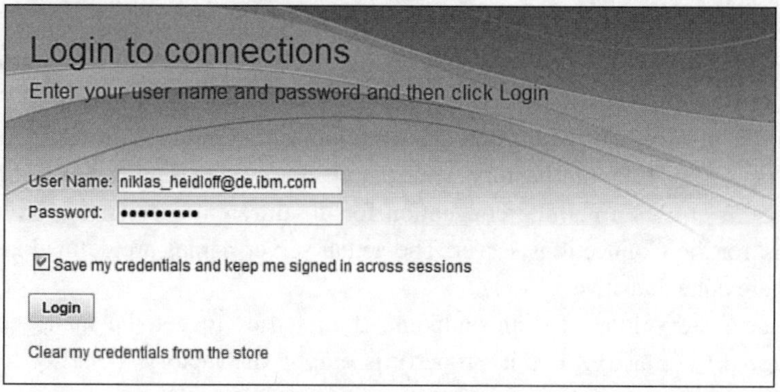

Figure 13.11   XPages authentication page example.

Access Endpoints

Now that you have configured everything, you can easily invoke REST calls. The REST calls are invoked from the server side, which eliminates issues such as cross domain access and authentication.

Listing 13.9 is an easy example for how to read the current Dropbox username.

Listing 13.9   A Dropbox OAuth Example XPage

```
<xp:button
  value="Call the Dropbox service - Authenticated"
  id="button4">
  <xp:eventHandler
    event="onclick"
    submit="true"
    refreshMode="complete">
    <xp:this.action>
             <![CDATA[#{javascript:
if(!dropbox.getOAuthProvider().acquireToken()) {
 viewScope.text = "Please, acquire a token before calling the service"
   return;
}
var svc = new sbt.GenericService(dropbox,"0/account/info/")
var account_info = svc.get(null,"json");
var user = account_info.email;
viewScope.text = user
             }]]>
    </xp:this.action>
  </xp:eventHandler>
</xp:button>
```

The variable `dropbox` is the name of the managed bean defined in **faces-config.xml**, which has the type **OAuthEndpointBean**.

In addition to using an explicit parameter holding the endpoint name, you can use the EndpointFactory. The EndpointFactory (`com.ibm.xsp.extlib.sbt.services.client.EndpointFactory`) uses a naming convention for the different servers. For example, it uses `connections` for the Connections server. The actual server names are defined as constants in this class and are not exhaustive.

When the factory looks for an endpoint, it first tries to get the managed bean name `extlib.endpoint.<name>`. If this property is empty, the factory looks for a bean named `<name>`.

In practice, naming the beans using the convention (`connections`, `sametime`, `dropbox`, and so on) is sufficient and easy. But a property exists in case you want to easily switch between servers (production, test, and more) if there are naming conflicts. For example, if you define a managed bean `connections` to point to the Greenhouse Connections install and a second one to point to Bleedyellow Connections, let's say `bleedyellowConnections`, the developer can define with the property **extlib.endpoint.connections** in **xsp.properties** which one to use at runtime as the default.

```
xsp.properties: extlib.endpoint.connections=bleedyellowConnections
```

To access the endpoint from JavaScript, there is a new @Function:

```
@Endpoint(name)
```

It returns the endpoint object named `name`.

The **OAuthEndpointBean** type has an `authenticate(boolean force)` to get a token if no token is stored in the token store database. The parameter `force` allows you to force a refresh of the token. With `isAuthenticated()`, you can check whether a token has already been acquired.

```
public boolean isAuthenticated() throws ServicesException
public void authenticate(boolean force) throws ServicesException
```

REST API Calls

To execute the actual REST service call, there is a generic service `com.ibm.xsp. extlib.ser-vices.client.GenericService` with `get`, `post`, `delete`, and `put` methods. Listing 13.8 uses this to execute a `get` request to https://api.dropbox.com/0/account/info/ to obtain the current user's account information. To find out the supported URLs, check out the service's website or product documentation, as shown in Table 13.1.

Table 13.1 Service Documentation

Service	Documentation
Dropbox	https://www.dropbox.com/developers/web_docs#api-specification
LotusLive	http://www-10.lotus.com/ldd/appdevwiki.nsf/ xpViewCategories.xsp?lookupName=API%20Reference
IBM Connections	http://publib.boulder.ibm.com/infocenter/ltscnnct/v2r0/ index.jsp?topic=/com.ibm.connections.25.help/c_api_welcome.html
IBM Social Business Toolkit	http://www-10.lotus.com/ldd/appdevwiki.nsf/dx/Activity_stream_ API_sbt

You can create a new instance of a service via the following constructor using `com.ibm.xsp.extlib.sbt.services.client.GenericService` or specialized services such as `DropboxService`. The endpoint is the managed bean defined in **faces-config.xml**.

```
public GenericService(Endpoint endpoint, String serviceUrl)
```

All services include the methods shown in Table 13.2.

Table 13.2   Available Methods

Object	Syntax
`public Object get`	`(Map<String,String> parameters, String format) throws ServicesException`
`public Object post`	`(Map<String,String> parameters, Object content, String format) throws ServicesException`
`public Object put`	`(Map<String,String> parameters, Object content, String format) throws ServicesException`
`public Object delete`	`(Map<String,String> parameters) throws ServicesException`

With the `parameters` parameter, name/value pairs can be defined that are added to the URL to be invoked.

The parameter format defines to which object type output should be converted. The different types are defined in `com.ibm.xsp.extlib.services.client.Serviceas`, shown in Table 13.3.

Table 13.3   Parameter Format

Format	Returns
`public static final String FORMAT_TEXT= "text"`	Returns `java.util.String`
`public static final String FORMAT_XML= "xml"`	Returns `org.w3c.dom.Document`
`public static final String FORMAT_JSON= "json"`	Returns `com.ibm.jscript.std.ObjectObject`

For the `post` and `put` methods, the actual content needs to be passed in. Depending on the type, different content types are used, as shown in Table 13.4.

Table 13.4 Content Types

Instance	Content Type
content instanceof IValue	contentType = "application/json"
content instanceof JsonObject	contentType = "application/json"
content instanceof Node	contentType = "application/xml"

Utilities for Parsing

REST services return mostly data in the format of JSON or XML (for example, Atom feed). Although JSON parsing in JavaScript is rather straightforward, it's a little bit tricky for XML (for example, XPath). Even for JSON, you have to write some code manually so it doesn't run in null pointer exceptions if certain parts of the tree don't exist. In any case, parsing JSON and XML is different when using standard JavaScript mechanisms.

The XPages ExtLib comes with several utilities to make parsing easier. You can run some samples that are part of the Social Enabler database. Figure 13.12 shows the page with JSON.

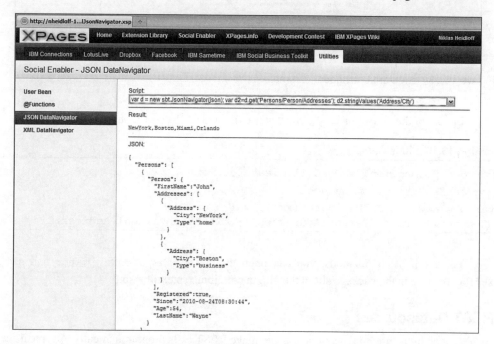

Figure 13.12 JSON data navigation example.

Figure 13.13 shows how a page displays as XML.

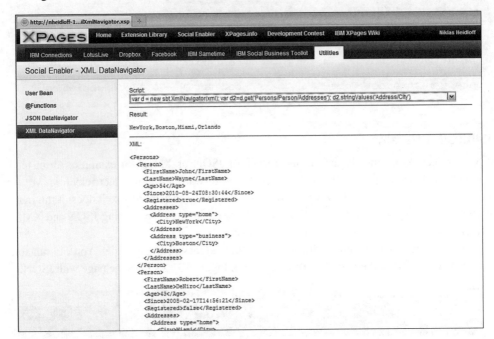

Figure 13.13   XML data navigation example.

In both of the preceding cases, you can use the same APIs (see Listing 13.10).

Listing 13.10   XML Sample

```
var doc:DOMDocument = DOMUtil.createDocument()
doc.setXMLString(something)
var d = new sbt.XmlNavigator(xml); var
d2=d.get('Persons/Person/Addresses'); d2.stringValues('Address/City')
```

For a full list of methods, you can open the classes `sbt.JsonNavigator` and `sbt.XmlNavigator` in the package **sbt** in the plugin com.ibm.xsp.extlibx.sbt.

REST Datasources

As described in the previous section, you can make REST calls programmatically. A typical scenario is developers wanting to display lists of objects. You can do this with the Core View Panel control, the Repeat control, or the Data View control from the XPages ExtLib. These controls not only display a list of objects but also allow paging, caching of objects, and other functionality like expand/collapse. Figure 13.14 illustrates what such a control can look like on an XPage.

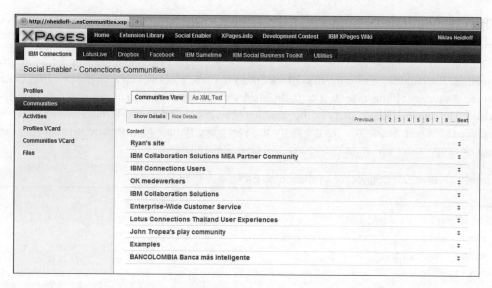

Figure 13.14   REST data in a view collection.

These controls require datasources. The XPages ExtLib comes with a set of additional data-sources provided by the **sbt** plugin, as shown in Figure 13.15.

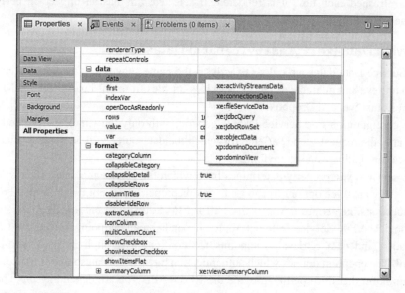

Figure 13.15   Additional social datasources.

The Connections Datasource (`xe:connectionsData`)

Listing 13.11 shows the XPages markup of a typical use case of the `xe:connectionsData` datasource. It is a simple use case that uses just the required properties to allow this datasource to function. The datasource uses the **maxBlockCount** to cache blocks of data. In the example, three blocks are cached. If this is set to 1 or 0, the blocks are disregarded each time a new data block is added. The **serviceURL** property is important here because the relative URL must be used and not include the server name. You must specify the **var** property here too, because it is used by the request scope under which the datasource will be made available.

Listing 13.11   IBM Connections Datasource Sample

```
<xe:connectionsData
 var="connectionsAtom1"
 serviceUrl="/communities/service/atom/communities/all"
 endpoint="connections"
 maxBlockCount="3">
</xe:connectionsData>
```

Additional properties are available for this datasource that may become useful outside the typical use case. You may use the **clearOnRendering** property to indicate whether the data should be refreshed each time it is rendered. If selected, this has an impact on performance because the default is not to refresh.

File Service Data (`xe:fileServiceData`) Datasource

The File Service Data datasource does exactly as the name suggests. It's a datasource that you can use to retrieve and interact with REST services for files from third parties like IBM Connections, IBM LotusLive, and Dropbox.

The configuration File Service Data is generic, with only the **var** property needing to be set. The var is the request scope variable for which the datasource will be made available in the XPage. You can set this value to anything.

The **serviceType** property determines from which file service the datasource will retrieve data. Now there are three options to choose from this property: `xe:connectionsFileData` for IBM Connections, `xe:lotusLiveFileData` for IBM LotusLive, and `xe:dropboxFileData` for Dropbox. The File Service Data datasource depends on an endpoint mechanism to perform authentication and data retrieval. Endpoints are configured through an application's **faces-config.xml**. The endpoint defines which authentication method the datasource is to use.

Be mindful that third parties provide the REST APIs you are depending on. These APIs may change without notice, although it's unlikely.

`xe:fileServiceData` Example for Connections

The Social Enabler samples database, **XPagesSBT.nsf**, contains examples for all three service types. Listing 13.12 shows the example for IBM Connections,, which comes from the **sbtFilesConnections.xsp** Custom Control. It uses the Lotus Greenhouse Connections server; the serviceUrl is specific to that server.

Listing 13.12 File Service Data Control Example for Connections

```
<xe:fileServiceData
 var="fileServiceData1"
 endpoint="connections"
 <xe:this.serviceType>
  <xe:connectionsFileData></xe:connectionsFileData>
 </xe:this.serviceType>
</xe:fileServiceData>
```

`xe:fileServiceData` for Dropbox

A similar connection is made to the Dropbox file service in Listing 13.13, which is the example from the **sbtFilesDropbox.xsp** Custom Control in the Social Enabler database.

Listing 13.13 File Service Data for Dropbox Example

```
<xe:fileServiceData
 var="fileServiceData1"
 endpoint="dropbox"
 <xe:this.serviceType>
 <xe:dropboxFileData></xe:dropboxFileData>
 </xe:this.serviceType>
</xe:fileServiceData>
```

`xe:fileServiceData` for LotusLive

Listing 13.14 is the example used for IBM LotusLive from the **sbtLotusLive.xsp** Custom Control.

Listing 13.14 File Service Data for LotusLive

```
<xe:fileServiceData
 var="fileServiceData1"
 endpoint="lotuslive"
 <xe:this.serviceType>
  <xe:lotusLiveFileData></xe:lotusLiveFileData>
```

Listing 13.14   (Continued)

```
</xe:this.serviceType>
<xe:this.urlParameters>
 <xe:urlParameter name="subscriberId">
  <xe:this.value>
   <![CDATA[${javascript:return userBean.lotusLiveSubscriberId;}]]>
  </xe:this.value>
 </xe:urlParameter>
 </xe:this.urlParameters>
</xe:fileServiceData>
```

For IBM LotusLive, the `subscriberId` needs to be passed in which is provided by the user bean.

Activity Stream Data (`xe:activityStreamData`)

The Activity Stream Data datasource is another new datasource to XPages by way of the ExtLib. It aims to be a conduit between XPages and use of Activity Streams, one of the Social Business corner stones, in real life applications.

Activity Streams is an open format specification for activity stream protocols, which syndicate activities taken in social web applications and services. The Activity Stream datasource aims to harness this. Listing 13.15 shows one such sample in Lotus Greenhouse (http://greenhouse.lotus.com/).

Lotus Greenhouse's activity stream is generated using the IBM Social Business Toolkit. This is a set of extensible tools and resources for incorporating social capabilities into your applications and business processes. The Social Business Toolkit works alongside the IBM Social Business Framework, which is the strategic model for a unified work experience across the IBM Collaboration Solutions product portfolio. Initially, the Social Business Toolkit delivers a set of tools that enable you to publish and retrieve events to the activity stream. The activity stream is a personal view of relevant updates and events that have been aggregated from multiple sources into a single stream of business information. XPages can then connect to these activity streams, like that in Lotus Greenhouse, using the Activity Stream Data datasource.

Listing 13.15 is a simple use case of this datasource. The **serviceUrl** property again is specific to the activity stream service in question, Lotus Greenhouse. The **endpoint** property specifies the name of the endpoint that the datasource needs to call to retrieve the actual bean. The **format** property then defines the output type of the result. The default output type is JSON, and in the example it is set to XML-Atom.

You can use many properties with this datasource to specifically tailor to a unique use case.

You can do basic filtering of the activity stream data using the **filterBy** property. More filtering options are available with operators and certain values, using the **filterOp** and **filterValue** properties, respectively. You can use the **appId** property to filter the stream based on the application ID, which by default gets all applications. And as with applications, you can filter the stream by a user's ID with the **userId** property.

You can use the **updateSince** property to show results from a specific date. This value can be expressed as a number, date, or text, which is passed as it is in a URL.

Listing 13.15   Sample Datasource Connection to Lotus Greenhouse

```
<xe:activityStreamsData
 var="activityStreams1"
 serviceUrl="/vulcan/shindig/rest/activitystreams"
 endpoint="greenHouse"
 format="atom">
</xe:activityStreamsData>
```

Proxies

Social applications often request information on other servers. This is no problem for code that runs on the Domino server, such as the REST calls (see Chapter 11, "REST Services"). Often, however, you need to access resources such as JavaScript or CSS files located on other servers/domains from the web browser. Because this opens potential security holes, most browsers implement the one domain security policy, which means that all requests need to go to the same domain. To accomplish this, proxies on the same server are typically used. IBM Lotus Domino comes with such a proxy server and the ExtLib with another ability to use proxies. These alternatives and the pros and cons are described next.

Domino Proxy

IBM Lotus Domino comes with an out-of-the-box proxy server. You can configure this proxy server using Domino Administrator and Security Settings and Policies. The advantage of this proxy is that it is available globally for all Domino applications, and it's easy to set it up because only configuration, not development, is needed.

Essentially as a first step, you define the URLs you want to allow applications to connect to in a Security Settings document, as shown in Figure 13.16.

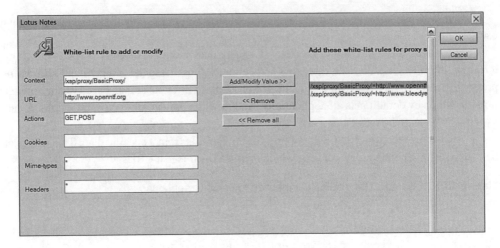

Figure 13.16   Setting a proxy in the Security Settings document.

In a second and last step, you use policies to define for which users these settings should be employed, as shown in Figure 13.7.

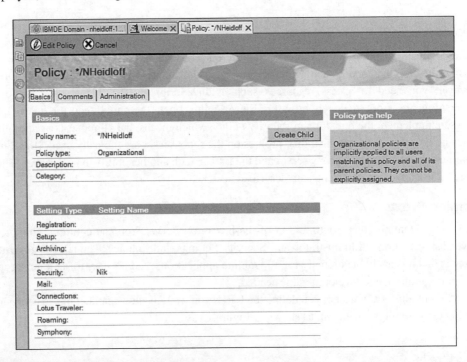

Figure 13.17   Final step to setting a proxy.

For this to work, users need to be authenticated so that the right policies can be found. After this, you can call URLs like this:

```
http://myDominoServer.de/xsp/proxy/BasicProxy/http/www.openntf.org/
dogear/atom?email=niklas_heidloff@de.ibm.com
```

ExtLib Proxies

In addition, you can implement your own proxy servers by building plugins with Java. One advantage is security, because you can control exactly what can and must not happen. Another advantage is that you can build this proxy and deploy it as an OSGi bundle (as the ExtLib as well). The disadvantage is that custom coding is needed.

The ExtLib contains some utilities that make it rather easy to implement proxies. Essentially, you have to implement the interface IProxyHandler.

```
com.ibm.xsp.extlib.proxy.IProxyHandler:
public interface IProxyHandler {    public void
service(HttpServletRequest request, HttpServletResponse response)
throws ServletException, IOException;}
```

For calls trying to connect to services defined in endpoints, there is a utility class `BasicProxyForEndpoint` (`com.ibm.xsp.extlib.sbt.proxy.BasicProxyForEndpoint`) that ensures, for example, that only calls to the endpoint's URL are allowed.

Register proxies programmatically via `com.ibm.xsp.extlib.proxy.ProxyHandlerFactory`, like this example from `com.ibm.xsp.extlib.sbt.fragment.SBTFragment`:

```
ProxyHandlerFactory.get().registerHandler("files", FileHandler.class);
```

After this, you can call the proxy using (`xsp/.proxy/files/`).

```
http://nheidloff-1/XPagesSBT.nsf/xsp/.proxy/files//DAS1.gif?type=drop-
box&path=/DAS1.gif&mimeType=image/gif&endpointName=dropbox
```

To learn more, check out `com.ibm.xsp.extlib.sbt.connections.proxy.ConnectionsProxyHandler` or `com.ibm.xsp.extlib.sbt.files.proxy.FileHandler` in the plugin.

User Profiles and Identities

Integrating between many systems can be complex and hard to maintain, particularly if the application code is tightly coupled with the other systems. For example, an application can choose to display the user picture coming from Connections by emitting a REST request to the Connections server to get the photo URL. But, if the application now needs to get the photo from a different source, you must change the calling code. Furthermore, calling a REST service every time you need a picture can be inefficient. Caching the photo URL and other user information is generally a good idea. Making this code loosely coupled and efficient, while being secured, is a hard task of the ExtLib.

User and People Beans

The ExtLib provides a social API that gives access to the users and their information. To make it easily consumable from an XPage, this API is exposed through two managed beans: **peopleBean** and **userBean**. Although the **peopleBean** requires an explicit user ID, the **userBean** works with the user being authenticated in the session. So the **userBean** is basically a shortcut for `people-Bean[@UserName()]` (or `peopleBean.getPerson(<userName>)` in Java).

Both beans export the user data by accessing their members is JavaScript (for example, `userBean.displayName`) or calling a method in Java (for example, `userBean.get-Field("displayName")`). The member names are completely generic, but a convention is used for some common ones:

```
displayName: The user display name
thumbnailUrl: A URL to the user picture
```

NOTE

See `com.ibm.xsp.extlib.social.Person` in the `com.ibm.xsp.extlib` plugin (not `com.ibm.xsp.extlibx.sbt` plugin) for a definition of these standard conventions.

Such beans make it easy to display user data.

Display the current user picture:

```
<xp:image url="#{userBean.thumbnailUrl}" id="image1"></xp:image>
```

Display the current user display name:

```
<xp:text escape="true" id="computedField4" value="#{userBean.display-
Name}"></xp:text>
```

Display the name of a specific user:

```
<xp:text escape="true" id="computedField24"
value="#{javascript:peopleBean.getPerson('CN=Frank
Adams/O=renovations').displayName}"></xp:text>
```

Extensions to User and People Beans

You can extend **userBean** and **peopleBean** to return information from other services. In the context of Social, this is important because in many scenarios, user profiles need to be extended with information from other Social services. Typical examples are unique IDs and quota information. For example, the LotusLive Files datasource in the **com.ibm.xsp.extlibx.sbt** plugin requires you to pass in a `subscriberId`, which is the unique ID of the current user. For this purpose, the managed bean **userBean** has a new variable `lotusLiveSubscriberId`, as shown in Listing 13.16.

Listing 13.16 LotusLive Subscribed ID Sample

```
<xe:fileServiceData
 var="fileServiceData1"
 endpoint="lotuslive"
 serviceUrl="files/basic/cmis/repository">
 <xe:this.serviceType>
  <xe:lotusLiveFileData></xe:lotusLiveFileData>
 </xe:this.serviceType>
 <xe:this.urlParameters>
  <xe:urlParameter name="subscriberId">
   <xe:this.value>
    <![CDATA[${javascript:return userBean.lotusLiveSubscriberId;}]]>
   </xe:this.value>
  </xe:urlParameter>
 </xe:this.urlParameters>
</xe:fileServiceData>
```

You can add your own variables to this bean by implementing the extension point `com.ibm.xsp.extlib.social.PersonDataProvider` in an Eclipse plugin. This extension point is defined in the core **com.ibm.xsp.extlib** plugin and the infrastructure in the `com.ibm.xsp.extlib.social` package. You can define an extension in your own plugin or fragment as shown in Listing 13.17.

Listing 13.17 A fragment.xml Sample for the Person Data Provider

```
    <extension point="com.ibm.commons.Extension">
    <service type="com.ibm.xsp.extlib.social.PersonDataProvider"
class="com.ibm.xsp.extlib.sbt.user.LotusLivePeopleDataProvider" />
</extension>
```

The custom class needs to extend `com.ibm.xsp.extlib.social.impl.`
`Abstract-PeopleDataProvider`, as shown in Listing 13.18.

Listing 13.18   The Abstract People Data Provider Extended

```
public class LotusLivePeopleDataProvider extends
AbstractPeopleDataProvider {
    public static class PeopleData extends PersonImpl.Properties {
        boolean privateData;
        String lotusLiveSubscriberId;
    }
    private static PeopleData EMPTY_DATA = new PeopleData();
    private final String SUBSCRIBER_ID = "lotusLiveSubscriberId";

    private PeopleData getPeopleData(PersonImpl person) {
        String id = person.getId();
        PeopleData data = (PeopleData)getProperties(id,
PeopleData.class);
        if(data!=null && data.privateData &&
!person.isAuthenticatedUser()) {
            data = null;
        }

        if(data == null) {
            synchronized(getSyncObject()) {
                data = (PeopleData)getProperties(id, PeopleData.class);
                if(data == null) {
                    data = readPeopleData(person);
                    if(data!=EMPTY_DATA) {
                        addProperties(id,data);
                    }
                }
            }
        }
        return data;
    }
    private PeopleData readPeopleData(PersonImpl person) {
        if(!person.isAuthenticatedUser()){
            return null;
        }
        Endpoint ep =
EndpointFactory.getEndPointUnchecked(EndpointFactory.SERVER_LOTUSLIVE);
```

```
        if(ep!=null) {
            try {
                if(ep.isAuthenticated()){
                    GenericService service = new
GenericService(ep,"/manage/oauth/getUserIdentity");
                    Object result = service.get(null, "json");
                    if(result instanceof FBSValue){
                        JsonNavigator jsonUtil = new
JsonNavigator(result);
                        PeopleData data = new PeopleData();
                        data.lotusLiveSubscriberId =
jsonUtil.stringValue("subscriberid");
                        return data;
                    }
                }
            } catch(ClientServicesException ex) {
                Platform.getInstance().log(ex);
            }
        }
        return EMPTY_DATA;
    }

    @Override
    public String getName() {
        return "LotusLive";
    }
    @Override
    protected String getDefaultCacheScope() {
        return "global"; // $NON-NLS-1$
    }
    @Override
    protected int getDefaultCacheSize() {
        return 300;
    }

    @Override
    public Class<?> getType(PersonImpl person, Object key) {
        if(SUBSCRIBER_ID.equals(key)){
            return String.class;
        }
        return null;
```

Listing 13.18   (Continued)

```
    }

    @Override
    public Object getValue(PersonImpl person, Object key) {
        if(SUBSCRIBER_ID.equals(key) && person.isAuthenticatedUser()){
            return getPeopleData(person).lotusLiveSubscriberId;
        }
        return null;
    }

    @Override
    public void enumerateProperties(Set<String> propNames) {
        super.enumerateProperties(propNames);
        propNames.add(SUBSCRIBER_ID);
    }

    @Override
    public void readValues(PersonImpl[] persons) {
      }
}
```

The method `public Object getValue(PersonImpl person, Object key)` needs to return the specific variable for a specific person. There is a convenience method `getSyncObject()` you can use to synchronize this call so that the same property is not read for the same person multiple times simultaneously.

There is also a second method you can implement to read all properties for all users together. This speeds up the performance, especially when profile information from multiple people is displayed: `public void readValues(PersonImpl[] persons)`.

Enablement of Extensions

Defining the extension and implementing the people datasource provider is not sufficient. In addition, you need to enable datasource providers per application and define the order in which they are invoked.

While running on the Domino platform, the Domino-related data providers are enabled by default. They give access to the following Domino data. Figure 13.18 shows how the `dumpObject` control displays the properties of the **userBean**.

UtilUserBean.xsp:

```
<xe:dumpObject id="dumpObject1" value="#{userBean}"></xe:dumpObject>
```

You can ignore the "Domino:" prefix in the property names. It's only an artifact for the dumpObject control. Note that this property list is not exhaustive and can grow over time based on application needs (see Figure 13.18).

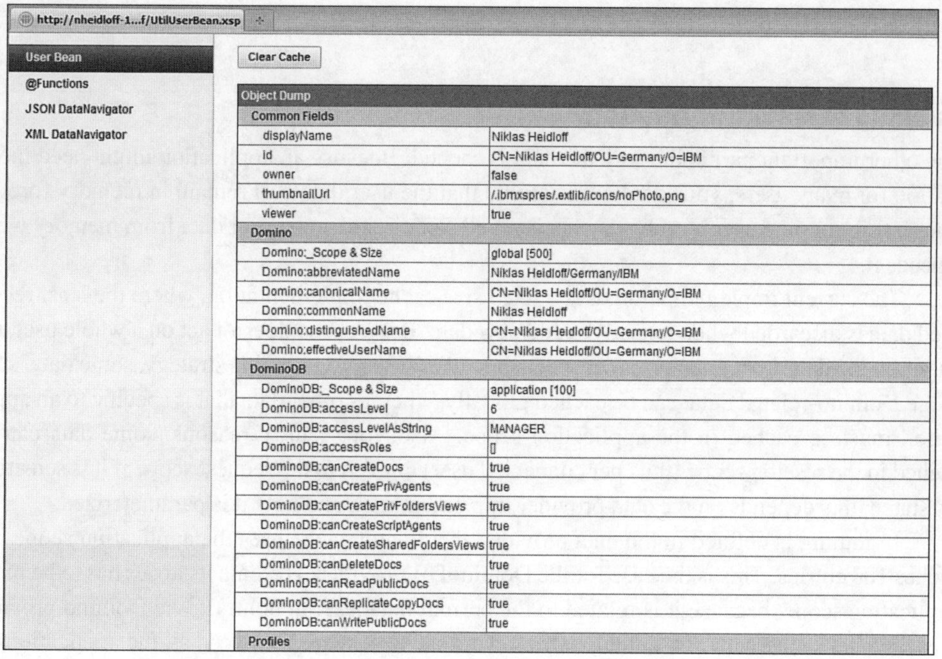

Figure 13.18 A userBean configuration example.

There are actually two Domino data providers: one for the global user data and one for the user data relative to the current database. This is because you can share the global user data across the databases, but you can't do that with the one relative to the database. Thus, the caching strategy (discussed later in this section) is different for these two data sets.

You can enable multiple providers at the same time. If nothing is set explicitly, only the default providers and the one defined within the application are activated. You must explicitly reference the other global providers in a property in **xsp.properties**.

```
extlib.people.provider=profiles;bluepages;lotuslive
```

The order is important because it defines the way the providers will be searched for a property value. For example, if the profiles provider returns a non-null value for **thumbNailUrl**, neither bluepages nor lotuslive are returned.

The default providers, like the Domino one or those defined within the application, are implicitly added at the beginning of the list. To move them at a different position, you can explicitly add them to the property in the **xsp.properties**.

```
extlib.people.provider=profiles;bluepages;lotuslive;domino;dominodb
```

Caching of User Information

The other important part is the way the data is cached. Because an application might need information for many users, you should not assume that the user data will remain in memory forever. The ExtLib runtime uses a cache mechanism and can discard some user data from memory when it needs it.

The current implementation uses a fixed size cache implementation, where the least recent used data is discarded when it needs to add new data. But a cache doesn't act on a whole user, but rather on the data from each provider independently. When you use this strategy, some data, such as the Domino-related data, can be cached globally, whereas other data that is specific to an application must be cached in the application scope. Also, for security reasons, some data can be cached in the session scope (thus per connected user) or even in the request scope if it is sensitive. As stated, this depends on the data provider implementation and how it is parameterized.

If nothing is defined in the data provider, the default cache uses the application scope and caches 100 entries. This is the case for the DominoDB provider. The data it carries has to be in the application scope, because it is related to the current database. In contrast, the Domino provider uses a global cache with 500 default entries. This cache is shared between all the applications to maximize the memory use.

You can change these default values by using the properties shown in Listing 13.19 in the **xsp.properties**.

Listing 13.19   Properties in xsp.properties for Changing Values

```
extlib.social.people.domino.cachescope=global
extlib.social.people.domino.cachesize=500
extlib.social.people.dominodb.cachescope=application
extlib.social.people.dominodb.cachesize=100
```

More generally, you can set both the scope and the size of a provider with a property (see Listing 13.20).

Listing 13.20   Available Method for Setting Scope and Size

```
extlib.social.people.<provider
name>.cachescope=none|global|application|session|request
extlib.social.people.<provider name>.cachesize=<int value>
```

The XPages infrastructure stores/caches users' profile information. To read the latest values, the infrastructure calls the two `clear` methods, which you can implement as in Listing 13.21.

Listing 13.21   Available Methods for Infrastructure Calls

```
public void clear()
public void clear(String id)
```

User Identities

Because there is no global identity for a particular user, a user might have multiple identities, one per server. For example, he can be John Doe/Boston/ACME in Notes, jdoe@acme.com in Lotus-Live, or John_Doe@gmail.com in Google+. Unfortunately (or fortunately), there is no direct, reliable way for getting one identity from the others. Generally, the identity has to go through a map implemented within the application or the underlying framework, like the XPages ExtLib.

To make this easier, the XPages ExtLib provides an `IdentityMapper` (`com.ibm.xsp.extlib.social.impl.IdentityMapper`) mechanism that can map between the Domino system identity and any other one, back and forth. For example, the **ProfilesDataProvider** that is feeding the **userBean** with data from Connections first asks the **PeopleService** for the Connections identity corresponding to the bean. If it gets a null response, it doesn't call the Connections services. Otherwise, it uses the mapped name to query Connections.

Similarly, the `EndpointFactory`, some possible identity targets ('facebook','-connections', ...) are defined as constants in the `IdentityMapper` class. But the list of possible targets is not limited by them.

Some convenience methods are available in the **userBean** and **peopleBean** to access user identities:

```
userBean.getIdentity('facebook');
```

There are also two @Functions to get user profile information from JavaScript:

```
@IdentityFromId(target,id)
```

This returns the user identity for a particular target (for example, Facebook) from a Domino ID.

```
@IdFromIdentity(target,identity)
```

This returns the user Domino ID for a particular target (for example, Facebook) and the user identity in this target.

The Social Enabler database (XPagesSBT.nsf) shows an `IdentityMapper` implementation in Listing 13.22.

Listing 13.22   demo.IdentityProvider.java

```
public class IdentityProvider implements IdentityMapper {
 public String getUserIdFromIdentity(String target, String identity) {
  if(StringUtil.equals(target,"facebook")) {
   if(StringUtil.equals(identity,"fadams@facebook.com")) {
    return "CN=Frank Adams/O=renovations";
   }
  }
  return null;
 }
public String getUserIdentityFromId(String target, String id) {
  if(StringUtil.equals(target,"facebook")) {
   if(StringUtil.equals(id,"CN=Frank Adams/O=renovations")) {
    return "fadams@facebook.com";
   }
  }
  return null;
 }
}
```

The result, Figure 13.19, is displayed on the XPage **UtilFunctions.xsp**.

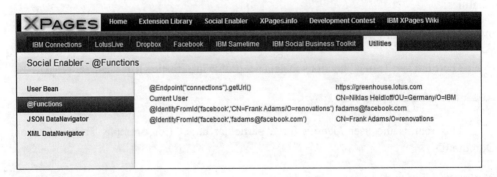

Figure 13.19   Identity mapper.

User Interface Controls

The **com.ibm.xsp.extlibx.sbt** plugin and the Social Enabler database come with a set of user interface controls. You can easily use these controls in custom applications.

There are two types of controls: library and custom. Library controls are implemented via plugins with Java, deployed via OSGi bundles, and globally available to all applications on a Domino server. Custom Controls live in a Notes Storage Facility (NSF) and are deployed as part of it.

Some of the following controls have been implemented as library controls, others as Custom Controls. Controls that are likely to be used as they are and that have few configuration options have been implemented as library controls. Controls that require a high level of customization and often even extensions or bigger changes have been implemented as Custom Controls. These Custom Controls work as they are for standard scenarios. For more specialized requirements, you must change their source code.

Files Controls for Dropbox, LotusLive, and Connections

The Social Enabler database, **XPagesSBT.nsf**, comes with three Custom Controls to access files from Dropbox, LotusLive, and Connections. In all cases, the files are read directly from the different services. There is no synchronization to the NSF happening, even though from the user interface perspective the files just look like Notes views.

Dropbox

Figure 13.20 shows a list of files and folders read from Dropbox and rendered in an XPage.

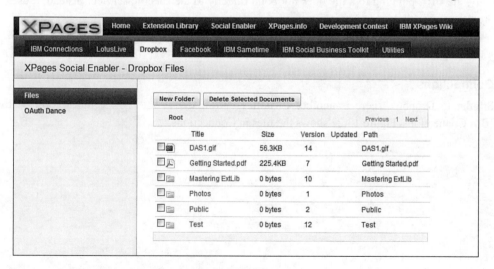

Figure 13.20　Files from Dropbox rendered in XPages.

You can access the same files through other Dropbox clients, such as the Dropbox web user interface shown in Figure 13.21.

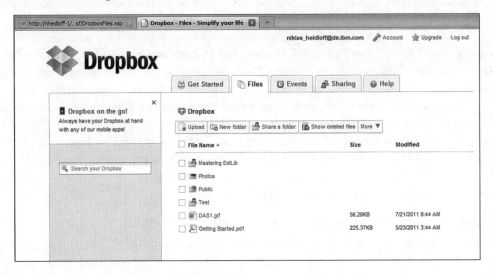

Figure 13.21   Files and folders in the Dropbox client.

Users can page through the list of files as in other Notes views. They can also open a folder, navigate back to the parent folder, and create new folders. They can also download files. Technically, the URL pointing to a file does not point directly to the specific service. Instead, it uses a proxy server so that it can use OAuth.

To use this control, you can simply drag and drop `<xc:sbtFilesDropbox>` `</xc:sbtFilesDropbox>` from the Designer palette.

Connections

Similar to Dropbox, there is another Custom Control, `<xc:sbtFilesConnections/>`, for IBM Connections. Figure 13.22 shows the files in Connections.

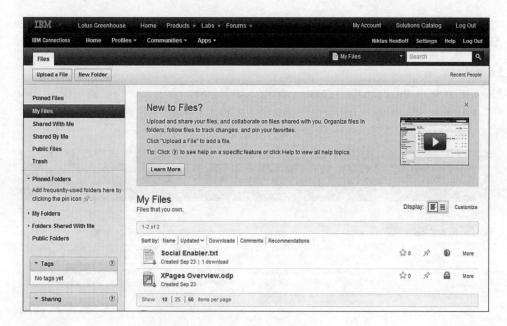

Figure 13.22 Connections Custom Control sample.

Figure 13.23 shows the same files in an XPage.

Figure 13.23 IBM Connections in XPages.

Unlike Dropbox, this Custom Control doesn't support folders because the Connections API does not allow it.

LotusLive

Last but not least, there is a third Custom Control for LotusLive, `<xc:sbtFilesLotusLive/>`, with similar functionality to the Connections files control. Figure 13.24 shows files in LotusLive.

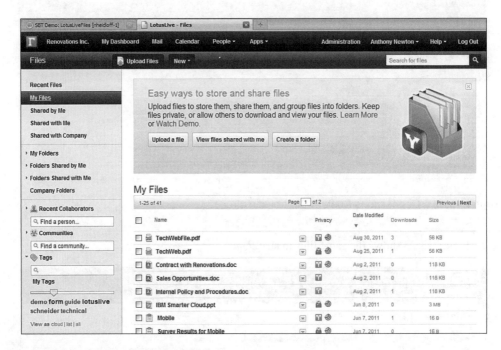

Figure 13.24   Sample files in LotusLive.

Figure 13.25 shows the same files in an XPage.

Figure 13.25   LotusLive files in XPages.

Sametime Controls

You access IBM Sametime from XPages applications using two library controls: a content type and two sample Custom Controls. The XPages **SametimeLiveName.xsp** and **SametimeWidgets.xsp** from the Social Enabler database, **XPagesSBT.nsf**, show these controls in action.

The Sametime Client Control (`xe:sametimeClient`)

This control creates the Sametime client. It holds the different Sametime parameters and is required on the page to use the Sametime features. If it is not on the page, or not rendered, the other ST controls behave as if they're not connected to Sametime. For example, it allows Sametime to be disabled when the target device is mobile.

The Sametime Widget Control (`xe:sametimeWidget`)

This control renders a Sametime widget based on its Dojo type and attributes. It is disabled if no Sametime client is rendered in the page.

`contentType="xs:st.livename"`

This is a content type to be assigned to a text column or a view column. Again, it has no effect if no Sametime client is rendered in the page. (The text is displayed without the Sametime widget.)

The `xe:sametimeClient` works with an endpoint, where the user/password is stored for the session. This endpoint can also leverage a `store` (optional), where the credentials can be held and reused later on. Users can close the browser and not have to log in again when they reconnect, as shown in Listing 13.23.

Listing 13.23   Login Dialog Sample for Sametime Client

```
<managed-bean>
  <managed-bean-name>PwdStore</managed-bean-name>
  <managed-bean-class>

com.ibm.xsp.extlib.sbt.security.password.store.BAMemoryPasswordStore
  </managed-bean-class>
  <managed-bean-scope>application</managed-bean-scope>
</managed-bean>
<managed-bean>
  <managed-bean-name>sametime</managed-bean-name>
  <managed-bean-class>
com.ibm.xsp.extlib.sbt.services.client.endpoints.BasicEndpointBean
  </managed-bean-class>
  <managed-bean-scope>session</managed-bean-scope>
  <managed-property>
    <property-name>url</property-name>
    <value>http://stweb.ibm.com</value>
  </managed-property>
  <managed-property>
    <property-name>passwordStore</property-name>
    <value>PwdStore</value>
  </managed-property>
```

The Social Enabler database contains two Custom Controls, sbtLoginDialog and sbtLoginSection, that provide a login UI as well as an example showing how to log in programmatically (see Listing 13.24).

Listing 13.24   Login Sample from SametimeLiveName.xsp

```
<xe:sametimeClient
  id="sametimeClient1"
  autoLogin="true"
  clientScriptFile="livename"
  autoTunnelURI="true">
</xe:sametimeClient>
Login Section:
<xc:sbtLoginSection
  id="sbtLoginSection1"
  sectionTitle="Login To Sametime"
```

```
    endpoint="sametime"
    label="Login To Sametime">
</xc:sbtLoginSection>
Login Dialog:
<xc:sbtLoginDialog
    id="loginDialog"
    dialogTitle="Login To Sametime"
    endpoint="sametime"
    label="Login To Sametime">
</xc:sbtLoginDialog>
Sametime logged as:
<xp:text
    escape="true"
    id="computedField4"
    value="#{sametime.user}">
</xp:text>
Here is an example with only the id:
<xp:text
    escape="true"
    id="computedField1"
    contentType="xs:st.livename">
    <xp:this.value><![CDATA[#{javascript:@Endpoint("sametime").
    getUserIdentity()}]]></xp:this.value>
</xp:text>
Here is an example with the id and an empty display name:
<xp:text
    escape="true"
    id="computedField2"
    contentType="xs:st.livename">
    <xp:this.value><![CDATA[#{javascript:@Endpoint("sametime").
    getUserIdentity()+"|"}]]></xp:this.value>
</xp:text>
Here is an example with the id and a display name set:
<xp:text
    escape="true"
    id="computedField3"
    contentType="xs:st.livename">
```

Listing 13.24   (Continued)

```
    <xp:this.value><![CDATA[#{javascript:@Endpoint("sametime").
    getUserIdentity()+"|[user display name]"}]]></xp:this.value>
</xp:text>
Here is an example using a sametime widget:
<xe:sametimeWidget
  id="sametimeWidget1"
  dojoType="sametime.LiveName">
  <xe:this.dojoAttributes>
    <xp:dojoAttribute
      name="userId">
      <xp:this.value><![CDATA[#{javascript:@Endpoint("sametime").
      getUserIdentity()}]]></xp:this.value>
    </xp:dojoAttribute>
  </xe:this.dojoAttributes>
</xe:sametimeWidget>
```

Connections Controls

There are library controls to display the IBM Connections business card for specific users and to display the card of a specific community.

Profiles VCard

You can invoke the business card inline or as a pop-up dialog (see Figure 13.26).

Figure 13.26   IBM Connection control sample.

The following sample shows how to use the controls. There is a client control, called Connections Client (`xe:connectionsClient`), that needs to be added to an XPage to use the other control.

The Connections Widget (`xe:connectionsWidget`) control expects to get passed in the username and ID. In addition, you can define whether to show the inline or pop-up version using the dojoType `"extlib.dijit.ProfilesVCardInline"`.

Alternatively, you can use the content type `contentType="xs:lc.vcard"`, as shown in Listing 13.25.

Listing 13.25   Connections Profiles VCard Sample

```
<xe:connectionsClient
  id="connectionsClient1"
  profilesVCard="true">
</xe:connectionsClient>
  Use content type
  <xp:text
    escape="true"
    id="computedField3"
    contentType="xs:lc.vcard"
    value="#{javascript:return
userBean.email+'|'+userBean.groupwareMail}">
  </xp:text>
  <xp:text
    escape="true"
    id="computedField2"
    contentType="xs:lc.vcard"
    value="#{javascript:return userBean.id+'|'+userBean.commonName}">
  </xp:text>
  Use widgets
  <xe:connectionsWidget
    id="connectionsWidget1"
    dojoType="extlib.dijit.ProfilesVCard">
    <xe:this.dojoAttributes>
      <xp:dojoAttribute
        name="userName"
        value="#{javascript:return userBean.groupwareMail}">
      </xp:dojoAttribute>
      <xp:dojoAttribute
        name="userId"
        value="#{javascript:return userBean.email}">
      </xp:dojoAttribute>
    </xe:this.dojoAttributes>
  </xe:connectionsWidget>
  <xe:connectionsWidget
    id="connectionsWidget2"
    dojoType="extlib.dijit.ProfilesVCardInline">
    <xe:this.dojoAttributes>
      <xp:dojoAttribute
        name="userName"
```

```
      value="#{javascript:return userBean.groupwareMail}">
    </xp:dojoAttribute>
    <xp:dojoAttribute
      name="userId"
      value="#{javascript:return userBean.email}">
    </xp:dojoAttribute>
  </xe:this.dojoAttributes>
</xe:connectionsWidget>
```

Communities VCard

On the page **ConnectionsCommunitiesVCard.xsp** is a sample showing how to display the VCard of a selected community, as shown in Figure 13.27.

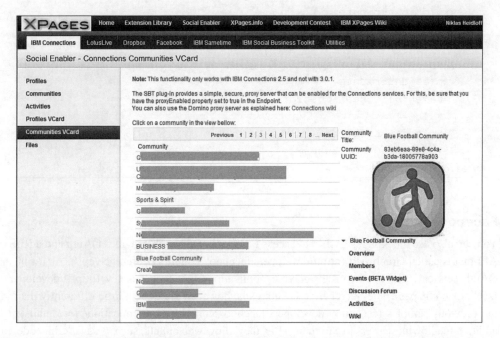

Figure 13.27　IBM Connections Control VCard sample.

For the communities VCard, you need to set the dojoType to `"extlib.dijit.Communi-tiesVCard"`, as shown in Listing 13.26.

Listing 13.26   Connection Sample with dojoType Set

```
<xe:connectionsClient
  id="connectionsClient1"
  communitiesVCard="true">
</xe:connectionsClient>
<xe:connectionsWidget
  id="connectionsWidget1"
  dojoType="extlib.dijit.CommunitiesVCard">
  <xe:this.dojoAttributes>
    <xp:dojoAttribute
      name="name"
      value="#{javascript:viewScope.cTitle}">
    </xp:dojoAttribute>
    <xp:dojoAttribute
      name="uuid"
      value="#{javascript:viewScope.cUuid}">
    </xp:dojoAttribute>
    <xp:dojoAttribute
      name="selectedWidgetId"
      value="">
    </xp:dojoAttribute>
  </xe:this.dojoAttributes>
</xe:connectionsWidget>
```

Facebook Controls

You can also use the XPages ExtLib to access Facebook. Facebook provides OAuth and a REST API that is called Graph API (http://developers.facebook.com/docs/reference/api/). As for other OAuth services, you need to register your applications first to get a key (https://developers.facebook.com/apps). The Server-Side OAuth calls, however, are done a little differently than in the previous samples (see http://developers.facebook.com/docs/authentication/ for details). In addition to allowing servers to call their APIs, they allow web clients, such as JavaScript code, to call their REST APIs directly. This functionality is used in the next samples.

Facebook comes with a set of social plugins—most importantly the Login button and the Like button—that can easily be embedded in websites. To make it even more convenient for you, the ExtLib comes with some predefined controls: the **Login** button, the **Like** button, and the **Comment** plugin. Figure 13.28 shows the **Like** button and the **Comment** plugin.

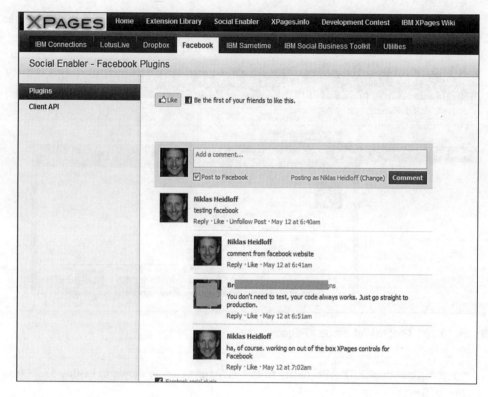

Figure 13.28 Facebook sample plugin.

You can add these controls to an XPage via drag and drop from the Designer palette. To use any Facebook controls or the Facebook JavaScript SDK, add the `xe:facebookClient` control and the Facebook application key to **faces-config.xml**, as described in Figure 13.28. Listing 13.27 shows how this might be configured.

Listing 13.27 Facebook Client Control Sample from FacebookPlugins.xsp

```
<xe:facebookClient></xe:facebookClient>
  <xe:facebookLikeButton
    href="#{javascript:context.getUrl()}">
  </xe:facebookLikeButton>

  <xe:facebookComments
    href="#{javascript:'http://heidloff.net'}"
    num_posts="5">
  </xe:facebookComments>
```

The next sample shows the login control and a Facebook dialog triggered using the JavaScript API (see Figure 13.29).

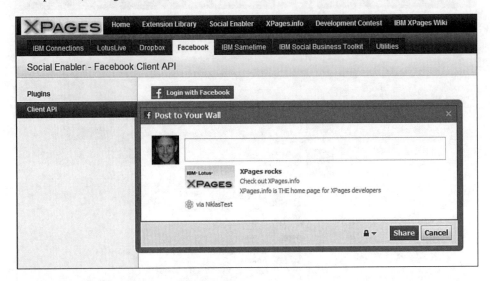

Figure 13.29   Post to Wall inside XPages.

You can call the REST APIs easily from JavaScript code, as shown in Listing 13.28 from **FacebookClientAPI.xsp**.

Listing 13.28   Facebook Login Button Configuration Sample

```
<xe:facebookClient></xe:facebookClient>
<xe:facebookLoginButton
   perms="email,user_checkins">Login with
Facebook</xe:facebookLoginButton>
<xp:button
   value="Show Login Status"
   id="button1">
   <xp:eventHandler
     event="onclick"
     submit="false">
     <xp:this.script><![CDATA[
FB.getLoginStatus(function(response) {
 if (response.session) {
  if (response.perms) {
```

```
    alert("User is logged in and granted some permissions.");
   } else {
    alert("User is logged in, but did not grant any permissions");
   }
  } else {
   alert("User is not logged in");
  }
 }, true);]]>
     </xp:this.script>
   </xp:eventHandler>
 </xp:button>

<xp:button
   value="Show current User"
   id="button2">
   <xp:eventHandler
     event="onclick"
     submit="false">
     <xp:this.script><![CDATA[
FB.api('/me', function(user) {
  if(user != null) {
   var image = document.getElementById('image');
   image.src = 'http://graph.facebook.com/' + user.id + '/picture';
   var name = document.getElementById('name');
   name.innerHTML = user.name
  }
});
]]></xp:this.script>
   </xp:eventHandler>
 </xp:button>
```

The code in the listing shows how to call the Facebook API **FB.getLoginStatus** to get the login status of the current user and how to use **FB.API** to open the Facebook dialog to post to Facebook.

IBM Social Business Toolkit

At Lotusphere 2011, there was a lot of talk about the IBM Social Business Framework. In the wiki, the toolkit is defined (http://www-10.lotus.com/ldd/appdevwiki.nsf/xpViewCategories.xsp?lookupName=IBM%20Social%20Business%20Toolkit):

> The IBM Social Business Toolkit is a set of extensible tools and resources for incorporating social capabilities into applications and business processes. Social capabilities include features and functionality that tap into the power of social interactions, business networks, community-based problem solving, and more. The Social Business Toolkit is evolving in parallel with the IBM Social Business Framework, a strategic model for a unified work experience across the IBM Collaboration Solutions product portfolio.
>
> Initially, the Social Business Toolkit delivers a set of tools that enable you to publish and retrieve events to the activity stream. The activity stream is a personal view of relevant updates and events that have been aggregated from multiple sources into a single stream of business information. As part of the Social Business Framework, the activity stream will eventually become a common component you can embed into multiple products across the product portfolio.
>
> In line with enhancing the activity stream, the Social Business Toolkit will expand to include extensibility areas such as embedded experiences, share box, and more. An embedded experience is a way of interacting with events, notifications, and business processes dynamically in context directly from an inbox, social home page, and other containers without having to log into and switch to another application or service. A share box is a gadget that you can embed into pages for creating and sharing information and custom content. A share box is an example of an embedded experience.

Since Lotusphere 2011, a first version of this toolkit has been deployed on Lotus Greenhouse that everyone can try. There is a sample user interface with an embedded experience (https://greenhouse.lotus.com/activitystream/) showing items from different sources in a so-called activity stream (see Figure 13.30).

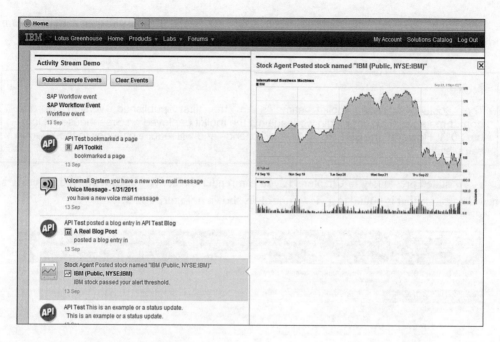

Figure 13.30   IBM Lotus Greenhouse activity stream.

There is also a REST API application (https://greenhouse.lotus.com/vulcan/shindig/client/testAPI.jsp), as shown in Figure 13.31, to add new entries to the activity stream or to get certain entries as JSON or XML.

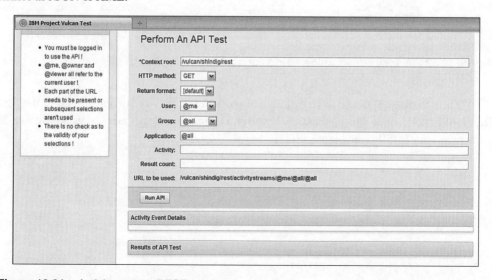

Figure 13.31   Activity stream REST service.

The ExtLib comes with some utilities to access the Social Business Toolkit activity stream from XPages.

NOTE

The Social Business Toolkit samples in the first published version of the **com.ibm.xsp.extlibx.sbt** plugin work against the toolkit deployed on Greenhouse in October 2011. However, the SBT REST APIs will change and will require changes to the XPages samples.

As stated previously in Chapter 11, you can render the activity stream on XPages using a new datasource that is bound to a view control, as shown in Figure 13.32.

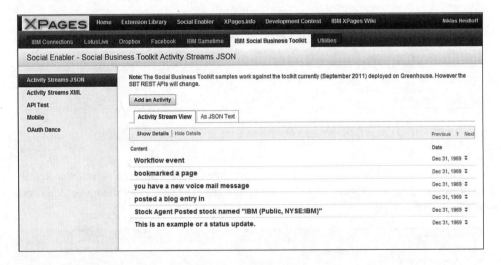

Figure 13.32   Activity stream rendered in XPages.

There is also an XPage to read from and write to the activity stream, similar to the SBT REST API application. This application, however, is done via XPages and shows how to use the APIs programmatically (see Figure 13.33).

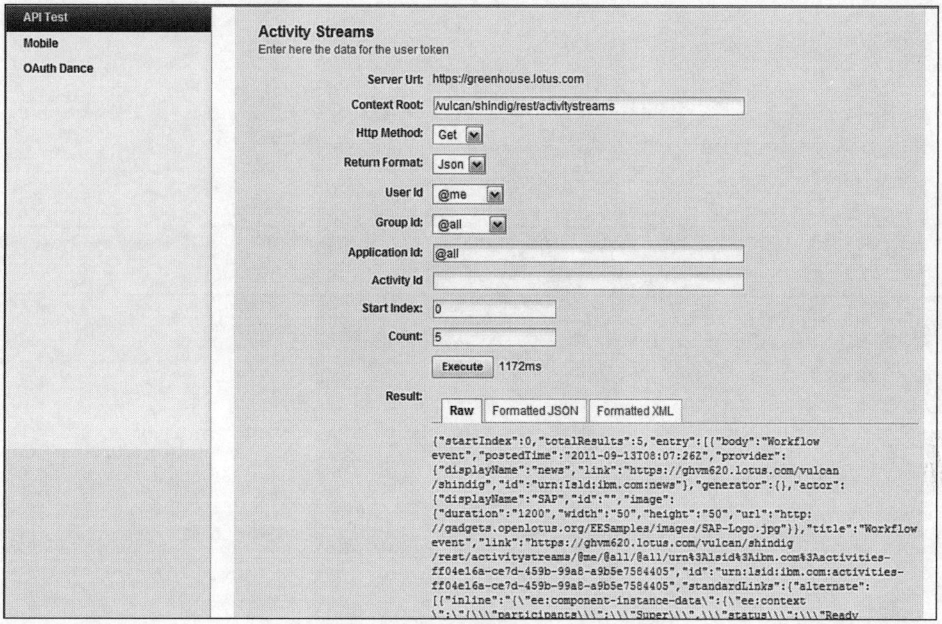

Figure 13.33 Activity stream configuration via XPages.

Conclusion

This chapter dealt with the exciting new social business tools out there and how to incorporate them into XPages using the ExtLib. The story isn't finished yet. Social business is always moving—quickly. Now you have the tools to keep up and evolve.

PART IV

Getting Under the Covers with Java

14 Java Development in XPages

CHAPTER 14

Java Development in XPages

For more than a decade, the role of the Java language in the toolset available to Notes and Domino developers has been increasing. Although Java was originally available for use only in agents, the platform has since added support for Java in LotusScript® through LS2J, Java script libraries, web services, composite applications, and—now that both the Lotus Notes Client and Domino Designer are based on Eclipse—extensions to the platform via plugin development.

With the addition of XPages to the platform, the capacity for inclusion of Java in Domino applications has never been easier or more powerful. This chapter provides a glimpse into some of the many ways Java can take your applications to the next level, as well as a few ways that you can get even more use out of some of the XPages Extension Library controls already described in previous chapters.

Benefits of Java Development

There are many advantages to the use of proprietary languages within any development platform. Both Notes Formula and LotusScript, for instance, were created specifically for the platform and are optimized for use within it. They contain little that does not apply to the platform. This not only provides certain runtime performance benefits, but also simplifies mastery of these languages, because the boundaries of what they contain are defined by the platform at the vendor's discretion.

In contrast, Java is comparatively infinite. Because the language was not defined with a specific development platform in mind, the foundation is generic, and specific capabilities of the language have been gradually added in layers atop that foundation. Java is arguably the best example in wide use today of a true object-oriented language, so its very nature allows for the creation of object hierarchies that are simply not possible in LotusScript.

Java has always been designed to be independent of specific operating systems. Code written in Java, therefore, can be compiled once and executed within any environment that supports Java. Although Notes and Domino have long excelled at shielding developers from designing applications specific to a given operating system, it is important to note that this same goal is fundamental to the nature of the Java language.

Perhaps the most significant advantage of Java, however, is the sheer number of people using it. The 2009 Global Developer Population and Demographics Survey (conducted by Evans Data Corporation) found the Java developer population to be in excess of 9 million people. Java also now runs natively on nearly every device imaginable. Because of the combination of these factors, envision nearly anything developers want their application to do, and it's likely that somebody, somewhere in the world, has already done it using Java. By leveraging the work that has already been done by others, developers can spend less time solving problems others have already solved and more time producing functionality that is truly unique to the application or its target audience.

Referencing Native Java in Server-Side JavaScript

There are several ways to leverage Java in an XPage. The easiest is to include references to portions of the core language directly within Server-Side JavaScript (SSJS) expressions.

A core concept in XPages development is the use of scope variables to store and retrieve objects. Each of these variables is an implementation of a Java construct known as a Map, which is conceptually similar to the List construct in LotusScript. It is possible, however, to manually create objects with a similar structure by using the native Java HashMap class.

When you're constructing a Java object from within SSJS expressions, you must use the fully qualified name of the class, including the package in which the class is stored, as shown in Listing 14.1. Java classes are organized into collections of related classes known as packages. This organization is similar in some respects to bundling related LotusScript classes or functions into a single script library. Java packages, by convention, are named using a period-delimited syntax that begins with the Internet domain of the code's origin in reverse order, followed by a hierarchy of the nature of the classes each package contains. For example, a package of utility classes for working with XML developed by ACME, Inc., might be named com.acme.util.xml. Similarly, all classes that make up the Extension Library are contained in packages whose name begins with com.ibm.xsp.extlib, with the exception of those whose package name begins with com.ibm.domino.services. The native HashMap class is contained in the package java.util. The full name of any Java class is its package name plus its simple name. Hence, the full name of the HashMap class is java.util.HashMap.

Listing 14.1   Accessing Java Classes Using SSJS

```
var myMap = new java.util.HashMap();
myMap.put("someKey", someValue);
sessionScope.put("nestedMap", myMap);
```

The technique demonstrated in Listing 14.1 allows scope variables to store entire hierarchies of objects. This provides an opportunity both for sophisticated performance management and for the inclusion of advanced functionality.

If classes from the same package will be referenced numerous times within the same expression, a call to the `importPackage` function can be made with the package's name as the parameter, allowing each class to then be referenced using just the class name rather than the fully qualified name, as seen in Listing 14.2.

Listing 14.2   Using the SSJS importPackage Directive

```
importPackage(java.util);
var firstMap = new HashMap();
var secondMap = new HashMap();
```

Use caution when importing Java packages within SSJS. If a class referenced by only its simple name exists in more than one imported package, the interpreter may be unable to produce the intended result. If, for example, ACME has created both a `com.acme.rss.Parser` class and a `com.acme.json.Parser` class, it would be inadvisable to import both packages and attempt to construct an instance of either `Parser` using only the class name.

For the same reason, a name collision can occur if a class name within an imported package is identical to any variable that's already defined, whether that variable is native to SSJS or has been declared within the application code. Although you can avoid both of these scenarios by clearly naming all variables and classes, it is important to be aware of this issue when using `importPackage`, particularly because of the volume of code created by others that can be referenced within an XPage. When in doubt, always use the full name of the class instead.

Using Java That Others Have Written

Because Java is such a widely used language, nearly any feature the developer would want to include in an XPage application has already been implemented by someone, and most likely open sourced. In particular, many commonly encountered problems or features have been addressed in libraries and exported using the Java Archive (JAR) format. Developers can simply import these JARs into an application and start using their features immediately, with no need for manual customization to make the library compatible with Domino.

One example of this open source library is called Apache POI, which provides programmatic generation and manipulation of spreadsheets, presentations, and other productivity documents. Because this is a necessary feature in many applications, the Apache POI library was created to provide a robust implementation of this functionality, offering a straightforward application programming interface (API) for creating, reading, and modifying these types of files.

Apache POI targets the Office Open XML (OOXML) document standard, which, as the name suggests, is based upon XML. In theory, therefore, you could manually handle these files using any XML parser or transformer—or even just low-level string manipulation. One indication of the complexity of these formats, however, is that the subcomponent of Apache POI that handles the spreadsheet format is known as Horrible Spreadsheet Format (HSSF). The developer may not want to deal with these XML formats directly. A far better practice is to leverage the work others have already done by importing this library into your own application, and letting it do the low-level file manipulation.

If you are running a version of Domino Designer older than 8.5.3, the first step in adding external Java code to an XPage application is to customize Designer to reveal more of its true nature as Eclipse. Eclipse segments its user interface into visual blocks known as views; the collection of views that is visible at any given time is known as a perspective. Few of the standard views display within the Domino Designer perspective; its default content consists solely of views IBM has created specifically to streamline interaction with the design of a Domino application. Each user can modify perspectives, however, and any installed view can be added to the current perspective.

One of the most useful views not included by default in the Domino Designer perspective prior to 8.5.3 is known as the Package Explorer. This view allows you to browse each application as a standard Eclipse project, which treats the design of the application as a folder structure. Some portions of the design of a Domino application can be found only by browsing it in this fashion; this also allows you to add files to the design that could not otherwise be included.

From the Window menu at the top of Designer, open the submenu labeled **Show Eclipse Views**. Then select the menu item labeled **Other**, as shown in Figure 14.1.

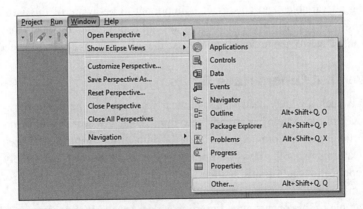

Figure 14.1　The option to select the Other perspective.

A window appears, displaying all installed views. This window includes a field allowing the list to be filtered. Type the phrase **Package Explorer** into this field, and the list of views is filtered to contain a single matching item, listed under the **Java** category (see Figure 14.2).

Figure 14.2 Finding the Package Explorer view.

Select this item, and then click **OK**. The Package Explorer view is added to the Domino Designer perspective. Once you have added the view to the perspective, you can drag it to an alternate location, if desired. For example, dragging it on top of the Application Navigator view causes both views to become tabs; this allows for rapid switching between Domino-centric design browsing and Eclipse-centric browsing, as shown in Figure 14.3.

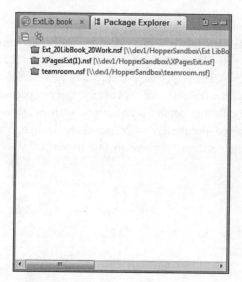

Figure 14.3 Anchoring the Package Explorer.

To avoid having to reopen the Package Explorer each time Designer is launched, return to the **Window** menu and select the menu item labeled **Save Perspective As**. A window appears, allowing an existing perspective to be selected or a new name to be entered. The current perspective, **Domino Designer**, is selected by default, as shown in Figure 14.4.

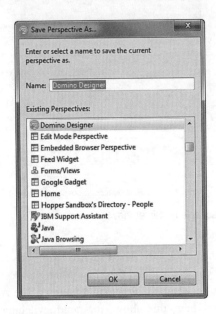

Figure 14.4   Naming and saving the perspective.

Click **OK**, and then confirm that the existing perspective should be overwritten. This causes the perspective, as it currently is displayed, to be loaded each time Designer is launched. Repeat this step any time you add or move views and want to retain the new perspective layout. Alternatively, you can save the changes as a completely new perspective by entering a new name prior to saving. However, Designer does not open to this perspective immediately. Designer only reopens to one of the factory default perspectives, such as Domino Designer or XPages. To reopen the newly named perspective after launching Designer, select **Window→Open Perspective→Other** and select the new perspective from the list.

Now that the Package Explorer displays within Designer, locate an open application within that view. The project corresponding to each application is listed by its filename, followed by an indication of the full location of the application, as shown in Figure 14.5.

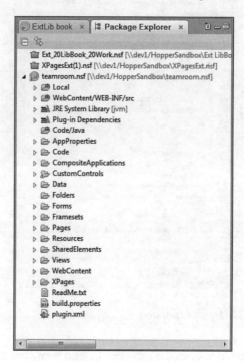

Figure 14.5   Viewing an application in Package Explorer.

One of the folders within a Domino application that is only accessible via the Package Explorer is **WebContent**. Expand this folder to locate the **WEB-INF** subfolder, as shown in Figure 14.6.

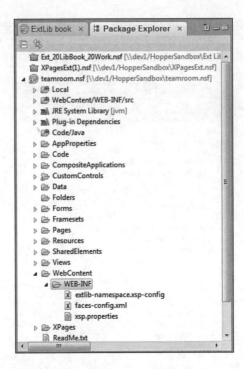

Figure 14.6   The WEB-INF folder expanded.

Right-click this subfolder, open the submenu labeled **New**, and then select the menu item labeled **Other**. Expand the **General** section and select **Folder**; then click the **Next** button. When prompted, enter a folder name of **lib** and click **Finish**, as shown in Figure 14.7. The **WEB-INF** folder now contains the new subfolder.

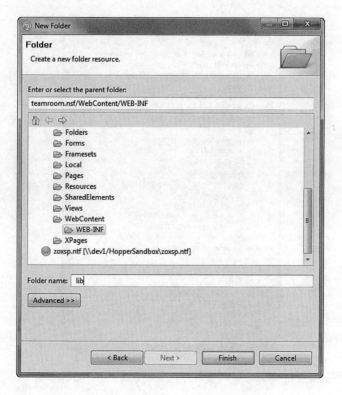

Figure 14.7 Creating a new folder in WEB-INF.

In a browser, visit the website for the Apache POI project (http://poi.apache.org/download.html). Download the latest stable release, and extract the archive contents. Within the extracted folder (as of this writing, Apache POI 3.7), delete the **docs** subfolder; you may want to simply move this subfolder elsewhere, because it contains documentation for the entire library API. Once you have moved or removed this subfolder, drag the parent folder to the **lib** folder previously created in Designer.

After you have imported the folder structure, expand all subfolders. Select all files with a **.jar** extension, and then right-click any of the selected files. Open the submenu labeled **Build Path**, and then select the menu item labeled **Add to Build Path**. The selected files no longer appear within the **lib** folder structure; instead, they now display beneath **Referenced Libraries** at the top of the project (see Figure 14.8).

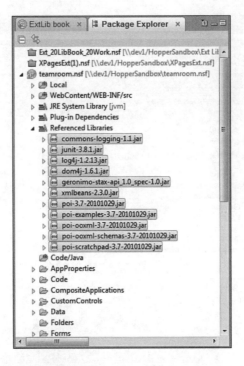

Figure 14.8   Adding JARs to the Build Path.

The Apache POI library is now bundled as part of the application, and any SSJS code within the application may reference classes defined by the library using code similar to the simple example in Listing 14.3.

Listing 14.3   Using Apache POI in SSJS

```
var workbook = new org.apache.poi.hssf.usermodel.HSSFWorkbook();
var createHelper = workbook.getCreationHelper();
var sheet = workbook.createSheet("new sheet");
var row = sheet.createRow(0);
var cell = row.createCell(0);
cell.setCellValue("Hello World!");
```

The code outlined in Listing 14.3 demonstrates that XPages allow a developer to leverage entire code libraries written by others, reducing the effort of performing complex operations to comparatively few lines of code.

Setting Up Domino Designer to Create Java Classes

Adding a custom class of your own to an XPage project is easy. Starting with version 8.5.3, Domino Designer exposes a Java design element that you can use to add your own Java classes. However, prior to this version, a few extra steps had to be taken to prepare the Notes Storage Facility (NSF) for Java development. This section reviews how to use both methods. First, for version 8.5.2 and prior, we'll create a class using the Package Explorer, just as a typical Java developer using Eclipse for any Java project might. Note that you can also use this method in version 8.5.3 and above if desired. You are not required to use the new Java design element in 8.5.3.

The previous section included instructions for adding a folder named **lib** to the **WEB-INF** folder contained within **WebContent**. Repeat those steps now to add a folder named **src** in the same location. Next, right-click the new folder, open the submenu labeled **Build Path**, and then choose the menu item labeled **Use as Source Folder**, as shown in Figure 14.9.

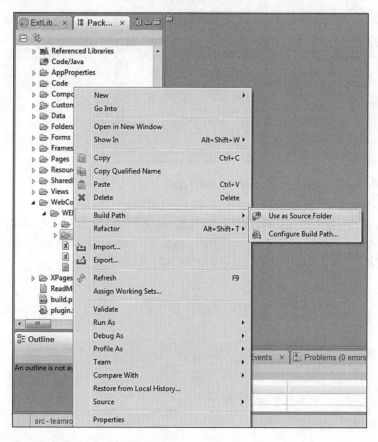

Figure 14.9   The Use as Source Folder option.

Although the folder still exists in the same logical location within the project, it will now display as an Eclipse source folder at the top of the project structure, displaying its relative location within the project, as shown in Figure 14.10.

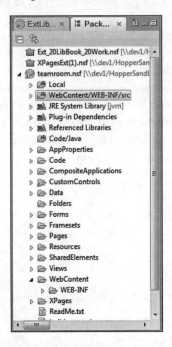

Figure 14.10   New relative location within the project.

The next step is to create a package that indicates the type of classes that will be added to the project. As previously described, package names conventionally start with an indication of the origin of the code and end with an indication of the nature of the code.

Before creating a package for the first time, it's a good idea to customize the Designer perspective to more easily create Java artifacts within an XPage project. In Designer, click the **Window** menu, and select **Customize Perspective**. In the dialog that appears, you can customize the items that appear on certain menus and submenus, such as when you right-click a Java source folder. In the dialog, under **Submenus**, select **New**. Then, in the **Shortcut Categories** box, find **Java** and highlight it so the list of Java shortcuts appears in the **Shortcuts** box. Place check marks next to **Class**, **Enum**, **Interface**, **Package**, and **Source Folder**, as seen in Figure 14.11.

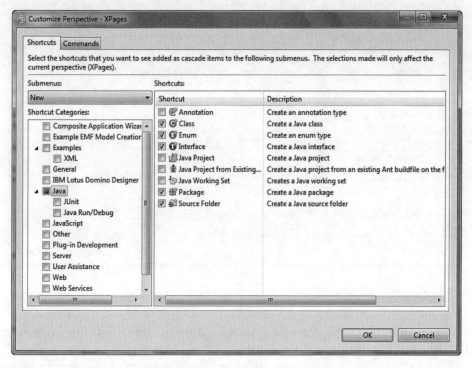

Figure 14.11 Shortcut Categories selection.

Then, back in the **Shortcut Categories** box, select **General**, and place a check mark next to **Folder** (see Figure 14.12).

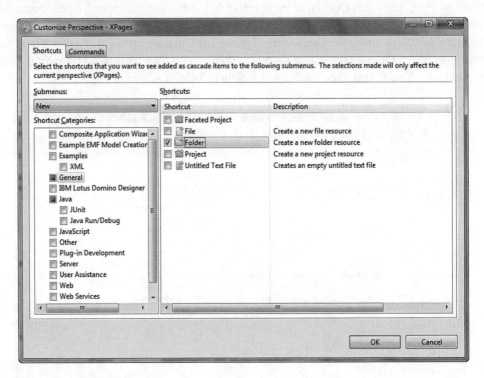

Figure 14.12   The Folder option.

Close the dialog, and then in **Package Explorer**, right-click the **WebContent/ WEB-INF/src** folder that has been added to the build path. Then expand the **New** submenu. You should see the list of items that have been added for Java development, making it easier to create new Java-related items (see Figure 14.13).

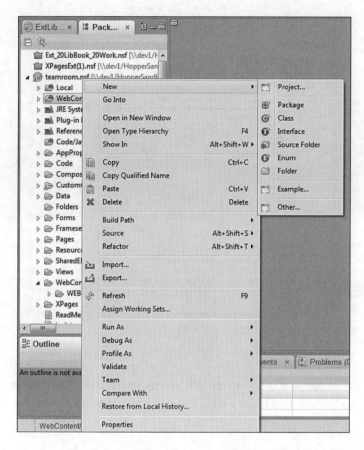

Figure 14.13 Easier access for creating new Java elements from the right-click context menu.

Now, you'll create, as an example, a package to contain utility classes for XPages applications that will be included in an OpenNTF project; to indicate both the nature of the code and its origin, name the package **org.openntf.xsp.util** by right-clicking on the **WebContent/ WEB-INF/src** folder as before and expanding the **New** submenu. From that submenu, select **Package**. A wizard page appears asking you to name the package. This is where you enter the **org.openntf.xsp.util** name and then click **Finish**, as seen in Figure 14.14.

Figure 14.14   New Java package.

After creating the package, right-click it, and select **New** and then **Class** to create a Java class. This opens the new Java Class wizard that walks you through creating the new class (see Figure 14.15).

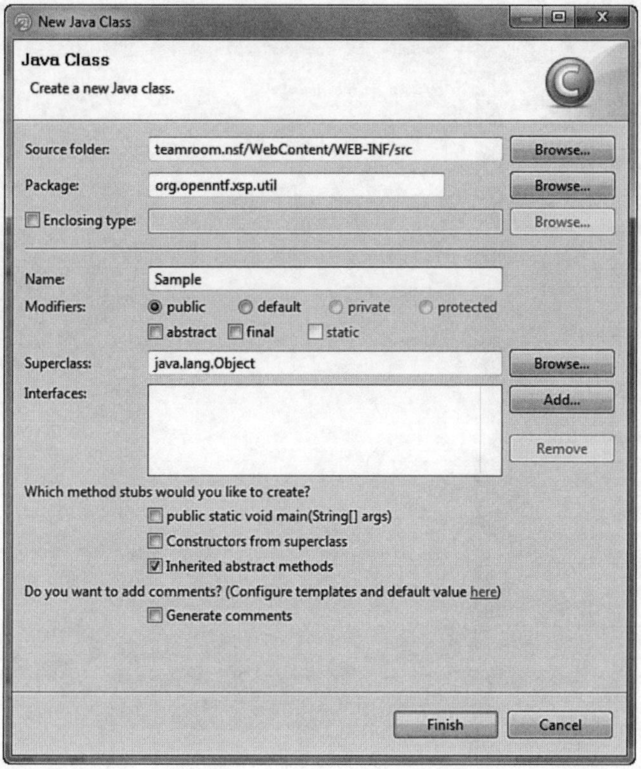

Figure 14.15 New Java Class dialog.

This new class opens in the Java editor, as seen in Figure 14.16. Once customized and saved, the new class is then accessible from within your XPages application, either through SSJS in the same manner demonstrated prior using Apache POI in SSJS, or even in more integrated ways, such as a Managed Java Bean.

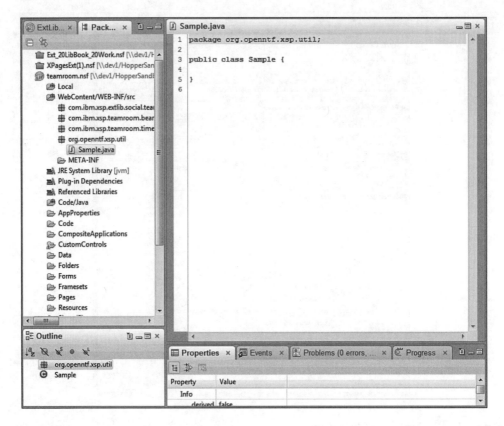

Figure 14.16   Ready to begin writing a Java class.

Introduction to Java Beans

Given the coffee motif of the Java language, the term Bean is used simply to indicate the role a class plays as a unit of Java. You may have also encountered the acronym POJO: Plain Old Java Object. A POJO is any Java class that doesn't conform to specific conventions. A Bean, on the other hand, conforms to specific—but easy—conventions:

- **It includes an argumentless constructor**—For those of you with a LotusScript background, this is similar to the way you can dim a variable as a `New NotesSession()` or a `New NotesUIWorkspace()`. You don't have to pass parameters, or arguments, to that declaration; you just create the new object and then interact with it later.

> **NOTE**
>
> This doesn't mean that a Bean can't also have constructors that do accept arguments; Java, after all, does support method overloading. But at a minimum, the class must support instantiation with no arguments.

- **Attributes of the object are accessible via predictably named getters and setters**— For example, if I create a `House` Bean, and one of its properties is `address`, the class includes a `getAddress()` method and a `setAddress()` method. The getter method accepts no arguments and returns the current value of the argument, in its proper type; the setter accepts one argument—the new value of the property—also in the proper type. You may wonder, why not just make the property public if you're always going to provide public getters and setters? This is because forcing reads/writes to call methods ensures that no change is made to the class members without the class knowing it is happening. This provides an opportunity to sanitize incoming data, for example, to ensure a property's value is not being set to invalid data, or if other class members' values or states are dependent upon another, it gives the class an opportunity to adjust accordingly. Enforcing this consistency across all classes allows for the utmost flexibility, while maintaining predictability.

> **NOTE**
>
> One deviation from the getPropertyName/setPropertyName convention is if the property is a boolean (true/false) value. In this case, the getter uses an `is` prefix instead of `get` (for example, `isForeclosed()` instead of `getForeclosed()`). The setter still uses `set` as its prefix.

- **The class is serializable**—Serialization is the process of storing the state of an object somewhere else. This could be in some flat file on the hard drive, a database record, or even just a different in-memory format. De-serialization, then, is the reconstruction of the object state from an alternate location. This is actually a key reason for the previous two conventions: Some process external to the class definition can parse the serialized state of an object and restore its state predictably, construct an instance with no arguments, and then call the setters for each of the attribute values it finds.

Everything in an XPage is a Bean. Every control—meaning every inputText, every panel, every repeat—is a Bean. Your code can interact with control instances in a predictable fashion. An inputText has a title property that stores a string; therefore, it must have a `getTitle()` method that returns a string and a `setTitle()` method that accepts a string. Just about every control has a `styleClass` string property, so it's generally safe to assume that, even in SSJS, you can call `getStyleClass()` and `setStyleClass()` regardless of which control you're interacting with.

There are many other advantages to the extent to which everything in XPages is based on Beans, like using abbreviated expression language (EL) syntax to bind read/write control attributes to a property of another Bean. To expand on the House and Address example, you can write an EL expression using the variable name associated with the instance of the House, let's say whiteHouse, and the property name that you want to access, such as address, in simple dot notation, like whiteHouse.address. EL knows to convert that into a call to the getAddress() method (when reading the value) or the setAddress() method (when assigning the value) of the whiteHouse instance of the House Bean.

Managed Beans

Now that you understand what a Java Bean is, what then, is a Managed Bean? Quite simply, a Managed Bean is nothing more than a regular Bean that is controlled, or managed, by the XPages runtime. The runtime decides if an instance of a given Bean is needed; when it is, it is created by the runtime by calling the argumentless constructor of the Bean's class. In XPages this occurs whenever a Managed Bean is referenced from within a bit of code, such as in SSJS or EL.

A Managed Bean can be any Java Bean that has been configured for use as a Managed Bean in the **faces-config.xml** file in the project. This file is located within the **WebContent/WEB-INF** folder of the NSF. To configure the Managed Bean for use, you add a bit of XML code to this file to identify the name, class, and scope of the Bean. The name is short; think of a variable or instance name that globally identifies the Bean throughout the application. For example, earlier this chapter referred to an instance of the House Bean as whiteHouse. This name could be the name of the Managed Bean in your application. The class is simply the fully qualified name of the class you want to serve as the basis for the Managed Bean. For example, this could be org.openntf.xsp.util.House if your House class was located within the org.openntf.xsp.util package.

Finally, the scope of the Managed Bean defines the lifetime that any one instance of the Bean will exist. The proper values here can be none, request, view, session, and application. None indicates that the Bean is not persisted beyond the code block where it is referenced. With this scope, if a Bean is referenced in a page event, such as in beforeRenderResponse, once the event has executed, the instance of the Bean is discarded. For request, view, session, and application, the lifetime can be directly correlated to the XPage scope object's requestScope, viewScope, sessionScope, and applicationScope. Just like these maps, the Managed Bean's life will be for the duration of the request, view, session, or entire application's lifetime (barring idle-timeout or other lifetime-limiting events). When designing Beans for specific scopes, such as application, take special care to design the Bean's instance to initialize itself and restore its state at any time. The Bean may not know when it is being destroyed or created outside of the constructor, so changes in state that need to be persisted should be saved in some fashion that if a new instance of the Bean is initialized, it can re-create the proper state for the Bean.

Listing 14.4 shows the content of the **faces-config.xml** file from the TeamRoom, with a Managed Bean defined.

Listing 14.4   A Sample faces-config.xml Deploying a Managed Bean

```
<?xml version="1.0" encoding="UTF-8"?>
<faces-config>
  <managed-Bean>
    <managed-Bean-name>CheckboxBean</managed-Bean-name>
    <managed-Bean-class>
      com.ibm.xsp.teamroom.Beans.CheckboxBean
    </managed-Bean-class>
    <managed-Bean-scope>view</managed-Bean-scope>
  </managed-Bean>
</faces-config>
```

The User and People Bean

The Extension Library includes some precreated Managed Beans that provide access to pieces of information that may be commonly used, such as user information. Access to these Beans is automatic once the Extension Library is installed. You can reference them in both SSJS and EL.

Probably the most used Bean from the Extension Library is the user Bean (`userBean`), which was discussed briefly in Chapter 13, "Get Social." The user Bean provides quick access to information about the current user, including the user's name and access level to the current database. To access the Bean, use the symbol `userBean`. Listing 14.5 shows how to access the Bean using SSJS.

Listing 14.5   Accessing the User Bean Using SSJS

```
<xp:this.loaded><![CDATA[${javascript:
  (userBean.accessLevel > lotus.domino.ACL.LEVEL_AUTHOR) &&
      userBean.canCreateDocs
}]]></xp:this.loaded>
```

Listing 14.6 shows how to access the Bean using EL.

Listing 14.6   Accessing the User Bean Using EL

```
<xp:button
  loaded=${userBean.canCreateDocs}>
</xp:button>
```

Table 14.1 describes each of the fields that are available from the user Bean.

Table 14.1   Field Values Available from the User Bean

Field	Purpose
commonName	Returns a string value of the current user's common name (for example, John Doe).
distinguishedName	Returns the string value of the current user's distinguished name.
abbreviatedName	Returns the abbreviated version of the current user (for example, John Doe/WWCorp).
canonicalName	Returns the canonical name of the current user (for example, CN=John Doe/O=WWCorp).
effectiveUserName	Returns the current effective username.
canCreateDocs	Returns true if the user is able to create documents in the current database.
canDeleteDocs	Returns true if the user is able to delete documents in the current database.
canCreatePrivAgents	Returns true if the user is able to create Private Agents in the current database.
canCreatePrivFoldersViews	Returns true if the user is able to create Private Views or Folders in the current database.
canCreateSharedFoldersViews	Returns true if the user is able to create Shared Views or Folders in the current database.
canCreateScriptAgents	Returns true if the user is able to create Java or LotusScript Agents in the current database.
canReadPublicDocs	Returns true if the user is able to read public documents in the current database.
canWritePublicDocs	Returns true if the user is able to write public documents in the current database.
canReplicateCopyDocs	Returns true if the user is able to replicate or copy documents in the current database.
accessLevel	Returns an integer value representing the user's current access level in the database. Use constant values in `lotus.domino.ACL` (for example, `lotus.domino.ACL.LEVEL_READER`).

Field	Purpose
accessLevelAsString	Returns a string value representing the user's current access level in the database. Returns a value of NOACCESS, DEPOSITOR, READER, AUTHOR, EDITOR, DESIGNER, or MANAGER.
accessRoles	Returns an array of the roles associated with the current user in the current database.
notesId	Returns the user's Notes ID as a string.
id	Returns the user's ID as a string.
emailAddress	Returns the user's e-mail address.
displayName	Returns the user's display address.
thumbnailUrl	Returns the user's avatar thumbnail URL.

The TeamRoom makes extensive use of the user Bean. In Listing 14.7, an excerpt from the Layout Custom Control shows the user Bean in action. In this example, a placebar action is displayed if the user's access to the TeamRoom application is greater than author access.

Listing 14.7 The User Bean in Action in the Layout Custom Control of the TeamRoom

```
<xe:this.placeBarActions>
  <xe:pageTreeNode
    title="TeamRoom Setup"
    page="setup">
    <xe:this.loaded><![CDATA[${javascript:
      userBean.accessLevel > lotus.domino.ACL.LEVEL_AUTHOR
    }]]></xe:this.loaded>
  </xe:pageTreeNode>
</xe:this.placeBarActions>
```

The people Bean retrieves information about a specific user other than the current user. A user's information is retrieved by passing the user's abbreviated username to the getPerson() method. The method returns an object that contains bits of the user's information using the fields specified in Table 14.1. The TeamRoom application also uses the people Bean. Listing 14.8 displays a code snippet from the home XPage to display the name of a document author.

Listing 14.8   Code Snippet from the Home XPage in the TeamRoom Using the People Bean

```
<xp:link
  id="authorLink">
    <xp:this.text><![CDATA[#{javascript:
      peopleBean.getPerson(@Name("[Abbreviate]",
        viewEntry.getColumnValue("From"))).displayName
    }]]></xp:this.text>
    <xp:this.value><![CDATA[#{javascript:
      "/members.xsp?profile=" + @Name("[Abbreviate]",
        viewEntry.getColumnValue("From"))
    }]]></xp:this.value>
</xp:link>
```

Conclusion

This chapter barely scratched the surface of using Java in an XPages application. It offered a glimpse into the extensibility of the XPages environment through the use of the Extension Library, and by extension the XPages Extensibility API that powers the entire Extension Library. You can find more information on the use of Java in XPages and programming with the Extensibility API online at the Lotus Notes and Domino Application Development Wiki at http://www-10.lotus.com/ldd/ddwiki.nsf as well as many other valuable sites across the Internet.

Resources

XPages.info

The website http://XPages.info/ is the best landing page for all things XPages. It contains reams of information on XPages ranging from the basics, the latest XPages blog posts, and videos, to listings of the best XPages resources and demos.

XPages Extension Library OpenNTF Project

The XPages Extension Library (ExtLib) project, http://extlib.openntf.org, is the most active and most downloaded on OpenNTF (http://www.openntf.org/). Not only is this project frequently updated with new releases, it has active **Feature Requests, Discussion**, and **Defects** sections. So no excuses—drop in, join us, and take part!

Also in the ExtLib project, each download contains a file called **XPages-Doc.zip**. Extracted, the file contains a self-contained website displaying information on each control, core controls, and ExtLib in a javadoc-like format.

Lotus Notes Domino 8.5.3 Upgrade Packs Documentation

Documentation for the Upgrade Packs is available from the Lotus Notes and Domino Application Development wiki (http://www-10.lotus.com/ldd/ddwiki.nsf). Once there, select the **Product Documentation** tab at the top, and then select from the table **8.5.3 UP1** under the **Versions** column for any of the products.

XPages Extension Library Wiki Documentation

Documentation for the IBM-supported version of the XPages ExtLib is also available from the Lotus Notes and Domino Application Development wiki (http://www-10.lotus.com/ldd/ddwiki.nsf). Select the **Product Documentation** tab, and then go to the **8.5.3 UP1** link on the same row as **Domino Designer XPages Extension Library**. There are more than 150 articles on the new controls as well as documents on installation and deployment.

On the table on the same **Product Documentation** tab, the **8.5.3 UP1** link for the Domino Data Service displays the documentation for the REST Services.

XPages Extensibility API Wiki Documentation

The Lotus Notes and Domino Application Development wiki also contains documentation on the XPages Extensibility application programming interface (API) (http://www-10 .lotus.com/ldd/ddwiki.nsf/xpViewCategories.xsp?lookupName=XPages%20Extensibility%20A PI), which underpins the XPages ExtLib. This is a vital reference if you need to build your own Extension Library.

Other Resources

Name	Link
Blog, Declan Lynch	http://www.qtzar.com/
Blog, Jeremy Hodge	http://www.hodgebloge.com/
Blog, Paul Withers	http://www.intec.co.uk/blog/
Blog, Tim Tripcony	http://www.timtripcony.com/
CSS Specification	http://www.w3.org/Style/CSS
Dojo Toolkit	http://dojotoolkit.org/
IBM Lotus Domino Designer Information Center	http://XPag.es/?DesignerInfo
J2EE 1.5 Specification	http://download.oracle.com/javaee/5/api
Java 1.5 Specification	http://java.sun.com/j2se/1.5.0/docs/api
JSF Specification	http://www.oracle.com/technetwork/java/javaee/javaserverfaces-139869.html
XPages Podcasts, The XCast	http://thexcast.net/

Index

A

access endpoints, 446-447
accessing
data services (from Domino
as a built-in service), 356
enabling services on
Domino servers,
357-359
relational data through
JDBC, 377-378
creating connections to
the RDBMS, 406-407,
409-410
installing JDBC
drivers, 379
Accordion Container, 229-231
properties, 230
Accordion control, 256-257
Accordion Pane, 229-231
actionFacet, Heading
control, 314

Activity Stream Data data
source, 454-455
adding
JDBC data sources to
XPages, 411
parameters to SQL
statements, 412
addOnLoad(), 97
advanced node types
beanTreeNode, 245
dominoViewEntriesTree-
Node, 247
dominoViewListTree
Node, 246
pageTreeNode, 242-245
repeatTreeNode, 245
All Documents, TeamRoom
template, 60
anchoring Package
Explorer, 493
AnonymousEndpointBean, 441

Apache POI, 491
SSJS, 498
APIs (application
programming interfaces), 377
appendSQLType(), 426
application development, 9
Application Layout, 9-10
TeamRoom template, 57-58
Application Layout control
within a Custom Control,
276-280
OneUI development,
264-266
banner property, 272
footer property, 269
legal property, 267-268
mastFooter property, 273
mastHeader
property, 273
navigation path, 268
placebar property,
270-271

515

XPages Extension Library

A Step-by-step Guide to the Next Generation of XPages Components

Paul Hannan, Declan Sciolla-Lynch, Jeremy Hodge, Paul Withers, Tim Tripcony

IBM Press

Safari
Books Online

FREE Online Edition

Your purchase of *XPages Extension Library* includes access to a free online edition for 45 days through the **Safari Books Online** subscription service. Nearly every IBM Press book is available online through **Safari Books Online**, along with thousands of books and videos from publishers such as Addison-Wesley Professional, Cisco Press, Exam Cram, O'Reilly Media, Prentice Hall, Que, Sams, and VMware Press.

Safari Books Online is a digital library providing searchable, on-demand access to thousands of technology, digital media, and professional development books and videos from leading publishers. With one monthly or yearly subscription price, you get unlimited access to learning tools and information on topics including mobile app and software development, tips and tricks on using your favorite gadgets, networking, project management, graphic design, and much more.

Activate your FREE Online Edition at informit.com/safarifree

STEP 1:   Enter the coupon code: CCEGFAA.

STEP 2:   New Safari users, complete the brief registration form.
Safari subscribers, just log in.

If you have difficulty registering on Safari or accessing the online edition,
please e-mail customer-service@safaribooksonline.com

 Addison Wesley AdobePress  ALPHA Cisco Press Press FINANCIAL TIMES IBM Press Microsoft Press New Riders O'REILLY

 Peachpit Press PRENTICE HALL que Redbooks SAMS SAS Publishing  vmware PRESS WILEY wrox